THE ENCYCLOPEDIA OF SAUCES FOR YOUR PASTA

(THE GREATEST COLLECTION OF PASTA SAUCES EVER IN ONE BOOK!)

PUBLISHER: MARCUS KIMBERLY PUBLISHING COMPANY

COPY EDITORS: ELEANOR DEDIC-AIEVOLI AND ENID WINGATE

COVER DESIGN: LISA BACCHINI

COPYRIGHT: 1989 BY CHARLES A. BELLISSINO

ISBN 1-879743-00-0

LIBRARY OF CONGRESS CATALOGUE IN PUBLICATION NUMBER: 89-85045
AUTHOR: CHARLES A. BELLISSINO
THE ENCYCLOPEDIA OF SAUCES FOR YOUR PASTA.
INCLUDES INDICES.

1ST PRINTING AUGUST 1991
2ND PRINTING NOVEMBER 1991
3RD PRINTING JUNE 1993

DEDICATED WITH LOVE TO MY FAMILY;
MY SON MARCUS AND DAUGHTER KIMBERLY,
WHO NOT ONLY GAVE ME CONSTANT ENCOURAGEMENT IN THE WRITING OF THIS BOOK,
BUT GRACIOUSLY ATE MY EXPERIMENTS.

CONTENTS

THERE ARE 142 RECIPES IN THE BOOK THAT CAN BE COOKED AN/OR PREPARED IN LESS TIME THAN IT TAKES THE PASTA TO COOK, AND THEY ARE SO MARKED, LOOK UNDER THE SAUCE NAME FOR THE PHRASE: (ANOTHER QUICKIE)

CHAPTER 10

SAUCES MADE FROM TOMATOES AND VEGETABLES 295

ACKNOWLEDGMENTS

IN THE MANUSCRIPT STAGE, AN AUTHOR CAN READ THROUGH THE SAME ERRORS DOZENS OF TIMES AND NEVER SEE THEM, IT IS WITH THIS IN MIND THAT I WISH TO ACKNOWLEDGE THE IMPORTANCE OF THE REVIEW AND CONTRIBUTIONS MADE BY ELEANOR DEDIC-AIEVOLI AND ENID WINGATE. MRS. DEDIC-AIEVOLI IS AN OUTSTANDING HIGH SCHOOL PRINCIPAL AND ENGLISH TEACHER, WHO RAISED MY GRAMMAR AND PUNCTUATION GRADE FROM A "C" TO AN "A". ENID WINGATE IS AN AVID CREATOR OF RECIPES.

A DEBT OF GRATITUDE I OWE TO MANY

THERE ARE TIMES IN OUR LIVES WHEN WE WISH TO ACKNOWLEDGE A KINDNESS OR A SHARED EVENT. AMONG THOSE MOMENTS IN MY LIFE ARE MANY WONDERFUL MEALS I'VE ENJOYED WITH FAMILY, FRIENDS, NEIGHBORS AND ACQUAINTANCES. FROM THESE MEALS OF SIMPLE FARE AND ELOQUENT DINNERS CAME A NUMBER OF THE OUTSTANDING RECIPES IN THIS BOOK. YOU NEVER KNOW WHEN YOU SIT DOWN TO A MEAL WHETHER IT WILL BE MEMORABLE OR EMINENTLY FORGETTABLE. AND THERE ARE TIMES WHEN YOU'LL BE COMPLETELY SURPRISED BY A DISH BECAUSE OF ITS OUTSTANDING TASTE. WHEN THAT HAPPENS, ASK FOR THE RECIPE! I BELIEVE THAT WHEN SOMEONE HONORS ME BY ASKING ME TO DINE IN THEIR HOME, THE GREATEST COMPLIMENT I CAN OFFER IS TO ASK FOR THE RECIPE. THAT VERY ACT LED ME TO MORE FULLY UNDERSTAND HOW PEOPLE ARE WILLING TO SHARE SOME OF THE THINGS THEY PRIZE THE MOST. AND HIGH AMONG THEIR PRIZED POSSESSIONS ARE FAVORITE PERSONAL AND FAMILY RECIPES.

TO A VERY LARGE EXTENT, EVERYONE WILL EAT THE FOODS THEY GREW UP WITH. SINCE MOST AMERICANS HAVE AN ETHNIC HERITAGE FROM SOMEWHERE ELSE, THAT SOMEWHERE ELSE IS THE BASIS OF THEIR FAMILY CUISINE. PENNSYLVANIA DUTCH EAT GERMAN STYLE FOODS, LOUISIANA CAJUNS EAT FRENCH STYLE FOODS. AMERICANS WITH A ITALIAN HERITAGE EAT THE FOODS OF ITALY. ELSEWHERE IN THIS BOOK, PARTICULARLY IN THE INTRODUCTION, YOU'LL DISCOVER THE WHERE'S AND WHY'S OF PASTA SAUCES AND THE ABSOLUTELY STAGGERING DIFFERENCES IN SAUCE INGREDIENTS AND PREPARATIONS IN ITALY. MY PATERNAL GRANDPARENTS CAME FROM THE SMALL VILLAGE OF ROCCA d'ASPIDE IN THE REGION OF CAMPANIA. SO THE SAUCES WE ATE WERE VARIATIONS OF TOMATO SAUCES, OR GARLIC AND OLIVE OIL SAUCES. IT WASN'T UNTIL I BECAME AN ADULT THAT I DISCOVERED YOU COULD PUT ANYTHING ELSE ON PASTA. THAT DISCOVERY WAS NOT ONLY STARTLING, BUT IT OPENED UP A WHOLE NEW WORLD OF FOODS TO ME. IT WAS THAT DISCOVERY THAT LED TO THIS BOOK.

AMONG THE BASIC LAWS OF THE UNIVERSE IS THIS ONE, FOR EVERY ACTION THERE IS AN EQUAL REACTION. AS IT BECAME KNOWN IN THE SOCIAL CIRCLES I TRAVELLED IN, THAT I WAS A COLLECTOR OF PASTA SAUCE RECIPES, THEY WERE FREQUENTLY OFFERED TO ME BY PEOPLE WHO HAD A RECIPE THEY LOVED AND WANTED TO SHARE IT WITH SOMEONE WHO COULD AND WOULD APPRECIATE THEIR GIFT. I AM GRATEFUL TO ALL WHO SHARED THEIR RECIPES WITH ME.

An Introduction to Pasta Sauces.

OR

A Sauce for the Goose may be Good for a Gander, but Don't Put it on My Pasta!

I, LIKE MILLIONS OF PEOPLE LOVE PASTA, AND DON'T WANT TO EAT IT WITH THE SAME SAUCE EVERY TIME. CONSIDER, IF YOU HAVE PASTA ONLY ONCE A WEEK, THAT'S FIFTY-TWO TIMES A YEAR. SURELY THERE'S AMPLE ROOM WITH THAT SCHEDULE TO TRY DIFFERENT SAUCES. IF YOU'RE READING THIS BOOK, I KNOW YOU AGREE WITH ME. MY MOTIVATION IN WRITING THIS BOOK WAS DUE PRIMARILY TO A STARTLING DISCOVERY* I MADE AS A YOUNG MAN. AND SECONDLY, BY THE REWARDS OF THE SEARCH FOR PASTA SAUCES. THE COOK LOOKING FOR A PASTA SAUCE MAY BE REQUIRED TO SEARCH VIRTUALLY ALL THE CATEGORIES OF A COOKBOOK, BECAUSE THERE SEEMS TO BE NO CLEAR CUT UNDERSTANDING OF "SAUCE" OR HOW IT IS TO BE APPLIED TO PASTA. AND THEREIN LIES THE WHY OF THIS BOOK.

IS A VEGETABLE MEDLEY WITH PASTA A SAUCE? OR IS IT PASTA WITH VEGETABLES? IS THAT THE SAME AS, OR CLOSE TO "PASTA PRIMAVERA"? ALMOST EVERYONE LIKES BACON AND EGGS; BUT WHEN IT IS BLENDED WITH PASTA, IT'S CALLED "PASTA ALLA CARBONARA", AND WHERE IN A COOKBOOK WOULD YOU LOOK FOR IT? SURELY NOT UNDER SAUCES. EXPERIENCE HAS PROBABLY CONVINCED YOU, AS IT HAS ME, THAT THERE IS NO STANDARD SYSTEM CURRENTLY IN USE ON HOW PASTA SAUCES ARE LISTED IN AMERICAN COOKBOOKS, OR FOR THAT MATTER, ITALIAN COOKBOOKS. AND NO ONE SEEMS TO KNOW HOW THEY SHOULD BE LISTED. AND . . . , (I LOVE THIS ONE!) IF AN AUTHOR GIVES YOU ONE HUNDRED WAYS TO PREPARE PASTA, HE OR SHE WILL PROCEED TO TELL YOU ONE HUNDRED TIMES HOW TO COOK IT. WHY?

* (SEE ACKNOWLEDGMENTS.)

SORTING OUT THE CONFUSION

A CURSORY EXAMINATION OF ALMOST ANY COOKBOOK, ESPECIALLY ONE ABOUT "PASTA" WILL GIVE YOU A CATEGORY OF SAUCES (IT IS GENERALLY A SMALL CATEGORY) AND THEN THE AUTHORS PROCEED TO BLITHELY LIST PASTAS WITH A SAUCE RECIPE ATTACHED WHEREVER AND WHENEVER THEY FANCY, EVEN IN THE PLETHORA OF "ITALIAN" COOKBOOKS CURRENTLY ON THE MARKET IT'S TRUE. WHY? IF A SAUCE IS GOOD SERVED OVER A STRING PASTA, LIKE SPAGHETTI, MAY IT NOT ALSO BE SERVED OVER A HOLLOW MACARONI OR THE OVAL LINGUINI? IF THAT IS TRUE, THEN WHY NOT LIST THAT SAUCE UNDER "SAUCES" AND THEN GIVE SPECIFIC PASTA RECOMMENDATIONS. HOME COOKS ARE SUBJECTED TO ABSOLUTE CONFUSION, NOT TO MENTION OBFUSCATION IN THE PLACEMENT OF PASTA SAUCES IN A COOKBOOK. THERE ARE GENERALLY NO INDEPENDENTLY LISTED SAUCES IN THE "PASTA" AND/OR "PASTA/RICE" CATEGORIES OF ANY COOKBOOK. INSTEAD, SAUCES ARE CONSIDERED PART OF THE DISH AND LISTED UNDER THE NAMES OF THE PASTA, (SPAGHETTI WITH/ OR RIGATONI WITH/ OR FETTUCCINE WITH/) SOMETIMES BY THE MAJOR NON PASTA INGREDIENT (BROCCOLI WITH/, ZUCCHINI WITH/) OR POSSIBLY BY SOME EUPHEMISTIC TERM LIKE "TIA ANGELINA'S FAVORITE TORTELLINI" OR FOR THE SEASON OF THE YEAR THE PRIMARY INGREDIENT IS HARVESTED, AS IN PASTA PRIMAVERA (SPRING, SPRINGTIME). THEN THERE ARE PLACE OR COMMUNITY NAMES (BOLOGNESE, MILANESE OR FLORENTINE, ETC.). AND LET'S NOT OVERLOOK THE EVER POPULAR OCCUPATIONAL NAMES, ALL PRECEDED BY THE GENERIC "PASTA" OR A SPECIFIC VARIETY AS "SPAGHETTI ALL' OR ALLA", A FEW OF THEM ARE; "WHORE'S" SAUCE (PUTTANESCA); "SAILOR'S" SAUCE (MARINARA), "FISHERMAN'S" SAUCE (ALLA PESCATORE), THE "POLICEMAN'S" SAUCE (ALLA CARABINIERE), THE "CHARCOAL VENDOR'S" SAUCE, (ALLA CARBONARA), THE "SHEPHERD'S" SAUCE (ALLA PASTORE), AND, WE CERTAINLY DON'T WANT TO OVERLOOK THE EVER POPULAR "CART DRIVER'S" SAUCE (ALLA CARRETTIERA); THIS SAUCE IS INTERESTING. I HAVE ELEVEN SAUCES WITH THAT NAME, ALL WITH DIFFERENT INGREDIENTS AND DIFFERENT METHODS OF PREPARATION. PLUS, WHILE TRACKING WITH A SINGLE INGREDIENT LIST FOR A "CART DRIVER'S SAUCE", I HAVE FOUND NO LESS THAN SEVEN SEPARATE AND NEAR IDENTICAL RECIPES ALL WITH DIFFERENT NAMES. BUT, REALIZE THAT SAUCES ARE REGIONAL IN ITALY, AND MORE OFTEN THAN NOT, EXTREMELY LOCALIZED: THEREFORE, IT'S NOT UNUSUAL TO FIND THE SAME SAUCE BEARING DIFFERENT NAMES. A CASE IN POINT WOULD BE SEAFOOD. MOST OF ITALY'S LARGEST CITIES ARE ON, OR CLOSE TO A COAST: AND A LARGE PORTION OF THEIR FOOD IS FROM THE SEA. FOR OUR EXAMPLE, LET'S SELECT NAPLES AND VENICE. WHAT ARE THE ODDS THAT YOU CAN FIND

THE SAME METHOD OF PREPARATION FOR SPECIFIC SEAFOODS IN BOTH CITIES? THE ANSWER IS SLIM TO NON-EXISTENT! IT IS ALMOST AS THOUGH THEY WERE DIFFERENT COUNTRIES. THAT DISTINCT LOCALIZED DIFFERENCE IN FOOD PREPARATION ALSO APPLIES TO THE INLAND CITIES, AND THEREIN LIES THE TALE. TO FURTHER ILLUSTRATE AND EMPHASIZE ITALY'S LOCALIZATION OF FOODS, I'LL SHARE THIS TIDBIT I CAME ACROSS WHILE GATHERING INFORMATION FOR THIS BOOK. BALSAMIC VINEGAR ONLY RECENTLY BECAME POPULAR THROUGHOUT ITALY, BUT ONLY AFTER IT BECAME POPULAR IN THE UNITED STATES. BEFORE THAT ROUND TRIP, VERY FEW PEOPLE MORE THAN TWENTY MILES DISTANT FROM MODENA KNEW ABOUT IT, AND FEWER STILL USED IT. ANYONE DISTANT FROM MODENA WHO KNEW ABOUT BALSAMIC VINEGAR CONSIDERED IT TO BE A MEDICINE AND NOT A FOOD. AMERICAN INTEREST IN BALSAMIC VINEGAR WAS CREATED ONLY AFTER AN EAST COAST GOURMET AND FOOD WRITER PRAISED BALSAMIC VINEGAR IN ONE OF HIS BOOKS (I DON'T KNOW WHO OR WHICH).

THE MEANING OF "SAUCE"

EVERYONE KNOWS WHAT SAUCE MEANS, RIGHT? WELL MAYBE. SAUCE IS A DRESSING FOR CERTAIN FOODS. IF WE DRIZZLE A LITTLE OIL OVER PASTA, WE HAVE DRESSED THE PASTA. CAN THAT BE A SAUCE? BY DEFINITION, YES. THEN BY EXTENSION, ANY COMBINATION OF INGREDIENTS USED TO DRESS FOOD CAN BE CALLED SAUCE. WE DO MAKE SOME DISTINCTIONS TO THAT PROCESS, WE HAVE DRESSINGS, TOPPINGS, ICINGS AND GRAVIES IN ADDITION TO SAUCES, THEY ARE USED IN SPECIFIC CASES. WE DON'T SAUCE A SALAD, BUT WE DO SAUCE ICE CREAM. WE PUT DRESSINGS ON SALADS, BUT NEVER ON ICE CREAM. WE PUT GRAVY ON SANDWICHES, BUT NEVER ON SALADS. WE SPLIT THE DIFFERENCE AND WILL PUT A DRESSING OR SAUCE ON A SANDWICH. WE ICE CAKES AND SOMETIMES WE'LL EVEN USE TOPPINGS. CONFUSED? ME TOO. WAIT TILL YOU TRY TO DEFINE A SALAD. BEFORE I WRITE MYSELF INTO A CORNER, LET ME ADDRESS THE REASON FOR THIS EXPLANATION. YOU'LL FIND IN THIS BOOK SOME VERY SIMPLE, AS WELL AS SOME VERY COMPLEX SAUCES. I WOULD LIKE TO AVOID READER COMMENTS THAT ANYTHING AS SIMPLE AS A LITTLE OIL AND CHEESE CANNOT POSSIBLY BE A SAUCE. IT IS! AND CONVERSELY, A LARGE NUMBER OF INGREDIENTS COOKED OR JOINED TOGETHER FOR THE BENEFIT OF MELDING THE FLAVORS, AND THEN USED TO DRESS (SERVE OVER) PASTA IS ALSO A SAUCE.

Have We Got a Sauce for You?

AS A POINT OF INFORMATION ON PASTA SAUCES USED IN ITALY. I HAVE READ, FROM THE EMINENT PASTA AUTHORITY OF ITALY, EVA AGNESI, A SIXTH GENERATION PASTA MAKER AND CURATOR OF THE "SPAGHETTI HISTORICAL MUSEUM" IN PONTEDASSIO, ITALY, THAT THERE MAY BE IN EXCESS OF 1,000 PASTA SAUCE RECIPES. CONSIDERING THAT I HAVE OVER FOUR HUNDRED SAUCES RECIPES AND THEIR VARIATIONS IN THIS BOOK: AND I REJECTED WHAT I BELIEVE TO BE A NEAR EQUAL NUMBER, I WOULD SUGGEST ONE THOUSAND SAUCES MAY BE A MODEST ESTIMATE.

Foreign Imports

DURING THE 16TH CENTURY, FOODS FROM AMERICA WERE BROUGHT TO EUROPE AND SUBSEQUENTLY INCORPORATED INTO EUROPEAN COOKERY. THERE THEY ESTABLISHED VERY DEEP ROOTS. THE TOMATO AND CORN (MAIZE) ARE SO FIRMLY ENTRENCHED IN ITALIAN COOKERY THAT IT WOULD ʳᵉ DIFFICULT TO IMAGINE ITALIAN FOOD WITHOUT THEM. A SHORT LIST OF AMERICAN FOODS THAT TRAVELLED TO EUROPE TO STAY INCLUDE THE TOMATO, POTATO, PIMENTO (RED PEPPER), KIDNEY BEAN, SQUASH, CORN (MAIZE), PEANUT, STRAWBERRY AND THE TURKEY. THEIR IMPACT ON ITALIAN COOKERY IS IRREVERSIBLE.

IN ITALY, THE TOMATO WAS FIRST REFERRED TO IN PRINT IN 1554 AND CALLED THE "GOLDEN APPLE" (POMO D'ORO). SMALL AND YELLOW, IT WAS USED IN SALADS UNTIL FURTHER AGRICULTURAL REFINEMENTS MADE IT LARGER AND JUICER: AND THAT TOOK THE BETTER PART OF TWO HUNDRED YEARS. SOMETIME DURING THAT PERIOD, THE TOMATO'S USE AS A PASTA SAUCE INGREDIENT WAS ESTABLISHED.

A Sauce Et Tu?

I BELIEVE A NOTE IN THE DEFENSE OF PASTA COOKBOOK AUTHORS IS PROBABLY CALLED FOR HERE. THERE ARE HUNDREDS OF DISHES IN WHICH PASTA AND AN ASSORTMENT OF INGREDIENTS ARE THE DISH, BUT NOT THE "SAUCE". HOWEVER, IF ..., WHAT THEY ARE OFFERING IS A PREPARATION METHOD THAT INCLUDES A LIST OF INGREDIENTS TO BE PREPARED SEPARATELY, AND THEN SERVED OVER THE PASTA, THAT CONSTITUTES A SAUCE. A SAUCE IS A DRESSING, WHETHER IT BE SIMPLE OR COMPOUND. THAT ALSO CREATES A PROBLEM WHEN ATTEMPTING TO CATEGORIZE A COOKBOOK AND IT CREATES A PROBLEM FOR THE READER. I'VE TRIED TO AVOID THAT TRAP BY STICKING TO SAUCES THAT CAN BE PREPARED SEPARATELY AND THEN ADDED TO A RECOMMENDED OR FAVORITE PASTA. I THINK I HAVE SUCCEEDED.

The Shape(s) You Love to Eat!

THERE DOES SEEM TO BE A STRONG RELUCTANCE BY COOKBOOK AUTHORS TO SEPARATE A PARTICULAR PASTA SHAPE FROM THE "DRESSING" INGREDIENTS. THAT CERTAINLY CAME ABOUT BECAUSE OF THE ITALIAN REGIONAL PREFERENCE FOR PARTICULAR SHAPES. SOUTHERNERS, ESPECIALLY SICILIANS, SEEM TO LOVE HOLLOW STRINGS AND MEDIUM TUBE SHAPED PASTA OVER OTHER VARIETIES, IN THE CENTRAL REGIONS AROUND ROME AND NAPLES, THE PREFERENCE SEEMS TO BE FOR SPAGHETTI AND OTHER SOLID STRING TYPES. IN NORTHERN AREAS, THE RIBBON TYPES, THE POTATO DUMPLING (GNOCCHI) AND THE BROAD FLAT OR SQUARE LASAGNA'S ARE THE PASTA OF CHOICE. A VERY WIDE VARIETY OF SMALL PASTA SHAPES ARE USED EXTENSIVELY IN BROTHS; AND EVEN IN THAT USE, THERE ARE REGIONAL PREFERENCES FOR PARTICULAR SHAPES.

ADDITIONALLY, THE USE OF OLIVE OIL, BUTTER, OR BOTH IS ALSO REGIONAL. THE FAR NORTH USES ONLY BUTTER; THE DEEP SOUTH USES ONLY OLIVE OIL, WHILE THE CENTRAL REGIONS COMBINE THEM OR USE THEM SEPARATELY ACCORDING TO THE TASTE THEY WANT. IT IS THESE PREFERENCES FOR THEIR FAVORITE PASTA SHAPE AND REGIONAL INGREDIENTS THAT ITALIAN COOKBOOKS AND BY EXTENSION, AMERICAN COOKBOOKS CLASSIFY PASTA. ALSO, IN BOTH ITALIAN AND AMERICAN COOKBOOKS, SAUCES INDEPENDENT OF THOSE GIVEN WITH SPECIFIC PASTA DISHES, WERE LIMITED TO MAYONNAISE, BECHAMEL, HOLLANDAISE AND A FEW SELECTED OTHERS. THOSE INCLUDE SAUCES FOR MEATS, FOWL AND FISH, FOR VEGETABLES, EGGS, DESSERTS AND PUDDINGS, AND POSSIBLY ONE OR TWO TOMATO SAUCES. OCCASIONALLY YOU MAY EVEN FIND A TOMATO SAUCE WITH A SPECIFIC AND RECOGNIZABLE NAME IN THE "SAUCE" CATEGORY.

WHERE IN THE WORLD DID THAT COME FROM?

A NATIONAL SAUCE FOR PASTA IN ITALY DOESN'T EXIST, PROBABLY BECAUSE ITALIANS COOK WITH SPONTANEITY. THEY DON'T FOLLOW RECIPES, THEY ARE NOT METHODICAL ADHERENTS TO THE FORMULA, THEY TEND TO "WING IT" ACCORDING TO WHAT'S IN THE PANTRY OR WHAT'S AVAILABLE AT THE MARKET. THEIR SAUCES WERE CREATED DURING A TIME WHEN THEIR MARKETS PRETTY MUCH CARRIED ONLY LOCAL PRODUCE, MEATS OR SEAFOOD. THOSE LIMITS MADE THEM VERY LOCAL, SOMETIMES LIMITED TO A SINGLE VILLAGE OR REGION; ALTHOUGH, IN MORE RECENT YEARS ONE OR TWO SAUCES HAVE COME CLOSE TO BEING NATIONAL IN SCOPE. TO KEEP THIS IN PROPER PERSPECTIVE BEAR IN MIND THAT "AMERICAN FOOD" WAS VERY LOCAL UNTIL THE COMING OF THE RAILROAD AND THE FURTHER DEVELOPMENT OF THE REFRIGERATED FREIGHT CAR.

ASIDE FROM GEOGRAPHICAL HAPPENSTANCE IN THE PLACEMENTS OF INGRED-IENTS, EACH REGION DEVELOPED ITS OWN UNIQUE RECIPES AND METHODS OF PREPARING SAUCES BECAUSE HISTORY AND ITALIAN GEOGRAPHY PLAYED A LARGE PART IN ESTABLISHING PREFERENCES. THERE ARE MANY AREAS WHERE THESE INFLUENCES ARE EVIDENT. IN THE VICINITY OF TRIESTE THERE ARE INFLUENCES FROM THE OLD AUSTRO-HUNGARIAN EMPIRE AS WELL AS FROM NEIGHBORING YUGOSLAVIA. SICILY, ALONG WITH PARTS OF CALABRIA, PUGLIA AND BASILICATA WAS FIRST OCCUPIED BY GREEKS (c. 750 B.C.), ABOUT THE TIME THE LATINS WERE GETTING SETTLED IN AND FOUNDING ROME (754 B.C.). IN FACT, THE ENTIRE SOUTHERN REGION WAS REFERRED TO BY EARLY LATINS (ROMANS) AS "MAGNA GRAECIA", (GREATER GREECE) AND ONE OF GREECE'S FAMED 3RD CENTURY B.C., PHYSICISTS AND MATHEMATICIANS, ARCHIMEDES, LIVED IN SYRACUSE (ITALIAN: SIRACUSA). SYRACUSE, WAS THE CONTEMPORARY RIVAL OF ATHENS.

LATER INVADERS OF ITALY WERE, PHOENICIANS, BYZANTINES, AND ARABS. ALSO DESERVING MENTION ARE A FEW OF THE MORE IMPORTANT TEUTONIC INVADERS WHOSE MARAUDING TRIBES OVERRAN MUCH OF ITALY, THE VANDALS, (FROM WHOM WE GET OUR WORD "VANDAL"), AS WELL AS THE LOMBARDS (C. 568 A.D.), GOTHS AND OSTROGOTHS. THE NON TEUTONIC CELTS AND HUN-GARIANS (MAGYARS), NOT TO MENTION THE ASIAN HUNS, WHO HAD LITTLE OR NO INTEREST IN EITHER FOOD OR GRACIOUS DINING JUST IN DESTRUCTION, HAD NO INFLUENCE UPON ITALIAN COOKERY AND ONLY STAYED FOR A SHORT VISIT.

MUCH LATER, SICILY AND THE SOUTHERN TIP OF THE PENINSULA AGAIN PLAYED UNWILLING HOSTS TO THE NORMAN FRENCH, AUSTRIAN HAPSBURGS AND THE SPANISH. ALL OF THEM LEFT SOME INFLUENCES UPON ITALY AND ITS CUISINE. ADDITIONALLY, WE CERTAINLY DON'T WANT TO FORGET THE MYSTERY TRIBES AND EARLIER OCCUPANTS OF THE NORTH AND CENTRAL ITALIAN PENINSULA, THE SABINES AND THE MORE IMPORTANT ETRUSCANS, WHO APPARENTLY ESTABLISHED THEMSELVES IN ITALY APPROXIMATELY 700 YEARS PRIOR TO THE ARRIVAL OF THE LATINS, AND WHO WERE TO A LARGE EXTENT TUTORS TO THE LATINS. THE RESIDUAL INFLUENCES FROM THE VARIOUS CONQUERING GROUPS THAT HELD PORTIONS OF ITALY FOR YEARS, IF NOT CENTURIES, ARE REFLECTED IN SEVERAL CHAPTERS OF THIS BOOK. AND THEN THERE ARE AREAS IN ITALY WHERE PASTA IS SELDOM IF EVER EATEN IN FAVOR OF LOCALLY GROWN RICE OR MAIZE; READ CORN MEAL, (ITALIAN: POLENTA).

TAKING THE PRECEDING INTO CONSIDERATION, IT WOULDN'T BE DIFFICULT TO BELIEVE THAT THERE ARE PROBABLY AS MANY PASTA SAUCES AS THERE ARE ITALIAN COOKS. AND THAT DOES NOT INCLUDE THE NUMBER OF CREATIVE AMERICAN COOKS WHO ARE IN CONSTANT SEARCH FOR SAUCES THAT OFFER THE TASTE THEY WANT TO EITHER ENHANCE A MEAL OR BE THE ENTREE.

Words, Words, Words,
That's Not What it Means to Me!

EVEN THE WORD "SAUCE" IS SUSPECT, ITALIANS DON'T HAVE A WORD THAT MEANS PASTA SAUCE; THEY USE A VARIETY OF TERMS. THE CLOSEST WORD ITALIANS, HAVE FOR A PASTA SAUCE IS "SUGO". I, FOR ONE, FIND "SUGO" VERY CONFUSING. IF IT HAS A MEANING FOR A SPECIFIC TYPE OR STYLE OF SAUCE, I HAVEN'T BEEN ABLE TO IDENTIFY IT. BESIDES THAT, I'M JUST BARELY GETTING A GRASP ON "RAGU". YOU'LL FIND ANY NUMBER OF ITALIAN COOKBOOKS IN WHICH THE AUTHOR WILL USE "SUGO", "RAGU" AND "SALSA", OR ACCORDING TO SOME AUTHORS, "SALSE" AND EVEN "ASCIUTTA" (MEANING DRY DOUGH OR WITHOUT BROTH), PLUS THE ETERNALLY POPULAR "ALLA" (IN THE STYLE OF) TO IDENTIFY A SAUCE FOR PASTA, OR IF THEY ARE GOING TO HAVE YOU ADD CREAM OR MILK, IT WILL BE CALLED BY THE PASTA NAME AND FOLLOWED BY "ALLA PANNA". RESTAURANTS LOVE THAT APPLICATION FOR ANY SAUCE THEY ADD MILK OR CREAM TO (i.e., RIGATONI ALLA PANNA). TO MAKE MATTERS WORSE, MANY AMERICANS OF ITALIAN HERITAGE, WILL CALL A SAUCE IN WHICH MEAT HAS SIMMERED, A GRAVY. SAUCE IS A FRENCH WORD, AND SALSA IS BOTH AN ITALIAN AND SPANISH WORD. SAUCE MOVED INTO ENGLISH, "SUGO" DID NOT. SALSA IS COMING AND I BELIEVE IN THE UNITED STATES; IT IS CORRECTLY APPLIED ONLY TO SPANISH OR MEXICAN SAUCES, PRINCIPALLY DUE TO THE RISING POPULARITY OF MEXICAN FOOD AND IT'S CORN CHIP DIPPING SALSAS.

Old Family Secret Recipes!

(Many of Them Really Are!! Read on to Discover Why.)

AMONG THE SAUCES OF ITALY ONLY A VERY FEW HAVE EVER ACHIEVED A DEGREE OF NATIONWIDE ACCEPTANCE. THERE ARE MANY REASONS FOR THIS, FOREMOST AMONG THEM WAS THE TRADITION OF PASSING RECIPES DOWN FROM ONE GENERATION TO ANOTHER BY DEMONSTRATION AND INSTRUCTION WITHIN THE FAMILY. DIALECTS AND REGIONAL PREFERENCES, AS WELL AS AVAILABILITY OF INGREDIENTS, SUBSTANTIALLY INTERFERED WITH ANY POSSIBLE NATIONWIDE COOKBOOK RIGHT UP UNTIL 1928 WHEN A LADY NAMED ADA BONI PUBLISHED HER COOKBOOK. IT WAS A REMARKABLE ACCOMPLISHMENT TO BRING INTO ONE BOOK THE STAGGERING ARRAY OF ITALIAN COOKERY. IT ALSO BRINGS INTO SHARP FOCUS FOR THOSE WHO ARE LOOKING, THE FACT THAT PROBABLY NINETY PERCENT OF THE ITALIANS WHO WOULD EVER EMIGRATE TO AMERICA WERE ALREADY HERE. THAT MEANT THAT THEIR RECIPES WERE PROBABLY IN THEIR HEADS AND NOT IN BOOKS, OR IF IN BOOKS, THEY WERE LIKELY WRITTEN IN DIALECT. COMPARE THAT INFORMATION TO AMERICA'S FIRST COOKBOOK TO ACHIEVE NATIONAL ACCEPTANCE, "FANNY FARMERS BOSTON SCHOOL OF COOKING" COOKBOOK, PUBLISHED IN 1897, ABOUT 30 YEARS EARLIER THAN ITALY'S FIRST TRULY NATIONAL COOKBOOK, (MISS FARMER'S COOKBOOK INTRODUCED THE USE OF STANDARD MEASUREMENTS IN RECIPES). FANNY HAD IT A LITTLE EASIER BECAUSE WE WERE NOT A NATION SPLIT BY DIALECTS, AMERICANS PRETTY MUCH SPOKE AND READ THE SAME LANGUAGE; AND MORE IMPORTANTLY, THANKS TO AMERICA'S RAILROADS AND THE REFRIGERATED RAIL CAR, COMMON FOODS WERE GENERALLY AVAILABLE THROUGHOUT THE COUNTRY DURING THEIR SEASON.

THE SAUCES WITH NAME RECOGNITION THAT HAVE REACHED ACCEPTANCE ON A NATIONAL LEVEL, BOTH HERE AND IN ITALY ARE THE TOMATO BASED "MARINARA SAUCE", THE MEAT BASED "BOLOGNESE" SAUCE AND POSSIBLY A BUTTER/CREAM (A.K.A. "ALFREDO", OR BY THE DESIGNATION "ALLA PANNA") SAUCE, OR THE LESS EXPENSIVE VERSION, THE MILK/FLOUR SAUCE KNOWN AS BALSAMELLA (BECHAMEL). THERE ARE IN THIS BOOK SEVERAL SAUCES BY EACH NAME OF THE ABOVE.

MAY I HAVE YOUR RECIPE?
JUST CHISEL IT ON THIS ROCK!

FROM A HISTORICAL PERSPECTIVE YOU MIGHT LIKE TO KNOW THAT THE ITALIANS PUBLISHED THE WORLDS FIRST COOKBOOK DURING THE FIRST CENTURY A.D. WHEN THE ROMAN, APICIUS, (HE WAS AN ITALIAN WASN'T HE? AFTER ALL THE LATINS, READ; ROMANS, DID CALL THEIR COUNTY, ITALY), WROTE HIS BOOK OF RECIPES, CALLED "DE RE COQUINARIA", MEANING "ON COOKERY". THE SECOND COOKBOOK TO HAVE A MAJOR IMPACT IN ITALY WAS WRITTEN BY A VATICAN LIBRARIAN IN 1475 NAMED BARTOLOMEO SACCHI (PEN NAME; PLATINA) AND TITLED "CONCERNING HONEST PLEASURE AND WELL-BEING". THE ABOVE-MENTIONED ITALIAN COOKBOOKS WERE WRITTEN IN LATIN (EXCEPT FOR MRS. BONI'S) AND WRITTEN DURING PERIODS IN WHICH THE GENERAL POPULACE COULD NOT READ. IN FACT, THE FIRST BOOK (AN ESSAY) EVER PUBLISHED IN WHAT WOULD BECOME STANDARD ITALIAN, WAS DANTE'S "DE VULGARI ELO-QUENTIA" ("ON THE VERNACULAR TONGUE"), WRITTEN IN 1305. IT WAS A SUCCESSFUL APPEAL FOR ITALY TO ADOPT THE NATIVE VERNACULAR (HIS OWN TUSCAN DIALECT), AND REPLACE LATIN AS THE LITERARY LANGUAGE OF ITALY. LATER IN HIS LIFE HE COMPLETED HIS CLASSIC "THE DIVINE COMEDY" ALSO IN THE TUSCAN DIALECT; AND THAT FIRMLY ESTABLISHED TUSCAN ITALIAN AS THE WRITTEN FORM OF ITALIAN. WHILE HIS WRITINGS MAY HAVE CHANGED THE DIRECTION OF LANGUAGE IN ITALY, THEY DID LITTLE OR NOTHING FOR ITALIAN COOKBOOKS UNTIL 1928.

AT'SA MY RECIPE!!!

EATING IN RESTAURANTS WHERE THE CHEF'S EGO ISN'T ALL PERVASIVE, YOU'LL GENERALLY FIND A "PASTA DELLA CASA" (PASTA OF THE HOUSE); THIS COULD MEAN ANYTHING, AND DOES. THE DISH COULD BE FROM A NEWLY DISCOVERED RECIPE, OR A SECRET "OLD FAMILY RECIPE", OR A RECIPE SOMEONE RECOMMENDED, POSSIBLY A FAVORITE OF A BETTER CUSTOMER, OR IT COULD BE A "CREATED SAUCE" BY THE HOUSE CHEF. OCCASIONALLY THE EGOS OF CHEFS WOULD HAVE US BELIEVE THEY HAVE CREATED A SAUCE THAT IN FACT MAY HAVE BEEN AROUND FOR SEVERAL HUNDRED YEARS. THAT OCCURS WHEN THEY DON'T READ BOOKS ABOUT THEIR CRAFT OR WHEN THEY OMIT OR ADD AN ITEM TO A RECIPE. DID IT CREATE A NEW SAUCE? WELL, MANY FAMOUS CHEFS DID THAT VERY THING QUITE SUCCESSFULLY, AND OC-CASIONALLY THEY WERE RIGHT. IN POINT OF FACT HOWEVER, THAT SHOULD BE CONSIDERED A VARIATION.

AMERICANS SEEM TO BE ON AN ENDLESS SEARCH FOR NEW TASTES. AMERICA IS UNLIKE MANY AREAS OF THE WORLD WHERE THE SAME FOODS HAVE BEEN SERVED FOR CENTURIES, IF NOT FOR THOUSANDS OF YEARS. THAT'S NOT OUR STYLE, CHANGE IS! MODIFICATIONS AND VARIATIONS ARE CENTRAL TO AMERICAN TASTE.

IN THIS QUEST, PASTA SAUCES FOR THE FIRST TIME COME INTO THEIR OWN. THERE ARE HUNDREDS OF FOOD ITEMS THAT CAN BE PART OF A PASTA SAUCE. TAKE ANY BASIC SAUCE RECIPE AND YOU MAY MODIFY IT SUBSTANTIALLY BY DROPPING OR ADDING A SINGLE INGREDIENT. WITH TOMATO SAUCES, THE TYPE OF TOMATO AND ESPECIALLY ITS PROCESSING WILL GIVE YOU A DIFFERENT TASTE, IF NOT A DIFFERENT SAUCE.

IN SELECTING RECIPES FOR THIS BOOK, I'VE SELECTED ONLY ITALIAN, AMERICAN AND MODIFIED AMERICAN SAUCES. I'VE AVOIDED SAUCES THAT MAY HAVE OTHER ETHNIC INFLUENCES. LET'S EXPAND ON THAT. THERE ARE EMI-GRANT ITALIANS OR NATURAL BORN CITIZENS OF ITALIAN HERITAGE IN PRACTICALLY EVERY COUNTRY OF THE WORLD. IN OUR OWN HEMISPHERE THEY'RE WELL REPRESENTED IN CANADA, MEXICO, CENTRAL AMERICA AND ALL OF SOUTH AMERICA. ADD TO THAT THAT SPAGHETTI, IF NOT OTHER PASTA VARIETIES, IS A WORLD WIDE FAVORITE. YOU'LL EVEN FIND ITALIAN RESTAURANTS IN JAPAN AND CHINA STAFFED BY LOCAL COOKS. EVERY COOK WILL AT SOME POINT BEGIN TO EXPERIMENT AND ADD LOCAL OR NATIONAL FAVORITE SEASONINGS. THE RESULT MAY BE A GREAT FAVORITE IN THAT COUNTRY, BUT NOT ELSEWHERE. IT IS THESE INFLUENCES I HAVE AVOIDED.

Whatta Ya Mean, I Can't Put It on Fish?

THE SAUCE RECIPES IN THIS BOOK ARE FOR PASTA! I'VE MADE ABSOLUTELY NO ATTEMPT TO OFFER SAUCES FOR USE ON ANYTHING OTHER THAN PASTA. WHILE I'LL NOT MAKE ANY FLAT STATEMENT THAT SOME OF THE SAUCES IN THIS BOOK CANNOT BE USED TO PREPARE, ACCOMPANY OR COMPLIMENT MEATS, FISH OR FOWL, THAT IS NOT MY INTENT.

WHILE THE NUMBER OF SAUCES IN THIS BOOK ARE EXTENSIVE, AND TO SOME POSITIVELY OVERWHELMING, I HAVE REALLY BEEN SELECTIVE, I'VE OMITTED ABOUT AS MANY RECIPES AS I'VE INCLUDED. THAT MEANS SEVERAL THINGS, AMONG THEM, IS THAT, IF THIS BOOK BECOMES A KITCHEN LIBRARY STAPLE, I CAN RENDER IT OBSOLETE BY WRITING A NEW EDITION WITH "NEW" AND "ADDED" RECIPES. THAT MAY HELP KEEP ME GAINFULLY EMPLOYED AND OFF THE STREET.

Pasta Stands Alone!

ONE OF THE TRULY INTERESTING FEATURES ABOUT PASTA, IS THAT IT WILL STAND AS THE ENTREE OF ANY AMERICAN MEATLESS MEAL. I QUALIFY THAT BECAUSE ITALIANS GENERALLY USE PASTA AS A SMALL FIRST (AMERICAN: SIDE) DISH, FOLLOWING THE ANTIPASTO AND/OR SOUP, BUT PRIOR TO SERVING THE VEGETABLES AND ENTREE. OF COURSE, THAT DOES HAVE ITS ADVANTAGES; IT MEANS THAT YOU CAN EAT PASTA EVERY DAY OF THE WEEK WITHOUT OVERDOSING.

WHILE YOURS TRULY AND MILLIONS OF OTHER AMERICANS MAY HAVE AN ITALIAN HERITAGE, WE ARE AMERICAN TO THE CORE. WE THINK, ACT AND EAT THAT WAY. AND THAT'S WHY WE TOO, LIKE MILLIONS OF AMERICAN FAMILIES, USE PASTA AS AN ENTREE, AND NOT AS A FIRST (SIDE) DISH. IN ACTUAL FACT, I RARELY SERVE PASTA IN ANY OTHER ROLE THAN AS THE ENTREE. IT CAN BE BEAUTIFULLY ACCOMPANIED WITH ONE OR TWO VEGETABLES. IF DESIRED, A SALAD BEFORE OR IN THE ITALIAN MANNER, FOLLOWING, THEN CAPPED OFF WITH FRESH FRUIT, OR OTHER LIGHT DESSERT. THESE ARE THE COMPONENTS OF AN ABSOLUTELY WONDERFUL MEAL.

YOU CAN'T FOOL ME,
MARCO POLO BROUGHT PASTA TO ITALY!
OR
YOU MEAN THIS STUFF HAS A HISTORY?

HERE ARE A FEW HISTORICAL NOTES ON PASTA YOU MIGHT FIND INTERESTING. IN THE LAND THAT WOULD BECOME KNOWN AS ITALY, A PEOPLE CALLED ETRUSCANS OCCUPIED THE NORTH-CENTRAL AREA BEFORE THE ARRIVAL OF THE LATINS. THEY WERE APPARENTLY FAMILIAR WITH A FORM OF PASTA OR NOODLES, BECAUSE DESIGN WORK ON SOME OF THEIR TOMBS SHOW BOTH THE TOOLS FOR PREPARATION AND THE INGREDIENTS. THE PARTICULAR TOMBS WITH THESE DESIGNS ARE DATED APPROXIMATELY 2,100 YEARS BEFORE MARCO POLO RETURNED FROM CHINA. AS REGARDS CHINA, THERE ARE CHINESE RECORDS THAT SHOW THEY WERE EATING A NOODLE TYPE FOOD ABOUT 7,000 YEARS AGO (THAT WAS BEFORE THE BEGINNING OF THE WORLD, IF WE ACCEPT THE HEBREW CALENDAR AS VALID).

HISTORICALLY IT IS KNOWN THAT THE GREEKS, ETRUSCANS, LATINS AND OSTROGOTHS ALL WERE FAMILIAR WITH AND ATE A FOOD MADE FROM A "PASTE". IN ALL PROBABILITY, ANY GROUP OF PEOPLE WHO HARVESTED GRAINS MAY HAVE DEVELOPED A "PASTE" (ITALIAN; PASTA) FROM GROUND GRAIN AND WATER. THAT'S ALL THERE IS TO IT; FLOUR AND WATER EQUAL PASTA. FLATTEN IT OUT, CUT INTO SHAPES, COOK SOME IN WATER FOR NOW AND DRY SOME FOR LATER USE.

THE FIRST EUROPEAN PUBLISHED REFERENCES TO PASTA CAME FROM AN UNKNOWN MEDIEVAL AUTHOR WHOSE BOOK OF MILK TARTS AND EGG PIES ALSO INCLUDED FORMULAS FOR MAKING VERMICELLI, TORTELLI AND TORTELLETTI.

IN ENGLAND DURING THE MIDDLE AGES, PASTA (MACARONI) WAS VERY POPULAR, IN FACT THE MACARONI CLUBS THAT FLOURISHED DURING THE 1700s MAY POSSIBLY HAVE TAKEN THEIR NAME FROM MACARONI BECAUSE OF ITS ASSUMED OR RECOGNIZED ELEGANCE. THIS CAME ABOUT IN PART BECAUSE THE WORD "MACARONI" WAS USED AT THAT TIME TO DESCRIBE THINGS OF ELEGANCE; THIS ASSUMES IT WAS FIRST EATEN AT COURT OR IN THE MANOR HOUSES OF ENGLAND. IF THE SERFS HAD BEEN THE FIRST TO EAT IT, THERE NEVER WOULD HAVE BEEN A "MACARONI CLUB", AND WE (AMERICANS) WOULD

NOT HAVE BEEN JESTED BY THE ENGLISH SOLDIERS WITH THE SONG, YANKEE DOODLE DANDY, A SONG THAT REQUIRED YOU TO "STICK A FEATHER IN YOUR CAP AND CALL IT MACARONI" (ELEGANT), A SONG WHICH WE TOOK AND CONVERTED FROM A CHIDING CHANTY TO A SONG OF PATRIOTISM. DURING THE EARLY 1800s EVEN THE KING OF ENGLAND (GEORGE IV) ATE PASTA, MOST LIKELY A BAKED MACARONI AND CHEESE, OR AS THE COURT MENU CALLED IT, (LA TIMBALE MACARONI A' LA NAPOLITAINE). TIMBALE IS A METHOD OF COOKERY. IN THIS METHOD, THE INGREDIENTS ARE PLACED IN TO A BUTTERED BOWL OR DEEP SIDED DISH; THAT DISH IS THEN SET ON A RACK IN A LARGER DISH OR PAN WITH A WATER LEVEL TO MATCH THE FOOD LEVEL AND THEN BAKED UNTIL SET. BAKED CUSTARDS ARE FREQUENTLY DONE THIS WAY.

MEANWHILE, BACK HOME IN AMERICA, OUR FIRST COMMERCIAL PASTA FACTORY WAS OPENED IN 1848 IN BROOKLYN, NEW YORK, BY A FRENCHMAN NAMED ANTOINE ZEREGA. HOW DO YOU LIKE THEM APPLES? I WILL ASSUME, YOU DON'T HAVE TO, THAT MR. ZEREGA PROBABLY LEARNED THE ART OF PASTA MAKING FROM AN ITALIAN. IF THERE IS ONE THING FRANCE HAS IN ABUNDANCE, IT'S ITALIANS. LOOK AT THE MANY ITALIAN NAMES AMONG FRANCE'S FAMOUS FASHION CLOTHING AND COSMETIC HOUSES. IN ADDITION LARGE NUMBERS OF ITALIANS COVER MUCH OF THE FRENCH SOUTH COAST, INCLUDING THE PRINCIPALITY OF MONACO, WHERE THE ROYAL FAMILY "GRIMALDI" IS OF ITALIAN ANCESTRY, AS WAS THE ISLAND OF CORSICA AND THE CORSICAN WHO ELEVATED HIMSELF STRAIGHT UP THE ARMY RANKS FROM CORPORAL, TO GENERAL, TO FIRST CONSUL, TO EMPEROR; NAPOLEON BONAPARTE (ITALIAN; BOUNAPARTE). CORSICA WAS CEDED TO FRANCE BY GENOA IN 1769, THE YEAR OF, AND ABOUT FOUR MONTHS BEFORE NAPPY'S BIRTH, FOLLOWING 400 YEARS OF CONTINUOUS ITALIAN (GENOESE) RULE. IN ADDITION, MUCH OF THE FRENCH RIVIERA RULED BY THE HOUSE OF SAVOY, INCLUDING THE CITY OF NICE, WAS CEDED TO FRANCE BY ITALY IN 1860 FOR SOME ASSISTANCE FROM FRANCE DURING ONE OF ITALY'S INNUMERABLE WARS AGAINST AUSTRIA. WHEREVER MR. ZEREGA LEARNED TO MAKE PASTA, HE BROUGHT HIS KNOW-LEDGE AND MADE HIS PRODUCT IN THE RIGHT PLACE. THE COMPANY IS STILL IN BUSINESS AND YOU MAY BE ABLE TO FIND HIS PASTA IN A GOOD QUALITY ITALIAN MARKET OR A GOURMET SHOP IN YOUR TOWN.

IN THE 1100s A.D., B.M.P., (i.e., before marco polo), AN ARAB GEOGRAPHER NAMED AL-IDRISI PUBLISHED A BOOK TITLED "ENTERTAINMENT FOR TRAVELLERS" AND DESCRIBED A FOOD FROM NEAR PALERMO, SICILY, MADE FROM FLOUR IN THE SHAPE OF THREADS AND CALLED "ITRIYAH" MEANING STRINGS. A MODIFIED VERSION OF THE WORD IS STILL USED IN SICILY TODAY TO IDENTIFY PASTA, IT IS: "TRII".

Pasta, is it Really Good for You?
Yes! Yes! Yes! and Yes Again!

WITH ALL THE RESEARCH GOING ON IN THE UNITED STATES AND THE WORLD REGARDING NUTRITION, ABOUT WHAT IS AND WHAT ISN'T GOOD FOR YOU, COMPLEX CARBOHYDRATES (READ PASTA) STAND OUT AS THE WINNER. PASTA IS EASILY DIGESTIBLE, IT RAPIDLY RELEASES ITS SUGARS, AND PROTEIN FOR QUICK USABLE ENERGY. THE VERY SMALL FAT CONTENT STAYS A LITTLE LONGER. LET ME REPEAT THAT! FROM COMPLEX CARBOHYDRATES (SUGARS) COMES QUICK AND USABLE ENERGY, AS WELL AS ESSENTIAL NUTRITION. PROTEIN HAS BEEN UNHORSED AS THE QUICK AND NOBLE ENERGY SOURCE OF HUMAN NUTRITION. IT HAS BEEN DETERMINED THAT A BALANCED DIET FOR HUMAN NUTRITION REQUIRES 55% TO 60% OF CALORIC INTAKE TO BE IN THE FORM OF SUGARS (COMPLEX CARBOHYDRATES). AND ..., PASTA NOT ONLY MEETS THAT NEED, BUT IT IS LOW IN CALORIES. ONE CUP OF COOKED PASTA (2 OUNCES DRY) IS RIGHT AT 200 CALORIES, (THE NUTRIENT CONTENT OF 2 OUNCES OF DRY PASTA PROVIDES ABOUT 10 GRAMS OF PROTEIN, 1 GRAM OF FAT AND 42 GRAMS OF CARBOHYDRATE), USE A SPRINKLING OF SAUCE AND HAVE A LIGHT, SATISFYING HIGH ENERGY ENTREE OF ABOUT 250 CALORIES. AS AN ADDED BONUS, IT IS VERY ECONOMICAL! WE'RE TALKING ABOUT NICKELS AND DIMES PER SERVING. (I WOULD HAVE SAID PENNIES, BUT THAT'S NO LONGER TRUE). EAT IT OFTEN, IT'S WONDERFUL AND SO GOOD FOR YOU.

WELL, WE BELIEVE WE'VE IDENTIFIED THE MAJOR PROBLEM AMERICAN COOKS HAVE WITH ITALIAN STYLE PASTA SAUCES, AND WE FURTHER BELIEVE THAT WITH THIS BOOK WE'VE PROVIDED THE SOLUTION. A PLACE FOR EVERY PASTA SAUCE AND EVERY PASTA SAUCE IN ITS PLACE. WE HAVE CATEGORIZED AND ALPHABETIZED SAUCES, AND HAVE RECOMMENDED PASTAS TO BE SERVED WITH THEM. INTERESTINGLY, THERE DOES SEEM TO BE A STRONG, IF NOT ABSOLUTE CORRELATION BETWEEN A TRADITIONAL SAUCE ON A PASTA AND ITS SHAPE. SOME SAUCES SIMPLY DO NOT COMPLIMENT PASTA OF DIFFERENT SHAPES IN THE SAME WAY. GENERALLY SPEAKING, THE MORE PUNGENT A SAUCE, THE PLAINER AND/OR THINNER THE PASTA SHAPE. HOWEVER, K.I.S., IS OUR GOAL (KEEP IT SIMPLE!). IF YOU LIKE A PARTICULAR SAUCE, PUT IT ON ANY PASTA SHAPE YOU LIKE.

LET'S JUST BUTTER IT THIS TIME!

A POINT WORTH REMEMBERING IF YOU USE PASTA AS A FIRST DISH, AS IN THE ITALIAN MANNER, YOU DON'T ALWAYS NEED A MULTI-INGREDIENT SAUCE. IT IS A COMMON PRACTICE IN ITALY TO EAT PASTA WITH ONLY A SPRINKLING OF OLIVE OIL OR MELTED BUTTER, WITH OR WITHOUT GRATED CHEESE. IF THAT SOUNDS GOOD TO YOU, GO FOR IT!

A FINAL NOTE ON HOW I DETERMINED THE MANNER OF CATEGORIZING IN THIS BOOK. I HAVE CHOSEN TO LIST A SAUCE BY THE DOMINANT INGREDIENT. THIS MEANS THAT A GROUPING OF SEAFOOD PIECES IN SEASONED WHIPPING CREAM IS LISTED UNDER CREAM SAUCES AND NOT SEAFOOD SAUCES. RIGHTFULLY, IT COULD BE EITHER, BUT SINCE THIS IS MY BOOK, I'VE EXERCISED AUTHORS LICENSE AND HAVE CHOSEN WHAT I LIKE!

AUTHORS NOTES:

INFORMATION YOU CAN'T LIVE WITHOUT!
OR
TERMS AND PHRASES YOU SHOULD KNOW.

MY BOOK REVIEWER, A MASTER OF ENGLISH PROSE, WHO IS BOTH ERUDITE AND ARTICULATE, WROTE THE FOLLOWING EVALUATION REGARDING THE UNIQUENESS OF OUR MEMORY JOGGER, THE SIMPLICITY OF OUR PAGE LAYOUT, THE EXACTNESS OF THE RECIPES, AND THE EASY FLOW OF OUR PREPARATION METHOD. HER CRITIQUE OF MY BOOK WAS NEATLY AND SUCCINCTLY SUMMED UP IN THE FOLLOWING QUOTATION:

"SIXE MINITS AGO I CUDDINT SPEL COOK, DEN I RED YER BOOK, NOW I AR WUN!"

TO THE BEGINNING COOK: FOLLOW THE RECIPE EXACTLY. AS YOU GAIN EXPERIENCE AND A FEELING OF CONFIDENCE IN THE KITCHEN, YOU THEN CAN EXERCISE THAT KNOWLEDGE AND BEHAVE AS AN EXPERIENCED COOK. EXPERIENCED COOKS IN GENERAL WILL USE A RECIPE AS A GUIDE AND ONLY FOLLOW THE RECIPE WHEN NECESSARY. PROFESSIONALS ALWAYS FOLLOW THE RECIPE BECAUSE CONSISTENCY IS ESSENTIAL. PROFESSIONAL COOKS AND CHEFS WILL VARY A RECIPE WHEN NECESSITY REQUIRES IT OR WHEN THEY ARE EXPERIMENTING. BEGINNING COOKS SHOULD NOT.

How to Use This Book

THE NUMBER OF SAUCES IN THIS BOOK MAY BE OVERWHELMING TO THE AVERAGE HOME COOK. IT WASN'T MEANT TO BE! I MEAN FOR THIS BOOK TO BE A WELCOME REFERENCE ADDITION TO YOUR LIBRARY AND A GENUINE SOURCE OF INSPIRED COOKING CHOICES FOR YOU. START IN THE CONTENTS PAGES, FIND A CATEGORY THAT CAPTURES YOUR ATTENTION, START WITH THE FIRST SAUCE IN THE CATEGORY OR READ THROUGH THEM UNTIL ONE RINGS YOUR BELL, THEN GO FOR IT. OR, YOU MAY SEARCH FOR A SAUCE BY INGREDIENT(S), OR SPECIFIC NAMES. TO DO SO SEE THE CROSS REFERENCED INDEX AT THE BACK OF THE BOOK.

BEAR IN MIND THAT THERE ARE 425 SAUCES, PLUS DOZENS OF VARIATIONS, THEREBY GIVING YOU WELL OVER FOUR HUNDRED SAUCES IN THIS THIS BOOK; AND IF YOU SERVE PASTA ONCE A WEEK, IT'LL TAKE YOU BETTER THAN SEVEN AND ONE HALF YEARS TO TRY EVERY SAUCE ONCE. THEREFORE, TO MAKE IT EASIER FOR YOU TO KEEP TRACK OF THE SAUCES YOU'VE TRIED, AND YOUR OPINION OF THEM, THERE IS A BOX NEAR THE SAUCE NAME THAT YOU MAY CHECK SO THAT YOU'LL KNOW IF YOU'VE TRIED THE SAUCE AND IF YOU WOULD USE IT AGAIN:

LOVED IT ( )
HATED IT ( )
MAYBE WE'LL TRY IT AGAIN ( )
WE'LL USE IT FOR UNWELCOME GUESTS ( )

KEY PHRASES

BLENDERIZE (ING)

YOU'LL COME ACROSS THIS WORD OFTEN. IT MEANS TO CHOP THE CANNED TOMATOES IN A BLENDER. A TWO OR THREE SECOND PUSH OF THE "PULSE" BUTTON IS ENOUGH TO DO THE JOB. IF YOU NEED THE THERAPY, YOU COULD DO IT WITH A KNIFE. I PREFER THE BLENDER.

IF YOU OWN A HAND HELD, HAND OPERATED "PROCESSOR", YOU MAY, WHEN THE SAUCE IS DONE, CHOP AND/OR PUREE THE TOMATOES, ALONG WITH EVERYTHING ELSE IN THE PAN. THAT WILL KEEP YOUR BLENDER CLEAN, BUT ..., YOU STAND A CHANCE OF WHIRLING SAUCE AROUND YOU, THE KITCHEN AND YOUR STOVE, USE CAUTION WITH THESE HAND HELD DEVICES.

TIMING

LOOK FOR THE WORDS (ANOTHER QUICKIE) UNDER THE SAUCE NAME TO INDICATE THAT IT MAY BE PREPARED OR COOKED IN LESS TIME THAN IT WILL TAKE THE PASTA TO COOK. HOWEVER, THAT IS TRUE ONLY WHEN THE INGREDIENTS HAVE BEEN PREPARED AND ARE LAYING OUT ON THE WORK SURFACE. ALL THAT IS THEN REQUIRED IS PLACING THEM INTO A PAN IN THE ORDER CALLED FOR AND COOKED TO TIME AND TEMPERATURE REQUIRED. TO QUOTE AN OLD MOTTO OF MY YOUTH "BE PREPARED", AND IF YOU DON'T LIKE THAT ONE, LET'S USE THE COAST GUARD MOTTO OF "SEMPER PARATUS" THAT MEANS YOU'RE "ALWAYS PREPARED", BEFORE THE PASTA WATER BOILS!

TO REPEAT: ANOTHER QUICKIE, IS A KEY PHRASE; I DON'T CARE IF YOUR SPOUSE IS SMIRKING, IN THIS BOOK IT MEANS THAT THE SAUCE TAKES LESS TIME TO PREPARE AND/OR COOK THAN THE PASTA. YOU'LL FIND THE PHRASE (ANOTHER QUICKIE) IMMEDIATELY UNDER THE NAME OF 142 SAUCES IN THIS BOOK. IT MEANS WHAT IT SAYS. FAST AND EASY. AND IT IS NOT TO BE CONFUSED WITH FAST AND LOOSE, WHICH I UNDERSTAND CAN BE APPLIED TO CERTAIN PEOPLE. AND ..., CERTAINLY TO NO ONE READING THIS BOOK. ALSO LOOK FOR THE TERM "LONG AND LOW", NO, THAT'S NOT A CHINESE DANCE TEAM! IT MEANS THAT THE SAUCE WILL REQUIRE A SUBSTANTIAL COOKING TIME, GENERALLY GREATER THAN ONE HOUR, (LONG AND LOW). IF THERE IS NO KEY PHRASE BENEATH THE NAME OF A SAUCE, THAT MEANS THE SAUCE CAN BE COOKED IN APPROXIMATELY 30 MINUTES. LET'S RECAP THEM:

(ANOTHER QUICKIE);	FASTER THAN YOUR PASTA WILL COOK: THIS DOES NOT APPLY TO FRESH PASTA OR ANGEL HAIR.
NO PHRASE;	THE SAUCE WILL COOK IN THIRTY MINUTES OR LESS.
(LONG AND LOW);	ONE TO SEVERAL HOURS COOKING TIME.

INGREDIENT PREPARATION

(SLOW OR FAST: YOUR CHOICE)

THE CHOPPING OF TOMATOES, AS WELL AS ALL FRESH HERBS, GARLIC, ONIONS CAN BE DONE SLOWLY AND ON OCCASION PAINFULLY, WITH A KNIFE OR SOME OTHER BRONZE AGE TOOL. OR, YOU CAN STEP INTO THE 20TH CENTURY AND GET THE JOB DONE WITH A BLENDER OR FOOD PROCESSOR. I DON'T BELIEVE IT MAKES A SIGNIFICANT DIFFERENCE TO THE END PRODUCT IF YOU LOVINGLY AND LABORIOUSLY MINCE A GARLIC CLOVE OR WHIRL IT IN A FOOD PROCESSOR ALONG WITH SEVERAL OTHER INGREDIENTS. THERE PROBABLY ARE FOLKS WHO WILL GIVE YOU AN ARGUMENT HERE. BUT, IF CHOPPING AND MINCING ARE NOT A THERAPEUTIC NEED, WHY NOT GET IT DONE AS QUICKLY, CLEANLY AND NEATLY AS POSSIBLE?

THERE IS ONE INGREDIENT THAT DOESN'T LEND ITSELF TO HIGH SPEED CHOPPING. ONIONS! I WOULD URGE CAUTION HERE. AN ONION CAN BE LIQUEFIED VERY QUICKLY, AND YOU WON'T LIKE WHAT IT DOES TO YOUR SAUCE. WITH ONIONS, I STILL PREFER TO PREPARE THEM WITH A KNIFE.

BACON

WHAT IS THERE YOU NEED TO KNOW ABOUT BACON, YOU'VE PROBABLY BEEN EATING IT FOR BREAKFAST AND IN B.L.T. SANDWICHES MOST OF YOUR LIFE. ON THE OUTSIDE CHANCE THAT YOU'RE NOT AWARE OF BACON CURES, I OFFER THIS. BACON COMES IN SEVERAL CURES, SWEET (SUGAR, BROWN SUGAR, HONEY, MAPLE SYRUP) OR SALT CURED, AS WELL AS WITH SMOKE CURES. SMOKING IS DONE WITH A VARIETY OF HARD WOODS AND/OR CORN COBS. SMOKING FROM SWEET HARD WOODS CAN ADD A SWEETNESS TO THE BACON, (IF THE SMOKE SMELLS SWEET, IT WILL IMPART THAT SWEETNESS), HICKORY WILL, CORN COBS WON'T. SINCE WE ARE GENERALLY ACCUSTOMED TO SWEETER BACON, BE ALERT TO THE FACT THAT THE ITALIAN VARIETY, PANCETTA IS SALT CURED AND GENERALLY WITH SPICES, SO THE TASTE IS SOMEWHAT DIFFERENT. OUR POINT IS THAT FOR YOU TO APPROXIMATE THE TASTE OF PANCETTA, WHEN YOU CAN'T FIND PANCETTA WHERE YOU LIVE, IS TO USE SALT PORK, OR SALT CURED BACON.

COUNTRY STYLE

COUNTRY STYLE, IN ITALIAN COOKERY, MEANS THAT THE PASTA, AFTER IT IS COOKED AND DRAINED, IS ADDED TO THE PAN IN WHICH YOU'VE COOKED YOUR SAUCE FOR A FEW ADDITIONAL MINUTES OF COOKING AND BLENDING WITH THE SAUCE. THIS APPEARS TO BE A SOUTHERN METHOD; ALTHOUGH IT IS USED IN MOST CREAM SAUCES, AND THEY ARE NORTHERN. WHILE I'VE AD-DRESSED ITS USE IN A FEW NON-CREAM SAUCES, I'VE DISREGARDED THE METHOD IN A LARGER NUMBER. IT CAN BE USED IN MOST OF THE SAUCES IN THIS BOOK. IF YOU LIKE THE METHOD, USE IT.

A SUGGESTION ON PANS, IF I MAY. IF YOU DO NOT HAVE TWO LARGE PANS, OR YOUR STOVE WILL NOT ACCOMMODATE TWO LARGE PANS, MAKE THE SAUCE IN A SMALL SAUCE PAN, COOK THE PASTA IN YOUR LARGE PAN, DRAIN, PUT BOTH THE PASTA AND SAUCE INTO THE LARGE PAN AND FINISH THE "COUNTRY STYLE" COOKING USING ONLY ONE LARGE PAN.

A VARIATION OF THIS METHOD IS USED QUITE OFTEN WITH VEGETABLES SUCH AS CAULIFLOWER OR BROCCOLI. THAT IS WHERE THE VEGETABLES AND THE PASTA ARE COOKED TOGETHER, PARTIALLY DRAINED AND THEN OLIVE OIL, GARLIC AND OR ONIONS ARE ADDED, WITH OR WITHOUT GRATED CHEESE, BLENDED AND SERVED.

CHEESES AND CHEESING

ASIDE FROM THE FACT THAT THE GRATING CHEESE OF PREFERENCE CHANGES FROM NORTH TO SOUTH, SO DOES ITS APPLICATION. NORTHERNERS SEEM TO HAVE A PREFERENCE FOR TOSSING HOT, DRAINED PASTA WITH THEIR GRATED CHEESE (GENERALLY PARMESAN), AND THEN ADDING THE SAUCE, AND TOSSING AGAIN. IF THEY ARE ALSO USING BUTTER (NORMALLY TRUE) THEY WILL TOSS THE PASTA WITH BUTTER FIRST, THEN THE GRATED CHEESE AND AGAIN WITH THE SAUCE.

SOUTHERNERS BY CONTRAST, TOSS THE PASTA WITH THE SAUCE AND THEN ADD COPIOUS AMOUNTS OF GRATED CHEESE (NORMALLY ROMANO) ON TOP, TO BE DRAWN UP WITH THE PASTA BY THE FORK FULL.

EGGPLANT

THE EGGPLANT COMES IN SEVERAL SIZES AND SHAPES; THE FAMILIAR LARGE SIZED DEEP PURPLE VARIETY, THE SMALL, SLENDER SIZED DEEP PURPLE JAPANESE VARIETY, AND NOW THE NEWEST VARIETY ON THE AMERICAN MARKET, THE MEDIUM SIZED WHITE VARIETY. THEY ALL SHOULD BE PEELED, SALTED AND TOWEL DRIED OR RINSED, OR SOAKED IN A BRINE BATH TO RID THEM OF THEIR CHARACTERISTIC BITTERNESS BEFORE USING IN ANY OF THE SAUCE RECIPES. THERE ARE SEVERAL RECIPES IN THIS BOOK THAT DO NOT REQUIRE THAT STEP. SINCE YOU'LL BE DOING THE COOKING, DO WHAT YOU LIKE. THE SMALL JAPANESE VARIETY MAY, IF VERY FRESH, BE PREPARED AND EATEN WITH SKIN ON. BOTH THE JAPANESE AND WHITE VARIETIES ARE VERY MILD AND MAY BECOME YOUR FAVORITES.

GARLIC

(OR WHAT "YOUR CHOICE" REALLY MEANS)

ON TO THE PURPOSE OF THIS ASIDE . . . , WHEN YOU SEE GARLIC AS AN INGREDIENT IN A SAUCE FOLLOWED BY THE WORDS (YOUR CHOICE), IT MEANS THAT HOW THE GARLIC IS ADDED TO THE SAUCE IS YOUR CHOICE, BECAUSE: GARLIC CAN BE HALVED, QUARTERED, SLICED, DICED, CHOPPED, MINCED, SMASHED, MASHED, CRUSHED, BRUISED, PRESSED, SHREDDED OR LEFT WHOLE. AND, YOU'LL FIND THOSE WHO WILL ARGUE WITH YOU ON THE RELATIVE MERITS OF DOING IT IN ANY OF THE ABOVE FASHIONS, I BELIEVE A WORD IS PROPERLY DUE HERE. IT DOESN'T MATTER TO ME HOW YOU PREPARE IT. YOUR CHOICE IS WHETHER YOU'LL WANT IT TO REMAIN IN THE FINISHED SAUCE. SOME DO, SOME DON'T. IF YOU DON'T WANT IT TO REMAIN IN THE SAUCE, THEN BY ALL MEANS LEAVE IT WHOLE OR SLIGHTLY CRUSHED, THEN REMOVE IT AT THE POINT OF YOUR PREFERENCE. THE MOST COMMON REMOVAL POINTS ARE, IMMEDIATELY AFTER BROWNING OR PRIOR TO SERVING.

A VERY GOOD METHOD FOR ADDING THE ESSENCE OF GARLIC TO A SAUCE IS TO HALVE A CLOVE, RUB THE BOWL, THEN DISCARD THE CLOVE. THIS WORKS ESPECIALLY WELL WITH UNCOOKED SAUCES LEFT TO MARINATE FOR SEVERAL HOURS.

I USE ALL THE ABOVE METHODS AND WHAT'S MORE, I BELIEVE EACH METHOD INFLUENCES THE END TASTE. IN SOME SAUCES I LOVE THE FLAVOR GARLIC ADDS, IN OTHER SAUCES, I WILL AVOID IT. IT CAN OVERPOWER AND RUIN AN OTHERWISE MARVELOUS SAUCE. USE YOUR OWN DISCRETION IN ADDING OR OMITTING GARLIC. BUT AS A CAUTION . . . , BE AWARE, THAT THERE IS NO SUBSTITUTE FOR GARLIC. IF YOU OMIT IT YOU MAY LOSE A SUBSTANTIAL PORTION OF THE SAUCE'S FLAVOR.

GREEN PEPPER

THROUGHOUT THIS BOOK I REFER TO "LONG GREEN MILDLY HOT PEPPERS" WHENEVER A RECIPE CALLS FOR FRESH HOT PEPPER(S). THAT MAY SEEM TO BE EXCESSIVE WORDING, AND YOU'RE RIGHT. BUT, HOT PEPPERS COME IN MANY SHAPES AND SIZES. THAT'S OK TOO, EXCEPT, THAT THE LONG ONES ARE MARKETED UNDER A VARIETY OF NAMES. THAT'S WHERE THE CONFUSION COMES IN. WHERE I LIVE THEY ARE MARKETED UNDER AT LEAST THREE NAMES, THE MOST FREQUENTLY USED IS, (LONG) ANAHEIM'S, AND WHO KNOWS WHAT THEY MAY BE CALLED WHERE YOU SHOP. IF I SELECTED ONE NAME FROM AMONG THE THREE USED WHERE I LIVE, YOU MIGHT NEVER BE ABLE TO FIND IT, SO I HOPE THAT THE DESCRIPTION, "LONG GREEN MILDLY HOT PEPPERS" WILL SERVE YOU WELL.

MUSHROOMS

MUSHROOMS ARE A WORLD FAVORITE, AND AS YOU'LL DISCOVER IN THIS BOOK, MANY OF THE RECIPES CALL FOR THE ADDITION OF MUSHROOMS. WHEN IT COMES TO PUTTING MUSHROOMS IN A SLOW COOKING TOMATO SAUCE HOWEVER, YOU MAY NOT LIKE THE END RESULT. I KNOW I DON'T. TRY IT ONCE, IF YOU FIND THE TASTE UNACCEPTABLE, THEN NOTE IT SOMEWHERE ON THE RECIPE PAGE TO OMIT THEM IN FUTURE PREPARATIONS.

ABOVE ALL, USE ONLY FRESH MUSHROOMS!

Onions

ONIONS COME WITH A VARIETY OF QUALITIES, SOME VERY SWEET AND SOME HOT ENOUGH TO BURN. THEY'RE ALL GOOD AND ALL HAVE SOME SWEETNESS, BUT SOME ARE SWEET TO THE TASTE WHEN RAW, THOSE ARE THE BEST FOR OUR COOKING USE. THE SWEETEST VARIETIES CURRENTLY ON THE MARKET ARE VIDALIAS, OUT OF VIDALIA, GEORGIA, THE WALLA WALLAS FROM WASHINGTON, THE MAUI SWEETS, FROM YOU KNOW WHERE AND FROM TEXAS, THE TEXAS 10-15.

TO SWEETEN A HOT ONION, PEEL, SLICE AND WASH THEM. MAYBE I'D BETTER EXPAND ON THAT, A NEW BRIDE MAY WASH THEM IN SOAPY WATER. TO WASH, SLICE THE ONION INTO THIN RINGS, SOAK THEM IN COLD WATER FOR ABOUT 10 MINUTES, SQUEEZE SEVERAL TIMES, DRAIN, ADD NEW COLD WATER AND REPEAT THE PROCESS TWO OR THREE TIMES.

OR,

YOU COULD SUBSTITUTE SHALLOTS FOR ONIONS IF YOU WISH. THE COST IS HIGHER, BUT THEY'RE IN THE SAME FAMILY AND VERY MILD.

Green Onions

KISSIN' KIN TO THE ONION IS THE GREEN ONION (CHIVE IN THE WEST AND SCALLION IN THE EAST), SAME ONION, DIFFERENT NAME. THEY MAY SUCCESSFULLY BE REPLACED IN ANY RECIPE WITH THE LEEK. LEEKS ARE CONSIDERABLY MILDER THAN THE GREEN ONION AND PREFERRED BY SOME.

OIL

WHERE A RECIPE CALLS FOR OIL, MAY I RECOMMEND YOU USE ONLY OLIVE OIL. IT ADDS A FLAVOR AND BOUQUET THAT SIMPLY CANNOT BE HAD WITH VEGETABLE OIL (AMERICAN VEGETABLE OILS ARE DESIGNED TO BE TASTE FREE). ANY GOOD OLIVE OIL WILL WORK, IT NEED NOT BE ONE OF THE VIRGIN TYPES. THEY ARE TOO EXPENSIVE FOR COOKING AND ARE BEST LEFT TO COLD USES, SUCH AS SALADS, ANTIPASTAS AND UNCOOKED PASTA SAUCES. SINCE OLIVE OIL IS A PRODUCT FROM VARIOUS OLIVE TYPES, ITS TASTE WILL DIFFER SUB-STANTIALLY FROM ONE GROWER/PRODUCER TO ANOTHER. SOME PRODUCERS WILL ALSO BLEND VARIETIES. A "COLD PRESS" TO HEATED PRESSING OF THE SAME OLIVE, WILL GIVE YOU A DIFFERENT TASTE, THE LATTER IS NOT MARKED ON THE CONTAINER. MY SUGGESTION IS TO TRY SEVERAL BRANDS UNTIL YOU FIND A TASTE YOU LIKE.

AMONG THE ADDED AND GENUINE BENEFITS OF OLIVE OIL IS THAT IT IS EASILY DIGESTIBLE. IT CONTAINS LINOLEIC ACID IN NEAR IDENTICAL PROPOR-TIONS TO MOTHER'S MILK (I READ THAT SOMEWHERE), AND THAT'S WHAT MAKES IT EASILY DIGESTIBLE. (TRY A SIDE DISH OF PASTA WITH ONLY A SPRINKLING OF OLIVE OIL INSTEAD OF BUTTER). ADDITIONALLY, OLIVE OIL IS HIGHEST IN MONOUNSATURATED FAT, THE KIND OF FAT THAT HAS A NEUTRAL EFFECT ON BLOOD CHOLESTEROL AND BENEFICIAL TO HDL (HIGH DENSITY LIPOPROTEIN) IN POSSIBLY REDUCING HIGH BLOOD PRESSURE. RECENT DEVELOP-MENTS FROM OLIVE OIL PRODUCERS HAVE ADDED A NEW, LIGHTER OLIVE OIL, CALLED "LIGHT" OR "EXTRA LIGHT", AND BROUGHT HAPPINESS TO THOSE WHO WOULD MAKE MORE EXTENSIVE USE OF OLIVE OIL BECAUSE OF ITS HEALTH GIVING BENEFITS. THE NEW LIGHTER OIL HAS THE WONDERFUL ABILITY TO BE USED IN BAKING AND HIGH TEMPERATURE COOKING WITHOUT BURNING AND WITHOUT ADDING OLIVE OIL'S DISTINCTIVE TASTE, YET RETAINING ALL ITS NUTRITIONAL VALUE.

PARSLEY

ANY VARIETY OF PARSLEY WILL WORK, NORMALLY BECAUSE IT IS USED FOR EYE APPEAL AND COLOR. HOWEVER, THERE WILL BE TIMES WHEN YOU'LL WANT THE PARSLEY TO ADD TASTE TO YOUR SAUCE. IN THAT INSTANCE I WOULD RECOMMEND THE USE OF BROAD LEAF (ITALIAN) PARSLEY. IT MAY BE DIFFICULT TO FIND IN SOME PARTS OF THE COUNTRY, BUT IF YOU CAN FIND IT, USE IT. IT HAS AN ADDED TASTE DIFFICULT TO DEFINE, BUT DISTINCTLY ITALIAN.

I WILL OFFER ONE CAVEAT HERE, NEVER USE CILANTRO, SOMETIMES CALLED MEXICAN OR CHINESE PARSLEY. IT WILL ADD A DISTINCTIVE FLAVOR THAT I FIND REMARKABLY SIMILAR TO DISHWASHING DETERGENT.

POTS AND PANS

I AM GOING TO ASSUME THAT YOU NEED NO INSTRUCTIONS FROM ME ON WHAT SIZE PAN OR SKILLET TO USE FOR MAKING A SAUCE OR COOKING YOUR PASTA. THAT WILL OBVIOUSLY BE DETERMINED BY YOUR COOKWARE. HOWEVER, THERE MAY BE AN OCCASION OR TWO WHEN I WILL MAKE SUCH A RECOMMENDATION. IF I DO, IT IS BECAUSE SOMETHING OTHER WILL NOT WORK, OR BE LESS THAN SATISFACTORY.

ROUX

ON A NUMBER OF OCCASIONS WHILE USING THIS BOOK, YOU'LL BE ASKED TO MAKE A ROUX. MOST EXPERIENCED COOKS KNOW HOW TO DO THAT. IF YOU DO NOT, THEN THIS IS FOR YOU. A ROUX IS THE BASE AND THICKENER FOR A SAUCE OR GRAVY. YOU MAY USE BUTTER, OR ANY OIL OF YOUR CHOICE. THE METHOD IS VERY SIMPLE, MELT 1 TO 2 TABLESPOONS OF BUTTER IN A SAUCE PAN. ADD AN EQUAL AMOUNT OF FLOUR, WHISK THE FLOUR IN THE MELTED BUTTER FOR SEVERAL MINUTES (DO NOT COLOR THE ROUX BY BROWNING FOR ANY SAUCE IN THIS BOOK*), ADD 1 CUP OF MILK TO EACH TABLESPOON OF FLOUR USED, WHISK MILK UNTIL SMOOTH AND ROUX THICKENS. REMOVE FROM HEAT, USE AS DIRECTED BY THE RECIPE.

*A ROUX (ROO) IS NOT ONLY A BASE AND THICKENER FOR MANY GRAVIES AND SAUCES, IT MAY ALSO BE THE COLORING AGENT WHEN IT IS BROWNED TO ANY DESIRED SHADE.

SALTING

I DO NOT ADD SALT TO A RECIPE USING CANNED TOMATOES. IN THE CANNING PROCESS ENOUGH SALT IS ADDED TO THE TOMATOES TO BRING OUT THE TASTE OF THE TOMATO AND CARRY IT THROUGH YOUR COOKING AND ONTO THE PLATE. FRESH TOMATOES DO REQUIRE SALTING. THERE ARE CURRENTLY MANY CANNED PRODUCTS COMING FROM THE CANNERS WITH LESS SALT AND/OR NO SALT. IF THERE IS NO DIETARY REASON FOR YOU TO AVOID SALT, DON'T.

SAUCE PREPARATION

A VERY LARGE NUMBER OF SAUCES CAN BE MADE AFTER THE PASTA HAS BEEN ADDED TO BOILING WATER AND IS MERRILY BUBBLING ALONG. CONTRARY TO MYTH AND BAD COOKS, TOMATO SAUCES DO NOT REQUIRE HOURS OF SIMMERING. THERE MAY BE AN OCCASIONAL ONE THAT WILL, BUT MOST ARE DONE IN ONE HALF HOUR AND MANY EVEN MORE QUICKLY. FRESH MEAT IN A SAUCE, WILL EXTEND ITS COOKING TIME CONSIDERABLY, BUT THAT IS BECAUSE YOU ARE COOKING THE MEAT AND NOT REALLY SIMMERING THE OTHER INGREDIENTS OF THE SAUCE TO THE BENEFIT OF THOSE INGREDIENTS.

LOOK FOR THE WORDS (ANOTHER QUICKIE) UNDER THE SAUCE NAME TO INDICATE THAT IT MAY BE COOKED IN LESS TIME THAN IT WILL TAKE THE PASTA TO COOK. HOWEVER, THAT IS GENERALLY TRUE ONLY WHEN THE INGREDIENTS HAVE BEEN PREPARED AND ARE LAYING OUT ON THE WORK SURFACE. ALL THAT IS THEN REQUIRED IS PLACING THEM INTO A PAN IN THE ORDER CALLED FOR AND COOKED TO TIME AND TEMPERATURE REQUIRED. LET ME REPEAT MYSELF WITH THIS QUOTE OF AN OLD MOTTO FROM THE DAYS OF MY YOUTH, "BE PREPARED", AND IF YOU DON'T LIKE THAT ONE, YOU MAY USE THE COAST GUARD MOTTO OF "SEMPER PARATUS" THAT MEANS YOU'RE "ALWAYS PREPARED", BEFORE THE PASTA WATER BOILS!

SAUCING

MOST OF THE RECIPES IN THIS BOOK WILL YIELD MORE SAUCE THAN NEEDED FOR ONE POUND OF PASTA. A NUMBER OF AMERICAN PACKERS, NOW PACK 1/2 AND 3/4 POUND PACKAGES (8 & 12 OUNCES), LOOK OUT FOR THOSE. ONE FULL RECIPE POURED OVER 12 OUNCES OF PASTA WILL MAKE YOUR OFFERING LOOK LIKE SOUP.

WHEN ADDING SAUCE TO YOUR PASTA, UNLESS OTHERWISE DIRECTED, START WITH ABOUT 1 CUP OF THE SAUCE YOU'VE MADE, YOU MAY ADD MORE SAUCE AS NEEDED, OR PLACE THE REMAINING SAUCE ON THE TABLE AND LET YOUR DINER'S ADD MORE IF THEY WISH TO. DON'T OVER SAUCE, THERE SHOULD BE A NICE COATING OF SAUCE ON THE PASTA AND NONE AT THE BOTTOM OF THE SERVING BOWL. IN ITALY THE COMMON PRACTICE IS TO USE A VERY SMALL AMOUNT OF SAUCE. THE DESIRED EFFECT IS LIGHTNESS.

TOMATOES: CANNED

WHEN IS A PEAR A PLUM? WHEN THE CANNER WANTS IT TO BE! PEAR AND PLUM SEEM TO BE INTERCHANGEABLE TERMS FOR THE SMALL TASTY ITALIAN TYPE TOMATO. AMERICAN CANNERS THAT USE A VARIETY NAME (S&W AND CONTADINA) CALL THEM PEAR TOMATOES, WHILE ITALIAN CANNERS (DELVERDE) CALL THEIRS PLUM TOMATOES. MOST AMERICAN CANNERS GET AROUND THE ISSUE BY LABELING THEIR PRODUCT "ITALIAN STYLE TOMATOES" AND PRINTING A PICTURE OF THE LITTLE TOMATOES ON THE LABEL. WHILE ITALIAN CANNERS JUST CALL THEIRS TOMATOES. IN GENERAL, ITALIANS USE "PLUM" AS THE PREFERRED VARIETY NAME.

TO ADD A BIT OF FURTHER CONFUSION TO THE COOK'S LIFE, THROUGHOUT AMERICA, THAT SAME TOMATO IS MARKETED FRESH AS "SALADETTE TOMATO" OR IN SOME GROCERY STORES AS "ROMA TOMATOES", PROBABLY BECAUSE NO ONE COULD AGREE ON PLUM OR PEAR.

Tomatoes: Canned and Seasoned

or

(Old Product with New Tastes)

RECENTLY TOMATO PACKERS HAVE BEGUN TO OFFER THAT OLD STANDARD, "STEWED TOMATOES" IN SEVERAL SEASONED VARIETIES, "ITALIAN STYLE" BEING AMONG THEM. ON OCCASION, THE ITALIAN STYLE STEWED TOMATO MAY BE JUDICIALLY USED AS A SAUCE BASE (IT IS VERY SWEET), OR SERVED AS A VEGETABLE JUST AS IT COMES FROM THE CAN.

CANNERS ARE ALSO OFFERING A VARIETY OF SEASONED TOMATOES, I.E., "ITALIAN FLAVORED", OR "ITALIAN SEASONED". I DON'T USE THEM, THEY ARE TOO EXPENSIVE FOR THE SMALL AMOUNT OF SEASONING ADDED, AND THEY OFTEN CONTAIN INGREDIENTS I DON'T WANT IN MY SAUCE, OR ARE TOO SALTY OR TOO SWEET. IT'S VERY EASY TO PREPARE A QUICK TOMATO SAUCE WITHOUT PAYING DEARLY FOR SOMEONE ELSE'S WORK.

Tomatoes: Fresh

ANY VARIETY OF FRESH TOMATO WILL MAKE A GOOD TOMATO SAUCE. VINE RIPENED TOMATOES HAVE THE ADDED BENEFIT OF MAKING AN UNCOOKED SAUCE WITH GREAT FRESH TOMATO FLAVOR. ADMITTEDLY VINE RIPENED TOMATOES MAY BE HARD TO COME BY IN SOME AREAS. COUNT YOURSELF LUCKY IF YOU HAVE A NEIGHBOR WHO LOVES GARDENING AND ALWAYS HAS A BUMPER CROP. POSSIBLY THE BEST TOMATO TO USE FOR UNCOOKED SAUCES WOULD BE THE LITTLE ITALIAN STYLE TOMATO, THEY ARE HIGH IN MEAT CONTENT AND SHORT ON JUICINESS; AND THEY ARE GENERALLY AVAILABLE THROUGHOUT THE YEAR. I ALSO LIKE A GOOD RIPE BEEFSTEAK TOMATO. IT HAS AN EVEN MIX OF BOTH, HIGH JUICE CONTENT AND HIGH MEAT CONTENT.

TOMATOES: CONDENSED

HERE WE'RE TALKING ABOUT TOMATO PASTE, TOMATO PUREE AND TOMATO SAUCE. THE LATTER HAS ITS USES WHEN ADDED TO SOMETHING ELSE, INCLUDING OTHER TYPES OF CANNED TOMATOES, IT CAN RARELY STAND ALONE.

PUREE IS NEARLY WORTHLESS. IT IS FIRST AND FOREMOST BITTER AND MUST BE SWEETENED. WHY BOTHER! I HAVE NEVER FOUND A BRAND THAT WAS ACCEPTABLE TO ME, DITTO FOR THE CANNED TOMATO PRODUCTS KNOWN AS "GROUND TOMATOES" AND "CRUSHED TOMATOES".

THE FLAVOR OF TOMATO PASTE VARIES INCREDIBLY BETWEEN CANNERS; SOME ARE ALMOST GOOD ENOUGH TO EAT STRAIGHT FROM THE CAN, OTHERS SHOULD BE THROWN OUT. SINCE CANNERS ADD ONLY A LITTLE SALT TO TOMATO PASTE, EVERYTHING THAT CAN AFFECT A GROWING CROP WILL SHOW UP IN TOMATO PASTE. STARTING WITH THE VARIETY OF TOMATO PLANTED, THE RICHNESS OF THE SOIL, THE AMOUNT OF SUNSHINE ON THE FIELD, THE AMOUNT AND QUALITY OF WATER, AND THE SUGAR CONTENT OF THE TOMATO AT POINT OF HARVEST. THE PASTE QUALITY YOU WANT TO AVOID IS BITTERNESS, I GUESS WHAT I SUGGEST IS THAT YOU TRY SEVERAL BRANDS UNTIL YOU FIND ONE WITH A TASTE YOU LIKE.

TOMATOES: SUN DRIED

ONE OF THE MORE RECENT CULINARY INTRODUCTIONS IN AMERICA OF THINGS ITALIAN IS THE SUN DRIED TOMATO. HERE THEY MOST LIKELY ARE DRIED IN DEHYDRATORS, AND THAT HAS NO IMPACT UPON THE TOMATOES TASTE OR FLAVOR. AMERICAN PACKERS OF DRIED TOMATOES ARE SEEKING A NICHE IN THE MARKET PLACE FOR THEIR PRODUCT; I DON'T BELIEVE IT WILL BE IN PASTA SAUCES. THE PHRASE SOME AMERICAN PACKERS USE TO DESCRIBE THEIR PRODUCT'S FLAVOR IS "INTENSE TOMATO FLAVOR". NOT TRUE! THE TOMATO FLAVOR IS COMPLETELY OVERWHELMED BY THE FLAVOR OF THE TOMATO'S SKINS, AND THAT IS BITTERNESS! FOR A MORE DESCRIPTIVE STORY ABOUT MY EXPERTISE IN MAKING THIS JUDGEMENT CALL, PLEASE READ THE INTRODUCTION TO THE FIRST SAUCE RECIPE IN CHAPTER 22.

IT IS VERY POSSIBLE THAT DRIED TOMATOES WILL FIND A HOME IN AMERICAN COOKERY. IF IT DOES, IT WILL BE AS AN INGREDIENT IN DISHES OTHER THAN PASTA.

Of Wines and Sauces

LET ME START BY SUGGESTING YOU DO NOT BUY "COOKING WINE" FOR ANY REASON. IT IS OVERPRICED, UNWARRANTED AND DEFINITELY UNNECESSARY. COOKING WINE IS SALTED WINE. THAT'S IT! SO BUY ANY WINE THAT YOU WOULD DRINK AND ENJOY, THEN USE THAT IN YOUR COOKING. CONSIDER THIS OLD FRENCH SAYING; THE BETTER THE WINE, THE BETTER THE SAUCE. ASIDE FROM THAT, IF YOU WOULDN'T DRINK IT, WHY WOULD YOU PUT IT IN YOUR FOOD? LET'S GET BACK TO COOKING WINE; IN THE MANOR HOUSES OF ENGLAND (AND PROBABLY ELSEWHERE IN EUROPE), IT BECAME A METHOD OF PREVENTING THE KITCHEN AND HOUSEHOLD STAFF FROM SIPHONING THE SHERRIES. THE SALT ONLY RUINED THE TASTE OF THE WINE WHEN DRANK. IT DID NO HARM TO THE FOOD TO WHICH SALT WOULD NORMALLY BE ADDED ANYWAY.

THERE ARE OCCASIONS WHEN AN AMOUNT OF WINE WILL BE AN EXCELLENT ADDITION TO A PASTA SAUCE. I THINK THEY ARE RARE. IF YOU'RE OF A MIND TO, WINE CAN BE ADDED TO ANY SAUCE. I DON'T LIKE THAT PHILOSOPHY. THEY CAN ADD TOO MUCH TO AN OTHERWISE BALANCED SAUCE. DEEP RED WINES WILL COLOR YOUR SAUCE, DRY WINES ARE USUALLY TART WINES AND THEY MAY ADD A QUALITY YOU DON'T WANT, AND SWEET WINES CAN ADD (WHAT ELSE?) UNWANTED SWEETNESS. SOMETIMES IT MAY BE BETTER FOR THE SAUCE IF YOU JUST ADD WATER.

THE SHAPE(S) OF YOUR PASTA

HERE WE COME TO GRIPS WITH THE SHAPE DESCRIPTIONS OF THE PASTAS GENERALLY AVAILABLE IN THE UNITED STATES. THERE ARE VERY EASILY 150 OR MORE SHAPES AND VARIETIES AVAILABLE SOMEWHERE IN MOST CITIES.

THE NUMBER OF SHAPES IN ITALY PROBABLY EXCEEDS 300, AND NEW DESIGNS ARE BEING SOUGHT BY PASTA MAKERS THROUGHOUT THE COUNTRY.

SINCE I HAVE INTRODUCED (IN THIS ONE SIDED DIALOGUE) THE TERMS, SHAPES AND VARIETIES, PERHAPS WE NEED TO ADDRESS THAT DISTINCTION. SHAPES ARE OBVIOUS, SPAGHETTI, RIGATONI, LASAGNA AND RAVIOLI ARE SOME OF THE BETTER KNOWN ONES. VARIETIES ARE FAIRLY NEW, NORMALLY OLD FAMILIAR SHAPES, MADE WITH ADDED VEGETABLE OR PROTEIN. SOME OF THE BETTER KNOWN ADDITIONS ARE, SPINACH, CARROT, TOMATO, PROTEIN; AND MORE ARE COMING.

NOW LET'S ADDRESS THE MANNER IN WHICH WE FOLLOW EVERY RECIPE WITH A RECOMMENDATION FOR ONE OR MORE PASTA SHAPES. WE'VE LISTED THE RECOMMENDED SHAPE(S), IN GROUP TYPES, FOLLOWED BY DIVISIONS WITHIN THE GROUPS AND THEN BY THE RECOGNIZED PRODUCT NAMES.

PASTA NAME PRIMER

MANY OF THE NAMES GIVEN TO PASTA SHAPES ARE NICKNAMES FROM LOCAL DIALECTS. THEY DESCRIBE SHAPES, AND/OR THEIR RELATIONSHIP TO WHATEVER, INCLUDING, HUMAN AND ANIMAL ANATOMY, WEARING APPAREL, BUGS AND OTHER ASSORTED CREEPY, CRAWLY THINGS. IT MAY NOT BE IMPORTANT TO KNOW THE ACTUAL TRANSLATIONS. MAY WE PARAPHRASE SHAKESPEARE WITH; WOULD A PASTA BY ANY OTHER NAME TASTE AS GOOD?

BUCATI: AN ADJECTIVE MEANING "WITH A HOLE", ERGO, BUCATINI MEANS HOLLOW PASTA, GENERALLY APPLIED TO LONG STRANDS, READ "FAT HOLLOW STRINGS".

CANNELLE: MEANING "PIPES" OR "REEDS" AND THE ROOT FOR NAMES LIKE CANNELLONI.

CAPELLI:	ROOT WORD FOR "HAIR", GENERALLY APPLIED TO VERY THIN STRINGS, SUCH AS ANGEL HAIR, ITALIAN; CAPELLI D'ANGELO (THAT'S A BOY ANGEL).
CAPPELLI:	TO COVER HAIR, YOU NEED "CAPPELLI", (I IS PLURAL, O OR A WOULD BE SINGULAR, RESPECTIVELY MALE AND FEMALE) THAT'S A HAT AS IN "PRIEST'S HATS" AND SEVERAL OTHERS.
CHITARRA:	MEANS "GUITAR" AND IN PARTICULAR, GUITAR STRING STYLE PASTA. NOT POSSIBLE SAYS YOU, GUITAR STRINGS ARE ROUND AND THIS PASTA IS SQUARE SHAPED. TRUE, YOU KEEN OBSERVER. BUT, SAYS I, 'TIS MADE BY PRESSING A THICK DOUGH THROUGH A SET OF WIRES THAT LOOKS LIKE A ZITHER, AND TO CONFUSE YOU WE'LL CALL IT GUITAR STRINGS.
CONCHIGLIE:	FOR OUR PURPOSES, IT MEANS SEA SHELLS, OF ANY SIZE AND TEXTURE.
DITALI:	THE ROOT WORD "THIMBLE" AS APPLIED TO THE FAMILY OF SHORT HOLLOW PASTAS OF VARIOUS DIAMETERS AND SHORT LENGTHS.
FARFALLE:	ROOT WORD FOR "BUTTERFLIES", AND OFFERING A WHOLE FAMILY OF SIZES. BETTER KNOWN HERE AS "BOWS".
FEDELINI:	A THIN TYPE OF SPAGHETTI, PROBABLY BETTER KNOWN AS SPAGHETTINI.
FETTUCCINE:	MEANS "SMALL RIBBON" FOR OUR PURPOSES, IT MEANS ANY OF THE LONG RIBBONS IN WIDTHS, FROM ABOUT 3/16" TO 1/2" INCH.
FUSILLI:	ROOT WORD MEANING "TWISTS" AND APPLIES TO ALL PASTA LOOKING LIKE A CORKSCREW.

GEMELLI:	"TWINS", LATIN GEMINI, GENERALLY USED TO DESCRIBE TWO PIECES OF PASTA TWISTED TOGETHER. OR ONE PIECE FORMED IN AN "S" PATTERN, AND THAT CREATES THE IMAGE OF TWO PIECES.
GNOCCHI:	ROOT WORD FOR "DUMPLING". WHEN HOMEMADE, THAT'S WHAT YOU GET, WHEN MADE COMMERCIALLY; IT RESEMBLES A WIDE SEA SHELL.
INI, INE, ELLI, ETTI AND OLI:	FOR OUR PURPOSES THESE ARE SUFFIXES FOR "TINY", "LITTLE" OR "SMALL".
LASAGNE:	ROOT WORD FROM THE LATIN FOR "POTS", HOW IT GOT FROM THAT TO A WIDE, CURLY EDGED PASTA IS ANYBODY'S GUESS.
LINGUINE:	IT MEANS "SMALL TONGUES", AND JUDGING FROM THE STANDARD LENGTH OF THEM, THE ORIGINAL MUST HAVE COME FROM A TALL BIRD WHOSE TONGUE WAS ATTACHED TO ITS BELLY BUTTON.
LISCI:	TAG ON WORD TO MANY PASTAS, IT MEANS "SMOOTH".
MACARONI:	THE GENERIC WORD FOR ALL PASTE PRODUCTS. RECENTLY IN THE UNITED STATES, THAT WORD HAS BEEN REPLACED IN GENERAL USE BY THE ITALIAN WORD FOR PASTE, PASTA. THIS IS FINE BECAUSE "MACARONI" IS MORE ACCURATELY APPLIED TO TUBE TYPES SUCH AS ELBOWS, DITALINI, ZITI AND EVEN SEA SHELLS, AS WELL AS THE LONG HOLLOW STRING TYPES.

MANICOTTI:	MEANING "SMALL MUFF". IF YOU WERE MEASURING IT AGAINST A REAL MUFF, IT WOULD BE. UNLESS YOU'RE INTO WATCHING OLD MOVIES, YOU'VE PROBABLY NEVER SEEN A REAL MUFF, THOSE WERE THE LARGE FURRY, TUBE THINGS LADIES KEPT THEIR HANDS IN WHEN IT WAS UNSEEMLY FOR WOMEN TO WEAR GLOVES IN COLD WEATHER, OR THEY WORE FASHION GLOVES, TOO THIN TO PROTECT AGAINST THE COLD. FOR OUR PURPOSES, IT MEANS A FAT TUBE TYPE OF PASTA, SOMETHING BIG ENOUGH TO STUFF.
MOSTACCIOLI:	ROOT WORD FOR "SMALL MOUSTACHES", HOW THEY RELATE TO THE PASTA SHAPE IS ONE OF THE MYSTERIES WE FIND IN NAMES.
ONE, ONI:	NOT ONE (WUN), BUT (OH-NEY) THE SUFFIX FOR LARGE. WHEN ANY PASTA SHAPE IS CHOSEN TO BE MADE AVAIL-ABLE IN SEVERAL SIZES THESE SUFFIXES COME INTO PLAY AS IN "PENNE", A SMALLER VERSION BECOMES "PENNINE", WHILE THE LARGER VERSION BECOMES "PENNONE".
PASTA FRESCA:	MEANS "FRESHLY MADE PASTA", BUT YOU KNEW THAT.
PENNE:	TRANSLATES AS "PENS", "FEATHERS" OR "QUILLS". FOR OUR PURPOSES, IT MEANS MEDIUM TUBES, CUT DIAGONALLY.
PERCIATELLI:	MEANS "SMALL PIERCED" PASTA. FOR OUR APPLICATION IT MEANS LONG HOLLOW STRINGS.
RAVIOLI:	A FILLED PILLOW TYPE PASTA, COMES IN SQUARE, ROUND OR TRIANGULAR SHAPES.
RICCIE:	A TAG ON WORD MEANING "CURLY". IT MAY ALSO BE THE PRIME WORD WITH A SUFFIX FOR DIMINUTIVE.
RIGATI:	THIS WORD MEANS THE PASTA IS COVERED WITH SMALL RIDGES, RIGATONI AS OPPOSED TO PENNE OR MOSTACCIOLI SAME SHAPE, DIFFERENT TREATMENT.

ROTE:	ROOT WORD FOR "WHEELS", AS IN ROTELLE, ET AL.

SPAGHETTI: FROM SPAGO, ROOT WORD FOR "A LENGTH OF STRING OR CORD". ALSO KNOWN AMONG THE TRIKE SET AS "PAS-KETTY" OR JUST PLAIN "SKETTY".

TAGLIATELLE: FROM THE ITALIAN VERB "TO CUT", HERE WE HAVE A FAMILY OF RIBBON PASTA VIRTUALLY INDISTINGUISHABLE FROM THE "FETTUCCINE" FAMILY. ALTHOUGH, IN COMMERCIAL MARKETING OF FRESH PASTAS, TAGLIATELLE SEEMS TO BE THE ODDS ON FAVORITE FOR THE RIBBON TYPES. OBVIOUSLY IT'S THE PRODUCER'S CHOICE.

TAGLIATI: A SUFFIX OR TAG ON WORD MEANING "SHORTER VERSION".

TORTELLINI OR TORTELLI: MEANING SMALL TWISTS; IT WAS DEVELOPED IN BOLOGNA AND WE UNDERSTAND THAT IT WAS CREATED IN HONOR OF A LADY'S BELLY BUTTON. IT DOES RESEMBLE ONE.

VERMICELLI: FROM THE LATIN ROOT FOR "LITTLE WORMS". I LIKED IT BETTER WHEN I DIDN'T KNOW WHAT IT MEANT.

ZITI/ZITA: THE ITALIAN PENCHANT FOR TONGUE IN CHEEK IR-REVERENCE STRIKES AGAIN; ZITI MEANS "BRIDEGROOM". AND THE SHAPE OF THE PASTA SUGGESTS A WAXING OR WILTING PENIS. BUT YOU DRAW YOUR OWN CONCLUSIONS.

SHAPES AND NAMES

STRING TYPES

THIN SOLID STRINGS:
ANGEL HAIR
  (AKA: CAPELLI D'ANGELO)
CAPELLINI
FEDELINI
SPAGHETTINI
VERMICELLI

SOLID STRINGS:	SPAGHETTI
	PERCIATELLINI
	CHITARRA
	SPAGHETTONI
HOLLOW STRINGS:	BUCATINI
	PERCIATELLI
	PERCIATELLONI
	MEZZA ZITA
OVAL STRINGS:	LINGUINE
	LINGUE
	FETTUCCELLE
	FETTUCCELLE OVALI
CURLY STRINGS:	FUSILLI
	FARMER'S

TUBE TYPES

STRAIGHT EDGED LONG TUBES:	ZITONI
	CANDELE
MEDIUM TUBES:	ZITI OR ZITA
	RIGATONI
	SQUARE
	ELICOIDALI
	CANNARONI LISCI
	GNOCCHETTI LISCI
	CANNARONI RIGITI
	GNOCCHETTI RIGATI
	MILLERIGHI
	TUFOLI
	FESTONATI
	MILLERIGHI GIGANTI
	GNOCCHETTI ZITA LUNGHI
	SEDANI RIGATI
	SEDANINI RIGATI
	TUBETTI LUNGHI
	TUBETTI LUNGHI RIGATI

MEZZANI
MEZZANI RIGATI
MACCARONCELLI

DIAGONAL CUT
MEDIUM TUBES:
PENNONI
PENNONI RIGATI
PENNE
PENNE RIGATI
PENNE ZITA
PENNE ZITA RIGATI
PENNETTE LUNGHI
PENNETTE LUNGHI RIGATI
MOSTACCIOLI
MOSTACCIOLI RIGATI

SHORT TUBES:
DITALI
  (AKA: SALAD MAC)
DITALINI
MEZZI RIGATONI
MEZZI TUFOLI
CARDINALI
TUBETTI
TUBETTI RIGATI
GNOCCHETTI ZITA
GNOCCHETTI ZITA RIGATI
MEZZI SEDANINI RIGATI

BENT SHORT TUBES:
PIPE RIGATI
LUMACONI RIGATI
LUMACHE MEDIE
LUMACHE MEDIE RIGATI
CORNETTI RIGATI
ELBOW MACARONI
GOBBETTI

STUFFABLE TUBES:
CANNELLONI
MANICOTTI

SHORT CURLY TYPES

SOLID TWISTS: SPIRALS OR SPIRALI
ROTELLE OR ROTELLI
ROTINI
GEMELLINI
SHORT FUSILLI

HOLLOW TWISTS: ELBOW TWISTS
GEMELLI
SPACCATELLA
SPAGHETTI TWISTS

RIBBON TYPES

THE ITALIANS USE THE FOLLOWING TERMS TO DESCRIBE A "NOODLE" PASTA. MANY ITALIAN COOKBOOKS WILL CALL FOR NOODLES, AND YOU GET TO CHOOSE THE WIDTH WHEN NO SPECIFIC NOODLE IS RECOMMENDED FOR THE SAUCE. SINCE WE HAVE SO MANY VARIETIES OF NOODLES IN THE UNITED STATES, A GIFT OF THE MANY CULTURES THAT MAKE UP AMERICA, WE CANNOT EFFECTIVELY USE THE WORD NOODLE, ADDITIONALLY, IN THE UNITED STATES, ANYTHING CALLED A "NOODLE" MUST HAVE AN EGG SOLIDS CONTENT WITH A MINIMUM OF 5-1/2%; COMMERCIALLY VERY FEW PASTAS ARE MADE WITH EGG, WHILE HOMEMADE PASTA ALMOST ALWAYS CONTAIN EGG. SO I'VE ELECTED TO USE THE WORD RIBBON WHEN REFERRING TO ANY OF THE FOLLOWING.

RIBBONS: FETTUCCINE
TAGLIATELLINI
TAGLIATELLE
NASTRI
EGG TAGLIATELLE
PAPPARDELLE

NARROW RIBBONS: TRENETTINE
TRENETTE
TAGLIARINI
TAGLIOLINI

BROAD RIBBONS:	LASAGNA
	ONDINI
	MAFALDINI
	TRINETTE
	MAFALDE
	MARGHERITE

SHELL TYPES

MEDIUM SHELLS:	SEA SHELLS
	CAVATELLI
	GNOCCHI
	(AKA: DUMPLINGS)

| STUFFABLE SHELLS: | LARGE SEA SHELLS |

FANCY TYPES

MEDIUM SIZED:	RADIATORE
	PRIEST'S HATS
	WAGON WHEELS
	ORECCHIETTE
	BOW TIES
	(AKA: TRIPOLINI)
	CANESTRINI
	CRESTE DI GALLO
	(AKA: COCK'S CRESTS)

FILLED PILLOW TYPES

SQUARES, ROUNDS AND TRIANGLES:	RAVIOLI
	RAVIOLINI
	CAPPELLETTI
	AGNOLOTTI

| TIED: | TORTELLINI |

CHAPTER 1

THE COOKING OF PASTA

"TENDER BUT FIRM" IS YOUR GUIDE LINE; THE ITALIAN PHRASE FOR THIS IS "AL DENTE", WHICH MEANS "TO THE TOOTH". USE ANY PHRASE YOU LIKE, JUST DON'T RUIN A SPLENDID SAUCE THAT YOU'VE LOVINGLY PREPARED BY SERVING IT OVER A MUSHY PASTA. YUK!!! AND MOST IMPORTANTLY IS THIS, QUALITY IN, QUALITY OUT. BUY A GOOD DOMESTIC OR IMPORTED PASTA. THE BEST PASTAS USE HARD DURUM SEMOLINA WHEAT. DON'T BUY ANYTHING ELSE.

*** LET THIS BE YOUR TOTAL PREPARATION GUIDE. ***

DON'T OVER COOK, DON'T OVER DRAIN AND DON'T OVER SAUCE!

DON'T RINSE! EVEN TO MAKE A PASTA SALAD, DON'T RINSE!

RINSING WILL REMOVE MOST, IF NOT ALL THE VITAMINS AND NUTRIENTS AS WELL AS THE SALT CLINGING TO THE SURFACE. A LITTLE SALT BRINGS PASTA TO LIFE, REMOVE IT AND YOU ALSO REMOVE MOST OF ITS FLAVOR. RINSING WILL ALSO REMOVE THE SURFACE STARCH. THAT MAY SLOW DOWN THE PASTA'S TENDENCY TO STICK, BUT IT DOES NOTHING TO IMPROVE THE PASTA. IF YOU WANT TO KEEP PASTA UNSAUCED, OR USE IT IN A SALAD, TOSS IT WITH A SMALL AMOUNT OF OLIVE OIL OR BUTTER.

METHOD: FILL A LARGE POT WITH WATER (HOT WATER WILL SAVE ON ENERGY USE), BRING TO A BOIL AND THEN ADD SALT. SALT ADDITION IS ALMOST ESSENTIAL, BUT A PERSONAL CHOICE. ASSUMING THERE ARE NO DIETARY CON-SIDERATIONS, ADD ONE TO TWO LEVEL TABLESPOONS OF SALT TO A GALLON OF WATER. IF SALT IS OMITTED THE ENTIRE TASTE WILL FALL UPON THE SAUCE, A DELICATE SAUCE CAN BE OVERWHELMED BY A BLAND AND TASTELESS (READ UNSALTED) PASTA. THAT MAY BE ACCEPTABLE WHERE SALT NEEDS TO BE LIMITED. KEEP IN MIND THAT PASTA IS ONLY FLOUR AND WATER, AND IF YOUR SAUCE

HAS LITTLE OR NO SALT, THEN YOU'LL PROBABLY HAVE A TASTELESS DISH. SALT IS NEEDED, IF ONLY SPARINGLY, TO GIVE LIFE TO THE PASTA AND BRING OUT THE FLAVOR.

COVERING THE POT IS AN OPTION, IF YOU COVER, DO SO ONLY TO BRING THE POT BACK TO A FULL BOIL. OTHER THAN THAT, YOU CAN EXPECT A BOIL OVER AND SOME STOVE CLEANING. YOU MAY ADD A LITTLE OIL TO PREVENT BOIL OVER IF YOUR POT IS TOO SMALL TO HAVE SEVERAL INCHES BETWEEN THE WATER LEVEL AND THE TOP OF THE POT. THIS IS A PERSONAL OBSERVATION, BUT THE BETTER QUALITY PASTAS DON'T SEEM TO HAVE A PROPENSITY TO FOAM OVER AND OUT OF THE POT.

USE A POT LARGE ENOUGH TO LET YOUR PASTA COME TO A ROLLING BOIL, EXTRA WATER IN THE POT HURTS NOTHING. TOO SMALL A POT MAY HURT YOUR PASTA.

I'M A FIRM BELIEVER IN DROPPING ALL THE PASTA INTO THE POT AT ONCE, STIR TO PREVENT THE PASTA FROM STICKING TO ITSELF AND THEN LET 'ER GO AT A FULL ROLLING BOIL FOR AT LEAST EIGHT MINUTES, STIRRING OCCASIONALLY, TEST, IF DONE, DRAIN, SAUCE AND SERVE.

IMPORTANT: START YOUR TIMING WHEN THE WATER RETURNS TO A FULL BOIL.

EACH MANUFACTURER GIVES YOU A TIME SUGGESTION FOR COOKING THEIR PASTA, BUT YOU MAY COOK MOST PASTAS SUCCESSFULLY AT EIGHT MINUTES. SHAPE WILL DETERMINE TO A LARGE EXTENT THE COOKING TIME. FINE ANGEL HAIR TYPES AND FRESH PASTAS WILL COOK VERY RAPIDLY, POSSIBLY TWO TO THREE MINUTES. HEAVY THICK SHAPES WILL REQUIRE UPWARD OF FIFTEEN MINUTES OR MORE. AS A RULE OF THUMB, IF THE MANUFACTURER SUGGESTS OVER EIGHT MINUTES, BEGIN TESTING AT THAT POINT.

LET'S GO OVER THIS ONE MORE TIME:

WATER:	4 TO 8 QUARTS (AVERAGE AT 6 QUARTS).
SALT:	1 TO 2 LEVEL TABLESPOONS TO EACH 4 QUARTS WATER.
TIME:	CHECK PASTA MAKER'S SUGGESTED TIME;
	IF OVER 8 MINUTES, BEGIN TESTING AT 8 MINUTES.
	IF LESS THAN 8 MINUTES, MONITOR CONSTANTLY AFTER THE FIRST TWO MINUTES.
TIMING:	START YOUR TIMING AFTER THE WATER RETURNS TO A BOIL.

ONE ADDITIONAL COMMENT ON SALTING. FRESH, HOMEMADE PASTAS COOK MUCH MORE RAPIDLY THAN DRY PACKAGED PASTA. AVERAGE COOKING TIME IS THREE TO FIVE MINUTES, AND THEY WILL ABSORB SALT MORE QUICKLY THAN DRIED PASTA. SO YOU MAY WISH TO USE LESS SALT WHEN COOKING HOMEMADE OR PREPACKAGED FRESH PASTA.

HOW MUCH DO I USE PER PERSON?

IF IT IS THE ENTREE, GENERALLY 4 TO 6 OUNCES OF DRY PASTA IS ENOUGH FOR THE AVERAGE EATER; THAT'S 2 TO 3 CUPS OF COOKED PASTA.

IF IT IS TO BE A SIDE DISH (ITALIAN; I PRIMI, MEANING FIRST COURSE), 2 OUNCES OF DRY PASTA WILL GIVE ONE CUP OF COOKED PASTA.

SINCE THE SHAPE OF THE PASTA WILL INFLUENCE THE END RESULT, YOU MAY NEED TO ADJUST THE ABOVE BASED ON YOUR PERSONAL EXPERIENCE. WITH SOME TYPES OF PASTA, ONE OUNCE MAY BE SUFFICIENT.

HERE IS A RECOMMENDATION WE WILL MAKE. WHEN USING VERY THIN STRINGS, SUCH AS ANGEL HAIR, USE LESS THAN HALF THE AMOUNT YOU WOULD NORMALLY COOK. THAT MEANS IF YOU WERE GOING TO USE ONE POUND OF SPAGHETTI, USE ONLY ONE HALF POUND OF ANGEL HAIR. THE EXPLANATION IS, THE THINNER THE PASTA, THE MORE STRINGS TO THE POUND AND MORE SURFACE TO COVER, THEREFORE, MORE SAUCE IS REQUIRED, OR LESS PASTA.

SAUCING

NOW THAT YOU KNOW WHAT AMOUNTS OF PASTA YOU'LL NEED TO FEED YOUR FAMILY AND/OR GUESTS, MAY I SUGGEST THAT WHEN ADDING YOUR SAUCE TO THE PASTA DO IT WITH SOME APLOMB, (IS THAT A DESSERT?). UNLESS OTHERWISE DIRECTED, START WITH ABOUT 1 CUP OF YOUR SAUCE; ADD MORE SAUCE AS NEEDED, OR PLACE THE REMAINING SAUCE ON THE TABLE AND LET THE DINERS ADD MORE IF THEY WISH TO. DON'T OVER SAUCE. THERE SHOULD NOT BE ANY SAUCE AT THE BOTTOM OF THE SERVING BOWL. THE EFFECT YOU'LL BE LOOKING FOR IS LIGHTNESS. AND THAT COMES FROM A LIGHT SAUCING MORE SO THAN A "LIGHT" SAUCE.

MOST OF THE RECIPES IN THIS BOOK WILL YIELD MORE SAUCE THAN NEEDED FOR ONE POUND OF PASTA (MANY AMERICAN PACKERS USE ONLY 3/4 POUND PACKAGES, 12 OUNCES, THERE ARE EVEN 8 OUNCE PACKAGES, SO READ THE PACKAGE WEIGHT WHEN YOU BUY. ONE POUND OF PASTA WILL ADE- QUATELY SERVE FOUR PEOPLE WHEN THE PASTA IS YOUR ENTREE, A 12 OUNCE PACKAGE WON'T.

Chapter 2

Sauces made from Butter and/or Olive Oil

You'll notice that in this category of sauces, occasionally some water or pasta water may be added to the oil. A shortage of oil will make a dry dish; too much oil will make an oily dish (what else?). Some added liquid gives you the balancing ability to prevent dry or oily dishes.

WE TRIED THIS SAUCE . . . AND

LOVED IT ( )
HATED IT ( )
MAYBE WE'LL TRY IT AGAIN ( )
WE'LL USE IT FOR UNWELCOME GUESTS ( )

GARLIC AND OIL

(ANOTHER QUICKIE)

PASTA SERVED WITH A SAUCE OF BUTTER OR OIL WITH GARLIC

LIKE MILLIONS OF AMERICANS WHO LOVE THE BOUQUET OF GARLIC AND ENJOY THE TASTE OF IT, YOU PROBABLY HAVE NO DESIRE TO SMELL LIKE IT. THEREFORE I AM SUGGESTING YOU START WITH ONE CLOVE OF GARLIC IN THIS SAUCE, THEN INCREASE THE NUMBER OF CLOVES UNTIL YOU REACH YOUR TOLERANCE LEVEL.

ABOUT YOUR OIL. IN A REAL EMERGENCY, A REGULAR VEGETABLE OIL COULD BE USED, SO COULD CORN, GRAPE SEED (2ND BEST TO OLIVE OIL IN TASTE) OR PEANUT OIL (BEST IN HIGH TEMPERATURE TOLERANCE). THE LATTER IS UNIMPORTANT IN ITALIAN COOKERY. THESE OILS ARE SECOND BEST WITH THIS DISH AND THE RESULTS WILL BE TOO.

WE'LL START THIS CHAPTER WITH THE BEST KNOWN SAUCE IN THIS CATEGORY. GARLIC SAUTEED IN OLIVE OIL IS A MATCH MADE IN HEAVEN, THERE IS A BOUQUET FROM FRESHLY SLICED GARLIC BEING SAUTEED IN AN OLIVE OIL THAT SIMPLY LIFTS YOUR SPIRITS AND BRIGHTENS YOUR OUTLOOK ON LIFE. IT IS AN INCREDIBLY SIMPLE SAUCE THAT ONLY TAKES A FEW MOMENTS TO PREPARE. YOU NEEDN'T START IT UNTIL YOUR PASTA IS MERRILY BOILING ALONG.

INGREDIENTS: 1/2 CUP OLIVE OIL
1 TO 5 CLOVES OF GARLIC, CRUSHED, SLICED OR MINCED
1 TABLESPOON CHOPPED FRESH PARSLEY (ITALIAN BROADLEAF, IF YOU CAN GET IT)
1/2 TEASPOON SALT

OPTIONAL ITEMS: PLEASE SEE NEXT PAGE!

64

1/2   CUP PASTA WATER (ADD ONLY IF OIL IS ABSORBED) FRESHLY GROUND BLACK PEPPER TO TASTE

METHOD: SAUTE THE GARLIC IN THE OIL UNTIL IT TURNS LIGHTLY GOLDEN, REMOVE AND DISCARD (IF USING CRUSHED) GARLIC, POUR OIL OVER THE DRAINED PASTA, ADD THE FRESH PARSLEY, (AND BLACK PEPPER IF USED) TOSS, ADD THE LIQUID (IF USED), TOSS AGAIN, SERVE.

RECOMMENDED PASTA: ALL STRING TYPES.

WE TRIED THESE SAUCES . . . AND

LOVED 1( ) 2( ) 3( ) 4( ) 5( ) 6( ) 7( ) 8( ) 9( )

HATED IT ( ) 2( ) 3( ) 4( ) 5( ) 6( ) 7( ) 8( ) 9( )

MAYBE WE'LL TRY IT AGAIN ( ) 2( ) 3( ) 4( ) 5( ) 6( ) 7( ) 8( ) 9( )

WE'LL USE ( ) 2( ) 3( ) 4( ) 5( ) 6( ) 7( ) 8( ) 9( ) FOR UNWELCOME GUESTS

THE FOLLOWING VARIATIONS FOR THE BASE SAUCE ON THE PRECEDING PAGE CAN BE USED ONE AT A TIME, NOT COMBINED.

VARIATIONS: 1. ADD 1/2 TO 1 TEASPOON CRUSHED RED PEPPER FOR "ZIP UND ZING. (ISN'T THAT A GERMAN CHORAL GROUP?). THIS ADDITION GIVES THE SAUCE A NEW APPLICATION, IT NOW MAY BE CALLED: "ROMAN STYLE".

2. A PIECE OF A LONG GREEN MILDLY HOT PEPPER, LEFT WHOLE OR MINCED. REMOVE BEFORE ADDING TO THE PASTA IF LEFT WHOLE.

3. ADD SEVERAL CHOPPED OR MINCED ANCHOVIES FOR A SALTY TANG, DISSOLVE THEM IN THE HOT OIL/BUTTER BEFORE ADDING YOUR PASTA.

4. ADD A PINCH OF DRY OREGANO TO GIVE IT A FULL BODIED THRUST.

5. ADD 2 TABLESPOONS EACH OF FRESH, CHOPPED BASIL AND OREGANO.

6. FOR A NUTTIER TASTE, ADD SOME CHOPPED WALNUTS OR PINE NUTS.

7. TARTNESS CAN BE ADDED WITH A TABLESPOON OF CAPERS.

8. FOR A TOTAL TASTE CHANGE AND A MUCH SWEETER ONE, REPLACE THE GARLIC WITH ONE MEDIUM ONION, FINELY CHOPPED OR THINLY SLICED.

9. 1/2 CUP CHOPPED ONIONS, A SMALL MEASURE OF CRUSHED RED PEPPER AND SALT PORK (OR BACON) WILL MAKE THIS A "GRICIANA STYLE" SAUCE.

RECOMMENDED PASTA: STRING TYPES, SOLID OR HOLLOW.

GARLIC AND BUTTER SAUCE

(ANOTHER QUICKIE)

NOW WE COME TO A SAUCE THAT IS SINFULLY RICH AND WONDERFUL TO EAT, A BUTTER SAUCE. BUTTER HAS A TASTE LIKE NOTHING ELSE IN THIS WORLD. IT HAS A BOUQUET WHEN MELTING THAT EXCITES THE PALATE AND OFFERS A PROMISE OF A SUPERLATIVE DISH.

HERE WE EMPLOY OUR ACRONYM K.I.S., KEEP IT SIMPLE. GARLIC AND BUTTER, AND MAYBE SOME CHEESE.

GARLIC SHOULD NOT BE BROWNED IN BUTTER, FOR SEVERAL REASONS. ONE, THERE ARE IMPURITIES (THEY BURN) AND WATER IN BUTTER; IT IS NOT PURE DAIRY FAT. SECONDLY, IF YOU DO BROWN THE GARLIC, YOU'VE OVERCOOKED THE BUTTER AND LOST ITS ESSENCE.

CHOOSE YOUR OWN PREFERENCE OF BUTTER HERE, SWEET OR REGULAR. THE ONLY DIFFERENCE IS ADDED SALT. EUROPEANS GENERALLY USE SWEET BUTTER; WHILE IN AMERICA, SALTED BUTTER IS THE STANDARD. WITH SWEET BUTTER THE ESSENCE AND BOUQUET WILL BE THERE, WHILE THE TASTE WILL BE A LITTLE FLAT.

A SUGGESTION HERE ON PREPARING THE GARLIC. IF YOU CRUSH THE CLOVE IT CAN EASILY BE REMOVED PRIOR TO SERVING. IF, ON THE OTHER HAND YOU WANT IT TO BE A PART OF THE DISH, SLICE OR MINCE IT.

INGREDIENTS: 1   OR MORE CLOVES OF GARLIC (SLICED, MINCED OR CRUSHED

            3/4   CUP BUTTER

            1   TEASPOON CHOPPED PARSLEY

                     (OPTION): FRESHLY GRATED PARMESAN CHEESE

METHOD: MELT THE BUTTER IN A SKILLET OR SAUCE PAN, ADD THE GARLIC, LET IT SIMMER FOR A MOMENT OR TWO. DON'T ALLOW THE BUTTER TO FRY THE GARLIC, AT THAT POINT YOU'VE LOST THE ESSENCE OF THE BUTTER AND IT WON'T IMPROVE BY ADDING ANYTHING.

POUR SAUCE OVER YOUR PASTA, ADD PARSLEY, TOSS AND SERVE. IF YOU ARE GOING TO ADD CHEESE, ADD IT WITH THE PARSLEY.

RECOMMENDED PASTA: RIBBON TYPES OR STRING TYPES.

GREEN SAUCE

(ANOTHER QUICKIE)

THIS SAUCE IS A VARIATION OF THE PRECEDING SAUCE, THE CHANGES ARE A SUBSTANTIAL INCREASE OF PARSLEY AND A LITTLE OLIVE OIL.

INGREDIENTS:
1	TABLESPOON OLIVE OIL
3/4	POUND BUTTER
1	CLOVE GARLIC, CRUSHED OR MINCED
1	WHOLE CHIVE, MINCED
2	CUPS CHOPPED PARSLEY (ITALIAN, IF YOU HAVE IT)
1/2	TEASPOON SALT
1/4	TEASPOON FRESHLY GROUND BLACK PEPPER

METHOD: SAUTE GARLIC AND GREEN ONION IN THE BUTTER/OIL FOR 3 MINUTES, (DISCARD CRUSHED GARLIC, IF USED) ADD, PARSLEY, SALT AND PEPPER, STIR TO COAT PARSLEY, REMOVE SAUCE FROM HEAT, POUR OVER PASTA, TOSS AND SERVE.

RECOMMENDED PASTA: STRING OR, CURLY TYPES.

NEAPOLITAN MUSHROOM SAUCE

(ANOTHER QUICKIE)

NEAPOLITANS ARE QUITE CREATIVE WHEN IT COMES TO THEIR PASTA SAUCES; THEY'LL USE ALMOST ANYTHING AVAILABLE, AND THIS IS ONE OF THE RECIPES THAT ALLOWS THEM TO DO IT, IT'S A VERY FLEXIBLE RECIPE. IF YOU ARE OUT OF MUSHROOMS, USE ANY VEGETABLE AVAILABLE.

INGREDIENTS:
1/2	CUP OLIVE OIL
1	CLOVE GARLIC, MINCED
1/2	POUND MUSHROOMS, SLICED
2	TABLESPOONS PARSLEY, CHOPPED
	SALT AND PEPPER TO TASTE
	FRESHLY GRATED ROMANO CHEESE

METHOD: SAUTE THE GARLIC FOR 2 MINUTES, ADD THE MUSHROOMS AND CONTINUE COOKING UNTIL DONE, ABOUT 3 TO 4 MINUTES. POUR SAUCE OVER PASTA, ADD PARSLEY, SALT AND PEPPER, TOSS AND SERVE WITH CHEESE ON THE SIDE.

RECOMMENDED PASTA: STRING TYPES.

SAGE SAUCE

THIS SAUCE IS FROM LOMBARDY; THE SAGE IS ONLY A FLAVORING FOR THE BUTTER THAT BECOMES THE SAUCE FOR PASTA AND VEGETABLES. IT IS ALSO ONE OF THE FEW PASTA DISHES THAT USES CABBAGE. IT'S EASY AND QUICK.

INGREDIENTS:

1	POUND CABBAGE SHREDDED (SAVOY OR NAPA)
2 1/2	CUPS NEW WHITE POTATOES, PEELED AND DICED
6	OUNCES BUTTER
2	CLOVES GARLIC, BRUISED
1	TABLESPOON FRESH SAGE (1 TEASPOON DRY)
	(IF DRY, DON'T CRUMBLE, SOAK LEAVES FIRST)
1	CUP ROMANO
1/2	TEASPOON FRESHLY GROUND BLACK PEPPER

YOU MAY SUBSTITUTE 1 CUP SHREDDED MOZZARELLA FOR THE ROMANO

METHOD: PLACE THE POTATOES AND CABBAGE TOGETHER IN ENOUGH WATER TO COVER, BRING TO A BOIL AND COOK FOR 20 MINUTES, DRAIN. MEANWHILE, SAUTE THE GARLIC AND SAGE IN THE BUTTER UNTIL GARLIC IS GOLDEN. DISCARD GARLIC AND SAGE, POUR THE FLAVORED BUTTER OVER THE PASTA, TOSS TO COAT, ADD VEGETABLES, BLACK PEPPER AND CHEESE, TOSS AND SERVE.

IF YOU ELECT TO USE A FRESH PASTA, IT MAY BE ADDED TO THE COOKING VEGETABLES DURING THE FINAL 5 MINUTES. THEN COMPLETE AS ABOVE.

RECOMMENDED PASTA: RIBBON TYPES.

SWEET BUTTER SAUCE

(ANOTHER QUICKIE)

THIS COULD BE PLACED IN THE UNCOOKED SAUCE CHAPTER, IT ISN'T COOKED, BUT IT IS MADE WITH BUTTER. SIMPLE, FAST AND VERY GOOD. FROM FAR NORTHEASTERN ITALY COMES THIS LIGHT DELIGHT.

INGREDIENTS: 6   TABLESPOONS SWEET BUTTER
3/4   CUP FRESHLY GRATED PARMESAN CHEESE
3   BUTTON MUSHROOMS, THINLY SLICED (CANNED OR RAW)
PINCH   NUTMEG
PINCH   FRESHLY GROUND BLACK PEPPER

METHOD: SOFTEN THE BUTTER (A FEW SECONDS IN A MICROWAVE WILL DO), PLACE COOKED PASTA IN THE SERVING BOWL, ADD BUTTER, TOSS TO COAT, ADD CHEESE, NUTMEG, BLACK PEPPER AND MUSHROOMS, TOSS AGAIN, SERVE.

RECOMMENDED PASTA: RIBBON TYPES.

BUTTER AND MARJORAM SAUCE

(ANOTHER QUICKIE)

ANOTHER LIGHT SAUCE FROM ITALY'S NORTHEAST. FRESH MARJORAM IS THE DESIRED HERB HERE. IF FRESH MARJORAM IS NOT AVAILABLE, THEN TRY IT WITH DRY MARJORAM. YOU'LL DISCOVER, THAT AS WITH ALL HERBS, THERE ARE WIDE TASTE DIFFERENCES BETWEEN FRESH AND DRIED HERBS.

INGREDIENTS:
6	TABLESPOONS BUTTER
1	TABLESPOON PINENUTS, CHOPPED
1	TABLESPOON CHOPPED FRESH MARJORAM
	OR
1	TEASPOON DRY MARJORAM
3/4	CUP FRESHLY GRATED PARMESAN CHEESE

METHOD: SAUTE THE PINENUTS AND MARJORAM IN THE BUTTER FOR 1 MINUTE, POUR SAUCE OVER PASTA, ADD CHEESE, TOSS AND SERVE.

RECOMMENDED PASTA: ANY OF THE FANCIES.

BROWN BUTTER SAUCE

(ANOTHER QUICKIE)

EVEN THOUGH I HAVE RECOMMENDED THAT YOU NOT BROWN GARLIC IN BUTTER, THERE ARE PEOPLE WHO DO LIKE THAT TASTE; THEREFORE, I HAVE INCLUDED THIS RECIPE.

INGREDIENTS: 8   TABLESPOONS BUTTER (YOUR CHOICE)
              2   CLOVES GARLIC, HALVED, BRUISED OR CRUSHED
                 FRESHLY GRATED PARMESAN CHEESE TO TASTE

METHOD: SAUTE THE GARLIC IN THE BUTTER UNTIL THE GARLIC HAS BROWNED. DISCARD THE GARLIC, POUR BUTTER OVER PASTA, TOSS AND SERVE WITH CHEESE ON THE SIDE.

RECOMMENDED PASTA: SHELLS, MEDIUM TUBES, STRING TYPES.

CARBONARA SAUCE

(ANOTHER QUICKIE)

THERE ARE ADDITIONAL CARBONARA RECIPES LISTED IN CHAPTER 3; THEY USE WHIPPING CREAM AS THE BASE LIQUID. HERE WE GET JUST BACON AND EGGS, NO CREAM. THIS ONE CERTAINLY OFFERS YOU FEWER CALORIES, TRY IT, YOU'LL LIKE IT.

THE HOT STEAMING PASTA WILL COOK THE BEATEN RAW EGGS, SO HAVE THEM READY AND AT ROOM TEMPERATURE IF POSSIBLE.

INGREDIENTS:
6 TO 8	SLICES SUGAR CURED BACON, COOKED CRISP. (USE A MICROWAVE OVEN IF YOU CAN)
3/4	CUP FRESHLY GRATED PARMESAN OR ROMANO CHEESE
3	EGGS, BEATEN
1	TEASPOON FRESHLY GROUND BLACK PEPPER

METHOD: TRY TIMING BACON AND PASTA TO FINISH COOKING TOGETHER. BLEND EGG, CHEESE AND BLACK PEPPER. POUR OVER DRAINED STEAMING PASTA, TOSS. ADD 2 TABLESPOONS OF THE HOT BACON OIL, TOSS AGAIN, GARNISH WITH CRUMBLED BACON, SERVE.

RECOMMENDED PASTA: STRING TYPES.

WE TRIED THIS SAUCE . . . AND

CARBONARA SAUCE TOO!

(ANOTHER QUICKIE)

PASTA CARBONARA IS THE ROMAN STYLE OF HAVING BACON AND EGGS. ROME IS A VERY LARGE CITY AND THE VARIATIONS OF THIS SAUCE ALONE MAY RUN INTO THE HUNDREDS. HERE WE FIND AN ADDITION OF ONIONS THAT WILL GIVE THIS SAUCE AN ADDED TOUCH OF SWEETNESS.

INGREDIENTS:
3	EGGS
1/2	CUP FRESHLY GRATED PARMESAN CHEESE
2	TABLESPOONS CHOPPED PARSLEY
	FRESHLY GROUND BLACK PEPPER TO TASTE
2	ONIONS (USE A SWEET VARIETY) CHOPPED
4	TABLESPOONS BUTTER
1/2	CUP WHITE WINE (PREFERABLY DRY)
6	SLICES SUGAR CURED BACON, DICED

METHOD: PLACE EGGS, GRATED CHEESE, PARSLEY AND BLACK PEPPER IN YOUR SERVING BOWL, BEAT WELL, SET ASIDE. SAUTE ONION IN BUTTER UNTIL TRANSPARENT, ADD WINE AND BACON, COOK AT A BOIL UNTIL WINE EVAPORATES, ABOUT 4 MINUTES. (IF SAUCE IS DONE BEFORE PASTA IS COOKED, REMOVE FROM HEAT). PLACE HOT DRAINED PASTA IN YOUR SERVING BOWL AND TOSS WITH EGG MIXTURE, ADD ONIONS, TOSS AGAIN, SERVE.

RECOMMENDED PASTA: STRING TYPES.

WE TRIED THIS SAUCE . . . AND

LOVED IT ( )
HATED IT ( )
MAYBE WE'LL TRY IT AGAIN ( )
WE'LL USE IT FOR UNWELCOME GUESTS ( )

ROMAN STYLE CARBONARA

(ANOTHER QUICKIE)

THIS SAUCE DIFFERS FROM THE PRECEDING BECAUSE OF THE USE OF GARLIC, IT ALSO USES DIFFERENT PROPORTIONS OF INGREDIENTS. THIS SAUCE WILL REQUIRE THE COOKING TO BE FINISHED IN A PAN OR PYREX SERVING DISH.

INGREDIENTS:
1	TABLESPOON LARD OR OLIVE OIL
5	SLICES SUGAR CURED BACON, MINCED
1	CLOVE GARLIC, CRUSHED
5	EGGS, LIGHTLY BEATEN
1/4	TEASPOON SALT
5	TABLESPOONS GRATED PARMESAN CHEESE
5	TABLESPOONS GRATED PECORINO CHEESE
	FRESHLY GROUND BLACK PEPPER TO TASTE

METHOD: SAUTE THE BACON AND GARLIC IN OIL, UNTIL GARLIC BROWNS, DISCARD GARLIC. SET BACON AND OIL ASIDE. BEAT THE EGGS, WITH SALT TO TASTE; BEAT IN CHEESE AND BLACK PEPPER TO TASTE. WHEN PASTA IS DONE, DRAIN AND PLACE PASTA IN PAN OR PYREX SERVING DISH; RETURN TO THE STOVE OVER LOW HEAT, ADD EGGS AND CHEESE, TOSS WHILE OVER HEAT, ADD BACON AND OIL, TOSS AGAIN, SERVE.

RECOMMENDED PASTA: MEDIUM TUBES.

78

BACON AND GARLIC SAUCE

(ANOTHER QUICKIE)

(THIS ONE IS NOT FOR EVERYBODY!)

NO OLIVE OIL, HERE THE BACON GIVES IT ALL: OIL, FLAVOR AND SUBSTANCE.

INGREDIENTS:

6 TO 8	SLICES SUGAR CURED BACON
1	CLOVE GARLIC, MINCED
1	TEASPOON FRESHLY GROUND BLACK PEPPER
2	TABLESPOONS FRESHLY GRATED PARMESAN

METHOD: CUT THE BACON INTO THIN, 1/4" PIECES, SAUTE THE BACON AND GARLIC UNTIL BACON CRISPS. ADD BLACK PEPPER. REMOVE FROM HEAT, POUR OVER YOUR PASTA, SPRINKLE WITH CHEESE, TOSS AND SERVE.

THIS SAUCE WILL BE ADEQUATE FOR ONE HALF POUND OF PASTA.

RECOMMENDED PASTA: STRING TYPES.

BASIL AND BUTTER SAUCE

(ANOTHER QUICKIE)

THIS SAUCE COULD BE CALLED B & B, BUT SOME OUTFIT IS ALREADY USING THAT, AND I DON'T WANT TO ENCOURAGE DRINKING IN THE KITCHEN, THAT'S WHY THEY PUT SALT IN THE COOKING WINE.

INGREDIENTS:

3	TABLESPOONS BUTTER
2	TABLESPOONS OLIVE OIL
1/2	CUP PASTA WATER
1/4	CUP FRESH BASIL, MINCED
	OR
2	TABLESPOONS DRIED
1/4	CUP FRESH PARSLEY, CHOPPED
1	CLOVE GARLIC (YOUR CHOICE)
1/2	TEASPOON SALT
1/2	TEASPOON NUTMEG
PINCH	FRESHLY GROUND BLACK PEPPER
2	TABLESPOONS GRATED PARMESAN CHEESE

METHOD: COMBINE, BUTTER, OIL, PASTA WATER, BASIL, PARSLEY, SALT AND NUTMEG. HEAT ALL THE INGREDIENTS OVER LOW HEAT FOR 2 OR 3 MINUTES, POUR OVER PASTA, TOSS, SPRINKLE WITH BLACK PEPPER AND CHEESE, SERVE.

RECOMMENDED PASTA: SEA SHELLS OR OTHER FANCY SHAPES.

LONG GREEN PEPPER SAUCE

(ANOTHER QUICKIE)

THIS SAUCE HAS A FLAVOR YOU'LL LOVE. THE LONG GREEN AND MILDLY HOT PEPPERS HAVE A VERY UNIQUE TASTE, TOTALLY DIFFERENT FROM OTHER HOT PEPPERS. ASIDE FROM USING THEM IN THIS SAUCE, THEY ARE WONDERFUL WITH SCRAMBLED EGGS OR AS SUBSTITUTIONS FOR BELL PEPPERS IN SOME TOMATO SAUCES. SO MUCH FOR THE ASIDE, ON TO THE SAUCE:

INGREDIENTS:

1/3	CUP OLIVE OIL
2	LONG GREEN PEPPERS, SEEDED AND MINCED
2	CLOVES GARLIC, MINCED
1/2	CUP FRESH PARSLEY, CHOPPED
1/2	TEASPOON SALT
1/2	CUP PASTA WATER OR HOT WATER

METHOD: SAUTE GREEN PEPPERS, SALT AND GARLIC UNTIL GARLIC TURNS SLIGHTLY GOLDEN. ADD THE PASTA WATER AND SIMMER FOR A FEW MINUTES, REMOVE FROM HEAT. POUR SAUCE OVER PASTA, ADD PARSLEY TOSS AND SERVE.

RECOMMENDED PASTA: STRING TYPES OR LONG FLAT TYPES.

MARINATED GARLIC SAUCE

(ANOTHER QUICKIE)

THIS IS AN INSTANT SAUCE, BUT YOU DON'T WANT TO USE IT AS QUICKLY AS YOU MAKE IT. WE'LL MAKE THIS IN A BLENDER AND ALLOW TIME FOR THE INGREDIENTS TO MELD BY MARINATING.

INGREDIENTS:

1	CUP V-8, TOMATO JUICE OR HOT CHICKEN BROTH (CHOOSE ONLY ONE, NOT ALL THREE)
2	TABLESPOONS OLIVE OIL
2	TABLESPOON MINCED SWEET OR MILDLY HOT PEPPER
1	TEASPOON DRY BASIL
3	CLOVES GARLIC (COULD BE PRESSED)
1/2	TEASPOON FRESHLY GROUND BLACK PEPPER

METHOD: PLACE ALL INGREDIENTS IN A BLENDER AND PROCESS TO LIQUEFY. MARINATE AT LEAST 30 MINUTES, OR ALL DAY. HAVE AT ROOM TEMPERATURE BEFORE ADDING TO YOUR PASTA, TOSS AND SERVE.

RECOMMENDED PASTA: STRING TYPES.

OLIVE OIL/BUTTER AND PINE NUT SAUCE

(ANOTHER QUICKIE)

THIS IS AN UNCOOKED SAUCE, QUICKLY PREPARED. TREAT THE GARLIC WITH RESPECT IN THIS SAUCE AS WELL AS ALL UNCOOKED SAUCES OR IT WILL GET ALL OF YOUR ATTENTION LATER IN THE EVENING. WE MEAN FOR YOU TO USE THE SMALLEST AMOUNT NECESSARY, OR RUB THE INTERIOR OF YOUR BLENDER OR FOOD PROCESSOR WITH GARLIC BEFORE BLENDING, THEN DISCARD THE GARLIC. IF YOU REALLY LIKE RAW GARLIC, USE BOTH CLOVES.

INGREDIENTS:
1/2 TO 2	CLOVES GARLIC
1/3	CUP PINE NUTS
SCANT 1/4	CUP ITALIAN PARSLEY
1/2	CUP GRATED ASIAGO OR PARMESAN CHEESE
1	TABLESPOON LEMON JUICE
1/2	TEASPOON SALT
PINCH	FRESHLY GROUND BLACK PEPPER
1/4	CUP OLIVE OIL
4	TABLESPOONS BUTTER

METHOD: COMBINE THE FIRST 7 INGREDIENTS IN YOUR PROCESSOR OR BLENDER. PROCESS UNTIL FINELY CHOPPED, ADD OIL, PROCESS UNTIL FAIRLY SMOOTH. TOSS HOT DRAINED PASTA WITH THE BUTTER UNTIL COATED, ADD THE SAUCE TOSS AGAIN, SERVE.

RECOMMENDED PASTA: NARROW RIBBON TYPES.

GARLIC AND ANCHOVY SAUCE

(ANOTHER QUICKIE)

THIS ANCHOVY QUICKIE COULD COME OUT ON THE SALTY SIDE. TO TONE IT DOWN, DRAIN THE ANCHOVIES ON PAPER TOWELS, THEN RINSE THEM UNDER COLD RUNNING WATER FOR A FEW SECONDS, DRAIN AGAIN, THEN USE AS DIRECTED.

INGREDIENTS:
3	TABLESPOONS BUTTER
3	TABLESPOONS OLIVE OIL
3	CLOVES GARLIC
1	SMALL CAN ANCHOVIES, DRAINED AND MASHED

METHOD: SAUTE GARLIC IN BUTTER AND OIL UNTIL LIGHTLY GOLDEN, REMOVE AND DISCARD GARLIC, ADD ANCHOVIES AND STIR UNTIL DISSOLVED. POUR SAUCE OVER PASTA, TOSS AND SERVE.

RECOMMENDED PASTA: THIN OVAL STRINGS.

BUTTER AND BLACK PEPPER SAUCE

(ANOTHER QUICKIE)

IF YOU LOVE BLACK PEPPER, I MEAN REALLY LOVE IT, THIS IS YOUR SAUCE. THERE ARE OCCASIONS AND SAUCES WHERE A LARGE USE OF BLACK PEPPER IS WELCOME. THEY ARE FEW AND FAR BETWEEN BECAUSE BLACK PEPPER IS SO DOMINANT; HOWEVER, THIS SAUCE WILL GIVE THE ADVENTURESOME COOK AN INTERESTING VEHICLE, SO GIVE IT A WHIRL. A NEW AND RISING STAR IN AMERICAN COOKERY IS THE GREEN PEPPERCORN; TRY THIS SAUCE BOTH WAYS, YOU MIGHT LIKE IT. THIS QUICKIE METHOD IS POPULAR THROUGHOUT ITALY, WITH EITHER BLACK PEPPER OR GRATED CHEESE, SOMETIMES BOTH, OR, SWAP THE BUTTER FOR OLIVE OIL.

INGREDIENTS: 1/2 POUND BUTTER (SWEET OR REGULAR)
                 1 TABLESPOON CRACKED BLACK PEPPERCORNS

METHOD: SOFTEN OR MELT THE BUTTER, TOSS WITH HOT DRAINED PASTA, ADD THE PEPPER, TOSS AGAIN, SERVE.

RECOMMENDED PASTA: NARROW RIBBON TYPES.

PAPRIKA SAUCE

THIS IS NOT FAR REMOVED FROM THE SAUCE YOU WOULD PREPARE FOR HUNGARIAN CHICKEN PAPRIKA, OR VEAL PAPRIKA. IN FACT IF YOU SWAPPED THE ASIAGO FOR A COUPLE OF ONIONS, AND THE OLIVE OIL FOR BACON OIL, YOU'D HAVE IT. THIS IS THE TYPE OF RECIPE THAT MAY HAVE ORIGINATED IN TRENTINO-ALTO ADIGE AND IS RELATED TO THE LARGE GERMAN SPEAKING, AUSTRO-ITALIAN POPULATION THERE. THE AUSTRIANS DEVELOPED A TASTE FOR PAPRIKA WHEN THE AUSTRO-HUNGARIAN EMPIRE WAS ONE OF THE BRIGHT LIGHTS OF EUROPEAN CULTURE, VIENNA IN PARTICULAR, AND BUDAPEST WERE FOR A WHILE THE CENTERS OF MUSIC, FOOD AND FASHION. WHEN THE EMPIRE DISSOLVED AND THE HUNGARIANS WENT HOME, PAPRIKA STAYED. HOWEVER, IF PAPRIKA IS NOT AMONG YOUR FAVORITE SEASONINGS, PASS ON BY.

INGREDIENTS:

4	TABLESPOONS OLIVE OIL
3	CLOVES GARLIC, CRUSHED
3	TABLESPOONS BUTTER
2	TABLESPOONS SWEET HUNGARIAN PAPRIKA
4	TOMATOES (B/P/C)
1/2	CUP WINE (IF TOMATOES ARE NOT JUICY)
1/2	TEASPOON SALT
	GRATED ASIAGO CHEESE

METHOD: SAUTE GARLIC IN THE OLIVE OIL UNTIL LIGHTLY GOLDEN, REMOVE AND DISCARD GARLIC, ADD BUTTER, WHEN MELTED, ADD PAPRIKA AND STIR CONSTANTLY FOR 2 MINUTES, ADD TOMATOES AND WINE IF NEEDED, ADD SALT, BRING SAUCE TO A BOIL, REDUCE HEAT AND SIMMER FOR 20 MINUTES. POUR SAUCE OVER PASTA, TOSS AND SERVE WITH CHEESE ON THE SIDE.

RECOMMENDED PASTA: MEDIUM OR SMALL, DIAGONAL CUT, TUBE TYPES.

WE TRIED THIS SAUCE . . . AND

LOVED IT ( )
HATED IT ( )
MAYBE WE'LL TRY IT AGAIN ( )
WE'LL USE IT FOR UNWELCOME GUESTS ( )

OLIVE AND ANCHOVY SAUCE

(ANOTHER QUICKIE)

THE OLIVES YOU CHOOSE TO USE IN THIS SAUCE WILL HAVE AN IMPACT HOW YOU TREAT THE ANCHOVIES. IF YOU HAVE SOME LARGE GREEN PIMENTO STUFFED OLIVES AVAILABLE (MARTINI SIZE), OR EVEN THE SMALL STUFFED ONES, SOMETIMES MARKETED AS, SALAD OLIVES, (THEY ARE SALTY). WITH THAT IN MIND, RINSE AND PAT DRY THE ANCHOVIES TO RID THEM OF SOME OF THEIR SALTINESS. MOST OTHER CANNED OLIVES (BLACK OR GREEN) WILL BE MILDER AND LESS SALTY.

INGREDIENTS:
1/2	CUP OLIVE OIL
2	CLOVES GARLIC (YOUR CHOICE)
1	OUNCE ANCHOVIES, MASHED (WITH OR WITHOUT CAPERS)
12	LARGE OR 18 SMALL OLIVES, CHOPPED
1/4	CUP THINLY SLICED MILDLY HOT PEPPER (ANY VARIETY)
1	TABLESPOON CHOPPED PARSLEY

METHOD: SAUTE GARLIC IN THE OLIVE OIL UNTIL LIGHTLY GOLDEN, ADD ANCHOVIES, WHEN THEY DISSOLVE, ADD OLIVES AND PEPPERS, COOK FOR 5 ADDITIONAL MINUTES. POUR SAUCE OVER PASTA, TOSS, GARNISH WITH PARSLEY, SERVE.

RECOMMENDED PASTA: THIN STRINGS.

WE TRIED THIS SAUCE . . . AND

LOVED IT ( )
HATED IT ( )
MAYBE WE'LL TRY IT AGAIN ( )
WE'LL USE IT FOR UNWELCOME GUESTS ( )

BUTTER AND BRANDY SAUCE

(ANOTHER QUICKIE)

IF YOU LIKE A SAUCE WITH A BRANDY OR WHISKEY BASE AS A CHANGE FROM WINE, SEE CHAPTERS 3 AND 8, FOR ADDITIONAL RECIPES. THIS SAUCE WILL DECIDEDLY TAKE ON THE TASTE OF YOUR CHOSEN BRANDY. MAKE SURE IT IS ONE YOU LIKE. IN FACT, YOU MAY UPGRADE BY USING COGNAC, OR SWEETEN THE SAUCE BY USING A LIQUEUR SUCH AS AMARETTO.

INGREDIENTS:
1/3	CUP SWEET BUTTER (SOFTENED)
1/2	CUP BRANDY
1/2	CLOVE GARLIC
1	CUP FRESHLY GRATED PARMESAN CHEESE
PINCH	WHITE PEPPER

METHOD: BLEND SOFTENED BUTTER AND BRANDY INTO A SOFT PASTE. RUB YOUR SERVING BOWL WITH GARLIC, DISCARD GARLIC, PLACE HOT DRAINED PASTA INTO THE BOWL, SPREAD THE CHEESE AND WHITE PEPPER OVER PASTA, TOSS UNTIL WELL BLENDED AND CHEESE HAS MELTED. ADD BUTTER AND BRANDY, TOSS AGAIN, SERVE.

RECOMMENDED PASTA: SHELL, SPIRAL OR FANCY TYPES.

CHAPTER 3

MEATLESS SAUCES MADE FROM CREAM

* (OF SPECIAL INTEREST.)

IF THERE ARE REASONS FOR YOU TO AVOID CREAM AND BUTTER, PASS RIGHT ON BY THIS CHAPTER. THERE'S NOTHING HERE FOR YOU. WELL, MAYBE, THERE ARE TWO RECIPES WITHOUT CREAM; ONE THAT MAY USE MILK ONLY (SEE "CREAMY SPINACH SAUCE"), AND ONE THAT USES CANNED MILK (SEE "CREAMY MILK SAUCE").

CREAM SAUCES GIVE YOU A LOT OF LATITUDE, AND IF USED WITHOUT DISCRETION, A LOT OF GIRTH. EVEN SO, THERE ARE TIMES WHEN YOU'LL WANT TO TAKE THE CALORIC BINGE.

CREAM SAUCES AND CREAMED SAUCES SHOULD BE A SIMPLE TOPIC, AFTER ALL HOW MANY THINGS CAN YOU DO WITH CREAM IN A SAUCE? THE ANSWER IS HUNDREDS, IF NOT THOUSANDS. ONE OF THE IMMEDIATELY CONFUSING ASPECTS, IS THAT CREAM ITSELF MAY NOT NECESSARILY BE AN INGREDIENT. SUCH IS THE CASE WHEN USING A BECHAMEL SAUCE (FRENCH), OR A BESCIAMELLA, (ITALIAN) ALTERNATELY SPELLED "BALSAMELLA". SAME SAUCE DIFFERENT DIALECT NAMES. IT'S THAT GOOD OLD STANDARD, THE "WHITE SAUCE"; USED IN SO MANY AMERICAN DISHES, FROM "CHICKEN A LA KING" TO "CREAMED BEEF ON TOAST" (GROUND OR CHIPPED), TO "BISCUITS AND GRAVY". IT SHOULD BE MADE FROM A FAT (BUTTER, MARGARINE, BACON OIL, SAUSAGE OIL, VEGETABLE OIL, LARD) FLOUR TO THICKEN AND MILK (OR, HALF AND HALF, WHIPPING CREAM, BUTTERMILK, CUT SOUR CREAM, YOGURT, OR EVEN A SYNTHETIC SOUR CREAM). OBVIOUSLY THERE ARE MANY OPPORTUNITIES FOR A COOK TO USE CREATIVITY HERE. I HAVE FOUND IN COOK BOOKS, AND WORSE, HAVE BEEN SERVED IN RESTAURANTS (WHERE I'VE FAILED TO ASK FOR IN-GREDIENTS) A WHITE SAUCE WITH FETTUCCINE PASTA. THAT WOULD HAVE BEEN ACCEPTABLE IF THE MENU HAD NOT REFERRED TO THE DISH AS "FETTUCCINE ALFREDO". THAT IS VERY SPECIFIC, IT REQUIRES BUTTER AND WHIPPING CREAM, WITH CHEESE AS THE THICKENING AGENT, NOT A WHITE SAUCE.

ALMOST ALL THE SAUCES IN THIS CATEGORY WILL BENEFIT FROM BEING PREPARED IN SOME TYPE OF PYREX SERVING DISH. BENEFIT HERE MEANS ONLY FEWER PANS TO WASH!!! CREAM SAUCES ARE GENERALLY COMPLETED OVER LOW HEAT WHILE YOU TOSS TO BLEND AND FINISH COOKING THE SAUCE. DO IT IN ANY MANNER THAT'S COMFORTABLE FOR YOU. FOR A MORE ELEGANT DINNER SETTING YOU MAY WISH TO FINISH A CREAM SAUCE IN A CHAFING DISH.

* YOU WILL FIND A NUMBER OF CREAM SAUCE RECIPES THAT CALL FOR GARLIC, BUT VERY FEW IN MY BOOK. I'LL LET YOU DECIDE TO ADD GARLIC TO ANY RECIPE NOT CALLING FOR IT ALL BY YOURSELF. REASON? THE GARLIC IN MOST CREAM SAUCE'S IS SELDOM COOKED, IT IS ONLY SOMEWHAT HEATED THROUGH, AND THE END RESULT IS WARM BUT RAW GARLIC. I SUSPECT THAT RAW GARLIC IS SOMEWHAT UPSETTING TO THE STOMACH OF MOST PEOPLE, AND MAY ALSO CAUSE A BURNING SENSATION. IF YOU LIKE IT, GO FOR IT! IF YOU DON'T, FOLLOW THE RECIPE.

* A LARGE NUMBER OF THE SAUCES IN THIS CHAPTER ARE INCREDIBLY RICH, THEREFORE, YOU WILL PROBABLY NOT BE ABLE TO EAT THE AMOUNT OF PASTA YOU MIGHT OTHERWISE EAT. SINCE CREAM SAUCES DO NOT REHEAT WELL, MAY I SUGGEST YOU ONLY COOK HALF THE AMOUNT OF PASTA YOU WOULD OTHERWISE PREPARE.

CREAM AND BUTTER SAUCE

(ANOTHER QUICKIE)

SINCE WE OPENED THIS CHAPTER WITH A COMMENTARY ABOUT CREAM SAUCES, LET'S BEGIN WITH THE BEST KNOWN AMONG THE MANY VARIATIONS OF CREAM SAUCES, A CREAM AND BUTTER SAUCE KNOWN AS THE SAUCE FOR "FETTUCCINE ALFREDO". BUT YOU NEED NOT LIMIT YOURSELF TO FETTUCCINE. GENERALLY, BUT NOT ABSOLUTELY, IN RESTAURANTS THIS WILL BE THE SAUCE SERVED WHEN THEY USE THE DESCRIPTION "ALLA PANNA" (WITH CREAM).

INGREDIENTS: 6   TABLESPOONS OF BUTTER (YOUR CHOICE)
              1   CUP WHIPPING CREAM
              1   CUP FRESHLY GRATED PARMESAN CHEESE*
              PINCH   OF GRATED NUTMEG (FRESH IF YOU HAVE IT)
                       SPRINKLE OF CHOPPED FRESH PARSLEY

* IT IS VERY IMPORTANT THAT THE CHEESE YOU USE BE FRESH. ONLY FRESH (READ: MOIST) CHEESE WILL MELT AND NOT TURN GUMMY.

SOME OF THE ABOVE INGREDIENTS MAY BE VARIED, REDUCE THE CHEESE AMOUNT AND INCREASE THE CREAM OR BUTTER AMOUNT FOR A THINNER SAUCE, OR YOU MAY USE HALF AND HALF FOR THE SAME EFFECT.

METHOD: MAY I SUGGEST THAT YOU PREPARE THIS SAUCE IN A PYREX CASSEROLE DISH.

1. AFTER YOU HAVE BROUGHT YOUR PASTA TO A BOIL, START YOUR SAUCE BY MELTING THE BUTTER, ADD THE CREAM AND ALLOW THEM TO SIMMER FOR A FEW MOMENTS.

PAY ATTENTION HERE, THIS PART IS TRICKY, IF YOU DO IT WRONG, YOU'VE GOT YUKKY STUFF!

Continued on next page

91

2.   DRAIN YOUR PASTA AND BLEND IT WITH THE CREAM AND MELTED BUTTER WHILE IT IT STILL UNDER HEAT, TOSS, REMOVE FROM HEAT, ADD THE CHEESE, NUTMEG AND PARSLEY, TOSS AGAIN AND SERVE.

YOU'RE GOING TO LOVE THIS DISH, IT IS RICH, RICH, RICH! IN FACT THE DISH IS SO LUXURIOUS THAT WHEN SERVING IT, MAY I SUGGEST THAT YOU ACCOMPANY IT WITH A STEAMED GREEN VEGETABLE SPRINKLED WITH A SELECTION FROM LEMON JUICE, OLIVE OIL OR LIME JUICE. FOLLOW WITH SHERBET AND COFFEE.

RECOMMENDED PASTA: NARROW OR MEDIUM RIBBON TYPES, OVAL STRINGS, SMALL FILLED PILLOWS AND SHELLS.

CREAM AND BUTTER SAUCE TOO!

(ANOTHER QUICKIE)

ALFREDO DIDN'T CREATE THIS ONE, BUT IT CERTAINLY IS A VARIATION, AND MOST LIKELY WOULD BE CALLED "ALLA PANNA" WHEN FOUND ON A MENU. LIKE ALL CREAM SAUCES, THIS ONE TOO IS NORTHERN, VERY SIMPLE AND VERY RICH.

INGREDIENTS: 1   CUP WHIPPING CREAM
               4   TABLESPOONS BUTTER
               1/2   CUP FRESHLY GRATED PARMESAN CHEESE

METHOD: MELT THE BUTTER IN THE CREAM, POUR SAUCE OVER PASTA, TOSS TO COAT, ADD CHEESE, TOSS AGAIN, SERVE.

RECOMMENDED PASTA: SMALL FILLED PILLOW TYPES.

CREAMED MUSHROOM SAUCE

(ANOTHER QUICKIE)

HERE IS ANOTHER CREAM SAUCE THAT NEED NOT BE STARTED UNTIL THE PASTA IS IN THE WATER, UNLESS YOU ARE USING FRESH PASTA. WITH FRESH PASTA, YOU'LL HAVE TO DO THEM SIMULTANEOUSLY, OR GET AN EXTRA SET OF HANDS. READY THE INGREDIENTS AND SET ASIDE.

INGREDIENTS:
3	TABLESPOONS BUTTER
2	CUPS OF WHIPPING CREAM
1/3	CUP FRESHLY GRATED PARMESAN CHEESE
1/2	POUND FRESH MUSHROOMS, THINLY SLICED
PINCH	WHITE PEPPER
	CHOPPED FRESH PARSLEY

METHOD: SAUTE THE MUSHROOMS IN THE BUTTER UNTIL THE ABSORBED BUTTER IS RELEASED BY THE MUSHROOMS (2 TO 3 MINUTES), ADD THE CREAM, BRING TO A BOIL; REDUCE HEAT TO A SIMMER, COOK 2 TO 3 MINUTES. STIR IN THE CHEESE, COOK 1 ADDITIONAL MINUTE. ADD YOUR COOKED PASTA TO THE PAN AND TOSS. SPRINKLE WITH SOME ADDITIONAL CHEESE AND PARSLEY. SERVE.

THIS IS ANOTHER CREAM SAUCE THAT COULD BENEFIT FROM BEING PREPARED IN A PYREX SERVING DISH.

RECOMMENDED PASTA: FILLED LITTLE PILLOW TYPES OR SHELL TYPES (DUMPLINGS TOO).

PEAS IN A POD SAUCE

(ANOTHER QUICKIE)

I GUESS YOU KNOW THAT MEANS FRESH PEAS. FROZEN PEAS WILL WORK, BUT NOT AS WELL; CANNED PEAS ARE A LOSER IN THIS SAUCE.

INGREDIENTS:
3	CUPS FRESHLY SHELLED PEAS (YOU CAN'T EAT THE PODS, THESE ARE NOT CHINESE SNOW PEAS!)
2	TABLESPOONS BUTTER
PINCH	NUTMEG
2	CUPS WHIPPING CREAM
1	WHOLE EGG, BEATEN
1	CUP FRESHLY GRATED PARMESAN CHEESE

METHOD: IF YOU ARE SURE OF THE COOKING TIME OF YOUR PASTA, YOU MAY COOK THE FRESH (OR FROZEN) PEAS ALONG WITH THE PASTA. COOK FRESH PEAS FOR 5 MINUTES; FOR FROZEN PEAS FOLLOW PACKAGE INSTRUCTIONS, IF YOU ARE HESITANT, STEAM THEM SEPARATELY.

PLACE CREAM, BUTTER, AND NUTMEG IN A SAUCE PAN AND BRING TO A BOIL, REMOVE PAN FROM HEAT, WHIP IN EGG AND CHEESE, RETURN TO HEAT, AND COOK UNTIL SLIGHTLY THICKENED. (IF SAUCE IS TOO THICK, THIN WITH MORE CREAM) ADD PEAS TO SAUCE IF THEY WERE NOT COOKED WITH PASTA. POUR SAUCE OVER DRAINED PASTA, TOSS AND SERVE.

RECOMMENDED PASTA: SMALL FILLED TYPES.

DELICATE PINK SAUCE

(ANOTHER QUICKIE)

A COMBINATION OF WHIPPING CREAM AND TOMATO PASTE GIVES YOU A LIGHT PINK COLORING AND A CREAMY TASTE. USE A PYREX OR CORNING WARE COOKING DISH TO PREPARE AND SERVE THIS DISH.

INGREDIENTS: 2   CUPS WHIPPING CREAM
2   LEVEL TABLESPOONS TOMATO PASTE (MEASURE, DON'T GUESS)
1/3   CUP FRESHLY GRATED PARMESAN CHEESE

METHOD: HEAT THE CREAM, DON'T BRING TO A BOIL, ADD TOMATO PASTE WHEN CREAM IS HOT; STIR TO DISSOLVE AND TO COLOR CREAM. ADD PASTA AND TOSS TO COAT, ADD CHEESE, TOSS AGAIN, SERVE.

RECOMMENDED PASTA: STRING TYPES.

CREAM AND TOMATO SAUCE

(PINK SAUCE TOO!)

NOTICE HOW CLEVERLY I WORKED IN THE PINK PART. IF YOU'VE EVER DONE ANY COLORING, THEN IT MUST BE OBVIOUS TO YOU THAT WHEN YOU MIX TOMATOES AND CREAM, THE RESULTING SAUCE COMES IN A SHADE OF PINK. BE THAT AS IT MAY, THIS SAUCE IS APPARENTLY OF NORTHERN ORIGIN.

INGREDIENTS:

4	TABLESPOONS BUTTER
1	SMALL ONION, MINCED
1	STALK CELERY, FINELY CHOPPED
1	CARROT, FINELY CHOPPED
1	16 OUNCE CAN TOMATOES
1	TABLESPOON FRESH BASIL (OR 1 TSP. DRY)
PINCH	WHITE PEPPER
1/2	CUP WHIPPING CREAM
	FRESHLY GRATED PARMESAN CHEESE TO TASTE

METHOD: SAUTE THE ONIONS, CELERY, AND CARROT UNTIL ONIONS ARE TRANSPARENT. BLENDERIZE THE TOMATOES; ADD TOMATOES, BASIL AND WHITE PEPPER TO THE VEGETABLES. PARTIALLY COVER AND SIMMER FOR 30 MINUTES. ADD THE CREAM, STIR TO BLEND, REMOVE FROM HEAT. POUR OVER PASTA, TOSS, SPRINKLE WITH PARMESAN AND SERVE.

RECOMMENDED PASTA: SMALL FILLED TYPES, SUCH AS CAPPELLETTI, RAVIOLINI, TORTELLINI.

97

WE TRIED THIS SAUCE . . . AND

LOVED IT ( )
HATED IT ( )
MAYBE WE'LL TRY IT AGAIN ( )
WE'LL USE IT FOR UNWELCOME GUESTS ( )

CREAM AND TOMATO SAUCE II

AN OBVIOUS VARIATION OF THE PRECEDING SAUCE. WE'LL OMIT SEVERAL INGREDIENTS AND AS A RESULT GET A DIFFERENT END PRODUCT. IT WILL STILL BE PINK, BUT WITH DIFFERENT TASTE.

INGREDIENTS:

1/4	POUND BUTTER
3	TABLESPOONS SWEET ONION, CHOPPED
1	MEDIUM CARROT, SHREDDED
1	STALK CELERY, FINELY CHOPPED
1	16 OUNCE CAN PEAR TOMATOES, BLENDERIZED
1/2	CUP WHIPPING CREAM

METHOD: PLACE ALL INGREDIENTS EXCEPT WHIPPING CREAM IN A SAUCE PAN, BRING TO A BOIL REDUCE HEAT AND SIMMER PARTIALLY COVERED FOR 1 HOUR. ADD WHIPPING CREAM TO HEAT THROUGH, REMOVE FROM HEAT. POUR SAUCE OVER PASTA, MIX WELL AND SERVE.

IF YOU WANT A SMOOTH SAUCE, SIEVE OR BLENDERIZE THE SAUCE WHEN THE COOKING IS COMPLETE, THEN POUR OVER YOUR PASTA.

RECOMMENDED PASTA: SMALL FILLED PILLOW TYPES OR GNOCCHI.

WE TRIED THIS SAUCE . . . AND

LOVED IT ( )
HATED IT ( )
MAYBE WE'LL TRY IT AGAIN ( )
WE'LL USE IT FOR UNWELCOME GUESTS ( )

FRESH TOMATO AND CREAM SAUCE

THERE IS A DIFFERENCE IN INGREDIENTS FROM THE PRECEDING RECIPES, BUT YOU STILL GET A PINK SAUCE.

INGREDIENTS:
2	TABLESPOONS BUTTER
2	CLOVES GARLIC, MINCED
3	POUNDS FRESH TOMATOES (B/P/C)
1	TEASPOON SALT
PINCH	FRESHLY GROUND BLACK PEPPER
2	TABLESPOONS BASIL, CHOPPED
1/2	CUP WHIPPING CREAM

METHOD: SAUTE GARLIC IN BUTTER FOR 1 MINUTE, ADD TOMATOES, SALT AND PEPPER. BRING TO A BOIL, REDUCE HEAT, LOOSELY COVER AND SIMMER FOR 25 MINUTES, ADD CREAM, STIR TO BLEND, COOK 5 ADDITIONAL MINUTES. POUR SAUCE OVER PASTA, TOSS AND SERVE.

RECOMMENDED PASTA: STRINGS OR LONG RIBBON TYPES.

99

PINK VODKA CREAM SAUCE

(ANOTHER QUICKIE)

IF YOU LEAVE SOMETHING GOOD ENOUGH TO EAT OR DRINK IN ITALY, SOMEONE WILL TRY IT IN A PASTA SAUCE, AND THAT'S WHAT HAS HAPPENED HERE. THIS IS AN ITALIAN STYLE SAUCE AND IT SEEMS TO BE A FAVORITE IN AND AROUND ROME. OF ALL THE HARD LIQUORS AROUND, VODKA IS THE MOST TASTELESS. IT ADDS NOTHING EXCEPT ALCOHOL. VODKA IS DISTILLED ALCOHOL, STEEPED IN, AND FILTERED THROUGH CHARCOAL, THEREFORE, WHAT-EVER YOU ADD TO VODKA IS THE FLAVOR. IN THIS SAUCE TOMATOES AND WHIPPING CREAM ARE THE FLAVORS. ASIDE FROM THAT, THE ALCOHOL IS EVAPORATED IN THE COOKING PROCESS.

INGREDIENTS:

2/3	CUP VODKA
PINCH	CRUSHED RED PEPPER
6	TABLESPOONS BUTTER
3/4	CUP PEAR TOMATOES, BLENDERIZED
3/4	CUP WHIPPING CREAM
1/2	CUP FRESHLY GRATED PARMESAN CHEESE

METHOD: STIR THE RED PEPPER INTO THE VODKA AND LET REST WHILE YOU SET YOUR PASTA TO BOILING. MELT THE BUTTER, ADD THE VODKA AND BRING TO A BOIL, ADD TOMATOES AND WHIPPING CREAM, RETURN SAUCE TO A BOIL, REDUCE HEAT AND ALLOW TO SIMMER FOR 5 MINUTES. DRAIN PASTA, ADD GRATED CHEESE AND TOSS, ADD SAUCE, TOSS AGAIN, SERVE.

RECOMMENDED PASTA: MEDIUM TUBE TYPES, STRAIGHT EDGED OR DIAGONAL CUT.

CREAM AND LEMON SAUCE

(ANOTHER QUICKIE)

ITALY IS A MAJOR PRODUCER OF CITRUS; THERE IS EXTENSIVE USE OF LEMON SPRINKLED ON FRESHLY COOKED VEGETABLES, OR ON SALADS, IN ICES, ICE CREAMS AND IN PASTRIES. THERE ARE ONLY A FEW OCCASIONS WHEN LEMON GETS INTO A PASTA SAUCE AND THIS IS ONE OF THEM. IT DOESN'T GET JUICE, JUST THE ZEST!

INGREDIENTS:
1	CUP WHIPPING CREAM
2	TEASPOONS GRATED LEMON ZEST (ONLY THE YELLOW)
2	TABLESPOONS ITALIAN PARSLEY, CHOPPED
2	TABLESPOONS BUTTER
2	TABLESPOONS GRATED PARMESAN CHEESE
PINCH	SALT

METHOD: WHILE PASTA IS COOKING, PLACE THE CREAM, LEMON ZEST, BUTTER, PARSLEY AND SALT IN A PYREX SERVING DISH. BRING IT TO BUBBLING AND WHEN THE BUTTER HAS MELTED, ADD THE FRESHLY DRAINED PASTA, TOSS UNTIL COATED, SPRINKLE ON THE CHEESE, TOSS AGAIN AND SERVE.

RECOMMENDED PASTA: RIBBON TYPES OR MEDIUM TUBE TYPES.

WE TRIED THIS SAUCE . . . AND

LOVED IT ( )
HATED IT ( )
MAYBE WE'LL TRY IT AGAIN ( )
WE'LL USE IT FOR UNWELCOME GUESTS ( )

CREAM AND LEMON SAUCE II

(ANOTHER QUICKIE)

THIS SAUCE LIKE THE PRECEDING USES THE ZEST, BUT DIFFERS BY ITS USE OF THE PULP. THIS IS A VERY LEMONY (IS THAT A WORD?) SAUCE. IT IS ABOUT AS SIMPLE AS THE PRECEDING SAUCE; IT ACTUALLY USES FEWER INGREDIENTS, BUT WITH DIFFERENT QUANTITIES, IT ALSO USES BRANDY AS A FLAVOR ENHANCER.

INGREDIENTS: 2   LEMONS
1   CUP WHIPPING CREAM
1/4   CUP BRANDY
2/3   CUP FRESHLY GRATED PARMESAN CHEESE

METHOD:

1. YOU CAN PREPARE THE LEMONS IN SEVERAL WAYS, YOU MIGHT CUT THEM IN HALF, SEPARATE THE SHELL INCLUDING THE PITH, FROM THE PULP, BY USING A LONG CITRUS PEELING TOOL, WITH THE SAME TOOL, REMOVE THE PITH FROM THE OUTER SHELL, THAT WILL LEAVE YOU WITH THE YELLOW PART (ZEST). MINCE THE ZEST, SLICE AND DICE THE PULP, REMOVING ALL SEEDS. OR,

2. GRATE THE ZEST OFF THE LEMONS, NOW JUICE THE LEMONS.

3. BRING WHIPPING CREAM, 1/2 THE LEMON ZEST AND LEMON PULP OR JUICE TO A LOW BOIL, KEEP AT THAT BOIL FOR 3 MINUTES, ADD BRANDY, COOK FOR 3 ADDITIONAL MINUTES. TOSS COOKED PASTA WITH GRATED CHEESE, ADD SAUCE, TOSS AGAIN, SERVE SPRINKLED WITH REMAINING LEMON ZEST.

RECOMMENDED PASTA: SOLID STRING TYPES, ANY SHAPE OR DIAMETER.

CREAM AND LEMON SAUCE III

HERE WE HAVE ANOTHER SAUCE FROM ITALY'S CITRUS ZONE. WITH THIS VERSION, WE'LL USE LEMON PEEL AND LEMON JUICE BLENDED WITH CREAM. IT SEEMS AS THOUGH THIS SHOULD BE A SUMMER SAUCE, BUT SINCE LEMONS ARE A YEAR ROUND ITEM, YOU CAN MAKE THIS ONE WHENEVER YOU'RE IN THE MOOD.

YOU MAY WANT TO PREPARE THIS SAUCE IN A CHAFING DISH OR SOME TYPE OF PYREX CASSEROLE DISH.

INGREDIENTS: 4   TABLESPOONS BUTTER
                1   CUP WHIPPING CREAM
                2   TABLESPOONS LEMON JUICE
                2   TABLESPOONS GRATED LEMON PEEL (YELLOW PART ONLY)

METHOD: MELT THE BUTTER IN THE WHIPPING CREAM, COOK FOR ABOUT 5 MINUTES, ADD LEMON JUICE AND BLEND IN WELL, ADD LEMON PEEL. NOW, EITHER POUR SAUCE OVER PASTA, TOSS AND SERVE. OR, ADD COOKED AND DRAINED PASTA TO THE SAUCE PAN, TOSS AND SERVE.

RECOMMENDED PASTA: NARROW RIBBON TYPES.

CREAM AND GREEN SAUCE

(ANOTHER QUICKIE)

THIS SAUCE IS NOT TOO FAR REMOVED FROM AN "ALLA PANNA" OR "ALFREDO" CREAM AND BUTTER SAUCE, IT USES CHIVES TO GIVE IT A DIFFERENT LOOK AND TASTE.

INGREDIENTS:

6	TABLESPOONS BUTTER
2	CLOVES GARLIC (YOUR CHOICE)
1	CUP CHIVES, SLICED FINE
1	CUP WHIPPING CREAM
1	CUP FRESHLY GRATED PARMESAN CHEESE
PINCH	FRESHLY GRATED NUTMEG
1/4	TEASPOON SALT OR TO TASTE

METHOD: SAUTE ONIONS IN THE BUTTER FOR ABOUT 2 MINUTES, ADD THE CREAM, NUTMEG AND SALT. BRING CREAM TO A BOIL, ADD THE FRESHLY DRAINED PASTA, TOSS TO COAT, ADD PARMESAN, TOSS AND SERVE.

RECOMMENDED PASTA: RIBBON TYPES OR MEDIUM TUBE TYPES.

CREAMY SPINACH SAUCE

IN THIS SAUCE, THE WHIPPING CREAM MAY BE OMITTED SHOULD YOU NEED TO AVOID IT; TO DO SO INCREASE THE MILK BY 1/2 CUP.

YOU'LL BE USING FRESH SPINACH FOR THIS SAUCE, AND WHILE IT WOULD BE POSSIBLE TO USE FROZEN, THE RESULTS WILL BE DIFFERENT. BESIDES, FRESH SPINACH NOW SEEMS TO BE AVAILABLE THROUGHOUT THE YEAR, GO WITH THE REAL THING. POPEYE WILL LOVE YOU FOR IT.

INGREDIENTS:

3/4	POUND FRESH SPINACH
6	TABLESPOONS SWEET BUTTER
1/3	CUP FLOUR
4	CUPS MILK
1	SMALL ONION, MINCED
1/2	TEASPOON SALT
2	CUPS SHREDDED SWISS CHEESE
1/4	CUP PARSLEY, CHOPPED
3	EGG YOLKS, BEATEN
1	CUP WHIPPING CREAM
PINCH	NUTMEG (FRESHLY GROUND IF YOU HAVE IT)

METHOD: WASH, STEM, AND STEAM THE SPINACH UNTIL JUST COOKED. DROP INTO COLD WATER TO STOP THE COOKING. NOW SQUEEZE VERY DRY. CHOP FINE, SET ASIDE. MAKE A ROUX OF THE BUTTER AND FLOUR BY ADDING THE FLOUR TO THE HOT, MELTED BUTTER, COOK FOR SEVERAL MINUTES, ADD MILK, ONION AND SALT. ATTEND CAREFULLY WHILE COOKING SAUCE ON LOW HEAT UNTIL ONION IS DONE; ABOUT 15 TO 20 MINUTES. ADD CHEESE, PARSLEY AND SPINACH, COOK UNTIL CHEESE MELTS. ADD BEATEN EGG YOLKS, WHIPPING CREAM AND NUTMEG. COOK SEVERAL ADDITIONAL MINUTES, BUT DO NOT ALLOW SAUCE TO BOIL. REMOVE FROM HEAT, POUR OVER PASTA, TOSS AND SERVE.

RECOMMENDED PASTA: RIBBON TYPES, OR ROUND AND OVAL STRINGS.

CREAMY SPINACH AND GORGONZOLA SAUCE

THIS IS A NORTHERN SAUCE WHOSE INGREDIENT LIST WOULD ALLOW ME TO PLACE IT IN ANY OF THREE DIFFERENT CATEGORIES. BUT SINCE IT SO NICELY COMPLIMENTS THE PRECEDING CREAM AND SPINACH SAUCE, I'VE PLACED IT HERE. WHILE THIS SAUCE CALLS FOR GORGONZOLA, YOU KNOW YOU MAY USE BLUE CHEESE IF YOU WISH, OR FOR THAT MATTER, YOU MAY EVEN USE CRUMBLED FETA CHEESE.

INGREDIENTS:

1	POUND SPINACH, WASHED AND STEMMED
4	TABLESPOONS BUTTER
6	OUNCES CRUMBLED GORGONZOLA CHEESE
1/3	CUP MARSALA WINE
1	CUP WHIPPING CREAM
1/4	CLOVE GARLIC, MINCED
PINCH	WHITE PEPPER
1/2	CUP FRESHLY GRATED ASIAGO CHEESE

METHOD: STEAM SPINACH IN THE WATER CLINGING TO IT AFTER WASHING, DRAIN AND SET ASIDE TO COOL. WHEN SPINACH IS COOL, SQUEEZE FAIRLY DRY AND THEN PUREE SPINACH IN A FOOD PROCESSOR OR BLENDER. DISSOLVE THE GORGONZOLA IN THE BUTTER OVER MEDIUM HEAT, ADD THE PUREED SPINACH, MARSALA, WHIPPING CREAM, GARLIC AND PEPPER, BRING TO A BOIL, REDUCE HEAT TO LOW AND COOK UNCOVERED FOR 10 MINUTES. POUR SAUCE OVER PASTA, TOSS AND SERVE WITH GRATED CHEESE ON THE SIDE.

RECOMMENDED PASTA: CURLY TYPES.

GORGONZOLA CREAMY CHEESE SAUCE

(ANOTHER QUICKIE)

THIS SAUCE HAS MORE GOING FOR IT THAN SIMPLY TAKING THE PRECEDING SAUCE AND REMOVING THE SPINACH, BUT NOT MUCH.   IT IS LESS SWEET BECAUSE THERE IS NO SWEET WINE, BUT IT DOES TAKE ON A SALTY CHARACTER DUE IN PART TO THE NATURE OF GORGONZOLA AND THE PARMESAN CHEESE. IF YOU DON'T HAVE GORGONZOLA CHEESE ON HAND YOU MAY CHOOSE TO USE ANY OF THE BLUE VEINED CHEESES.

FOR A SIMILAR SAUCE SEE CHAPTER 11, THE DIFFERENCES ARE ENOUGH TO WARRANT PLACING THEM IN DIFFERENT CATEGORIES.   THIS SAUCE USES FOUR TIMES THE WHIPPING CREAM, AND HAS A FEWER INGREDIENTS WHICH MAKES IT A VERY CREAMY SAUCE.   THE OTHER GETS MORE OF ITS CHARACTER FROM THE GORGONZOLA.

INGREDIENTS:

5	OUNCES CRUMBLED GORGONZOLA CHEESE
3	TABLESPOONS BUTTER
1	CUP WHIPPING CREAM
1	FRESH SAGE LEAVE OR TINY PINCH OF DRY SAGE
	FRESHLY GRATED PARMESAN CHEESE

METHOD: MELT BUTTER IN THE WHIPPING CREAM, ADD CRUMBLED GORGONZOLA, BLEND OVER MEDIUM HEAT STIRRING CONSTANTLY UNTIL CHEESE MELTS ADD SAGE, SIMMER FOR 2 MINUTES, ADD COOKED AND DRAINED PASTA TO THE SAUCE PAN, TOSS TO BLEND; SERVE WITH GRATED CHEESE ON THE SIDE.

RECOMMENDED PASTA: VERY THIN STRINGS OR NARROW RIBBONS.

CREAMY MILK SAUCE

(USING EVAPORATED MILK)

HERE IS A CREAM SAUCE THAT USES NEITHER CREAM, NOR A THICKENING AGENT SUCH AS CHEESE, EGGS OR FLOUR. IT USES CANNED EVAPORATED MILK. THE TASTE SO TYPICAL OF CANNED EVAPORATED MILK IS OVERCOME BY THE SEASONING.

I SEE NO REASON WHY THIS SAUCE COULD NOT BE MADE USING CONDENSED MILK, IT'S A LITTLE CREAMIER, A LITTLE SWEETER, A LITTLE BETTER TASTING AND A LITTLE MORE EXPENSIVE. IT'S WORTH A TRY.

INGREDIENTS:

2	CANS EVAPORATED MILK
2	TABLESPOONS OLIVE OIL
2	CLOVES GARLIC, MINCED
2	TABLESPOONS ONION, MINCED
1	YELLOW BELL OR MILDLY HOT PEPPER
1	RED BELL OR MILDLY HOT PEPPER
	(SEEDED AND CUT INTO STRIPS)
1	TABLESPOON DIJON MUSTARD
1	TEASPOON DRY BASIL OR THYME
1/2	TEASPOON SALT
PINCH	CRUSHED RED PEPPER
1/2	CUP FRESHLY GRATED PARMESAN CHEESE

METHOD: BRING EVAPORATED MILK TO A BOIL, REDUCE HEAT TO SIMMER, COOK ABOUT 10 MINUTES. MEANWHILE, SAUTE GARLIC, ONION AND PEPPERS IN OLIVE OIL UNTIL ONION IS TRANSPARENT, ADD MUSTARD, BASIL, SALT AND CRUSHED RED PEPPER. COOK FOR 1 ADDITIONAL MINUTE, ADD THE HOT MILK, BLEND WELL. POUR SAUCE OVER PASTA, SPRINKLE WITH CHEESE, TOSS AND SERVE.

RECOMMENDED PASTA: CURLY TYPES.

WHITE SAUCE

THIS IS THE CHEAP VERSION OF AN "ALFREDO (BUTTER/CREAM) SAUCE". IT PROBABLY WON'T HAPPEN OFTEN, BUT THERE ARE TIMES WHEN YOU MAY WANT TO USE THIS SAUCE. TRY IT ON A STUFFED PASTA SUCH AS RAVIOLI OR A LASAGNE. OR YOU MAY USE THIS WHITE SAUCE AND A TOMATO SAUCE (MAY I RECOMMEND THE STANDARD CANNED AMERICAN TOMATO SAUCE, OR TOMATO SAUCE #24) FOR A BAKED CANNELLONI. IF YOU CHOOSE TO DO THIS LITTLE EXTRA, THE EFFORT WILL ADD SUBSTANTIALLY TO YOUR MEAL. PLACE THE TOMATO SAUCE UNDER THE CANNELLONI (RESERVE A FEW SPOONFULS), SPREAD THE WHITE SAUCE ON TOP, THEN SPRINKLE THE REMAINING TOMATO SAUCE OVER THE WHITE SAUCE, ADD SOME GRATED PARMESAN AND MOZZARELLA CHEESE, BAKE FOR 30 MINUTES AT 350 DEGREES. (JUST BEFORE SERVING, IF YOU'LL SPRINKLE A LITTLE CHOPPED PARSLEY OVER THE PASTA, YOU'LL GET A GREEN, WHITE AND RED ITALIAN COLORS EFFECT.)

INGREDIENTS:

3	TABLESPOONS BUTTER
3	TABLESPOONS FLOUR
1/2	TEASPOON SALT
1 3/4	CUPS HALF AND HALF

METHOD: PREPARE A ROUX BY HEATING THE BUTTER TO BUBBLING, ADD THE FLOUR AND COOK FOR A FEW MINUTES.

WHISK IN THE HALF AND HALF AND STIR UNTIL SAUCE THICKENS. REMOVE FROM HEAT.

RECOMMENDED PASTA: IF YOU'VE A MIND TO, THIS SAUCE MAY BE USED AS IS OVER A FAVORITE PASTA.

109

CREAM AND BOURBON SAUCE

WHISKEY IS NOT A NORMAL PASTA SAUCE INGREDIENT, BUT YOU KNOW THAT. ASIDE FROM THAT, BOURBON IS PURE AMERICAN WHISKEY. IN FACT, I SEEM TO RECALL HAVING READ SOMEWHERE THAT BOURBON IS THE ONLY WHISKEY EVER DEVELOPED IN THE UNITED STATES. BOURBON GOT ITS NAME FROM THE KENTUCKY COUNTY THAT BROUGHT IT TO LIFE, BOURBON COUNTY. BE THAT AS IT MAY, HERE'S A SAUCE THAT WEDS IT TO CREAM AND MAKES IT WORK. BOURBON IS NOT AN ABSOLUTE, YOU MAY USE A SCOTCH WHOSE TASTE YOU ENJOY OR RYE WHISKEY. THE ALCOHOL EVAPORATES RAPIDLY DURING THE COOKING PROCESS, BUT THE TASTE REMAINS, SO MAKE SURE YOU REALLY LIKE THE TASTE OF THE WHISKEY YOU CHOOSE.

INGREDIENTS:
4	OUNCES MUSHROOMS, SLICED
3/4	CUP WHISKEY
1 1/2	CUPS WHIPPING CREAM
3	TABLESPOONS BUTTER
1	CLOVE GARLIC, BRUISED
1/4	CUP CHOPPED PARSLEY
PINCH	SALT
PINCH	NUTMEG
	FRESHLY GRATED PARMESAN CHEESE

METHOD:

1. SOAK THE MUSHROOM SLICES IN THE WHISKEY FOR ABOUT AN HOUR.

2. SAUTE THE GARLIC AND PARSLEY IN THE BUTTER OVER LOW HEAT FOR 2 TO 3 MINUTES. REMOVE AND DISCARD THE GARLIC. REMOVE THE MUSHROOMS FROM THE WHISKEY, ADD THEM TO THE BUTTER AND SAUTE MUSHROOMS FOR 2 MINUTES, ADD THE REMAINING WHISKEY, COVER AND SIMMER UNTIL MOST OF THE WHISKEY HAS EVAPORATED. ADD THE WHIPPING CREAM, SALT AND NUTMEG; BRING CREAM TO A NEAR BOIL. REMOVE FROM HEAT, POUR OVER YOUR PASTA, TOSS AND SERVE WITH GRATED CHEESE ON THE SIDE.

RECOMMENDED PASTA: THIN STRING TYPES.

110

CREAM AND BRANDY SAUCE

(ANOTHER QUICKIE)

FROM BOURBON TO BRANDY, I'LL WAGER THIS SAUCE TO BE A DANDY! WELL, NOW YOU KNOW WHY I WRITE COOK BOOKS AND NOT POETRY. AGAIN, I OFFER YOU A CAVEAT, USE A BRANDY WHOSE TASTE YOU ENJOY. THE BRANDY AND CREAM ARE USED UNCOOKED, SO IF THE HEAT FROM THE PASTA DOESN'T EVAPORATE THE ALCOHOL, IT WILL BE IN THE SAUCE.

INGREDIENTS:

1/4	CUP BRANDY
1	EGG YOLK
1	CUP WHIPPING CREAM
1	CUP FROZEN PEAS, OR FRESH
1/4	CUP BUTTER
1/4	TEASPOON SALT
2	TABLESPOONS CHOPPED PARSLEY

METHOD: LIGHTLY BEAT THE YOLK INTO THE BRANDY, ADD THE CREAM AND BEAT UNTIL WELL MIXED, SET ASIDE. SAUTE THE PEAS IN BUTTER FOR 5 TO 6 MINUTES, REMOVE FROM HEAT, ADD SALT AND PARSLEY. FOLD PEAS INTO CREAM SAUCE, POUR SAUCE OVER PASTA, TOSS AND SERVE.

RECOMMENDED PASTA: STRING TYPES.

EGGS AND CREAM SAUCE

(ANOTHER QUICKIE)

HOLY CHICKEN FAT BATMAN, LOOK AT THE YOLKS! LOTS OF EGG YOLKS FOR THIS SAUCE. TRY MAKING THIS ONE WHEN YOU WANT A MERINGUE PIE OR A FLUFFY TAPIOCA FOR DESSERT.

YOU'LL FINISH COOKING THIS IN THE SERVING DISH ON THE STOVE AND OVER HEAT, SO USE A PYREX OR CORNING CASSEROLE DISH FOR THE SAUCE.

INGREDIENTS:
6	OUNCES SWEET BUTTER
3/4	CUP WHIPPING CREAM
1/4	TEASPOON SALT
PINCH	WHITE PEPPER
6	EGG YOLKS, BEATEN
1	CUP FRESHLY GRATED PARMESAN CHEESE

METHOD: WITH YOUR PASTA MERRILY BOILING AWAY, START THE SAUCE BY SLOWLY MELTING THE BUTTER IN YOUR SERVING DISH WHEN BUTTER IS BUBBLING, ADD THE CREAM AND BRING TO A NEAR BOIL, ADD SALT AND PEPPER, ADD PASTA, TOSS TO COAT. DRIZZLE THE BEATEN EGG YOLKS OVER THE PASTA AND TOSS AGAIN; FINALLY ADD THE GRATED CHEESE, TOSS AGAIN AND SERVE.

RECOMMENDED PASTA: MEDIUM TUBE TYPES.

SWEET PEPPERS AND CREAM SAUCE

THIS SAUCE SEEMS TO HAVE MANY OF THE FLAVORS OF THE CONDENSED MILK SAUCE, BUT THE TWO SAUCES ARE WORLDS APART IN TASTE.

INGREDIENTS:

4	TABLESPOONS BUTTER
1	ONION, CHOPPED
1	BELL PEPPER, SEEDED AND DICED
1	YELLOW BELL OR WAX PEPPER, SEEDED AND DICED
1	RED BELL PEPPER, SEEDED AND DICED
1/2	TEASPOON SALT
1	CUP WHIPPING CREAM
1	TABLESPOON CHOPPED PARSLEY
1/2	GRATED PARMESAN CHEESE

METHOD: SAUTE THE ONION AND PEPPERS IN THE BUTTER UNTIL PEPPERS ARE COOKED, ABOUT 5 TO 8 MINUTES, ADD CREAM, BRING SAUCE TO A BOIL, COOK FOR 5 ADDITIONAL MINUTES, REMOVE SAUCE FROM HEAT AND POUR OVER PASTA, TOSS, ADD PARSLEY AND GRATED CHEESE, TOSS AGAIN, SERVE.

RECOMMENDED PASTA: MEDIUM SHELL OR CURLY TYPES.

WE TRIED THIS SAUCE . . . AND

LOVED IT ( )
HATED IT ( )
MAYBE WE'LL TRY IT AGAIN ( )
WE'LL USE IT FOR UNWELCOME GUESTS ( )

MUSHROOMS WITH PEAS SAUCE

(ANOTHER QUICKIE)

THIS SAUCE IS QUITE LIGHT DESPITE THE CREAM. THE PEAS ARE THERE FOR COLOR EFFECT ONLY; THERE AREN'T ENOUGH OF THEM TO ADD SUBSTANCE.

INGREDIENTS:

2	TABLESPOONS FROZEN OR FRESH PEAS
1/3	CUP SLICED MUSHROOMS
1/4	POUND BUTTER
1/2	CUP WHIPPING CREAM
1/2	CUP FRESHLY GRATED PARMESAN CHEESE

METHOD: COOK PEAS IN A LITTLE WATER, DRAIN AND SET ASIDE. SAUTE MUSHROOMS IN THE BUTTER FOR 3 MINUTES, POUR BUTTER, MUSHROOMS AND PEAS OVER PASTA, TOSS, ADD GRATED CHEESE, TOSS AGAIN SERVE.

RECOMMENDED PASTA: USE 8 OUNCES OF ANY RIBBON TYPE PASTA.

CHOCOLATE CREAM SAUCE

(ANOTHER QUICKIE)

EUROPEANS LOVE CHOCOLATE AND EAT MORE OF IT THAN AMERICANS. SOME STUDIES I'VE READ SHOW THE BRITISH AS THE NUMBER ONE CONSUMERS, FOLLOWED BY THE BELGIANS AND THEN THE SWISS. EUROPEANS EVEN EAT CHOCOLATE SPREAD ON BREAD AT BREAKFAST (WITH AND WITHOUT NUTS). THE AUSTRIANS MAKE A LIQUEUR OUT OF IT, SO THAT THEY MAY DRINK IT STRAIGHT. IN MOST OTHER EUROPEAN COUNTRIES THEY HAVE FOUND A WAY TO ADD IT TO THEIR COFFEE. THE SICILIANS ADD IT TO SOME CAPONATA RECIPES. SUFFICE IT TO SAY, THAT AT SOME POINT, SOMEONE WAS GOING TO PUT IT ON PASTA. WELL HERE'S THE SAUCE THAT DOES IT. I DON'T KNOW WHERE THE SAUCE ORIGINATED, BUT I SUSPECT IT'S EITHER FAR NORTHERN, OR SICILIAN.

INGREDIENTS:
1	CUP WHIPPING CREAM
4	OUNCES BITTER CHOCOLATE, SHREDDED OR CHOPPED
1/3	CUP BRANDY (USE ONE YOU LIKE)
PINCH	FRESHLY GRATED NUTMEG
	FRESHLY GRATED PARMESAN CHEESE

METHOD: HEAT THE WHIPPING CREAM, ADD SHREDDED CHOCOLATE. STIR OVER LOW HEAT UNTIL THE CHOCOLATE HAS DISSOLVED. ADD BRANDY AND CONTINUE TO SIMMER FOR 3 ADDITIONAL MINUTES, STIR IN THE NUTMEG, REMOVE SAUCE FROM HEAT, POUR SAUCE OVER PASTA, TOSS AND SERVE WITH GRATED CHEESE ON THE SIDE.

RECOMMENDED PASTA: STRING TYPES.

MAZZARESE STYLE SAUCE

(ANOTHER QUICKIE)

MAZZARESE IS NOT A COMMUNITY, BUT A PLACE, SORT OF CLUB HOUSE, OR POSSIBLY THE DINING ROOM AT A COUNTRY CLUB. I DON'T KNOW WHERE OR HOW THIS SAUCE WAS DEVELOPED; BUT IT DOES HAVE AN INTERESTING CHARACTER; IT IS ESSENTIALLY AN OLIVE PASTE, THINNED WITH WHIPPING CREAM. IF YOU ARE NOT A GARLIC LOVER, YOU'LL NEED TO EXERCISE CAUTION WITH THE AMOUNT USED; IT DOESN'T GET COOKED, ONLY WARMED.

INGREDIENTS:

2	DOZEN PITTED RIPE OLIVES
6	TABLESPOONS OLIVE OIL
1	TABLESPOON PINE NUTS
3/4	CUP WHIPPING CREAM
1	THIN SLICE TO 1 CLOVE GARLIC, MINCED
1	TEASPOON CHOPPED BASIL LEAF

METHOD: PLACE OLIVES, OLIVE OIL AND PINE NUTS INTO A FOOD PROCESSOR OR BLENDER AND PUREE. PLACE MIXTURE IN A SMALL SKILLET, ADD CREAM AND GARLIC. BLEND THOROUGHLY WHILE BRINGING SAUCE TO A BOIL. REMOVE FROM HEAT, POUR SAUCE OVER PASTA, TOSS, ADD CHOPPED BASIL, TOSS AGAIN, SERVE.

RECOMMENDED PASTA: HOLLOW STRINGS.

WE TRIED THIS SAUCE . . . AND

LOVED IT ( )
HATED IT ( )
MAYBE WE'LL TRY IT AGAIN ( )
WE'LL USE IT FOR UNWELCOME GUESTS ( )

ALMOND CREAM SAUCE

(ANOTHER QUICKIE)

CHAPTER 6, IS FULLY DEDICATED TO NUT SAUCES; THIS IS A CREAM SAUCE WITH NUTS, AND THAT'S WHY IT'S HERE AND NOT THERE. NUT SAUCES ARE NORTHERN AND CREAM SAUCES ARE ALSO NORTHERN. THIS ONE IS NO DIFFERENT, IT'S NORTHERN TOO.

INGREDIENTS:
2 TABLESPOONS BUTTER
2 1/2 CUP CHOPPED OR CRUSHED PLAIN UNSALTED ALMONDS
1/2 CUP WHIPPING CREAM
2 EGG YOLKS
1 TEASPOON GRATED FRESH LEMON PEEL

METHOD: MELT THE BUTTER, ADD THE NUTS, STIR AND SET ASIDE. PLACE IN A MIXING BOWL THE WHIPPING CREAM, EGG YOLKS AND LEMON PEEL. WHISK 'TILL SMOOTH. MIX THE BUTTER/NUTS AND CREAM/EGGS, BLEND WELL, POUR SAUCE OVER PASTA, TOSS AND SERVE.

RECOMMENDED PASTA: RIBBON TYPES.

CHAPTER 4

SAUCES MADE FROM CREAM AND MEAT OR SEAFOOD

CARBONARA SAUCE #1

HOT DOG, PASTA WITH BACON AND EGGS. HOT DOG IS AN EXPRESSION, DON'T USE ONE. ONCE AGAIN, A SAUCE THAT YOU'LL FINISH IN THE PAN. IF YOU HAVE A PYREX CASSEROLE DISH, USE IT.

IF THERE ARE REASONS FOR YOU TO AVOID CREAM AND BUTTER, BUT YOU STILL WANT TO TRY BACON AND EGGS ON YOUR PASTA, SEE THE CARBONARA SAUCE IN CHAPTER 2.

CARBONARA IS ONE OF THOSE TRADESMEN'S NAMES THAT GETS ATTACHED TO A PASTA SAUCE. IN THIS CASE, ANY SAUCE WITH BACON AND EGGS QUALIFIES. CARBONARA REFERS TO VENDORS OF CHARCOAL, HOW AND WHY THIS SAUCE GETS THIS APPLICATION IS OPEN TO INTERESTING SPECULATION.

INGREDIENTS: 4 TO 6   SLICES OF LEAN BACON CUT INTO 1/2 INCH WIDE PIECES (IF YOU CAN FIND IT USE ITALIAN BACON, IT'S CALLED PANCETTA)
3   CLOVES GARLIC
1/3   CUP WHIPPING CREAM
1   LARGE EGG PLUS 1 EGG YOLK
2/3   CUP FRESHLY GRATED PARMESAN CHEESE
GOOD SIZED PINCH OF WHITE PEPPER

METHOD: PLACE GARLIC AND BACON INTO A PAN, COOK BACON UNTIL IT'S THE WAY YOU LIKE IT. NOW, DRAIN OFF ALL BUT 2 TABLESPOONS OF OIL AND DISCARD THE GARLIC.

ADD CREAM TO THE BACON, STIR AND SET ASIDE.

WHISK THE EGG AND EGG YOLK ALONG WITH 1/2 THE CHEESE.

COMBINE ALL INGREDIENTS, PASTA, BACON/CREAM AND EGG/CHEESE MIX-
TURE, TOSS WHILE UNDER HEAT TO COOK THE EGG, SERVE WITH
REMAINING CHEESE.

RECOMMENDED PASTA: STRING TYPES.

CARBONARA SAUCE #2

IF YOU LIKE THE FIRST RECIPE FOR PASTA CARBONARA, THEN YOU'LL LIKE THIS ONE TOO! IT'S ANOTHER SAUCE OF BACON AND EGGS, THIS TIME WE'LL OMIT THE GARLIC, USE BUTTER AND INCREASE THE EGG AND CREAM AMOUNTS.

INGREDIENTS:

1	TABLESPOON OLIVE OIL
2	TABLESPOONS BUTTER
6	SLICES OF BACON, CUT INTO 1/2" PIECES (IF YOU USE AMERICAN BACON INSTEAD OF ITALIAN PANCETTA, DRAIN THE BACON OIL OFF AND DISCARD.)
4	EGG YOLKS
1/2	CUP WHIPPING CREAM
1/3	CUP FRESHLY GRATED PARMESAN CHEESE
1/4	TEASPOON SALT
	LOTS OF FRESHLY GROUND BLACK PEPPER, TO TASTE

METHOD: IF USING AMERICAN BACON, COOK UNTIL CRISP, DRAIN, DISCARD OIL AND SET ASIDE.

IF USING PANCETTA, SAUTE IN OIL/BUTTER UNTIL GOLDEN, SET ASIDE WITH THE OIL/BUTTER.

BEAT THE EGG YOLKS, BLEND IN THE CREAM, CHEESE, SALT AND PEPPER. TOSS YOUR COOKED HOT PASTA WITH THE EGG MIXTURE, ADD THE BACON AND THE OIL/BUTTER, TOSS AGAIN AND SERVE.

RECOMMENDED PASTA: STRING TYPES.

CARBONARA SAUCE #3

WITH THIS SAUCE WILL ADD A LITTLE ITALIAN SAUSAGE AND HAM INSTEAD OF BACON. SO INSTEAD OF BACON AND EGGS, YOU'LL HAVE TO LIVE WITH HAM AND EGGS.

INGREDIENTS:

1	LINK OF ITALIAN SAUSAGE OR 4 OUNCES OF ROPE STYLE
4	OUNCES HAM, CANADIAN BACON OR PROSCIUTTO, MINCED
4	TABLESPOONS BUTTER
3	WHOLE EGGS, BEATEN
1/2	CUP FRESH PARSLEY, CHOPPED
1/3	CUP FRESHLY GRATED PARMESAN CHEESE
	FRESHLY GROUND BLACK PEPPER

METHOD: STRIP THE CASING FROM THE SAUSAGE, CRUMBLE SAUSAGE AND FRY FOR ABOUT 5 MINUTES. DRAIN SAUSAGE OIL FROM PAN, REPLACE WITH BUTTER, ADD HAM AND COOK FOR 2 ADDITIONAL MINUTES.

WHIP TOGETHER OR IN A BLENDER WHIRL THE EGGS, PARSLEY, CHEESE AND BLACK PEPPER (YOU MAY DO THIS WHILE THE SAUSAGE IS COOKING).

POUR EGG MIXTURE OVER HOT PASTA AND TOSS, ADD THE SAUSAGE AND HAM, TOSS AGAIN, SERVE.

RECOMMENDED PASTA: STRING TYPES.

UMBRIAN STYLE CREAM SAUCE

UMBRIA IS IN THE VERY CENTER OF THE ITALIAN PENINSULA. SOMEWHAT BECAUSE OF THAT THE UMBRIANS WILL BALANCE THE INFLUENCES OF THE NORTH AND SOUTH, IT SHOWS UP IN THIS SAUCE WHERE WE'LL BE USING SOUTHERN ITALIAN SAUSAGE AND THE NORTHERN PREFERENCE FOR CREAM TO CREATE THIS SAUSAGE AND CREAM SAUCE.

INGREDIENTS:
1/2	POUND ITALIAN SAUSAGE
1	CUP WHIPPING CREAM
1/4	CUP FRESH GRATED PARMESAN CHEESE
PINCH	GRATED NUTMEG

METHOD: STRIP THE CASING FROM THE SAUSAGE, CRUMBLE AND SAUTE SAUSAGE UNTIL LIGHTLY BROWNED, ADD THE CREAM, BRING TO A GENTLE BOIL AND COOK FOR 5 MINUTES. POUR SAUCE OVER PASTA, ADD CHEESE AND NUTMEG, TOSS AND SERVE.

YOU MAY DRAIN THE SAUSAGE OIL BEFORE ADDING THE CREAM, REPLACE IT WITH 2 TABLESPOONS OF BUTTER.

RECOMMENDED PASTA: 8 OUNCES OF ANY MEDIUM TUBE TYPE (TO USE 1 POUND OF PASTA, DOUBLE THE INGREDIENTS).

CREAM FLORENTINE SAUCE

I DON'T REALLY KNOW WHERE THIS SAUCE ORIGINATED, BUT ALL INDICATORS POINT TO IT BEING NORTHERN. THE TERM "FLORENTINE", DOES NOT BY ITSELF INDICATE THAT THE SAUCE ORIGINATED IN FLORENCE, OR FOR THAT MATTER, TUSCANY. FLORENTINE IS USED AS AN ADJECTIVE AND GIVEN TO SAUCES AND PASTA DISHES CONTAINING SPINACH. AN EXCELLENT ALTERNATE GREEN FOR THIS SAUCE WOULD BE SWISS CHARD. IF YOU CHOOSE TO USE SWISS CHARD, I GUESS YOU COULD CALL THE SAUCE, CREAM HELVETIAN.

INGREDIENTS:

4	CUPS FRESH SPINACH, WASHED AND CHOPPED OR, 2-10 OUNCE PACKAGES FROZEN SPINACH
4	TABLESPOONS BUTTER
2	ONIONS, CHOPPED
2	CLOVES GARLIC, MINCED
2	TEASPOONS FLOUR
1/2	TEASPOON DRY BASIL
1/2	TEASPOON GROUND NUTMEG (FRESH, IF YOU HAVE IT)
8	OUNCES CREAM CHEESE OR BLENDERIZED RICOTTA
1 1/2	CUPS HALF AND HALF
4	SLICES BACON, COOKED CRISP, DRAINED AND CRUMBLED
1/4	CUP PINE NUTS
1/4	GRATED PARMESAN CHEESE

METHOD: STEAM FRESH SPINACH IN THE WATER CLINGING TO THE WASHED LEAVES, UNTIL COOKED, ABOUT 3 MINUTES, DRAIN, (IF USING FROZEN, JUST THAW AND DRAIN), SET ASIDE.

SAUTE ONION AND GARLIC IN BUTTER UNTIL ONION IS TRANSPARENT. ADD AND BLEND IN THE FLOUR, STIR IN THE CREAM CHEESE, ADD BASIL AND NUTMEG, STIR IN, WHISK IN HALF AND HALF, STIRRING UNTIL SAUCE COMES TO A NEAR BOIL AND THICKENS. ADD SPINACH TO HEAT THROUGH, REMOVE FROM HEAT, POUR SAUCE OVER PASTA, TOSS, SPRINKLE WITH BACON, PINE NUTS AND GRATED CHEESE. TOSS AGAIN IF DESIRED, SERVE.

RECOMMENDED PASTA: MEDIUM TUBE TYPES, OR FANCY SHAPES.

CREAM AND SEAFOOD SAUCE.

THERE ARE A NUMBER OF ITALIAN RECIPES THAT USE THE TERM "TUTTO MARE" TO DESCRIBE THEIR CONTENTS. TUTTO MARE, MEANS "ALL SEA", AND BY EXTENSION, MEANS THAT THE SAUCE CONTAINS AN ASSORTMENT OF SEAFOOD. SOME DO, SOME DON'T. THIS SAUCE FEATURES THREE SEAFOOD ITEMS, OYSTERS, SCALLOPS AND SHRIMP; THE FOLLOWING SAUCE OFFERS TWO, SHRIMP AND CRABMEAT.

INGREDIENTS:

1/4	CUP WATER
1	TABLESPOON CORNSTARCH
2	SMALL GREEN ONIONS WITH STEMS
2	MEDIUM CLOVES GARLIC
8	SMALL OYSTERS (FRESH IF POSSIBLE)
1/4	POUND SCALLOPS (FRESH IF POSSIBLE)
1	POUND SHRIMP (COOK AND DEVEIN IF FRESH)
1/4	CUP BUTTER
1 1/4	CUPS WHIPPING CREAM
2	TEASPOONS LEMON JUICE (FRESH IF POSSIBLE)
1/2	TEASPOON SALT
1/8	TEASPOON WHITE PEPPER
2	TABLESPOONS CHOPPED FRESH PARSLEY
	LEMON WEDGES

METHOD: MIX WATER AND CORN STARCH, SET ASIDE. SLICE THE ONIONS AND MINCE THE GARLIC, SET ASIDE. IF USING FRESH OYSTERS, SCRUB AND OPEN THEM OVER A BOWL TO SAVE THE OYSTER LIQUOR.

HEAT BUTTER, SAUTE OYSTERS FOR 1 TO 2 MINUTES, REMOVE FROM PAN. PLACE SCALLOPS AND SHRIMP INTO PAN, SAUTE FOR 2 TO 3 MINUTES, REMOVE FROM PAN.

BRIEFLY SAUTE GARLIC IN PAN DRIPPINGS, ADD THE WHIPPING CREAM, BRING TO A LOW BOIL. ADD CORNSTARCH AND BLEND. STIR IN LEMON JUICE, SALT AND WHITE PEPPER. ADD THE OYSTERS, SCALLOPS AND SHRIMP, COOK UNTIL SEAFOOD ITEMS ARE JUST HEATED THROUGH. TOSS SAUCE WITH YOUR PASTA, GREEN ONIONS AND PARSLEY. SERVE WITH LEMON WEDGES ON THE SIDE.

RECOMMENDED PASTA: STRING TYPES OR SHELLS.

WE TRIED THIS SAUCE . . . AND

CREAM AND SEAFOOD SAUCE TOO!

(ANOTHER QUICKIE)

SHRIMP AND CRAB MEAT ARE THE FEATURED SEAFOOD IN THIS SAUCE, IF FRESH CRAB IS OUT OF SEASON WHEN YOU WANT TO TRY THIS ONE, GO WITH IMITATION CRAB, IT'S QUITE GOOD FOR OCCASIONAL USE.

INGREDIENTS:

1	CUP WHIPPING CREAM
2	CUPS HALF AND HALF
1 1/2	CUPS SLICED MUSHROOMS
1/4	CUP BUTTER
1/3	CUP SHREDDED FONTINA OR MOZZARELLA CHEESE
1/2	CLOVE GARLIC, MINCED
1	TABLESPOON CHOPPED PARSLEY
	SALT AND FRESHLY GROUND BLACK PEPPER TO TASTE
6	OUNCES PRECOOKED AND TINY SHRIMP
8	OUNCES CRAB MEAT, DICED
1	CUP FRESHLY GRATED PARMESAN CHEESE

METHOD: PLACE ALL INGREDIENTS EXCEPT LAST THREE INTO A LARGE SAUCE PAN, BRING TO A BOIL WHILE STIRRING FREQUENTLY, ADD COOKED AND DRAINED PASTA ALONG WITH THE SHRIMP AND CRAB MEAT, COOK FOR 1 MINUTE, STIR IN GRATED CHEESE, SIMMER SAUCE FOR 2 ADDITION MINUTES UNTIL ALL THE CHEESE HAS MELTED, SERVE.

RECOMMENDED PASTA: SHELL OR CURLY TYPES.

PINK CREAM SAUCE

(ANOTHER QUICKIE)

CONFUSION REIGNS AGAIN; I REALLY DON'T LIKE PINK FOOD UNLESS IT IS SWEET LIKE ICE CREAM, CAKE OR CANDY. PINK SAUCE IS NOT EXCITING. BESIDES THAT, I REALLY DON'T KNOW WHERE THIS ONE SHOULD BE PLACED. IT HAS CREAM, IT HAS TOMATOES, IT HAS VEGETABLES AND IT HAS BACON. THAT QUALIFIES IT TO FIT IN ANY OF FOUR DIFFERENT CHAPTERS. TO COMPOUND THE PROBLEM, THERE ARE SEVERAL CREAM RECIPES IN CHAPTER 3 THAT WILL GIVE YOU A PINK SAUCE.

INGREDIENTS:

1	8 OUNCE CAN OF TOMATO SAUCE (YOU CAN MAKE YOUR OWN IF YOU'RE INCLINED TOO; SEE CHAPTER 8, TOMATO SAUCE #24)
6	SLICES BACON (USE PANCETTA IF YOU HAVE IT)
2	TABLESPOONS BUTTER
3/4	CUP WHIPPING CREAM
1/2	PACKAGE FROZEN PEAS
1/4	CUP GRATED PARMESAN CHEESE

METHOD: SAUTE THE BACON, YOU NEEDN'T BROWN IT, ADD BUTTER, TOMATO SAUCE, WHIPPING CREAM AND PEAS. BRING TO A BOIL, REDUCE HEAT TO LOW AND COOK FOR ABOUT 5 MINUTES.

POUR SAUCE OVER HOT PASTA, ADD THE CHEESE, TOSS AND SERVE.

OPTION: YOU MAY OMIT THE BACON FROM THIS SAUCE. REPLACE THE LOST OIL BY INCREASING THE BUTTER BY 2 TABLESPOONS.

RECOMMENDED PASTA: RIBBON TYPES.

LOBSTER CREAM SAUCE

HERE IS THE PERFECT SAUCE FOR THOSE SYNTHETIC LOBSTER TAILS (A.K.A. PHONY PHISH). BUT WHO CARES, THEY ARE VERY TASTY AND MUCH LESS COSTLY THAN THE GENUINE ARTICLE. THIS IS A DISH YOU COULD LOVE TO HAS NICE EYE APPEAL WITH THE LOBSTER CUT INTO MEDALLIONS AND LAID ACROSS THE PASTA. AN ADDED BONUS WHEN SERVED AS SUGGESTED ARE THE COLORS OF THE ITALIAN FLAG, THE RED COLORING OF THE LOBSTER, THE WHITE OF THE SAUCE AND PASTA AND THE GREEN TOUCH FROM THE PEAS.

INGREDIENTS:

2	TABLESPOONS ONION, CHOPPED
1	CLOVE GARLIC, MINCED
1/2	CUP BUTTER
3/4	CUP SHERRY
1/4	CUP AMARETTO
1/2	CUP FLOUR
DASH	CAYENNE PEPPER
2	CUPS HALF AND HALF
2	CUPS FROZEN PEAS
1	POUND ARTIFICIAL LOBSTER TAILS
1/4	CUP SLICED ALMONDS, TOASTED OR SAUTEED IN BUTTER

METHOD: BECAUSE THERE ARE SEVERAL NEAR SIMULTANEOUS STEPS INVOLVED IN THE PREPARATION OF THE SAUCE, I'M GOING TO NUMBER THEM TO HELP LESSEN ANY CONFUSION:

1. BUTTER THE LOBSTER TAILS AND SET ASIDE.

2. COOK OR MICROWAVE PEAS AND SET ASIDE.

3. PREHEAT THE BROILER WHILE YOU SAUTE ONION AND GARLIC IN THE BUTTER UNTIL ONION IS TRANSPARENT. REMOVE ONION AND GARLIC, SET ASIDE.

130

4. ADD AND WHISK FLOUR IN THE REMAINING BUTTER TO MAKE A ROUX, COOK FOR A FEW MINUTES, WHISK IN THE HALF AND HALF UNTIL YOU HAVE A SMOOTH SAUCE, RETURN THE ONION AND GARLIC, WHISK IN SHERRY, AMARETTO. AND CAYENNE,

5. ADD PEAS AND SIMMER WHILE YOU BROIL THE LOBSTER TAILS. POUR SAUCE OVER THE PASTA, TOSS AND SET ON INDIVIDUAL SERVING PLATES.

6. SLICE LOBSTER TAILS IN MEDALLIONS (CUT ACROSS LOBSTER FROM TOP TO BOTTOM) PLACE CUT LOBSTER ON TOP OF THE PASTA, SPRINKLE WITH ALMONDS, SERVE.

RECOMMENDED PASTA: STRINGS, ROUND OR OVAL TYPES

CREAM AND CAVIAR SAUCE

(ANOTHER QUICKIE)

IF CAVIAR IS ONE OF YOUR FAVORITE SNACK FOODS, THEN I'M SURE YOU'LL ENJOY THIS SAUCE. IF YOU HAVE DIFFICULTY IN LOCATING GOLDEN CAVIAR, YOU MAY SUBSTITUTE 1/2 CUP OF COOKED AND FLAKED SALMON (GENERALLY CANNED) OR SHREDDED LOX.

(FOR A SIMPLER CAVIAR SAUCE SEE THE FOLLOWING SAUCE.)

INGREDIENTS:

2	TABLESPOONS SWEET BUTTER
2	TABLESPOONS SHALLOTS, MINCED
2	CUPS WHIPPING CREAM
	SALT AND WHITE PEPPER TO TASTE
1	TEASPOON DRIED DILL WEED
1	CUP SOUR CREAM
2	TABLESPOONS GOLDEN CAVIAR

METHOD: SAUTE SHALLOTS IN THE BUTTER FOR A MINUTE, ADD THE WHIPPING CREAM, BRING TO A BOIL AND COOK UNTIL CREAM BEGINS TO THICKEN AND SLIGHTLY COLOR. ADD SOUR CREAM, DILL AND CAVIAR, STIR TO BLEND. REMOVE FROM HEAT, POUR SAUCE OVER PASTA, TOSS AND SERVE.

RECOMMENDED PASTA: OVAL STRINGS, RIBBONS OR ANGEL HAIR. IF YOU USE ANGEL HAIR, USE ONLY 2 TO 3 OUNCES.

WE TRIED THIS SAUCE . . . AND

SIMPLE CAVIAR SAUCE

(ANOTHER QUICKIE)

THE QUICKIE PHRASE MAY BE WISHFUL THINKING, I MEAN IT TO MEAN, THAT THE SAUCE CAN BE COOKED IN LESS TIME THAN IT TAKES THE PASTA TO COOK. AND WHERE I USE THE PHRASE, IT'S GENERALLY TRUE. WITH THIS SAUCE YOU'LL BE USING ANGEL HAIR OR SOMETHING SIMILAR, AND THAT STUFF COOKS IN SECONDS (ACTUALLY 2 TO 4 MINUTES.)

YOU MAY USE GOLDEN CAVIAR OR ANY OF THE BLACK VARIETIES FOR THIS SAUCE; LET YOUR WILLINGNESS TO SPEND MONEY BE YOUR GUIDE.

INGREDIENTS:
1/4 CUP BUTTER
1 TEASPOON LEMON JUICE
1/4 CUP WHIPPING CREAM
2 TABLESPOONS MINCED PARSLEY
1 OUNCE CAVIAR

METHOD: SLOWLY MELT THE BUTTER, ADD LEMON JUICE AND PARSLEY. REMOVE FROM HEAT, ADD THE CREAM AND BLEND WELL, POUR SAUCE OVER PASTA, TOSS AND SERVE.

RECOMMENDED PASTA: VERY THIN STRINGS. (USE 4 TO 6 OUNCES OF PASTA).

HAM AND CREAM SAUCE

WHEN I WAS A YOUNGSTER I RECALL READING A COMIC DEFINITION OF "AN ETERNITY" THE SCENARIO IS ONE WHERE TWO PEOPLE ARE TRYING TO EAT THEIR WAY THROUGH THE REMAINS OF A WHOLE HOLIDAY HAM. AS A YOUNGSTER WHOSE MOTHER BAKED WHOLE HAMS FOR CHRISTMAS I CAN CERTAINLY ATTEST TO THE TRUTH OF THAT DEFINITION. THIS IS AN AMERICAN RECIPE; AND IT DOES SEEM TO BE A WAY OF FINALLY GETTING RID OF THE CHRISTMAS HAM. IF YOU'RE THE TYPE WHO'LL EAT HAM WITH ANYTHING, THIS IS YOUR SAUCE.

INGREDIENTS:

1	10 OUNCE PACKAGE FROZEN PEAS
1	TABLESPOON BUTTER
2	TABLESPOONS ONION, CHOPPED
1 1/2	CUPS WHIPPING CREAM
1 1/2	POUNDS COOKED HAM, DICED
	PARMESAN CHEESE

METHOD: SAUTE ONION IN BUTTER UNTIL TRANSPARENT, SET ASIDE. COOK PEAS IN SMALL AMOUNT OF WATER, DON'T DRAIN. ADD SAUTEED ONION, CREAM AND HAM, BRING TO A BOIL. REDUCE HEAT TO LOW AND COOK FOR 5 MINUTES OR UNTIL SAUCE THICKENS. REMOVE FROM HEAT, POUR SAUCE OVER PASTA, TOSS AND SERVE. OFFER CHEESE ON THE SIDE.

RECOMMENDED PASTA: SHELL TYPES OR FANCIES.

Lazio Style Creamy Ham Sauce

WHILE THE ITALIANS MIGHT BE INCLINED TO PUT TRUFFLES (THE REAL ONES, NOT THE CANDY) INTO THIS SAUCE, MOST ITALIANS, AND THE MAJORITY OF AMERICANS COULD NOT AFFORD IT. THEREFORE, WE'LL USE MUSHROOMS. THIS WILL BE COMPLETED "COUNTRY STYLE", THAT IS IN THE SAUCE PAN. IF YOU WISH, USE A PYREX OR CORNING CASSEROLE DISH.

INGREDIENTS:

3	TABLESPOONS BUTTER
18	BUTTON MUSHROOMS
1/2	CUP PROSCUITTO, MINCED
1	CUP WHIPPING CREAM
2	EGG YOLKS, LIGHTLY BEATEN
1/2	CUP SHREDDED SHARP PROVOLONE OR GRATED DRY SHARP PROVOLONE
PINCH	FRESHLY GRATED NUTMEG

METHOD: HAVE YOUR PASTA NEAR DONE BEFORE STARTING THE SAUCE. BLEND WHIPPING CREAM AND EGG YOLKS, SET ASIDE. SAUTE THE MUSHROOMS IN BUTTER UNTIL DONE, ABOUT 4 MINUTES. LEAVE YOUR SAUCE PAN ON THE HEAT, ADD HOT DRAINED PASTA, AND THE CREAM AND EGG MIXTURE, BLEND WELL. ADD SHREDDED OR GRATED CHEESE, BLEND UNTIL MELTED, SPRINKLE WITH NUTMEG, TOSS AGAIN, SERVE.

RECOMMENDED PASTA: SHORT TUBE TYPES OR HOLLOW TWISTS.

135

EMILIAN STYLE CREAM SAUCE

(ANOTHER QUICKIE)

THIS SAUCE COMES FROM NORTH CENTRAL ITALY, THE EMILIA-ROMAGNA REGION. AND IT IS A TOUGH ONE TO CATEGORIZE; IT COULD ACTUALLY FIT INTO SEVERAL CHAPTERS BECAUSE IT HAS NEAR EQUAL AMOUNTS OF TOMATOES, VEGETABLES, CHEESE, BUTTER AND CREAM.

INGREDIENTS:

3/4	CUP BUTTER
3/4	CUP PEAR TOMATOES (B/P/C)
1/4	CUP PEAS, COOKED
1/4	CUP SWEET PEPPER STRIPS, ROASTED AND PEELED
1/4	POUND PROSCIUTTO, MINCED
1/2	CUP WHIPPING CREAM
1/2	CUP FRESHLY GRATED PARMESAN CHEESE

METHOD: MELT THE BUTTER OVER MEDIUM HEAT, ADD TOMATOES, COOK FOR 8 MINUTES. ADD PEAS, SWEET PEPPERS AND PROSCIUTTO, COOK 2 ADDITIONAL MINUTES. REMOVE FROM HEAT AND MOMENTARILY SET ASIDE. POUR CREAM OVER THE DRAINED PASTA, TOSS, ADD CHEESE, TOSS AGAIN. ADD TOMATO MIXTURE, TOSS AGAIN, SERVE.

RECOMMENDED PASTA: RIBBON TYPES.

SAUSAGE AND CREAM SAUCE

WE'RE GOING TO GIVE YOU A LOT OF LATITUDE WITH THIS SAUCE. YOU MAY USE ANY MILD SAUSAGE WHOSE TASTE YOU ENJOY, ITALIAN, POLISH, HUNGARIAN, SWEDISH, BRITISH BANGERS, GERMAN BRATWURST OR AMERICAN PORK SAUSAGE. DON'T USE HIGHLY COLORED OR SEASONED SAUSAGE SUCH AS PORTUGESE LINGUICA OR MEXICAN CHORIZO.

INGREDIENTS:

1/2	POUND SAUSAGE, SKINNED AND CRUMBLED OR MINCED
1	SHALLOT, MINCED
2	TABLESPOONS BUTTER
3/4	CUP WHIPPING CREAM
1/4	TEASPOON FRESHLY GROUND BLACK PEPPER
	SALT TO TASTE

METHOD: SAUTE SHALLOTS FOR 1 MINUTE, ADD SAUSAGE. COOK AT LEAST 10 MINUTES. ADD CREAM, BLACK PEPPER AND ANY SALT, COOK FOR 2 MINUTES. POUR SAUCE OVER PASTA, MIX AND SERVE.

RECOMMENDED PASTA: SMALL SHELLS, CURLY TYPES OR FANCIES.

BOLOGNA STYLE CREAMED MEAT SAUCE

THIS SAUCE LOOKS SUSPICIOUSLY LIKE A THINNED FILLING FOR A SMALL FILLED PILLOW PASTA. WHO KNOWS, THAT MAY BE HOW IT CAME ABOUT. SOME LEFTOVER FILLING, THIN IT. TOSS IT WITH A LITTLE PASTA AND VOILA! A NEW SAUCE. THIS SAUCE USES FIVE KINDS OF MEAT, COOKED AND THEN GROUND AND FINALLY MIXED WITH A VARIETY OF SWEET SPICES AND CREAM. AMONG OTHER THINGS THE BOLOGNESE LIKE TO COOK THEIR PASTA IN CHICKEN BROTH; IF YOU WISH TO TRY IT, DO SO. IF YOU DON'T HAPPEN TO HAVE A GALLON OF CHICKEN STOCK ON HAND, USE ABOUT 8 BOUILLON CUBES TO ONE GALLON OF WATER.

TRY USING THIS MIXTURE AS A FILLING FOR RAVIOLI AND OTHER FILLED PASTAS BY OMITTING THE CREAMS AND ADDING 2 EGG YOLKS.

INGREDIENTS:

6	OUNCES TURKEY BREAST (USE FRESH OR PRECOOKED)
2	OUNCES PROSCUITTO
1	VEAL SWEETBREAD, BLANCHED AND CLEANED
4	OUNCES PORK
4	OUNCES BEEF
1/4	POUND BUTTER
2	TABLESPOONS FRESHLY GRATED PARMESAN CHEESE
1/2	TEASPOON SALT
PINCH	GROUND NUTMEG
PINCH	GROUND CINNAMON
1	CUP WHIPPING CREAM
1	CUP HALF AND HALF
	(USE ONLY IF ADDITIONAL THINNING IS NEEDED)

METHOD: DICE ALL THE MEATS INTO 1/4 INCH CUBES, SAUTE THE MEAT IN THE BUTTER UNTIL COOKED. REMOVE FROM HEAT AND PROCESS IN FOOD PROCESSOR OR GRIND UNTIL FAIRLY SMOOTH. RETURN THE MEAT TO THE COOKING PAN, ADD THE CHEESE, SALT, NUTMEG, CINNAMON AND WHIPPING CREAM, BLEND UNTIL WELL MIXED. BRING SAUCE TO A LOW BOIL, ADD THE COOKED AND DRAINED PASTA, TOSS WELL, SERVE.

RECOMMENDED PASTA: NARROW RIBBON TYPES.

CREAMY SHRIMP SAUCE

(ANOTHER QUICKIE)

FOR THIS SAUCE YOU MAY USE THE TINY PRECOOKED SALAD SHRIMP SO PREVALENT IN AMERICAN SUPERMARKETS. IF TEDIOUS LABOR IS THERAPY FOR YOU, START WITH 1 POUND OF FRESH UNSHELLED TINY SHRIMP.

INGREDIENTS:

1/2	CUP WHIPPING CREAM
1/4	POUND BUTTER
8	OUNCES PRECOOKED PEELED SHRIMP
	FRESHLY GROUND BLACK PEPPER TO TASTE

METHOD: BRING WHIPPING CREAM AND BUTTER TO A BOIL, ADD SHRIMP TO HEAT THROUGH, POUR SAUCE OVER PASTA. TOSS, ADD BLACK PEPPER, TOSS AGAIN, SERVE.

RECOMMENDED PASTA: RIBBON TYPES.

140

CREAMED ANCHOVY SAUCE

(ANOTHER QUICKIE)

SPEED, TANG AND LASTING FLAVOR ARE THE CHARACTERISTICS OF THIS SAUCE. SO IF YOU LOVE ANCHOVY, OR SAUCES WITH A SALT TANG, THIS ONE IS FOR YOU.

ONE OF THE VERY INTERESTING CHARACTERISTICS OF CREAM SAUCES IS THE DOGMA ASSOCIATED WITH THEM. THERE ARE TWO DISCIPLINES INVOLVED IN THE PREPARATION OF A CREAM SAUCE. THE FIRST REQUIRES THAT NO CREAM BE MADE PART OF A SAUCE WITHOUT ITS BEING REDUCED TO NEAR ESSENCE. THE SECOND MAINTAINS THAT MERELY WARMING THE CREAM IS ADEQUATE. I DON'T LEAN TOWARD EITHER BUT RATHER USE THEM BOTH. IF THE CREAM IS WHAT WILL KEEP THE SAUCE LIQUID WITHOUT FURTHER LIQUID ADDITIONS, THEN DON'T REDUCE IT. IF HOWEVER, THE SAUCE IS TO HAVE A CREAM TASTE, BUT NOT FULLY LIQUID, THEN REDUCE. REDUCING REQUIRES THAT THE CREAM BE BOILED AWAY TO ABOUT HALF THE AMOUNT ADDED. IN THIS SAUCE, YOU'LL ONLY GET IT VERY WARM.

INGREDIENTS:

1	1 OUNCE CAN OF ANCHOVIES, DRAINED ON PAPER TOWELS
4	TABLESPOONS BUTTER
1	CUP WHIPPING CREAM
	CHOPPED PARSLEY FOR GARNISH

METHOD: MASH AND STIR TO DISSOLVE THE ANCHOVIES IN THE BUTTER OVER LOW HEAT. ADD THE CREAM, BRING TO A LOW BOIL, SIMMER FOR 5 MINUTES. POUR SAUCE OVER PASTA, TOSS, GARNISH WITH PARSLEY, SERVE.

RECOMMENDED PASTA: VERY THIN STRINGS.

SAN REMO SAUCE

SAN REMO IS JUST BARELY INSIDE ITALY, IN LIGURIA, VERY NEAR THE FRENCH BORDER, AND ON THE ITALIAN RIVIERA. IT OFFERS THIS SAUCE WITH A MIXTURE OF ASSORTED NUTS, OLIVES, CHEESE, HAM, PESTO, BUTTER AND CREAM. I HAVE THE FEELING THAT SOMEONE CLEANED OUT A REFRIGERATOR, OR DIDN'T KNOW WHEN TO STOP. WHATEVER THE RATIONALE FOR CREATING THIS SAUCE, IT WORKS.

IF YOU LIKE THIS SAUCE, SEE CHAPTER 6 FOR MORE RECIPES USING NUTMEATS.

INGREDIENTS:

1/4	CUP BUTTER
1/2	CUP TOMATO SAUCE, OR
1	TABLESPOON TOMATO PASTE AND 7 TABLESPOONS WATER
1/2	CUP WHIPPING CREAM
1/3	CUP PESTO SAUCE
8	OLIVES (YOUR CHOICE), CHOPPED OR SLICED
2	TABLESPOONS PINE NUTS, CHOPPED
8	WALNUT HALVES, GRATED
4	OUNCES HAM (PROSCUITTO IF POSSIBLE), CHOPPED
1/2	CUP FRESHLY GRATED PARMESAN CHEESE

METHOD: PLACE BUTTER AND TOMATO SAUCE IN A SAUCE PAN, COVER AND SIMMER FOR 10 MINUTES, REMOVE FROM HEAT. ADD CREAM AND PESTO SAUCE, BLEND WELL, ADD OLIVES, NUTS AND HAM. SPRINKLE DRAINED PASTA WITH GRATED CHEESE AND TOSS. POUR SAUCE OVER PASTA, TOSS AGAIN, SERVE.

RECOMMENDED PASTA: OVAL STRINGS.

Chapter 5

Uncooked Herb Sauces

Basil

Basil must be one of God's kitchen herbs. As a fresh herb it has no equal and no counterpart. Freshly picked sprigs of basil in a kitchen add an essence that is pure delight. Pesto is the northern Italian way of trying to capture that most elusive bouquet and put it on a plate. It doesn't always work. What does work is that pesto cannot be made from anything other than fresh basil! Anything else is a different product, period.

There are dozens of uses for pesto as a seasoning preparation for your kitchen, but in this chapter it's a pasta sauce. And, like many Italian sauces, it is simple. Let's keep it that way. Recall our favorite acronym K.I.S., keep it simple.

BASIL SAUCE

(PESTO)

(ANOTHER QUICKIE)

(ALSO SEE VARIATIONS ON NEXT PAGE)

BASIL, THAT WARM AND WONDERFUL KING OF THE MINT FAMILY, AND KEY INGREDIENT IN PESTO.   WHILE WE'LL ALLOW THAT THERE ARE SOME ALTERNATES, NONE CAN MATCH THE BOUQUET OF BASIL; IT CAN FAIRLY LIFT YOU OFF THE GROUND.   PESTO MEANS TO "BEAT", THAT IS TO MASH TO A PASTE, AND THAT'S THE WAY WE'LL DO IT, ONLY WE'LL DO IT WITH A BLENDER OR FOOD PROCESSOR.   THAT'S MUCH EASIER THAN USING A MORTAR AND PESTLE AND A WHOLE LOT FASTER.

MY PERSONAL EXPERIENCE WITH PASTA PREPARED WITH PESTO IS THAT IT IS NOT SALVAGEABLE.   MAKE ONLY WHAT WILL BE EATEN, IT IS NO GOOD COLD AND CANNOT BE REHEATED.

INGREDIENTS:	2	CUPS LIGHTLY PACKED BASIL LEAVES
	1/2	CUP OLIVE OIL
	1	OR MORE SLICES FROM A CLOVE OF GARLIC. NOT WHOLE CLOVES UNLESS YOU'RE A CERTIFIED GARLICHOLIC (IS THAT A WORD?).
		SALT TO TASTE

THE ABOVE ARE THE COMPONENTS OF A CLASSIC PESTO. IT IS LIGHT AND WONDERFUL JUST AS ABOVE; HOWEVER, MANY COOKS LIKE TO INCLUDE ONE OR BOTH OF THE FOLLOWING OPTIONS.

OPTIONS:	3/4	CUP FRESHLY GRATED PARMESAN CHEESE
	1 TO 2	TABLESPOONS PINENUTS

NOTE: IF YOU PREFER NOT TO ADD RAW GARLIC TO THE PESTO, PRESS IT FOR ITS OIL OR RUB THE BLENDING BOWL WITH A HALVED GARLIC CLOVE.

METHOD: PLACE BASIL, OLIVE OIL, GARLIC AND SALT IN A BLENDER OR FOOD PROCESSOR AND PROCESS UNTIL SMOOTH.

IF YOU ARE GOING TO ADD PINE NUTS, ADD THEM BEFORE PROCESSING. STIR IN THE OPTIONAL CHEESE AFTER PROCESSING.

RECOMMENDED PASTA: STRING TYPES, OVAL, THIN, OR RIBBON TYPES.

BOGUS PESTO'S

(ANOTHER QUICKIE - 9 OF 'EM)

FOR WANT OF A BETTER WORD, WE'RE STUCK WITH THIS AS A DESCRIPTION OF AN ALTERNATE PESTO. WHILE THE FOLLOWING INGREDIENTS ARE A FAR CRY FROM THE EXCITING TASTE OF BASIL, THEY'RE NOT BAD. MAY I SUGGEST THAT YOU NOT ADD DRY BASIL TO THE FOLLOWING. DRY BASIL JUST DOESN'T GET IT.

DARN NEAR ANY GREEN CAN BE USED FOR A BOGUS PESTO. I KNOW THAT SOUNDS PREPOSTEROUS, BUT I'VE USED THE FOLLOWING, THEY ARE:

ASPARAGUS (NEEDS TO BE RAW AND CHOPPED FINE BEFORE
　　PROCESSING OR BLENDING)
BROCCOLI
ENDIVE (HAS A NICE TART TANG)
ESCAROLE (HAS A SLIGHT BITTER BITE, DISCARD OUTER LEAVES)
PARSLEY (ANY VARIETY)
ROMAINE LETTUCE
SPINACH (WE ALL NEED MUSCLES)
WATERCRESS
ZUCCHINI SQUASH

ALL THE ABOVE NEED TO BE FRESH.

INGREDIENTS:	2	CUPS OF ANY OF THE ABOVE
	1/2	CUP OLIVE OIL
	1	THIN GARLIC SLICE OR CLOVE(S)
		SALT TO TASTE

OPTIONS:	3/4	CUP FRESHLY GRATED PARMESAN CHEESE
	1	TABLESPOON PINE NUTS, WALNUTS OR ALMONDS

METHOD: PLACE SELECTED GREENS, GARLIC AND OIL INTO A BLENDER OR PRO-CESSOR, ADD ANY OPTIONAL NUT CHOICE. PROCESS UNTIL FAIRLY SMOOTH. TRANSFER TO A SMALL BOWL, ADD THE CHEESE AND MIX. SPOON ON TO YOUR PASTA, TOSS AND SERVE.

RECOMMENDED PASTA: STRING TYPES.

SICILIAN PARSLEY SAUCE

(ANOTHER QUICKIE)

THIS SAUCE HAS A RAW GARLIC BITE THAT MAY OVERPOWER THE CASUAL GARLIC USER. IT ALSO APPEARS TO BE DESIGNED TO HOLD YOUR FRIENDS AND NEIGHBORS AT BAY. IT'S MY UNDERSTANDING THAT IN SICILY THE GARLIC AND PARSLEY ARE FREQUENTLY USED ALONE AS THE PASTA DRESSING. WOW! THAT'S TOO MUCH FOR ME, THEREFORE I'M SUGGESTING THE ADDITION OF OLIVE OIL PLUS A LITTLE SALT AND PEPPER.

INGREDIENTS: 2   OR MORE CLOVES GARLIC, MINCED
             1   CUP PARSLEY, MINCED
             3   TABLESPOONS OLIVE OIL
                 SALT AND FRESHLY GROUND BLACK PEPPER TO TASTE

METHOD: PLACE GARLIC AND PARSLEY IN A PROCESSOR AND PROCESS UNTIL FINELY CHOPPED OR MINCE BY HAND. BLEND WITH OLIVE OIL, SALT AND PEPPER TO TASTE. POUR SAUCE OVER LIGHTLY DRAINED PASTA, TOSS AND SERVE.

RECOMMENDED PASTA: SOLID OR HOLLOW STRINGS, MEDIUM TUBE TYPES.

CREAMY PARSLEY SAUCE

(ANOTHER QUICKIE)

THIS SAUCE WORKS WELL WITH ANY VARIETY OF PARSLEY, ALTHOUGH ITALIAN PARSLEY ADDS A LITTLE EXTRA UNIQUENESS.

INGREDIENTS:

1	CUP PARSLEY
1/4	CUP WATER
1	TABLESPOON DRIED MINCED ONION
2	TABLESPOONS WHIPPING CREAM
1	TABLESPOON LEMON JUICE
1/4	TEASPOON BLACK PEPPER
	SALT TO TASTE

(IF YOU WISH, A DIJON MUSTARD MAY BE SUBSTITUTED FOR THE CREAM. SOME DIJON MUSTARDS HAVE A VERY STRONG VINEGAR TASTE AND MAY NOT BE SATISFACTORY.)

METHOD: COMBINE ALL INGREDIENTS IN A BLENDER OR FOOD PROCESSOR AND PROCESS UNTIL FAIRLY SMOOTH.

RECOMMENDED PASTA: SPIRAL TYPES.

GREEN SAUCE II

(ANOTHER QUICKIE)

THIS SAUCE IS PRETTY VERSATILE, IT WILL LEND ITSELF TO OTHER USES IN YOUR KITCHEN. IT IS SLIGHTLY ACIDIC AND IT'S A GOOD SUMMER SAUCE.

INGREDIENTS:

1	TABLESPOON FRESH PARSLEY
1	TABLESPOON WATER CRESS OR CILANTRO OR ENDIVE
1	TABLESPOON CAPERS
3	TABLESPOONS LEMON JUICE
1/2	CLOVE GARLIC
1/4	TEASPOON SALT
6	TABLESPOONS OLIVE OIL

METHOD: DROP ALL INGREDIENTS INTO A BLENDER OR PROCESSOR, WHIP UNTIL FAIRLY SMOOTH. POUR OVER PASTA, TOSS AND SERVE.

RECOMMENDED PASTA: STRING TYPES.

GREEN SAUCE TOO!

THIS ONE IS VERY SIMILAR TO THE PRECEDING SAUCE, YOU'LL ADD A COUPLE OF INGREDIENTS AND PROCESS IN YOUR PROCESSOR UNTIL YOU HAVE A LIGHT PASTE; THAT WILL BE YOUR SAUCE.

INGREDIENTS:

1	BUNCH PARSLEY, WASHED AND STEMMED (SHAKE DRY)
1/3	CUP BREAD CRUMBS
1/2	CUP WATER OR DRY WHITE WINE
2	ANCHOVY FILLETS
1	SMALL GERKIN (OR 1 TEASPOON SWEET PICKLE RELISH)
2	CLOVES GARLIC, CHOPPED
1	TEASPOON CAPERS
1	CHIVE ONION, MINCED
1/2	TEASPOON SALT
PINCH	FRESHLY GROUND BLACK PEPPER
1/2	CUP OLIVE OIL

METHOD: PLACE ALL INGREDIENTS INTO A FOOD PROCESSOR AND PROCESS UNTIL FINELY MINCED, ADD OIL AND CONTINUE TO PROCESS UNTIL YOU HAVE A SMOOTH, BUT LIGHT PASTE. ADD ADDITIONAL OIL IF NEEDED, ALLOW THE PASTE TO MARINATE FOR ONE OR MORE HOURS. ADD PASTE TO HOT, DRAINED PASTA, TOSS AND SERVE.

RECOMMENDED PASTA: FANCY TYPES, NARROW RIBBONS, OR MEDIUM TUBE TYPES.

WE TRIED THIS SAUCE . . . AND

SAGE SAUCE TOO!

(ANOTHER QUICKIE)

THIS SAUCE ALSO IS FROM LOMBARDY, BUT THIS TIME IT IS SHORN OF ALL THE OTHER INGREDIENTS AND GETS DOWN TO BASICS. BUTTER AND FRESH SAGE, (K.I.S.). WHILE SAGE, A PREFERRED HERB IN NORTHERN COOKERY IS THE HERB USED HERE, I BELIEVE THAT ONE OF THE SOUTH'S FAVORITE HERBS, FRESH OREGANO WOULD WORK EQUALLY AS WELL.

INGREDIENTS: 2/3   CUP CHOPPED FRESH SAGE LEAVES
                1/2   CUP BUTTER, SWEET OR REGULAR

METHOD: MELT THE BUTTER, POUR IT OVER YOUR HOT, DRAINED PASTA AND TOSS. ADD THE SAGE, TOSS AGAIN, SERVE.

RECOMMENDED PASTA: STRINGS, SPIRALS OR FILLED PILLOW TYPES.

CHAPTER 6

SAUCES MADE FROM NUT MEATS
OR
COOKING WITH NUTS!

(IS THAT A DEROGATORY EXPRESSION?)

THERE MAY BE SOME TRUTH IN THAT, BUT FOR SAFETY'S SAKE WE'LL CALL IT COOKING WITH NUT MEATS. ITALY AND WESTERN EUROPE USE EXTENSIVE AMOUNTS OF NUT MEATS IN THEIR COOKING. MARZIPAN (ALMOND PASTE) IS AN ABSOLUTE MUST IN MUCH OF WESTERN EUROPE. IT IS USED AS A CANDY/PASTRY UNTO ITSELF, AS WELL AS IN PASTRIES AND ASSORTED OTHER DESSERTS. ITALIANS HAVE INCORPORATED NUT MEATS IN MANY OF THEIR FOODS, INCLUDING, BUT NOT LIMITED TO SALAMI, VARIETY LUNCH MEATS; ASSORTED ENTREES SUCH AS MEAT ROLLS (BRACIOLA), BAKED GOODS AND DESSERTS. THE NORTHERN ITALIANS MAKE PASTA SAUCES FROM NUT MEATS, AND THAT IS THE SUBJECT OF THIS CHAPTER. IN ITALY, YOU'RE APT TO FIND NUT MEATS IN JUST ABOUT ANY FOOD.

WE TRIED THIS SAUCE . . . AND

LOVED IT ( )
HATED IT ( )
MAYBE WE'LL TRY IT AGAIN ( )
WE'LL USE IT FOR UNWELCOME GUESTS ( )

SLIVERED ALMOND SAUCE

(ANOTHER QUICKIE)

ALMONDS ARE ONE OF THE FAVORITE NUTS USED IN ITALIAN COOKERY, ALONG WITH HAZELNUTS, ESPECIALLY WHEN USED IN CANDY MAKING, BAKING OR LIQUEURS. THEY ALSO ENJOY SAUCES WITH NUTS ON THEIR PASTAS. CHUNKY NUT PASTA SAUCES HAVEN'T YET MADE MOVED INTO AMERICAN COOKING. WITH THAT IN MIND, WE NOW WILL OFFER YOU SEVERAL.

INGREDIENTS:
4 TABLESPOONS BUTTER
1/2 CUP SLIVERED ALMONDS
1 SLICE FROM A LOAF OF ITALIAN OR FRENCH BREAD
1/2 CLOVE GARLIC
3 TABLESPOONS FRESH PARSLEY, CHOPPED

METHOD: USE SWEET OR SOUR DOUGH BREAD, TEAR THE BREAD SLICE INTO SMALL PIECES, PLACE IT IN YOUR BLENDER/PROCESSOR ALONG WITH THE GARLIC AND PARSLEY. PROCESS UNTIL WELL CHOPPED. MELT THE BUTTER, ADD THE NUTS AND BREAD CRUMB MIX, SAUTE UNTIL THE NUTS AND BREAD CRUMBS TURN LIGHTLY GOLDEN. LAY OVER YOUR PASTA, TOSS AND SERVE.

RECOMMENDED PASTA: RIBBON TYPES.

MINCED ALMOND SAUCE

(ANOTHER QUICKIE)

THIS IS ANOTHER BUTTER AND CREAM SAUCE ("ALLA PANNA" OR AS IN "ALFREDO") FOR AN ADDED TEXTURE, YOU'LL ADD MINCED ALMONDS. YOU MAY ELECT TO CHOP THE ALMONDS TO ANY DEGREE OF CHUNKINESS THAT IS APPEALING TO YOU; THERE IS NO HARD FAST RULE HERE.

INGREDIENTS:
- 8   OUNCES ALMONDS, MINCED OR CHOPPED
- 1   CUP WHIPPING CREAM
- 1/2   POUND BUTTER
- 1/2   CUP FRESHLY GRATED PARMESAN CHEESE, OR MIX WITH ASIAGO OR ROMANO OR ALL THREE

METHOD: BRING WHIPPING CREAM, BUTTER AND ALMONDS TO A LOW BOIL, ADD 1/2 THE CHEESE, STIR TO MELT, POUR SAUCE OVER PASTA, TOSS. ADD REMAINING CHEESE, TOSS AGAIN, SERVE.

RECOMMENDED PASTA: MEDIUM TUBE TYPES, OR BREAK ANY LONG HOLLOW PASTA INTO 3 INCH LENGTHS.

PINE NUT SAUCE

(ANOTHER QUICKIE)

THIS IS PRETTY MUCH THE SAME AS SLIVERED ALMOND SAUCE WITH TWO EXCEPTIONS, A DIFFERENT NUT AND YOU'LL USE DRY ITALIAN OR FRENCH BREAD CRUMBS.

INGREDIENTS:
1/4	POUND BUTTER
1/2	CUP PINE NUTS
1/2	CUP DRY BREAD CRUMBS FROM ITALIAN OR FRENCH BREAD
1/2	CLOVE GARLIC, MINCED
3	TABLESPOONS FRESH PARSLEY, USE WHOLE UNCHOPPED LEAVES

METHOD: SAUTE THE PINE NUTS, GARLIC AND THE BREAD CRUMBS IN THE BUTTER UNTIL NUTS BEGIN TO COLOR. ADD THE PARSLEY, REMOVE FROM HEAT, LAY OVER PASTA, TOSS AND SERVE.

RECOMMENDED PASTA: RIBBON TYPES.

WALNUT SAUCE #1

(ANOTHER QUICKIE)

THIS IS AN UNCOOKED SAUCE THAT HAS A VERY ENJOYABLE TASTE WITH AN INTERESTING TEXTURE. THIS ONE AND THE FOLLOWING WALNUT SAUCES ARE POPULAR IN NORTHWESTERN ITALY IN AND AROUND THE RIVIERA COUNTRY.

INGREDIENTS:

1	CUP WALNUTS
1/2	CUP OLIVE OIL
1/2	TEASPOON SALT
1/4	CUP WHIPPING CREAM
1/4	CUP RICOTTA CHEESE
2	TABLESPOONS FRESH PARSLEY
	GRATED PARMESAN CHEESE

METHOD: PLACE WALNUTS, OLIVE OIL, RICOTTA CHEESE, PARSLEY AND SALT INTO A BLENDER OR PROCESSOR; RUN AT HIGH SPEED UNTIL MIXTURE IS SMOOTH. SLOWLY ADD WHIPPING CREAM. POUR OVER HOT PASTA AND TOSS. SPRINKLE WITH PARMESAN CHEESE AND SERVE.

RECOMMENDED PASTA: RIBBON TYPES, OR FILLED PILLOW TYPES.

WE TRIED THIS SAUCE . . . AND

LOVED IT ( )
HATED IT ( )
MAYBE WE'LL TRY IT AGAIN ( )
WE'LL USE IT FOR UNWELCOME GUESTS ( )

WALNUT SAUCE #2

(ANOTHER QUICKIE)

1, 2, 3 AND IT'S DONE. IF YOU KEEP SHELLED WALNUTS IN YOUR FREEZER FOR OTHER USES, TRY THIS QUICKIE.

INGREDIENTS:
1	CUP WALNUTS
1/2	CUP OLIVE OIL
1	CLOVE GARLIC (YOUR CHOICE)
1/4	TEASPOON SALT
PINCH	FRESHLY GROUND PEPPER.

METHOD: BLEND ALL INGREDIENTS IN A BLENDER OR FOOD PROCESSOR UNTIL SMOOTH; HAVE SAUCE AT ROOM TEMPERATURE WHEN ADDED TO YOUR HOT, DRAINED PASTA.

RECOMMENDED PASTA: STRING TYPES.

LIGURIAN WALNUT SAUCE

(ANOTHER QUICKIE)

INGREDIENTS:

8	OUNCES WALNUT MEATS
1/3	CUP PINENUTS
1/2	CLOVE GARLIC
3	TABLESPOONS PARSLEY
1/2	CUP RICOTTA CHEESE
1/2	CUP OLIVE OIL

METHOD: PLACE ALL INGREDIENTS INTO A BLENDER OR FOOD PROCESSOR, TURN ON AND PROCESS UNTIL SMOOTH. POUR OVER PASTA, TOSS AND SERVE.

RECOMMENDED PASTA: SMALL FILLED PILLOW TYPES OR RIBBON TYPES.

CREAMY WALNUT SAUCE #1

ALMOST UNCOOKED. READ THE NUT PREPARATION CHOICES FIRST, THEN YOU'LL NEED TO DECIDE, COOKED OR UNCOOKED.

INGREDIENTS: 1 1/2   CUPS WALNUT MEATS
1/2   CLOVE GARLIC
1/4   TEASPOON SALT
PINCH   WHITE PEPPER
1   CUP WHIPPING CREAM

METHOD: YOU MAY: 1.   ROAST THE WALNUTS AT 350 DEGREES FOR 10 MINUTES
2.   SAUTE THEM IN BUTTER UNTIL LIGHTLY COLORED
3.   USE THEM UNCOOKED

EACH METHOD WILL GIVE YOU A DIFFERENT TASTE.

NOW THEN, PLACE YOUR WALNUTS, THE GARLIC, SALT AND PEPPER IN A BLENDER OR PROCESSOR AND WHIRL UNTIL SMOOTH.   ADD WHIPPING CREAM AND HIT PULSE BUTTON A TIME OR TWO JUST TO BLEND.   POUR SAUCE OVER PASTA, TOSS AND SERVE.

RECOMMENDED PASTA: PILLOW OR RIBBON TYPES.

CREAMY WALNUT SAUCE #2

(ANOTHER QUICKIE)

THIS IS A FULLY COOKED NUT SAUCE, IN FACT IT COMES CLOSE TO BEING THE BUTTER AND CREAM SAUCE KNOWN AS "ALFREDO" OR DESIGNATED BY RESTAURANTS AS "ALLA PANNA" SAUCE WITH NUTS ADDED.

INGREDIENTS:

1/2	POUND BUTTER
1/2	CLOVE GARLIC, MINCED
1/2	TEASPOON DRY BASIL OR FRESH CHOPPED PARSLEY
1	TABLESPOON PINENUTS, CHOPPED
3/4	CUP CHOPPED WALNUTS (MEASURE AFTER CHOPPING)
2	CUPS WHIPPING CREAM
1	CUP FRESHLY GRATED PARMESAN CHEESE
1/2	TEASPOON FRESHLY GROUND BLACK PEPPER

METHOD: SAUTE GARLIC AND PARSLEY FOR 3 MINUTES IN THE BUTTER, ADD PINENUTS AND WALNUTS, COOK 2 ADDITIONAL MINUTES. ADD CREAM, BRING CREAM TO A BOIL, REDUCE HEAT TO SIMMER, SLOWLY ADD PARMESAN CHEESE UNTIL MELTED AND BLENDED, ADD BLACK PEPPER. REMOVE FROM HEAT, POUR OVER PASTA, TOSS AND SERVE.

RECOMMENDED PASTA: STRINGS, RIBBON TYPES AND STUFFED LARGE TUBES.

WE TRIED THIS SAUCE . . . AND

LOVED IT ( )
HATED IT ( )
MAYBE WE'LL TRY IT AGAIN ( )
WE'LL USE IT FOR UNWELCOME GUESTS ( )

CREAMY WALNUT SAUCE #3

(ANOTHER QUICKIE)

YOU MAY TAKE LIBERTIES WITH THIS SAUCE. THAT IS, YOU MAY HAVE YOUR WAY WITH IT (DOES THAT SOUND NAUGHTY?). I MEAN, YOU MAY OMIT THE SALT AND PEPPER, AND TRY IT SLIGHTLY SWEETENED BY USING A LITTLE SUGAR.

INGREDIENTS:

2/3	CUP WALNUTS, FINELY CHOPPED OR MINCED
1/2	CUP WHIPPING CREAM
PINCH	THYME, CRUSHED
PINCH	GROUND CINNAMON
2	TABLESPOONS FRESHLY GRATED PARMESAN CHEESE
	SALT AND PEPPER TO TASTE
3	TABLESPOONS BUTTER

METHOD: PLACE ALL INGREDIENTS INTO A MIXING BOWL, WHISK UNTIL WELL BLENDED. TOSS THE HOT DRAINED PASTA WITH THE BUTTER TO COAT, ADD THE SAUCE, TOSS AGAIN, SERVE.

RECOMMENDED PASTA: MEDIUM STRAIGHT EDGED TUBE TYPES.

WE TRIED THIS SAUCE . . . AND

LOVED IT ( )
HATED IT ( )
MAYBE WE'LL TRY IT AGAIN ( )
WE'LL USE IT FOR UNWELCOME GUESTS ( )

WALNUT AND BASIL SAUCE

(ANOTHER QUICKIE)

ANOTHER OF THE NEAR PESTO SAUCES FROM NORTH CENTRAL ITALY, THIS SAUCE USES EQUAL AMOUNTS OF BASIL AND WALNUTS.

INGREDIENTS:
1	CUP FRESH BASIL LEAVES (LOOSELY PACKED)
1	CUP BROKEN WALNUTS
1/2	CUP FRESHLY GRATED PARMESAN CHEESE
1/2	CUP OLIVE OIL
1/2	TEASPOON SALT

METHOD: PLACE ALL INGREDIENTS INTO A BLENDER OR FOOD PROCESSOR AND PROCESS UNTIL SMOOTH. POUR SAUCE OVER PASTA, TOSS AND SERVE.

RECOMMENDED PASTA: STRING TYPES.

COOKED NUT SAUCE

WITH THIS SAUCE WE'RE GOING TO GIVE YOU A WIDE TASTE RANGE. THE ITALIANS MAKE EXTENSIVE USE OF PINE NUTS, WALNUTS, ALMONDS, HAZELNUTS (FILBERTS) AND CHESTNUTS. PICK ONE THAT YOU LIKE. SPEAKING OF CHESTNUTS, ON ONE OCCASION WHEN MY WIFE AND I WERE IN ITALY, WE WERE STROLLING THROUGH A PARK IN VERONA WHEN I POINTED OUT THE CHESTNUT TREES THAT WERE LADEN WITH RIPE AND FALLING CHESTNUTS. WE BEGAN TO PICK THEM OFF THE GROUND. ABOUT THE TIME WE HAD PICKED UP A HUNDRED OR SO, WE REALIZED THERE WAS NOTHING WE COULD DO WITH THEM. WE WERE STAYING IN A HOTEL ROOM WITHOUT A KITCHENETTE AND HAD NO WAY TO PREPARE THEM. CUSTOMS WAS CERTAINLY NOT GOING TO LET US BRING THEM INTO THE UNITED STATES. SO WE CONTINUED OUR STROLL, DISCRETELY DROPPING CHESTNUTS WHEN WE WERE SURE WE NOT BEING WATCHED BY ANYONE WHO WOULD QUESTION OUR SANITY.

INGREDIENTS:
1 DOZEN OF ANY OF THE ABOVE, MINCED
2 TABLESPOONS OLIVE OIL
3 TABLESPOONS BUTTER
1/4 TEASPOON SALT
1 TABLESPOON TOMATO PASTE
1 CUP WATER
FRESHLY GROUND BLACK PEPPER TO TASTE GRATED PARMESAN CHEESE

METHOD: SAUTE THE NUTS IN THE OLIVE OIL/BUTTER AND SALT FOR 2 MINUTES, ADD TOMATO PASTE AND WATER. BRING SAUCE TO A SLOW BOIL FOR ABOUT 10 MINUTES, POUR SAUCE OVER PASTA. SEASON WITH PEPPER AND GRATED CHEESE TO TASTE, TOSS AND SERVE.

RECOMMENDED PASTA: NARROW RIBBON TYPES.

MACADAMIA NUT SAUCE

(ANOTHER QUICKIE)

WE BOTH KNOW THAT MACADAMIA NUTS ARE FROM HAWAII, SO WE'LL TAKE THIS DECIDEDLY NON ITALIAN NUT MEAT AND MAKE AN AMERICAN PASTA SAUCE FROM IT. THIS SAUCE IS MADE IN THE SAME WAY YOU'D MAKE A PESTO SAUCE, IT'S JUST MORE EXPENSIVE.

INGREDIENTS:

3/4	CUP OLIVE OIL
1	CUP LOOSELY PACKED BASIL LEAVES
1/2	CLOVE GARLIC
1	CUP MACADAMIA NUT MEATS
1/2	TEASPOON SALT
PINCH	TEASPOON WHITE PEPPER
1/3	CUP FRESHLY GRATED PARMESAN CHEESE

METHOD: TOSS ALL INGREDIENTS EXCEPT THE CHEESE INTO A BLENDER OR FOOD PROCESSOR AND PROCESS UNTIL FAIRLY SMOOTH. MOVE THE SAUCE TO A SMALL BOWL, ADD THE CHEESE AND MIX BY HAND OR POUR YOUR SAUCE OVER THE HOT DRAINED PASTA. TOSS, ADD GRATED CHEESE AND TOSS AGAIN, SERVE.

RECOMMENDED PASTA: OVAL STRINGS OR RIBBONS.

CHAPTER 7

UNCOOKED TOMATO AND/OR VEGETABLE SAUCES

I THINK YOU'RE GOING TO LIKE THIS CHAPTER. THESE SAUCES ARE LIGHT AND COOL AND ABSOLUTELY WONDERFUL IN HOT SUMMER WEATHER. THEY ARE NOT PASTA SALADS! IN MOST OF THE RECIPES IN THIS CHAPTER, THE SAUCES SHOULD BE AT ROOM TEMPERATURE PRIOR TO BLENDING THEM WITH HOT PASTA.

IF YOU'VE READ MY INTRODUCTION, YOU'LL RECALL A SAUCE REFERRED TO AS "CART DRIVERS SAUCE". WELL, HERE IS WHERE IT FITS IN (ONLY THE UNCOOKED VERSION), ALONG WITH SUCH OTHER DISTINGUISHED TERMS AS: "SUMMER SAUCE", "FRESH SAUCE", "FRESH TOMATO AND BASIL SAUCE".

THE FOLLOWING RECIPES OFFER A VARIETY OF TASTE VARIATIONS BECAUSE THE DIFFERENT FLAVORING INGREDIENTS AND THEIR MELDING CREATE SUBTLE, BUT TANTALIZING TASTE DIFFERENCES IN THE SAUCES.

NOT ALL UNCOOKED SAUCES WILL BE FOUND IN THIS CHAPTER. BY DEFINITION, PESTO, ITS BOGUS COUNTERPARTS, AND SOME OF THE NUT AND CHEESE SAUCES BELONG HERE. HOWEVER, EXERCISING AUTHORS' LICENSE, I'VE LISTED THEM UNDER HERB SAUCES, NUT SAUCES AND CHEESE SAUCES.

THIS IS ONE GROUP OF SAUCES WHERE GARLIC LOVERS AND THOSE THAT ONLY TOLERATE IT ARE APT TO SQUARE OFF. YOUR CHOICES INCLUDE INCORPORAT-ING FRESHLY MINCED GARLIC CLOVE(S) INTO THE SAUCE, OR BRUISING THEM SO THAT THEY MAY BE REMOVED PRIOR TO SERVING. OR SIMPLY RUB THE MARINATING BOWL WITH HALVED CLOVES SO THAT ONLY A LIGHT HINT OF GARLIC PERMEATES THE SAUCE (MY CHOICE). YOU COULD ALSO PRESS THEM TO EXTRACT THE OIL.

IN THE FOLLOWING SAUCES, THE OLIVE OIL OF CHOICE IS EXTRA VIRGIN. THAT IS NOT AN ABSOLUTE. IF YOU ARE A USER OF REGULAR OLIVE OIL (DESIGNATED AS 100% PURE), EXTRA VIRGIN WILL GIVE YOU A TASTE PUNCH YOU MAY NOT LIKE.

*****COOKS' ALERT*****
(B/P/C)
MEANS: BLANCHED, PEELED AND CHOPPED

CART DRIVERS SAUCE

(ANOTHER QUICKIE)

THE ADVANTAGE OF THIS SOUTHERN FAVORITE OVER THE MOST OF THE FOLLOWING UNCOOKED SAUCES IS THAT THIS ONE HAS NO MARINATING TIME. IT'S A MIX AND USE SAUCE. THE ROMANS ALSO LAY CLAIM TO A VERSION OF A "CART DRIVERS SAUCE". I SUSPECT THE ROMAN MULE CART TEAMSTERS WERE EITHER UNIONIZED, OR LAID BACK THEY HAD TIME TO COOK THEIR VERSION. LOOK FOR IT IN CHAPTER 8, "MEATLESS TOMATO SAUCES".

INGREDIENTS:
1	CLOVE GARLIC, HALVED OR MINCED*
1/4	CUP OLIVE OIL
1 1/2	POUNDS FRESH TOMATOES (B/P/C)
1/4	CUP FRESH BASIL, CHOPPED
3/4	TEASPOON SALT
1/4	TEASPOON FRESHLY GROUND BLACK PEPPER

METHOD: RUB SERVING BOWL WITH GARLIC HALVES, DISCARD GARLIC, OR ADD MINCED GARLIC, OLIVE OIL, TOMATOES, BASIL, SALT AND PEPPER. BLEND WELL AND SET ASIDE. COOK AND DRAIN PASTA. ADD HOT COOKED PASTA TO THE SAUCE, TOSS AND SERVE.

*IF YOU CHOOSE TO MINCE THE GARLIC, SIMPLY ADD IT ALONG WITH THE OTHER INGREDIENTS.

RECOMMENDED PASTA: HOLLOW STRING TYPE.

MARECHIARO STYLE SAUCE

THERE ARE TIMES WHEN THE NAME OF A SAUCE BRINGS ON TOTAL CONFUSION. MARECHIARO CAN BE TRANSLATED TO MEAN CLEAR SEAS OR BRIGHT WATERS, OR CLEAR WATERS, OR BRIGHT SEAS, OR POSSIBLY A COLLOQUIALISM WITH A MEANING UNRELATED TO EITHER. I'M INCLINED TO BELIEVE THAT THE NAME COMES FROM A NEAPOLITAN WATERFRONT DISTRICT. THE PECULIARITY IS THAT THIS SAUCE POSSESSES THE INGREDIENTS TO BE A "MARINARA" AND ISN'T, PERHAPS IT ISN'T BECAUSE THIS VERSION IS UNCOOKED. IT IS AN EXCELLENT SAUCE WITH OR WITHOUT THE OLIVE OIL.

INGREDIENTS:
8	PEAR TOMATOES (B/P/C) AND DRAINED
1	CLOVE GARLIC, LIGHTLY CRUSHED
1	TABLESPOON CHOPPED BASIL
1/4	TEASPOON DRY OREGANO
3	TABLESPOONS FRESHLY GRATED PARMESAN CHEESE
1/2	TEASPOON SALT
1/4	TEASPOON FRESHLY GROUND BLACK PEPPER
1/2	CUP OLIVE OIL (OPTIONAL)

METHOD: BLEND ALL INGREDIENTS IN A BOWL, ALLOW TO REST FOR 1 HOUR. REMOVE AND DISCARD GARLIC, POUR SAUCE OVER PASTA, TOSS AND SERVE.

RECOMMENDED PASTA: MEDIUM, STRAIGHT EDGED TUBE TYPES.

TOMATO AND HERB SAUCE

(ANOTHER QUICKIE)

THERE IS AN INTERESTING PROCEDURE TO THIS SAUCE THAT SEPARATES IT FROM THE OTHER SAUCES IN THIS CATEGORY, A SINGLE ITEM IS ADDED TO THE SAUCE, HOT. THAT'S THE OLIVE OIL. THE INFUSION OF HOT OIL INTO THE ROOM TEMPERATURE SAUCE, BRINGS TO LIFE THE AROMATICS OF THE HERBS. DON'T, BUT IF YOU NEED TO USE DRY HERBS INSTEAD OF FRESH, USE 1/3 THE AMOUNT CALLED FOR. THERE IS NO MARINATING TIME REQUIREMENT FOR THIS SAUCE; MAKE IT WHILE PASTA IS COOKING.

INGREDIENTS:
12	PEAR TOMATOES (B/P/C) DICED AND DRAINED
3	TABLESPOONS CHOPPED FRESH BASIL
3	TABLESPOONS CHOPPED PARSLEY
3	TABLESPOONS CHOPPED FRESH ROSEMARY
1	TABLESPOON CHOPPED FRESH MINT
1	TABLESPOON CHOPPED FRESH SAGE
1/2	TEASPOON SALT
	FRESHLY GROUND BLACK PEPPER TO TASTE
1/3	CUP OLIVE OIL

METHOD: MIX ALL INGREDIENTS, EXCEPT OLIVE OIL IN A HEAT PROOF MIXING BOWL; SET ASIDE. WHEN READY TO USE, HEAT THE OLIVE OIL UNTIL VERY HOT, POUR OLIVE OIL INTO THE TOMATO MIXTURE AND BLEND. POUR SAUCE OVER PASTA, TOSS AND SERVE.

RECOMMENDED PASTA: ANY ONE YOU LIKE.

CHOPPED TOMATO AND OLIVE SAUCE

(ANOTHER QUICKIE)

EAT THIS ONE ON FRIDAY NIGHT WHEN YOU'RE GOING TO STAY HOME AND CURL UP WITH A GOOD BOOK OR WATCH A MOVIE ON YOUR VCR. THE AMOUNT OF GARLIC IN THIS RECIPE WILL DEFINITELY NOT MAKE YOU A POPULAR PERSON WITH WHOM TO HAVE A FACE TO FACE CONVERSATION. AND IF YOU'RE NOT A GARLIC AFICIONADO, YOU MAY EVEN FEEL A BURNING SENSATION IN YOUR STOMACH (TUMMY, IF YOU'RE FEMALE).

INGREDIENTS:
6	PEAR TOMATOES (B/P/C)
4	CLOVES GARLIC, MINCED
6	RIPE OLIVES, GREEN OR BLACK
	(OIL CURED IF YOU HAVE THEM)
1/4	LONG GREEN MILDLY HOT PEPPER, MINCED
2	TABLESPOONS OLIVE OIL
1	TABLESPOON LIME JUICE
1/4	TEASPOON SALT
1/4	FRESHLY GROUND BLACK PEPPER
1	TABLESPOON PARSLEY, CHOPPED

METHOD: YOU'LL WANT THE TOMATOES TO BE FAIRLY DRY FOR THIS SAUCE, SO DRAIN THEM AFTER CHOPPING. BLEND REMAINING INGREDIENTS AND TOMATOES. POUR SAUCE OVER PASTA, TOSS AND SERVE.

RECOMMENDED PASTA: VERY THIN STRING TYPES (4 TO 6 OUNCES ONLY).

FRESH UNCOOKED TOMATO SAUCE

(JUICY VERSION)

THESE UNCOOKED SAUCES COME IN TWO BASIC VERSIONS. ONE IS TO SEED AND DRAIN THE TOMATO OF ITS LIQUID AND SOFT PULP, THEREBY USING ONLY THE TOMATO MEAT, AND GETTING A DRIER SAUCE. THE SECOND IS TO USE THE ENTIRE TOMATO SANS ITS SKIN. BOTH VERSIONS HAVE THEIR DEFENDERS; THIS SAUCE AS YOU HAVE KEENLY NOTED, IS THE LATTER.

INGREDIENTS:

1	POUND FRESH BEEFSTEAK TOMATOES (B/P/C)
2	TABLESPOONS FRESH BASIL (CHOPPED)
1	TABLESPOON FRESH PARSLEY (CHOPPED)
1/2	TEASPOON SALT
1/4	TEASPOON FRESHLY GROUND BLACK PEPPER
1	CLOVE GARLIC (YOUR CHOICE)
1/2	CUP OLIVE OIL

METHOD: BLANCH, PEEL AND CHOP TOMATOES, (DO NOT SEED OR DRAIN) ADD SALT, PEPPER, BASIL AND PARSLEY AND BLEND. ADD OIL AND GARLIC. ALLOW TO MARINATE FOR A LEAST ONE HOUR AT ROOM TEMPERATURE.

(SINCE I DON'T LIKE ABSOLUTELY RAW GARLIC, I CHOOSE TO RUB THE MARINATING BOWL WITH A HALVED CLOVE, THEN DISCARD THE REMAINDER. YOU MAY DO WHAT YOU LIKE.)

BLEND OR TOSS THE SAUCE WITH YOUR DRAINED, STEAMING HOT PASTA AND SERVE.

IF YOU CHOOSE, PREPARE THIS SAUCE ONE OR MORE DAYS IN ADVANCE, COVER WELL AND REFRIGERATE. ALLOW IT TO WARM TO ROOM TEMPERATURE BEFORE USING.

RECOMMENDED PASTA: STRING TYPES, MEDIUM TUBE TYPES OR SHELL TYPES.

FRESH TOMATOES AND BASIL SAUCE #1

(ANOTHER QUICKIE, WELL ALMOST)

(THIS IS THE NOT SO JUICY, AND THE NO WAITING VERSION)

THIS SAUCE IS FOR REAL BASIL LOVERS, THE AMOUNT USED IS QUITE LARGE, QUICKLY MIXED AND IMMEDIATELY EATEN. THAT GIVES THE SAUCE A PUNGENCY THAT WILL SATISFY THE BASIL TASTE OF THE KINGLY HERB'S GREATEST FAN. INTERESTINGLY, BASIL TENDS TO ELUDE THE COOK'S CREATIVE ABILITY TO CAPTURE ITS ELUSIVE BOUQUET AND GET IN ONTO THE PLATE. THIS SAUCE COMES CLOSER TO ACCOMPLISHING THAT FEAT THAN GENOA'S FAMED PESTO SAUCE.

INGREDIENTS:
2	POUNDS FRESH PEAR TOMATOES (B/P/C)
2	CUPS FRESH BASIL, CHOPPED
6	TABLESPOONS OLIVE OIL
1	CLOVE GARLIC (YOUR CHOICE)
3/4	TEASPOON SALT
PINCH	FRESHLY GROUND BLACK PEPPER

METHOD: BLANCH, PEEL, SEED AND CHOP THE TOMATOES; SET INTO A COLANDER TO DRAIN. BLEND ALL THE INGREDIENTS WELL, POUR OVER HOT PASTA, TOSS AND SERVE.

RECOMMENDED PASTA: THIN STRING TYPES.

FRESH TOMATO AND BASIL SAUCE #2

THE ADDED INGREDIENTS IN THIS SAUCE GIVE IT A PIQUANCY OVER THE TASTE OF THE PRECEDING RECIPE; THAT MAY BE GOOD IF YOU LIKE PIQUANCY. (BESIDES THAT, PIQUANCIES ARE HARD TO FIND, I THINK THEY ONLY COME OUT AT NIGHT).

INGREDIENTS:

2	POUNDS FRESH PEAR TOMATOES (B/P/C)
1	CUP CHOPPED FRESH BASIL LEAVES
3	TABLESPOONS WINE VINEGAR (SHERRY VINEGAR, IF YOU HAVE IT)
3	OUNCES CAPERS (DRAINED AND RINSED)
	SALT AND FRESHLY GROUND BLACK PEPPER
1	CUP OLIVE OIL

METHOD: COMBINE PREPARED TOMATOES WITH BASIL. MARINATE AT ROOM TEMPERATURE FOR 1 OR MORE HOURS. BLEND VINEGAR, CAPERS, SALT AND PEPPER INTO TOMATO/BASIL MIXTURE.

COOK PASTA, DRAIN AND TOSS WITH OLIVE OIL. ADD THE TOMATO SAUCE, TOSS AGAIN AND SERVE.

RECOMMENDED PASTA: ANGEL HAIR OR OTHER FINE STRING TYPE PASTA.

174

SUMMER SAUCE

I'M NOT SURE WHY THIS IS CALLED A SUMMER SAUCE, THERE ARE NO INGREDIENTS LISTED THAT CANNOT BE FOUND IN MOST MAJOR MARKETS ALL YEAR ROUND. THE MOST OBVIOUS ASSUMPTION IS THAT WE WOULD PROBABLY NOT EAT AN UNCOOKED, ROOM TEMPERATURE SAUCE DURING THE OTHER THREE SEASONS.

INGREDIENTS:

1	POUND FRESH PEAR TOMATOES (B/P/C)
1	MEDIUM ONION (CHOPPED)
6	GREEN OLIVES (PITTED)
2	MEDIUM CLOVES OF GARLIC (MINCED)
1/3	CUP FRESH PARSLEY (CHOPPED)
2	TEASPOONS CAPERS (DRAINED)
2	TABLESPOONS FRESH BASIL (CHOPPED)
1/2	TEASPOON PAPRIKA
1/4	TEASPOON DRIED OREGANO OR 1 TEASPOON FRESH OREGANO
1	TABLESPOON RED WINE VINEGAR
1/2	CUP OLIVE OIL

METHOD: TOSS ALL THE ITEMS EXCEPT VINEGAR AND OIL TOGETHER, THEN ADD VINEGAR, AND TOSS. ADD OIL AND STIR UNTIL WELL MIXED. MARINATE IN REFRIGERATOR SEVERAL HOURS OR OVERNIGHT. ADD COLD SAUCE TO FRESHLY COOKED AND HOT PASTA, SERVE.

RECOMMENDED PASTA: STRING TYPES.

SUMMER SAUCE TOO!

THIS POPULAR ROMAN SAUCE IS QUITE SIMILAR TO THE PRECEDING, BUT I THINK IT BETTER LIVES UP TO ITS NAME. IT SHOULD BE "SUN COOKED" IN THE SAME MANNER YOU'D MAKE SUN TEA.

INGREDIENTS:
1/2	CLOVE GARLIC
2	POUNDS RIPE PEAR TOMATOES (B/P/C)
2	TABLESPOONS CAPERS
1	CUP SLICED OR HALVED RIPE BLACK OLIVES
1/4	CUP CHOPPED FRESH BASIL LEAVES
1/2	CUP OLIVE OIL
1/2	TEASPOON SALT
	FRESHLY GROUND BLACK PEPPER TO TASTE
2	TABLESPOONS EXTRA VIRGIN OLIVE OIL

METHOD: RUB THE MARINATING BOWL WITH THE GARLIC, DISCARD GARLIC, ADD ALL INGREDIENTS EXCEPT THE LAST. MIX WELL, COVER (WITH A SCREEN IF POSSIBLE), SET OUT IN THE SUN FOR 2 TO 3 HOURS (IF THAT'S NOT POSSIBLE, MARINATE INDOORS FOR 3 TO 4 HOURS). TOSS THE HOT DRAINED PASTA WITH THE 2 TABLESPOONS OIL, ADD THE SAUCE, TOSS AND SERVE.

IF YOU PLAN TO SERVE THE PASTA AT ROOM TEMPERATURE, TOSS THE PASTA WITH THE 2 TABLESPOONS OLIVE OIL, LET THE PASTA AND THE SAUCE COOL SEPARATELY BEFORE MIXING AND TOSSING.

RECOMMENDED PASTA: SHELLS OR MEDIUM TUBES.

SUMMER SAUCE III

(ANOTHER QUICKIE)

FEWER INGREDIENTS IN THIS SAUCE MAKE IT A LITTLE LIGHTER THAN THE PRECEDING SUMMER SAUCES. IT IS ALSO SERVED IMMEDIATELY UPON BLENDING, AND ONE OF THE VERY FEW, IF NOT THE ONLY UNCOOKED SAUCE TO ALLOW GRATED CHEESE. YOU MAY WISH TO HOLD OFF ON ADDING CHEESE UNTIL YOU'VE TASTED THIS SAUCE ON PASTA. THE CHEESE MAY DOMINATE THE DISH.

INGREDIENTS:
6	FRESH PEAR TOMATOES (B/P/C)
1/4	CLOVE GARLIC, MINCED (OR RUB BOWL)
1	TABLESPOON MINCED FRESH BASIL LEAVES
2	TABLESPOONS CHOPPED PARSLEY (ITALIAN IF POSSIBLE)
1	TEASPOON SALT
PINCH	OF FRESHLY GROUND BLACK PEPPER TO TASTE
1/4	CUP SCANT MEASURE, OLIVE OIL
	FRESHLY GRATED ROMANO CHEESE

METHOD: TOSS ALL SAUCE INGREDIENTS TOGETHER, POUR OVER PASTA WHEN DRAINED. TOSS AND SERVE WITH GRATED CHEESE ON THE SIDE.

RECOMMENDED PASTA: OVAL STRINGS.

177

COLD CHOPPED TOMATO SAUCE

WELL, COLD MAY BE AN UNWARRANTED ADJECTIVE, ACTUALLY BOTH THE SAUCE AND THE PASTA ARE TO BE AT ROOM TEMPERATURE WHEN YOU BLEND THEM. THIS SAUCE COMES VERY CLOSE TO BEING A SALAD DRESSING. VINEGAR AND LEMON ARE THE CULPRITS, BUT THEY DO ADD THEIR MAGIC.

INGREDIENTS:
2	POUNDS FRESH PEAR TOMATOES (B/P/C)
1	CLOVE GARLIC (YOUR CHOICE)
1	LEMON, JUICE AND ZEST
1	TEASPOON SALT
PINCH	FRESHLY GROUND BLACK PEPPER
1/2	CUP OLIVE OIL
3	TABLESPOONS WINE VINEGAR (WHITE OR RED)
3	TABLESPOONS FRESH BASIL, CHOPPED
2	TABLESPOONS PARSLEY, CHOPPED

METHOD: ONE OR MORE HOURS BEFORE THE MEAL, TOSS 1/2 THE OLIVE OIL AND ALL THE ABOVE INGREDIENTS. BLEND WELL, SET ASIDE. COOK PASTA, DRAIN, POUR THE REMAINING 1/2 OF THE OLIVE OIL OVER THE PASTA. TOSS TO COAT, SET ASIDE. THIS WILL PREVENT THE PASTA FROM STICKING WHILE IT IS COOLING WITHOUT RINSING. WHEN YOU ARE READY TO SERVE, MIX PASTA AND MARINATED SAUCE, TOSS AND SERVE.

RECOMMENDED PASTA: MEDIUM TUBES, SHELLS AND SPIRAL TYPES.

Fresh Tomato/Pepper Sauce

HERE'S A SAUCE WITH FRESH PEPPERS THAT WILL USE ALL THE COLORS AVAILABLE. IF YOU CAN'T FIND A COLOR, DON'T PUNT, PASS. THE TASTE EACH ONE OFFERS SHOULD NOT BE DOUBLED UP. YOU'LL SERVE THIS SAUCE AT ROOM TEMPERATURE OVER HOT, STEAMING PASTA, SO START THIS SAUCE IN THE MORNING FOR TONIGHT'S DINNER.

INGREDIENTS:

1	GREEN BELL PEPPER
1	YELLOW PEPPER, SWEET OR MILDLY HOT
1	SWEET RED PEPPER
1	LONG GREEN MILDLY HOT PEPPER
1/3	CUP OLIVE OIL
1	TABLESPOON RED WINE VINEGAR
3	PEAR TOMATOES (B/P/C)
6	CHIVES WITH TOPS, SLICED
1	CLOVE GARLIC, MINCED
1	TEASPOON OREGANO
1	TEASPOON SALT
PINCH	FRESHLY GROUND BLACK PEPPER
1/3	CUP SHREDDED MOZZARELLA OR PROVOLONE

METHOD: SEED AND THINLY SLICE THE PEPPERS, ADD AND BLEND ALL REMAINING INGREDIENTS EXCEPT THE CHEESE, MIX WELL AND ALLOW TO MARINATE ALL DAY OR OVERNIGHT (IF OVERNIGHT IS CHOSEN, REFRIGERATE). POUR THE ROOM TEMPERATURE SAUCE OVER HOT DRAINED PASTA, TOSS, ADD THE CHEESE, TOSS AGAIN AND SERVE.

THE EXTENDED MARINATING TIME IS IMPORTANT TO TONE DOWN THE PEPPERS.

Continued on next page

179

A COUPLE ADDITIONAL POINTS: YOU MAY ALSO SERVE THE PASTA AT ROOM TEMPERATURE. IF YOU WISH TO, COOK IT, DRAIN IT, COAT IT BY TOSSING WITH 1/4 CUP OLIVE OIL, COVER AND LET IT COOL. IF YOU REFRIGERATE THE SAUCE, BRING IT OUT EARLY ENOUGH TO RISE TO ROOM TEMPERATURE BEFORE SERVING. IT SHOULDN'T BE COLD.

RECOMMENDED PASTA: SHELL TYPES OR OTHER FANCIES.

COLD TOMATO/PEPPER SAUCE

THIS IS SLIGHTLY DIFFERENT THAN THE PRECEDING SAUCE AND EXPECTED TO BE COLD AND WELL MARINATED WHEN ADDED TO YOUR HOT, STEAMING PASTA.

INGREDIENTS:

4	PEAR TOMATOES (B/P/C)
1	GREEN BELL PEPPER, SEEDED AND CHOPPED
1	SWEET RED PEPPER, SEEDED AND CHOPPED
4	RIBS FROM THE HEART OF CELERY WITH LEAVES, CHOPPED
1 1/2	TEASPOON SALT
PINCH	FRESHLY GROUND BLACK PEPPER
1	SCANT TEASPOON DRY OREGANO LEAF
2	TABLESPOONS CHOPPED FRESH BASIL
2	TABLESPOONS RED WINE VINEGAR
2	TABLESPOONS OLIVE OIL, PLUS
2	TABLESPOONS OLIVE OIL.

METHOD: MIX ALL INGREDIENTS, EXCEPT LAST ITEM, IN A BOWL, COVER AND REFRIGERATE OVERNIGHT OR MIX IN THE MORNING AND CHILL ALL DAY. COOK AND DRAIN PASTA, TOSS WITH 2 TABLESPOONS OLIVE OIL, SET BOWL ON THE TABLE AND ALLOW DINERS TO SCOOP SAUCE OVER THEIR HOT PASTA.

RECOMMENDED PASTA: MEDIUM TUBES, SQUARE OR DIAGONAL CUT.

COLD SAUCE GREEK STYLE

THIS IS AN OIL FREE SHRIMP SAUCE OF POSSIBLE SOUTHERN ORIGIN. HERE, BY "GREEK STYLE", WE MEAN THE USE OF A GREEK CHEESE, IN THIS CASE, FETA CHEESE.

INGREDIENTS:

1	POUND COOKED BABY SHRIMP
1	POUND FETA CHEESE, PATTED DRY AND CRUMBLED
4	CHIVE ONIONS, MINCED
1 1/2	TEASPOONS DRY OREGANO LEAVES
1	16 OUNCE CAN PEAR TOMATOES, BLENDERIZED
	OR
8	FRESH PEAR TOMATOES (B/P/C)
	SALT AND PEPPER TO TASTE

METHOD: COMBINE ALL INGREDIENTS IN A BOWL, ALLOW TO MARINATE AT ROOM TEMPERATURE FOR ONE HOUR OR MORE, POUR SAUCE OVER PASTA, BLEND AND SERVE.

RECOMMENDED PASTA: MEDIUM TUBE TYPES, OR FANCIES.

FRESH HERB AND VEGETABLE SAUCE

(ANOTHER QUICKIE)

BECAUSE THIS SAUCE USES SEVERAL HERBS AND VERY FEW VEGETABLES, IT SHOULD ONLY BE MADE WITH FRESH HERBS. IF YOU OR A NEIGHBOR ARE NOT REAL GARDENERS WITH A PASSION FOR GROWING FRESH HERBS, IT'S IMPROBABLE THAT YOU'D HAVE OR COULD BUY ALL THE FRESH HERBS NEEDED, SO, IN ANTICIPATION OF THAT, I WILL FOLLOW THE FRESH HERB MEASUREMENTS WITH A (DRY MEASUREMENT).

INGREDIENTS:

4	CHIVE LEAVES, MINCED OR (1/2 TEASPOON DRY)
8	BASIL LEAVES, MINCED OR (1/2 TEASPOON DRY)
4	SAGE LEAVES, MINCED OR (1/4 TEASPOON DRY)
1/2	CLOVE GARLIC, MINCED
1/4	CUP MINCED FRESH PARSLEY
1	WHITE RADISH OR 2 PEELED RED ONES, MINCED
1	HEART OF CELERY, FINELY CHOPPED
4	PEAR TOMATOES (B/P/C) AND DRAINED
1/3	CUP OLIVE OIL
1/2	TEASPOON SALT
PINCH	BLACK PEPPER

METHOD: PLACE ALL INGREDIENTS INTO A BOWL, MIX WELL, LET REST WHILE PASTA IS COOKING. POUR SAUCE OVER HOT, DRAINED PASTA, TOSS AND SERVE.

RECOMMENDED PASTA: HOLLOW STRING TYPES.

FRESH ZUCCHINI SAUCE

(ANOTHER QUICKIE)

THE UBIQUITOUS ZUCCHINI HAS BECOME A STAR, A VEGETABLE WHOSE ENTRY INTO AMERICAN CUISINE, COUPLED WITH ITS ABILITY TO PRODUCE IN PROFUSION, HAS FORCED THE AMERICAN GARDENER AND CREATIVE COOK TO HAVE THEIR WAY WITH IT. AS A RESULT, THERE ARE SEVERAL COOKBOOKS FULLY DEDICATED TO THE RECIPES FOR ZUCCHINI. IT IS NOW CERTAINLY ONE OF AMERICA'S FAVORITE AND VERSATILE VEGETABLES. IT CAN AND DOES PLAY A ROLE IN EVERY COURSE OF THE AMERICAN MEAL; IT LENDS ITSELF BEAUTIFULLY TO PARTICIPATION IN APPETIZERS, SOUPS, SALADS, SAUCES, ENTREES, BREADS AND DESSERTS. WHAT OTHER VEGETABLES CAN BE USED IN THAT BROAD AN APPLICATION? (I MUST ADMIT CARROTS COME CLOSE). IN THIS BOOK THERE ARE SEVERAL RECIPES THAT MAKE USE OF THE ZUCCHINIS POTENTIAL AS A PASTA SAUCE INGREDIENT. LOOK FOR THEM IN THE VEGETABLE CATEGORY. THIS RECIPE GIVES YOU THE OPPORTUNITY TO USE IT AS AN UNCOOKED PASTA SAUCE.

INGREDIENTS:

1/2	CLOVE GARLIC
1/4	OLIVE OIL
2	CUPS SHREDDED ZUCCHINI
2	CHIVES, FINELY CHOPPED
2	TABLESPOONS CHOPPED PARSLEY
1	TEASPOON SALT
1/4	TEASPOON OREGANO LEAF

METHOD: RUB INTERIOR OR A SMALL BOWL WITH THE GARLIC CLOVE, DISCARD. PLACE REMAINING INGREDIENTS INTO THE BOWL, MIX WELL AND ALLOW TO REST WHILE PASTA IS COOKING. POUR SAUCE OVER HOT, DRAINED PASTA, TOSS AND SERVE.

RECOMMENDED PASTA: STRINGS.

OLIVE AND ANCHOVY SAUCE II

(ANOTHER QUICKIE)

IN PARTS OF SOUTHERN ITALY, THIS SAUCE IS KNOWN AS A "BLACK SAUCE" OBVIOUSLY DUE TO THE FACT THAT IT LOOKS THAT WAY WHEN YOU USE BLACK OLIVES. IT'S PRETTY SIMPLE . . . , OLIVES, OIL AND ANCHOVIES.

INGREDIENTS: 2 DOZEN RIPE OLIVES (YOUR CHOICE OF COLOR) CHOPPED
1/3 CUP OLIVE OIL
4 ANCHOVY FILLETS, MASHED
1/4 CUP CHOPPED PARSLEY

METHOD: BLEND ALL INGREDIENTS AND ALLOW TO REST WHILE PASTA IS COOKING. POUR SAUCE OVER PASTA, TOSS AND SERVE.

RECOMMENDED PASTA: HOLLOW STRING TYPES.

185

MOZZARELLA AND ANCHOVY SAUCE

(ANOTHER QUICKIE)

THIS LITTLE DEVIL USES SEVERAL EGG YOLKS ALSO, THE YOLKS ARE COOKED BY THE HOT PASTA AND THE SEASONING COMES FROM THE ANCHOVY.

INGREDIENTS:

2	TABLESPOONS BUTTER, MELTED
3	EGG YOLKS, LIGHTLY BEATEN
4	ANCHOVY FILLETS, FINELY CHOPPED
1/2	CUP SHREDDED MOZZARELLA
2	TABLESPOONS CHOPPED PARSLEY
	FRESHLY GROUND BLACK PEPPER TO TASTE

METHOD: BLEND ALL INGREDIENTS, ADJUST SEASONING WITH BLACK PEPPER. POUR SAUCE OVER HOT, DRAINED PASTA, TOSS AND SERVE.

RECOMMENDED PASTA: MEDIUM DIAGONAL CUT TUBE TYPES.

CHAPTER 8

MEATLESS SAUCES MADE FROM TOMATOES

WAIT A MINUTE HERE, AUTHOR! TOMATOES ARE USED AS VEGETABLES, AND CHAPTER 13 IS THE VEGETABLE SAUCE CHAPTER! I KNOW, I KNOW! WELL, WE BOTH KNOW THAT THE TOMATO IS A FRUIT, AND DO YOU REALLY CARE? THE QUESTION IS, WHY AM I GIVING IT A SEPARATE CHAPTER? PROBABLY BECAUSE IT IS SUCH A MONSTER CATEGORY; THERE ARE DOZENS UPON DOZENS OF TOMATO SAUCE RECIPES. ALL DO NOT QUALIFY AS MERE VARIATIONS. WITH MOST SAUCES, AS WELL AS TOMATO SAUCES, A SINGLE ITEM ADDED OR OMITTED CREATES A VARIATION. THE END TOTAL COULD BE AN UNACCEPTABLE NUMBER OF SAUCES. AT THE SAME TIME, I DON'T WANT TO GIVE YOU A SAUCE BASE OF TOMATOES AND OLIVE OIL FOLLOWED BY A LIST OF THIRTY OR FORTY ITEMS AND SAY PICK SEVERAL OF THE INGREDIENTS YOU LIKE!

SO, FOR WANT OF A BETTER METHOD, I HAVE NUMBERED THE SAUCES IN THIS CATEGORY THAT DO NOT HAVE NAME RECOGNITION BEYOND "TOMATO SAUCE". AND THOSE AMOUNT TO TWO DOZEN, PLUS. IN ADDITION, THERE ARE ANOTHER TWO DOZEN, PLUS, WITH RECOGNIZED NAMES, NOW THEN I'LL SAY, "PICK THE ONE(S) YOU LIKE".

"ARE YOU KIDDING, WHAT AM I GOING TO DO WITH 53 TOMATO SAUCES?"

YOU MAY, IF YOU WISH, IGNORE THIS CHAPTER. HOWEVER, IF YOU'D RATHER NOT, THEN LET'S LOOK AT THIS CATEGORY AND EXAMINE THE REASONING IF IT EXISTS, BEHIND THIS LARGE NUMBER OF SAUCES, ALL MEATLESS AND WITH TOMATOES.

WHERE DID ALL THOSE SAUCES COME FROM?

A WORD OR TWO OF HISTORY MIGHT HELP EXPLAIN IT. THE SOUTHERN ITALIANS WERE THE LARGEST GROUP OF ITALIANS TO ARRIVE HERE (THEY WERE THE TOMATO AND OLIVE OIL GROUP, THE BUTTER AND CREAM GROUP HAD NO REASON TO LEAVE, AT LEAST UNTIL CALIFORNIA'S VINEYARDS AND GOLD FIELDS BECKONED.) ADD TO THAT THAT PASTA SAUCES IN ITALY WERE, AND TO A GREAT EXTENT STILL ARE EXTREMELY LOCAL, THEY CHANGED VILLAGE BY VILLAGE, FROM THE VALLEY FLOOR'S TO THE HILL TOP'S, AND FROM FISHING VILLAGE TO FISHING VILLAGE AROUND THE EASTERN, SOUTHERN, WESTERN AND ISLAND COAST LINES.

IT IS A FACT THAT EVEN TODAY FROM ALMOST ANY VANTAGE POINT, WHETHER ON A VALLEY FLOOR OR HIGH ON A HILLSIDE YOU MAY LOOK IN ANY DIRECTION AND SEE DOZENS OF VILLAGES, ALL PROMINENTLY IDENTIFIED BY A STEEPLE OR BELL TOWER OF THE VILLAGE CHURCH (I DON'T BELIEVE THAT A VILLAGE EXISTS IN ITALY WITHOUT IT'S OWN PARISH).

THE SOUTHERNERS WERE THE FIRST TO SHARE THEIR RECIPES WITH AMERICA, AND THEY, MORE SO THAN THE NORTHERNERS, USED TOMATOES AS THEIR BASIC SAUCE INGREDIENT AND I MEAN BASIC, BASIC TO PRACTICALLY EVERY-THING THEY COOKED AND ESPECIALLY PASTA SAUCES.

SINCE OUR SUBJECT IS TOMATOES, LETS THINK FRESH.   EACH VARIETY OF TOMATO HAS ITS OWN FLAVOR AND IT WILL SHOW UP IN THE FINISHED SAUCE. BUY ITALIAN STYLE PEAR (IN YOUR AREA THEY MAY BE "SALADETTE" OR "ROMA") TOMATOES IF POSSIBLE, IF NOT USE WHAT IS AVAILABLE. IF CANNED, MY PARTICULAR FAVORITE IS THE ITALIAN PEAR TOMATO. HOWEVER, READ THE LABEL, BECAUSE MANY PACKERS WILL PACK A BASIL LEAF IN THEIR CANNED PEAR TOMATOES.   THAT'S OK EXCEPT; THAT IT WILL GIVE AN UNWANTED FLAVOR TO ANY SAUCE NOT REQUIRING BASIL.

I OCCASIONALLY USE CANNED TOMATO SAUCE (GENERALLY AS A THICKENING AGENT, IT WILL ALLOW YOU TO REDUCE COOKING TIME).   I RARELY USE TOMATO PASTE AND NEVER USE TOMATO PUREE. THE LATTER IS TOO BITTER FOR MY TASTE AND WILL IN MOST INSTANCES REQUIRE A SWEETENER, (READ SUGAR, HONEY OR SYRUP).   I DON'T BELIEVE THAT IT SHOULD EVER BE NECESSARY TO SWEETEN A TOMATO SAUCE WITH ANYTHING OTHER THAN A GOOD SWEET ONION (VIDALIA OR WALLA WALLA ARE EXCELLENT VARIETIES) OR FRESH YOUNG CARROT.

IF I MAY INTERJECT A NOTE ABOUT SWEETENERS IN YOUR SAUCE, IF THE RECIPE DOES NOT USE ENOUGH ONION AND/OR CARROT TO PROVIDE A NATURAL SWEETNESS TO THE SAUCE (APPROXIMATELY 2 TABLESPOONS OF EITHER TO 1 POUND OF TOMATOES), THE ADDITION OF A SWEETENER MAY BE NECESSARY. MY PERSONAL FAVORITE IS A SORGHUM SYRUP.   BUT I WILL LEAVE THAT DECISION ENTIRELY UP TO YOU; YOU WILL BE SAMPLING YOUR SAUCE AND THEREFORE YOU ARE THE BEST JUDGE. I WILL SUGGEST THAT IF A SWEETENER IS TO BE ADDED, START WITH 1/2 TEASPOON AND WORK UP FROM THERE.   I BELIEVE THAT SWEETENING MAY BE NEEDED WITH SOME VARIETIES OF FRESH TOMATOES; POSSIBLY NONE WILL BE NEEDED WITH PREMIUM LABEL CANNED TOMATOES, I.E., HUNTS, S&W, LIBBYS, DEL MONTE, CONTADINA, PROGRESSO,

STOKLEY AND SEVERAL OTHER MAJOR LABELS. LESSER LABELS, I.E., 2ND, 3RD AND SOMETIME 4TH GRADE PRODUCTS RECEIVE THOSE LABELS BECAUSE THEY ARE NOT OF THE QUALITY, OR DO NOT POSSESS THE NATURAL SWEETNESS NEEDED FOR FIRST LABELED PRODUCTS. THAT GENERALLY MEANS THE CANNER ADDS SUGAR.

IF YOU'VE EVER WONDERED ABOUT THE DIFFERENT LABEL QUALITIES, YOU MIGHT BE SURPRISED TO DISCOVER THAT IN MOST CASES, IT IS DETERMINED BY THE LENGTH OF TIME THE FRUIT OR VEGETABLE IS OFF THE TREE OR PLANT. MOST FIRST LABELED PRODUCTS ARE CANNED WITHIN MINUTES TO 36 HOURS OF THE TIME THEY ARE PICKED. BY THEN THE NATURAL SUGARS PRESENT IN THEM ARE AT A ROLLING GALLOP IN THEIR CONVERSION TO STARCH; AND THAT CAUSES A DETERIORATION IN FLAVOR AND QUALITY. THAT'S ALSO WHY SO MUCH SUGAR IS ADDED TO LOWER QUALITY LABELS.

PERHAPS YOU'RE ONE OF THE MANY PUZZLED OVER THE TERM PEAR AND/OR PLUM TOMATO? THEN LET'S EXAMINE THE QUESTION, WHEN CAN A PEAR BE A PLUM? THE ANSWER IS WHENEVER THE CANNER WANTS IT TO BE! AS NEAR AS I CAN DETERMINE, PEAR AND PLUM SEEM TO BE INTERCHANGEABLE TERMS FOR THE SMALL MEATY TOMATO. PEAR IS THE MOST PREVALENT IN THE UNITED STATES, WHILE IN ITALY, PLUM APPEARS TO BE THE PREFERRED NAME. WHEN SOLD FRESH IN MANY STORES IT IS REFERRED TO AS THE "ROMA" TOMATO, IN OTHER STORES AS THE "SALADETTE" TOMATO. AND WHEN SOLD IN CANS, BOTH PLUM (DELVERDE AN ITALIAN IMPORT) AND PEAR (S&W, CONTADINA) ARE USED. MOST AMERICAN CANNERS IGNORE THE QUESTION AND SIMPLY CALL THEIRS "ITALIAN STYLE TOMATOES", WHILE MOST ITALIAN CANNERS JUST SIMPLY USE TOMATOES. I DON'T BELIEVE THERE'S A DIFFERENCE.

IN THE FOLLOWING RECIPES WHEN FRESH TOMATOES ARE USED, IT MEANS TOMATOES THAT HAVE BEEN BLANCHED, SKINNED AND POSSIBLY SEEDED. I SAY POSSIBLY SEEDED BECAUSE THERE MAY BE TIMES WHEN YOU'LL WISH TO LEAVE THE SEEDS IN. BOTH THE TOMATO'S SKIN AND ITS SEEDS ARE BITTER. THE SKIN IS ESPECIALLY SO. AS FOR THE SEEDS, WELL IF YOU SEED THE TOMATO WITHOUT SIEVING, YOU ALSO LOSE THE SOFT PULP. I LIKE IT, AND I BELIEVE IT ADDS SOMETHING TO THE END PRODUCT THAT OTHERWISE WOULD BE LOST. THIS IS ESPECIALLY TRUE IN UNCOOKED SAUCES, AND THAT IS A SEPARATE CHAPTER. BUT IF YOU WANT TO GET RID OF THE SEEDS, SIEVING WILL DO IT.

A FEW OF THE FOLLOWING TOMATO SAUCES ARE DESIGNED TO BE PREPARED, POSSIBLY LIGHTLY COOKED AND THEN PLACED OVER OR ADDED TO PREPARED,

STUFFED OR LAYERED PASTA, POSSIBLY WITH OTHER INGREDIENTS FOR FURTHER COOKING OR BAKING. SOME, AFTER BRIEF COOKING, ARE READY TO BE TOSSED WITH YOUR COOKED PASTA. OTHERS NEED TO BE COOKED SLOWLY FOR A LONG PERIOD OF TIME. I'M NOT SURE WHY IT WORKS OUT THIS WAY, BUT SINCE IT DOES LETS MAKE USE OF IT.

A WORD ABOUT "MARINARA" SAUCES

THE NAME "MARINARA" IS APPLICABLE TO THE SEA. THEREFORE A MARINARA SAUCE SHOULD BE A SAUCE CONTAINING SEAFOOD, BUT WITH FEW EXCEPTIONS, DOESN'T. THE NAME MEANS "SAILOR'S" SAUCE. AND THAT MAY BE EXPANDED TO INCLUDE ANY OF THE TERMS APPLICABLE TO SAILING MEN. SEAMEN, NAVY MEN, FISHERMEN OR MERCHANT MARINERS. SINCE MOST RECIPES CALLED "MARINARA" DO NOT CONTAIN SEAFOOD THAT MAKES THE DESIGNATION A CONTRADICTION IN TERMS.

MY RESEARCH OF "MARINARA" SAUCE INGREDIENTS THROUGH DOZENS AND DOZENS OF "MARINARA" SAUCE RECIPES HAVE CONVINCED ME THERE IS NO ABSOLUTE FORMULA. I BELIEVE THAT IN MANY CASES WHEN SOMEONE IS ASKED THE NAME OF THEIR RED (TOMATO) SAUCE. IF THEY DON'T NAME IT AFTER SOMEONE IN THE FAMILY (MAMA'S, AUNT WHAT'S HER NAME, OR THEMSELVES.) PROBABLY SAY "MARINARA" ONLY BECAUSE THEY KNOW THE NAME, AND THAT THE NAME IS APPLICABLE TO RED SAUCES. MY RESEARCH HAS ALSO SHOWN THAT IN THE PREPONDERANT NUMBER OF "MARINARA" RECIPES THE NAME APPEARS TO BE RELATED TO THE INCLUSION OF THE HERBS, BASIL AND OREGANO, PLUS GARLIC IN A TOMATO BASE. BEYOND THAT I CAN'T FIND A COMMON TREAD. INTERESTINGLY, THE REMAINING NUMBER OF "MARINARA" RECIPES IN MY FILES USE NO HERBS. THOSE WITHOUT THE HERBS, BASIL AND OREGANO, USE ONLY OLIVE OIL, GARLIC, FRESH OR CANNED PEAR TOMATOES, AND OCCASIONALLY A SMALL MEASURE OF TOMATO PASTE. I AM CONVINCED THAT IN THE UNITED STATES, THE NAME "MARINARA" APPEARS TO HAVE BECOME A GENERIC TERM FOR TOMATO SAUCE.

A VERY GOOD SAUCE CAN BE MADE FROM TOMATOES (FRESH OR CANNED), GARLIC AND OLIVE OIL. THAT'S ALL! THE PROBLEM IS THE LACK OF A NATURAL SWEETENER (ONION/CARROT) AS A RESULT THE TASTE COULD BE SOMEWHERE BETWEEN BITTER AND TART. HERE IS THE TYPE OF "MARINARA" THAT WOULD REQUIRE A SWEETENER. IF I MAY REPEAT, IN THIS SITUATION, MY PREFERENCE FOR A SWEETENER WOULD BE A SORGHUM SYRUP OVER GRANULATED SUGAR OR HONEY. SORGHUM SYRUP IS VERY SWEET WITHOUT AN IDENTIFYING TASTE WHEN SMALL MEASUREMENTS ARE USED.

Salting

I DON'T ADD SALT TO CANNED TOMATOES WHEN USED IN A MEATLESS SAUCE. HOWEVER, IF FRESH TOMATOES ARE TO BE USED, SALT. IF OTHER FRESH INGREDIENTS ARE BEING USED, SOME SALT MAY BE NEEDED.

***

THE DESIGNATION:
(B/P/C)
FOLLOWING FRESH TOMATOES MEANS
BLANCHED, PEELED AND CHOPPED

WE TRIED THIS SAUCE . . . AND

LOVED IT ( )
HATED IT ( )
MAYBE WE'LL TRY IT AGAIN ( )
WE'LL USE IT FOR UNWELCOME GUESTS ( )

SICILIAN STYLE TOMATO SAUCE

THIS SAUCE IS PROBABLY MY OVERALL FAVORITE, IT'S SIMPLE AND VERY TASTY. IT USES NO HERBS, THE SAUCE IS SWEETENED WITH CARROT AND ONION WITH A HINT OF GARLIC.

INGREDIENTS:
3	TABLESPOONS OLIVE OIL
1	CLOVE GARLIC, CRUSHED OR MINCED
2	TABLESPOONS ONION, MINCED
2	TABLESPOONS CARROT, SHREDDED
1	28 OUNCE CAN WHOLE PEELED TOMATOES, BLENDERIZED

METHOD: SAUTE GARLIC, ONION AND CARROT IN OLIVE OIL UNTIL OIL IS GOLDEN IN COLOR. ADD THE TOMATOES, BRING SAUCE TO A BOIL, LOOSELY COVER, REDUCE HEAT TO SIMMER, COOK FOR 25 MINUTES. POUR SAUCE OVER PASTA. TOSS AND SERVE.

RECOMMENDED PASTA: STRING TYPES OR MEDIUM TUBES.

CENTRAL PENINSULA (ABRUZZI & MOLISE)

STYLE TOMATO SAUCE

(LONG AND LOW)

THIS IS VERY SIMILAR TO THE PRECEDING SAUCE; THE PRINCIPAL CHANGE IS THE TRADE OF GARLIC FOR ONION. IT APPEARS THAT IN CENTRAL ITALY, COOKS WILL TRADE GARLIC FOR THE SWEETER ONION AS FREQUENTLY AS THEY'LL SWAP OLIVE OIL FOR BUTTER, OR USE EQUAL PORTIONS OF BOTH. THE EXTENDED COOKING TIME FOR THIS SAUCE, GIVES IT A CONCENTRATED FLAVOR. THE SAUCE ALSO APPEARS TO BE SUITABLE FOR A WIDER SELECTION OF PASTA TYPES.

INGREDIENTS:

1/2	CUP OLIVE OIL
1/2	SWEET ONION, CHOPPED
1	MEDIUM CARROT, SHREDDED
1	STALK CELERY, FINELY CHOPPED
1	TEASPOON SALT
2	POUNDS PEAR TOMATOES (B/P/C) BLENDERIZED

METHOD: SAUTE THE ONION IN OLIVE OIL UNTIL TRANSPARENT, ADD CARROT AND CELERY, SAUTE FOR 2 MINUTES, ADD SALT AND TOMATOES, BRING SAUCE TO A BOIL, REDUCE HEAT, COVER AND SIMMER FOR 1 AND 1/2 HOURS. POUR SAUCE OVER PASTA, TOSS AND SERVE.

RECOMMENDED PASTA: STRINGS OR MEDIUM TUBES.

SWEET AND LIGHT SAUCE

THIS LITTLE HONEY USES THE SAME INGREDIENTS AS THE PROCEEDING SAUCE, BUT THE PREPARATION METHOD IS DIFFERENT AND THEREFORE THE END PRODUCT IS DIFFERENT.

INGREDIENTS:

2	POUNDS PEAR TOMATOES (B/P/C) BLENDERIZED
1	MEDIUM CARROT, SHREDDED
1	STALK CELERY, FINELY CHOPPED
1/2	MEDIUM ONION, CHOPPED
1	TEASPOON SALT
1/2	CUP OLIVE OIL

METHOD: PLACE TOMATOES, CARROT, CELERY, ONION AND SALT IN SAUCE PAN, BRING MIXTURE TO A BOIL, REDUCE HEAT, COVER AND SIMMER FOR 30 MINUTES. ADD OLIVE OIL, COOK AN ADDITIONAL 15 MINUTES. POUR SAUCE OVER PASTA, TOSS AND SERVE.

RECOMMENDED PASTA: STRINGS AND MEDIUM TUBE TYPES.

ROMAN STYLE "CART DRIVER'S" SAUCE

THIS IS A FAST, LIGHT AND VERY TASTY SAUCE. EVERY VILLAGE AND TOWN IN ITALY HAD CART DRIVERS, TODAY THEY'VE BEEN REPLACED BY TRUCKS OR PICKUP/MINIVAN TRUCKS AND THE THREE WHEELED SCOOTERS WITH A SMALL BED. HOWEVER, WAY BACK, WHEN THESE MULE DRIVING TEAMSTERS WERE ON THE ROAD, THEIR MIDDAY MEALS HAD TO BE SIMPLE ROADSIDE DINING. THE CART DRIVER HAD TO BRING HIS TRANSPORT TO A HALT WHILE HE PREPARED HIS MEAL, SO IT NOT ONLY HAD TO BE SIMPLE, BUT REASONABLY QUICK. THE LARGE NUMBER OF THESE WIDESPREAD CART DRIVER'S IS WHY YOU'LL FIND SO MANY VERSIONS OF THIS SAUCE. ADDITIONALLY, ROADSIDE RESTAURANTS WERE IN SHORT SUPPLY, AND CART DRIVER'S WERE WELL DOWN ON THE WAGE SCALE, SO, MOST LIKELY THEY COULDN'T AFFORD TO EAT AT A RESTAURANT.

JUDGING FROM THE AMOUNT OF GARLIC IN THIS SAUCE, THE GUY WHO CREATED THIS RECIPE MUST HAVE SLEPT WITH HIS MULE.

INGREDIENTS:

1	16 OUNCE CAN PEAR TOMATOES, BLENDERIZED
1 1/2	CUPS FRESH BASIL LEAVES, CHOPPED
4	CLOVES GARLIC, MINCED
1/3	CUP OLIVE OIL
	FRESHLY GROUND BLACK PEPPER TO TASTE

METHOD: PLACE ALL INGREDIENTS INTO A SAUCE PAN. BRING TO A BOIL, LOWER HEAT SLIGHTLY AND COOK FOR 15 MINUTES. POUR SAUCE OVER PASTA, TOSS AND SERVE.

RECOMMENDED PASTA: THIN STRING TYPES.

NORTHERN STYLE LIGHT SAUCE

FEATHER LIGHT MIGHT SEEM AN INAPPROPRIATE COMPARISON FOR A SAUCE, BUT A TASTE TEST WILL GET YOUR ATTENTION. IF LIGHT IS YOUR STYLE, GO FOR IT. IF YOUR INTO HEAVIES, YOU OWE THIS ONE A TRY.

INGREDIENTS: 2   POUNDS PEAR TOMATOES (B/P/C) BLENDERIZED

1	ONION, PEELED AND LEFT WHOLE
1	TEASPOON SALT
1/4	POUND BUTTER

METHOD: PLACE ALL INGREDIENTS INTO A SAUCE PAN. BRING TO A BOIL, REDUCE HEAT TO SIMMER, COVER AND COOK FOR 45 MINUTES. DISCARD ONION. POUR SAUCE OVER PASTA, TOSS AND SERVE.

RECOMMENDED PASTA: STRINGS, MEDIUM TUBE TYPES OR HOMEMADE GNOCCI.

NORTHERN STYLE SIMPLE SAUCE

THE FLAVOR IN THIS SAUCE COMES FROM TWO SEPARATE SOURCES, LIGHTLY SAUTEED GARLIC AND UNCOOKED FRESH BASIL. IT COULD BECOME ONE OF YOUR FAVORITES.

INGREDIENTS:
1/3	CUP OLIVE OIL
2	CLOVES GARLIC, MINCED OR THINLY SLICED
1	14 1/2 OUNCE CAN PEAR TOMATOES, CHOPPED WITH JUICE
1	TABLESPOON CHOPPED FRESH BASIL LEAVES

METHOD: SAUTE GARLIC IN OLIVE OIL UNTIL LIGHTLY GOLDEN. ADD TOMATOES, BRING SAUCE TO A BOIL. REDUCE HEAT AND SIMMER FOR 20 MINUTES. REMOVE SAUCE FROM HEAT, ADD BASIL AND STIR. POUR SAUCE OVER PASTA, TOSS AND SERVE.

VARIATIONS: OMIT THE BASIL AND DOUBLE UP ON THE GARLIC.
OR
TO DOUBLE THE SAUCE. OMIT THE BASIL. DOUBLE UP AGAIN THE GARLIC TO 8 CLOVES. AND ONCE ON THE TOMATOES TO A 28 OUNCE CAN.

RECOMMENDED PASTA: ANY ONE YOU LIKE.

NEAPOLITAN TOMATO SAUCE

THIS SAUCE IS TRADITIONALLY SERVED AS A SMOOTH SAUCE, TO DO THIS WITH CANNED WHOLE OR DICED TOMATOES, YOU'LL NEED TO SIEVE THEM AND DISCARD THE SEEDS.

INGREDIENTS:

1	28 OUNCE CAN PEAR TOMATOES (SIEVED)
3	TABLESPOONS OLIVE OIL
	(YOU MAY EXCHANGE BUTTER FOR 1/2 THE OIL)
1	TEASPOON BASIL, DRIED OR 2 TABLESPOONS FRESH
3	TABLESPOONS FRESH PARSLEY, CHOPPED
	GRATED PARMESAN CHEESE.

METHOD: HEAT OIL AND BUTTER, ADD TOMATOES AND DRIED BASIL. BRING TOMATOES TO A BOIL, REDUCE HEAT TO LOW, COOK PARTIALLY COVERED FOR 30 MINUTES. ADD FRESH BASIL IF USED, AND PARSLEY. REMOVE FROM HEAT, POUR OVER PASTA, TOSS AND SERVE WITH CHEESE.

RECOMMENDED PASTA: STRING TYPES.

PIZZAIOLA SAUCE

THE REAL DIFFERENCE BETWEEN THIS SAUCE AND THE NEAPOLITAN IS THE HERB PLUS A LITTLE GARLIC AND CHUNKIER TOMATOES.

INGREDIENTS:

1	28 OUNCE CAN PEAR TOMATOES, CHOPPED
2	CLOVES GARLIC (YOUR CHOICE)
1	TABLESPOON OLIVE OIL
1	TEASPOON DRIED OREGANO OR MARJORAM
3	TABLESPOONS FRESH PARSLEY, CHOPPED
	GRATED PARMESAN CHEESE

METHOD: HEAT OIL AND COOK GARLIC UNTIL LIGHTLY GOLDEN. IF YOU USED CRUSHED GARLIC CLOVES, DISCARD THEM NOW. ADD TOMATOES AND MARJORAM, BRING TO A BOIL, REDUCE HEAT TO LOW, COOK FOR 30 MINUTES. REMOVE FROM HEAT, STIR IN PARSLEY, POUR OVER PASTA AND TOSS, SERVE WITH CHEESE.

RECOMMENDED PASTA: STRING TYPES.

MARINARA SAUCE #1

(SAILORS SAUCE)

THIS IS ONE OF THE SAUCES I'VE KNOWN AND LOVED FROM MY YOUTH. ADMITTEDLY IT'S NAME LEAVES A LOT OPEN TO INTERPRETATION. MANY OF THE RECIPES YOU'LL FIND UNDER THIS NAME DO HAVE SOME SEAFOOD ITEM(S) ADDED. EQUALLY AS MANY SEEM TO IGNORE THE MEANING OF THE NAME, AND THAT MAY POSSIBLY BE EXPLAINED BY THE STORIES ABOUT THIS SAUCE. ONE OF THE STORIES SUGGESTS ITS NAME MAY HAVE COME ABOUT WHEN SEAMEN'S WIVES SEEING THEIR MEN'S BOATS ON THE HORIZON RETURNING TO PORT, RUSHED HOME TO PREPARE THIS SAUCE FOR THEIR FIRST HOME COOKED MEAL IN DAYS OR EVEN MONTHS. ANOTHER STORY, ALTHOUGH SOMEWHAT LESS LIKELY, MAY HAVE COME ABOUT WHEN SAILORS FOUND THEMSELVES IN STORMY SEAS WITH NO FISH ON BOARD, BUT WITH A GALLEY FILLED WITH TOMATOES, HERBS AND OLIVE OIL AND MADE THE BEST OF IT. (I KNOW, I KNOW, THAT ONE'S REACHING!)

INGREDIENTS:

1/3	CUP OLIVE OIL
1	ONION, CHOPPED
2	CLOVES GARLIC, MINCED
4	CUPS FRESH TOMATOES (B/P/C)
	OR, 1 - 28 OUNCE CAN PEAR TOMATOES, BLENDERIZED
1	TABLESPOON PARSLEY, CHOPPED
1/2	TEASPOON DRY BASIL
	OR
1	TABLESPOON FRESH BASIL, CHOPPED
1	TEASPOON SALT (WITH FRESH TOMATOES ONLY)
1/4	TEASPOON FRESHLY GROUND BLACK PEPPER
1/2	TEASPOON DRY OREGANO, OR 1 TSP FRESH
3	TABLESPOONS TOMATO PASTE
	GRATED PARMESAN CHEESE

METHOD: SAUTE GARLIC AND ONIONS IN OLIVE OIL UNTIL LIGHTLY GOLDEN. ADD TOMATOES, PARSLEY, BASIL, SALT AND PEPPER. BRING SAUCE TO A BOIL, REDUCE HEAT TO SIMMER, PARTIALLY COVER AND COOK FOR 30 MINUTES. (20 MINUTES FOR CANNED TOMATOES), ADD TOMATO PASTE AND OREGANO, COOK AN ADDITIONAL 15 MINUTES. POUR SAUCE OVER PASTA, TOSS AND SERVE WITH CHEESE ON THE SIDE.

RECOMMENDED PASTA: STRING AND OVAL TYPES.

MARINARA SAUCE #2

HERE IS OUR SECOND MARINARA OFFERING IN THIS CATEGORY OF MEATLESS TOMATO SAUCES, YOU'LL DISCOVER THERE IS A SLIGHT DIFFERENCE IN INGREDIENTS. HOWEVER, A SMALL CHANGE IN THE INGREDIENTS IS NOT THE TOTAL DIFFERENCE, THERE IS ALSO A DIFFERENCE IN THE METHOD AND THE TIME AT WHICH THE INGREDIENTS ARE ADDED, THAT GIVES YOU A DIFFERENT END PRODUCT. CONFUSED BY THE PROLIFERATION OF MARINARA RECIPES? WELL SO AM I. YOU'LL ALSO FIND A MARINARA IN TOMATOES WITH MEAT SAUCES AND IN SEAFOOD SAUCES. THE ACTUAL DESIGNATION OF MARINARA APPEARS TO BE RELATED TO THE INCLUSION OF THE HERBS, BASIL AND OREGANO, PLUS GARLIC IN A TOMATO BASE. BEYOND THAT I CAN'T FIND A COMMON TREAD.

INGREDIENTS:

3	TABLESPOONS OLIVE OIL
1	SMALL ONION, CHOPPED
1	CLOVE GARLIC, SLICED
1/2	STALK CELERY, MINCED
1	TABLESPOON FRESH PARSLEY, CHOPPED
1	28 OUNCE CAN ITALIAN STYLE TOMATOES
1/2	CAN TOMATO PASTE (OR, 1 - 8 OUNCE CAN TOMATO SAUCE)
1/2	TEASPOON BASIL, DRIED*
1/2	TEASPOON OREGANO, DRIED*
1	BAY LEAF (IF YOU DON'T LIKE IT, DON'T USE IT)

METHOD: SAUTE ONION, GARLIC, CELERY AND PARSLEY IN THE OLIVE OIL UNTIL ONION IS TRANSPARENT. ADD THE BLENDERIZED TOMATOES, TOMATO PASTE. BRING SAUCE TO A BOIL, REDUCE HEAT AND SIMMER PARTIALLY COVERED FOR 30 MINUTES. ADD DRIED BASIL AND DRIED OREGANO DURING LAST 10 MINUTES OF COOKING. POUR SAUCE OVER PASTA, TOSS AND SERVE.

*IF YOU USE FRESH BASIL, OR OREGANO, ADD THEM AFTER YOU HAVE REMOVED THE SAUCE FROM HEAT AND BEFORE YOU PLACE THE SAUCE ON YOUR PASTA. (USE 1 TABLESPOON EACH OF ANY FRESH HERB).

RECOMMENDED PASTA: ANY SHAPE YOU LIKE.

MEDITERRANEAN TOMATO SAUCE

(ANOTHER QUICKIE)

THIS SAUCE IS IN GENERAL USE ALONG THE WEST COAST BETWEEN THE APENNINES AND THE TYRRHENIAN SEA. THE ANCHOVIES WILL DISSOLVE IN THE COOKING PROCESS, THEY THEREFORE ARE REALLY A SEASONING AGENT. THIS SAUCE WILL REQUIRE HIGH HEAT AND CONSTANT MONITORING, SO, DON'T PUT THIS ONE ON AND WALK AWAY FROM THE STOVE.

INGREDIENTS:

1 1/2	POUNDS FRESH TOMATOES (ABOUT 4 LARGE) B/P/C AND WELL DRAINED
12	PITTED GREEN OLIVES (SLICED)
4 TO 6	FLAT ANCHOVIES (MASHED)
2	CLOVES GARLIC (YOUR CHOICE)
1/4	CUP OLIVE OIL
1/2	CUP CHOPPED FRESH PARSLEY
1	TABLESPOON DRAINED CAPERS
2	TEASPOONS OF CHOPPED FRESH BASIL (IF DRIED USE 1/2 TEASPOON)
1/2	TEASPOON DRIED OREGANO
1/2	TEASPOON SALT
1/4	TEASPOON DRIED HOT PEPPER FLAKES

METHOD: PREPARE THE ABOVE INGREDIENTS AND SET ASIDE. START THE SAUCE AFTER YOUR PASTA IS AT A ROLLING BOIL.

HEAT THE OIL, ADD GARLIC AND SAUTE FOR 1 MINUTE. ADD TOMATOES, PARSLEY, CAPERS, BASIL, OREGANO, SALT, PEPPER FLAKES, OLIVES AND ANCHOVIES. BRING THE SAUCE TO A BOIL UNTIL VISIBLE LIQUID HAS BEEN EVAPORATED AND SAUCE IS SLIGHTLY THICKENED. POUR OVER DRAINED PASTA, TOSS AND SERVE.

RECOMMENDED PASTA: STRING TYPES.

WE TRIED THIS SAUCE . . . AND

LOVED IT ( )
HATED IT ( )
MAYBE WE'LL TRY IT AGAIN ( )
WE'LL USE IT FOR UNWELCOME GUESTS ( )

WHORES SAUCE

(PUTTANESCA)

WITH IRREVERENT TONGUE IN CHEEK, SINNERS GET TOP BILLING IN ITALY, AT LEAST IN CAMPANIA. THERE IS OBVIOUSLY SOME REASONING BEHIND THIS SAUCES NAME, BUT I DON'T KNOW WHAT IT IS. I HAVE READ THAT HOOKERS IN NAPLES HAD A FONDNESS FOR THIS PARTICULAR SAUCE, AND THAT IT WAS OFFERED AT THEIR FAVORITE TRATTORIA'S IN THE RED LIGHT DISTRICTS. IF YOU DON'T BUY THAT, HOW ABOUT THIS ONE, MAYBE BECAUSE IT COULD BE MADE BETWEEN TRICKS ON A SLOW DAY.

INGREDIENTS:

1/4	CUP OLIVE OIL
1	ONION, CHOPPED
1	CLOVE GARLIC, SLICED
1/2	TEASPOON CRUSHED RED PEPPER
1	28 OUNCE CAN PEAR TOMATOES, BLENDERIZED
1	8 OUNCE CAN TOMATO SAUCE
1/3	CUP RIPE OLIVES, GREEN OR BLACK, SLICED OR SLIVERED
1	TABLESPOON CAPERS
1/2	TEASPOON OREGANO
2	OUNCES ANCHOVIES, CHOPPED
1/4	CUP FRESH PARSLEY, CHOPPED

METHOD: SAUTE ONION, GARLIC AND CRUSHED RED PEPPER IN OLIVE OIL UNTIL ONION IS TRANSPARENT. ADD TOMATOES, TOMATO SAUCE, OLIVES, CAPERS AND OREGANO. BRING TO A BOIL, LOOSELY COVER AND COOK ON LOW HEAT FOR 20 MINUTES. ADD PARSLEY AND ANCHOVIES, REMOVE FROM HEAT. POUR SAUCE OVER DRAINED PASTA, TOSS AND SERVE.

IF YOU WISH FOR A LITTLE ADDED ZIP, YOU MAY SUBSTITUTE 1 LONG GREEN MILDLY HOT PEPPER FOR THE ONION.

RECOMMENDED PASTA: THIN STRING TYPES.

BEER AND ANCHOVY SAUCE

YOU AND I BOTH KNOW THAT WINE IS THE NATIONAL BEVERAGE IN ITALY, BUT THEY ARE ALSO GREAT BEER PRODUCERS AND BEER CONSUMERS, AT LEAST IN THE NORTH, AND LIKE COOKS IN COUNTRIES THE WORLD OVER, THEY ENJOY THEIR OCCASIONAL RECIPES USING BEER. THERE ARE INDICATIONS THAT THIS SAUCE ORIGINATED IN THE CENTRAL REGION OF UMBRIA. BUT, THEN AGAIN IT COULD ALSO HAVE COME FROM ANY OF THE SEVEN REGIONS COMPRISING ITALY'S NORTHERN BORDER.

INGREDIENTS:

4	TABLESPOONS OLIVE OIL
1	CLOVE GARLIC, LIGHTLY CRUSHED
1	YELLOW BELL PEPPER, SEEDED AND DICED
1/4	CUP CHOPPED PARSLEY
6	OLIVES, YOUR CHOICE, HALVED
PINCH	DRY MARJORAM
4	ANCHOVY FILLETS, MASHED
1	POUND FRESH PEAR TOMATOES (B/P/C) DRAINED
1/2	CUP BEER
	FRESHLY GRATED PARMESAN CHEESE

METHOD: SAUTE THE GARLIC, BELL PEPPER, PARSLEY, OLIVES, MARJORAM AND ANCHOVIES IN THE OLIVE OIL FOR 3 MINUTES. ADD THE TOMATO, COOK FOR 5 ADDITIONAL MINUTES, ADD THE BEER, COVER AND SIMMER SAUCE FOR 10 MINUTES. POUR SAUCE OVER PASTA, TOSS AND SERVE WITH GRATED CHEESE ON THE SIDE.

RECOMMENDED PASTA: STRINGS.

FRESH TOMATO AND BASIL SAUCE

THE AMOUNT OF FRESH BASIL IN THIS SAUCE WILL CAPTURE YOUR IMAGINATION. THERE IS A LOVELY QUALITY ABOUT BASIL THAT SPRINGS FORTH FROM A PLATE WHEN ADDED AS IT IS IN THIS SAUCE; AFTER THE SAUCE IS DONE, AND JUST BEFORE SERVING.

INGREDIENTS:

3	TABLESPOONS OLIVE OIL
1	ONION, CHOPPED
1	CLOVE GARLIC, SLICED
2	POUNDS FRESH ITALIAN TYPE TOMATOES (B/P/C)
1/4	CUP FRESH PARSLEY, CHOPPED
1	TEASPOON SALT
1	CUP FRESH BASIL LEAVES, CHOPPED

METHOD: SAUTE IN THE OLIVE OIL, GARLIC AND ONIONS. ADD TOMATOES, PARSLEY AND 1/2 THE BASIL. BRING SAUCE TO A BOIL, REDUCE HEAT TO LOW AND COOK PARTIALLY COVERED FOR 30 MINUTES OR UNTIL SOMEWHAT THICKENED, REMOVE FROM HEAT. ADD THE REMAINING BASIL LEAVES. POUR SAUCE OVER PASTA, TOSS AND SERVE.

RECOMMENDED PASTA: STRING, RIBBON OR MEDIUM TUBE TYPES.

FRESH TOMATO AND BASIL SAUCE TOO!

ITALIANS SEEM TO BE DIVIDED IN THEIR LIKES OF HAVING TOMATO SAUCES SMOOTH RATHER THAN CHUNKY. THIS IS ONE OF THE SMOOTH VERSIONS, AND IT'S A GOOD ONE.

INGREDIENTS:

3	TABLESPOONS OLIVE OIL
3	TABLESPOONS BUTTER
1/2	CUP FRESH BASIL, TORN IN HALVES
1 1/2	POUNDS FRESH TOMATOES
1	TABLESPOON ONION, FINELY CHOPPED
1/2	TEASPOON SALT
PINCH	FRESHLY GRATED BLACK PEPPER
	GRATED PARMESAN CHEESE

METHOD: SLICE OR DICE THE TOMATOES, SET ASIDE. SAUTE ONION IN OLIVE OIL AND BUTTER UNTIL TRANSPARENT. ADD TOMATOES, SALT AND PEPPER. COOK AT MEDIUM HIGH HEAT FOR ABOUT 30 MINUTES. STRAIN THE COOKED TOMATOES THROUGH A SIEVE OR COLANDER. REHEAT THE SAUCE TO A BOIL. NOW, POUR SAUCE OVER YOUR PASTA AND TOSS. ADD THE FRESH BASIL AND CHEESE, TOSS AGAIN AND SERVE.

RECOMMENDED PASTA: HOLLOW STRING TYPES.

THE POLICEMAN'S SAUCE

WHY NOT? THERE ARE SAUCES NAMED FOR A DOZEN OR MORE OCCUPATIONS, FROM CART DRIVERS TO HOOKERS TO SEAMEN AND SHEPHERDS. IT WOULDN'T SURPRISE ME TO COME ACROSS SAUCES HONORING BUTCHERS, BAKERS AND CANDLESTICK MAKERS. IN THIS CASE IT IS NAMED AFTER THE LOCAL GENDARMES, OR AS THEY SAY IN ITALY, ALLA CARABINIERE. THERE IS ONE INTERESTING TOUCH TO THIS SAUCE, AND THAT IS THE HANDLING OF A PART OF THE HERBS GENERALLY DISCARDED. HERE YOU'LL USE IT AS A FLAVORING BEFORE DISCARDING.

INGREDIENTS:

12	STEMS STRIPED OF THEIR LEAVES. SIX OR MORE STEMS FROM BASIL, SIX OR FEWER STEMS FROM PARSLEY. CRUSH THE STEMS, TIE THEM TOGETHER.
4	TABLESPOONS OLIVE OIL
3	ONIONS, CHOPPED
6	TOMATOES ((B/P/C)
1	TEASPOON SALT
PINCH	CRUSHED RED PEPPER
4	TABLESPOONS BUTTER
3	TABLESPOONS CHOPPED FRESH BASIL LEAF
	FRESHLY GRATED ASIAGO CHEESE

METHOD: SAUCE THE ONIONS IN OLIVE OIL UNTIL JUST BEGINNING TO COLOR, ADD TOMATOES, SALT, CRUSHED PEPPER AND THE TIED STEMS. BRING SAUCE TO A BOIL, LOWER HEAT ENOUGH TO KEEP SAUCE A AT LOW BOIL UNTIL WATER HAS EVAPORATED OR FOR 15 MINUTES. REMOVE AND DISCARD STEMS. ADD BUTTER AND COOK FOR 2 ADDITIONAL MINUTES. POUR SAUCE OVER PASTA, TOSS AND SERVE WITH THE FRESH CHOPPED BASIL AND CHEESE ON THE SIDE.

RECOMMENDED PASTA: MEDIUM TUBES, DIAGONAL CUT.

VESUVIUS STYLE SAUCE

THIS SAUCE APPEARS TO BE ONE OF THE VERY FEW, IF NOT THE ONLY SAUCE RECIPE THAT DOES NOT CALL FOR PEELED TOMATOES. IT DOES USE TOMATOES, JUST UNPEELED. TOMATO SKINS ARE TART TO BITTER AND WILL INFLUENCE YOUR SAUCE, SO TASTE BEFORE SERVING AND CORRECT TO YOUR TASTE BY ADDING A SMALL AMOUNT OF SYRUP, SUGAR OR HONEY.

INGREDIENTS:

1	POUND PEAR TOMATOES, CHOPPED
1/2	CUP OLIVE OIL
1	TEASPOON FRESH CHOPPED BASIL
1	TEASPOON FRESH OREGANO, CHOPPED
1/2	TEASPOON SALT
1	CUP SHREDDED MOZZARELLA CHEESE
3/4	CUP FRESHLY GRATED PARMESAN CHEESE

METHOD: HEAT OIL, ADD TOMATOES, BASIL, OREGANO AND SALT. BRING TO A BOIL, LOWER HEAT SLIGHTLY, COOK AT A ROLLING FOR 15 MINUTES. ADD COOKED PASTA TO THE SAUCE IN THE SAUCE PAN, TOSS. ADD MOZ-ZARELLA AND PARMESAN AND COOK UNTIL CHEESES MELT. SERVE.

RECOMMENDED PASTA: CURLY TYPES.

OIL FREE TOMATO SAUCE

THIS SAUCE HAS A BENEFIT TO ANY ONE WHO MUST KEEP THEIR CALORIC INTAKE LOW OR AVOID FATS OF ANY KIND, IT HAS NO OIL. IF THAT IS NOT A PROBLEM FOR YOU, ADD 4 TABLESPOONS OF OLIVE OIL OR BUTTER.

INGREDIENTS: 1   28 OUNCE CAN PEAR TOMATOES, BLENDERIZED
2   ONIONS, CHOPPED
1   TEASPOON DRY BASIL

METHOD: PLACE ALL INGREDIENTS INTO A SAUCE PAN. BRING TO A BOIL. REDUCE HEAT, COVER AND SIMMER FOR 20 MINUTES. POUR SAUCE OVER PASTA, TOSS AND SERVE.

RECOMMENDED PASTA: ANY ONE YOU LIKE.

FRESH TOMATOES AND ONION SAUCE

A VERY SIMPLE, FAST AND FLAVORFUL SAUCE. ONIONS AND TOMATOES ARE COMPLIMENTARY TO ONE ANOTHER, AND WITH ONLY LIGHT SEASONING ADDED, NOTHING INTERFERES WITH THE MELDING OF THE SUGAR OF THE ONION AND THE ACID OF THE TOMATOES.

INGREDIENTS: 2 POUNDS FRESH PEAR TOMATOES (B/P/C)
     6   TABLESPOON BUTTER
     2   ONIONS, CHOPPED
     3/4 TEASPOON SALT
     1/4 TEASPOON FRESHLY GROUND BLACK PEPPER
        FRESHLY GRATED PARMESAN CHEESE

METHOD: SAUTE THE ONIONS IN THE BUTTER UNTIL WELL COATED. COVER THE PAN AND SIMMER FOR 6 MINUTES. ADD TOMATOES, SALT AND PEPPER, RAISE HEAT TO HIGH, AND COOK FOR 6 ADDITIONAL MINUTES. MONITOR AND STIR CONSTANTLY. POUR SAUCE OVER PASTA, TOSS AND SERVE WITH GRATED CHEESE ON THE SIDE.

RECOMMENDED PASTA: STRING TYPES.

SIENA STYLE SAUCE

SIENA IS IN TUSCANY, IN CENTRAL ITALY, IT'S A VERY OLD COMMUNITY, AND WAS A MEDIEVAL COMMERCIAL CENTER. THE CITY STARTED OUT AS AN ETRUSCAN SETTLEMENT, THAT MEANS PRE-ROMAN. IT IS ALSO THE HOME OF ONE OF THE PICTORIAL LAND MARKS OF ITALY, THE TOWER OF MANGIA IN SIENA'S PUBLIC SQUARE. I DON'T KNOW WHAT THIS HAS TO DO WITH THE SAUCE RECIPE, BUT IT DOES GIVE YOU A LITTLE BACKGROUND ABOUT SIENA. WHAT MAKES THIS SAUCE A LITTLE DIFFERENT IS IT'S METHOD OF PREPARATION.

INGREDIENTS:

2	POUNDS PEAR TOMATOES (B/P/C) AND DRAINED
	OR
1	28 OUNCE CAN, CHOPPED AND DRAINED
2	TABLESPOONS CHOPPED CARROTS
2	TABLESPOONS CHOPPED CELERY
3	TABLESPOONS CHOPPED ONION
1	TABLESPOON CHOPPED BASIL
2/3	TEASPOON SALT (ONLY WITH FRESH TOMATOES)
PINCH	FRESHLY GRATED BLACK PEPPER
1/2	CUP OLIVE OIL
3	TABLESPOONS CHOPPED ONION
1/2	CUP GRATED PARMESAN CHEESE

METHOD: PLACE TOMATOES, CARROTS, CELERY, ONION, BASIL, SALT, AND PEPPER INTO A SAUCE PAN. BRING TO A BOIL, REDUCE HEAT AND SIMMER FOR 30 MINUTES. AT THIS POINT YOU MAY SIEVE THE SAUCE OR BLENDERIZE IT TO GET A SMOOTH SAUCE. SAUTE THE SECOND PORTION OF ONION (3 TABLESPOONS) IN THE OLIVE OIL UNTIL THE ONION IS TRANSPARENT. ADD THE TOMATO SAUCE, BLEND WELL, REMOVE FROM HEAT. POUR SAUCE OVER PASTA, TOSS, ADD THE CHEESE, TOSS AGAIN, SERVE.

RECOMMENDED PASTA: STRING OR RIBBON TYPES.

TOMATOES AND BALSAMIC VINEGAR SAUCE

DURING THIS DECADE, BALSAMIC VINEGAR HAS BEEN ONE OF THE NEWER FLAVORINGS AVAILABLE TO AMERICAN COOKS. FOR THAT MATTER, A WHOLE CATEGORY OF FLAVORED VINEGARS AND OILS HAVE ARRIVED ON SCENE. BALSAMIC VINEGAR IS A CENTURIES OLD VINEGAR OF MODENA, ITALY. IT IS ALWAYS AGED AND AS A RESULT IS VERY CONCENTRATED, THEREFORE YOU ONLY NEED SMALL AMOUNTS TO DO THE JOB. DEPENDING UPON THE AGE OF YOUR VINEGAR, YOU'LL USE A COUPLE TEASPOONS TO A FEW DROPS. BALSAMIC IS GENERALLY AVAILABLE FROM ABOUT THREE YEARS OF AGE, UP TO, AND OVER ONE HUNDRED YEARS OF AGE, AND PRICED ACCORDINGLY. INTERESTINGLY, FEW ITALIANS OUTSIDE OF MODENA WERE AWARE OF BALSAMIC VINEGAR. IT'S MARKETABILITY IN ITALY DEVELOPED ONLY AFTER THE VINEGAR BECAME POPULAR IN AMERICA. THIS IS A CLASSIC EXAMPLE OF A PRODUCT NOW WIDELY ACCEPTED, BOTH IN AMERICA AND ITALY, THAT ONLY A FEW YEARS AGO WAS UNKNOWN MORE THAN FIFTY MILES AWAY FROM THE COMMUNITY THAT CREATED IT. ONCE AGAIN WE SEE THE FORCES AT WORK THAT ALLOW THE SAME SAUCE TO BE CREATED IN A DOZEN DIFFERENT LOCALS, EACH WITH A DIFFERENT NAME AND USING IDENTICAL OR NEAR IDENTICAL INGREDIENTS.

INGREDIENTS:

1/2	CUP OLIVE OIL
3	CLOVE GARLIC, MINCED OR THINLY SLICED
2 1/2	TEASPOONS DRY ROSEMARY, CRUSHED
	OR, 1/2 THAT AMOUNT IF USING FRESH LEAVES
1	16 OUNCE CAN PEAR TOMATOES, CHOPPED AND DRAINED
2	TEASPOONS BALSAMIC VINEGAR

METHOD: SAUTE YOUR GARLIC IN THE OLIVE OIL UNTIL LIGHTLY GOLDEN. ADD THE TOMATOES AND DRY ROSEMARY, COOK FOR ABOUT 12 MINUTES, REMOVE FROM HEAT, POUR SAUCE OVER THE PASTA, TOSS. *SPRINKLE THE VINEGAR OVER THE SAUCED PASTA, TOSS AGAIN, SERVE. (IF YOU CHOOSE TO USE FRESH ROSEMARY, SAUTE IT ALONG WITH THE GARLIC.)

*YOU MAY CHOOSE TO SPRINKLE THE VINEGAR OVER THE DRAINED PASTA AND TOSS BEFORE ADDING THE SAUCE.   THERE WILL BE A TASTE DIFFERENCE.

RECOMMENDED PASTA: MEDIUM DIAGONAL CUT TUBE TYPES.

TOMATOES AND WINE VINEGAR SAUCE

AS PASTA SAUCES GO, THERE ARE A NUMBER THAT REQUIRE THE ADDITION OF WINE VINEGAR. VINEGARS ARE SUBJECT TO THE SAME TASTE VARIATION AS THE WINES THEY'RE PREPARED FROM, SO, MAKE SURE YOU LIKE THE TASTE OF YOUR VINEGAR BEFORE USING THIS RECIPE.

INGREDIENTS:

1/3	CUP OLIVE OIL
1	CUP PEAR TOMATOES (B/P/C)
1/2	CUP CHOPPED MUSHROOMS
2	TABLESPOONS CHOPPED PARSLEY
1	TEASPOON MINCED CAPERS
	SALT AND PEPPER TO TASTE
1/4	SCANT CUP WINE VINEGAR

METHOD: PLACE ALL INGREDIENTS EXCEPT VINEGAR IN A SAUCE PAN. BRING SAUCE TO A BOIL, REDUCE HEAT TO SIMMER FOR 8 MINUTES. ADD VINEGAR, COOK 2 ADDITIONAL MINUTES. POUR SAUCE OVER PASTA, TOSS AND SERVE.

RECOMMENDED PASTA: STRINGS OR CURLY TYPES.

POMMAROLA SAUCE

THIS SAUCE IS OCCASIONALLY REFERRED TO AS A "TRADITIONAL SAUCE", OR BASIC SAUCE.   I DON'T KNOW WHO'S TRADITION THEY MEAN, NEAPOLITAN? SICILIAN? CALABRIAN? OR JUST SOUTHERN?

INGREDIENTS:

2	TABLESPOONS OLIVE OIL
1	SMALL ONION, CHOPPED
1	16 OUNCE CAN PEAR TOMATOES, BLENDERIZED
3	TABLESPOONS TOMATO PASTE
1	TABLESPOON CHOPPED BASIL
	OR
1	TEASPOON DRY BASIL
1/2	TEASPOON FRESHLY GROUND BLACK PEPPER

METHOD: SAUTE ONION IN OLIVE OIL UNTIL TRANSPARENT.   ADD ALL REMAINING INGREDIENTS.   BRING SAUCE TO A BOIL, REDUCE HEAT AND SIMMER FOR 40 MINUTES. POUR SAUCE OVER PASTA, TOSS AND SERVE.

IF YOU WANT A VERY SMOOTH SAUCE, PRESS SAUCE THROUGH A SIEVE OR RUN IN A BLENDER FOR A MINUTE OR TWO.

RECOMMENDED PASTA: STRING TYPES.

POMMAROLA SAUCE TOO!

THIS SAUCE TOO, IS A BASIC SAUCE, IT OFFERS A VARIATION OF THE INGREDIENTS THAT CHARACTERIZE THE PRECEDING SAUCE, IT DROPS THE ONION, BUT INCREASES THE AMOUNT OF TOMATOES, AND THAT WILL GIVE YOU A LIGHTER, MORE DELICATELY FLAVORED SAUCE, AND A LITTLE LESS SWEET.

INGREDIENTS:

2 1/2	28 OUNCE CANS OF PEAR TOMATOES
	OR, 3 POUNDS FRESH PEAR TOMATOES (B/P/C)
2	TABLESPOONS OLIVE OIL
1	CLOVE GARLIC, CRUSHED
1	TABLESPOON DRY BASIL
1/2	TEASPOON FRESHLY GROUND BLACK PEPPER
1	TEASPOON SALT (ONLY W/FRESH TOMATOES)

METHOD: SAUTE GARLIC IN OLIVE OIL UNTIL LIGHTLY GOLDEN. REMOVE AND DISCARD GARLIC. ADD TOMATOES, BASIL, PEPPER (AND SALT). BRING SAUCE TO A BOIL, LOOSELY COVER, REDUCE HEAT, AND SIMMER FOR 30 MINUTES. LADLE SOME OF THE SAUCE OVER YOUR PASTA, TOSS AND SERVE.

REFRIGERATE OR FREEZE REMAINING SAUCE FOR ANOTHER DAY.

RECOMMENDED PASTA: ANY SHAPE YOU LIKE.

FILLET OF TOMATO SAUCE

(YOU REALLY SHOULD USE FRESH TOMATOES FOR THIS SAUCE)

FILLETED TOMATO SAUCE MEANS THAT THE TOMATOES ARE QUARTERED, DRAINED OF THEIR JUICES AND THEN COOKED QUICKLY. THAT WILL GIVE YOU A LIGHT TOMATO SAUCE WITH FILLETS OF TOMATO. DEPENDING UPON THE TASTE YOU WANT, USE PANCETTA FAT, OR PROSCIUTTO FAT, RENDERED. IF NEITHER ONE IS AVAILABLE, YOU MAY USE ANY HAM FAT, SALT PORK OR BACON OIL. IF YOU CHOOSE TO YOU MAY OMIT THE RENDERED FAT AND BUTTER, AND GO WITH THE OLIVE OIL.

INGREDIENTS:

1/4	CUP FAT RENDERED, DISCARD SOLIDS.
2	TABLESPOONS OLIVE OIL
1	TABLESPOON BUTTER
2	ONIONS, CHOPPED
1	TABLESPOON CHOPPED FRESH BASIL OR, 1 TEASPOON DRIED
2	POUNDS FRESH TOMATOES, BLANCHED, PEELED, QUARTERED AND DRAINED, OR;
1	28 OUNCE CAN PEAR TOMATOES, QUARTERED AND DRAINED.
1/2	TEASPOON SALT
1/4	TEASPOON FRESHLY GROUND BLACK PEPPER

METHOD: WHEN THE OILS ARE READY, SAUTE ONIONS AND BASIL FOR 5 MINUTES, ADD TOMATOES, SALT AND PEPPER. BRING SAUCE TO A BOIL, LOWER HEAT TO MEDIUM, COOK FOR 10 TO 15 MINUTES. POUR SAUCE OVER PASTA, TOSS AND SERVE.

RECOMMENDED PASTA: NARROW RIBBONS OR STRINGS.

GREEN TOMATO SAUCE

WE MAY BE PLAYING FAST AND LOOSE WITH THE WORD SAUCE HERE, YOU'LL REALLY BE SERVING FLOURED AND FRIED TOMATOES IN WITH THE PASTA. SO, IF YOU CAN'T WAIT FOR YOUR TOMATOES TO RIPEN IN THE SPRING, OR IF YOU WANT TO MAKE GOOD USE OF THE FEW UNRIPENED TOMATOES LEFT ON THE VINE IN THE FALL, THIS SAUCE IS FOR YOU.

INGREDIENTS:
1	CUP FLOUR
1	TABLESPOON SALT
6	GREEN TOMATOES (SLIGHTLY YELLOWING IF POSSIBLE)
6	TABLESPOONS OLIVE OIL
	BLACK PEPPER TO TASTE
2	TABLESPOONS BUTTER

METHOD: BLEND FLOUR AND SALT, SET ASIDE. SLICE THE TOMATOES INTO 1/2" INCH SLICES. DIP OR SHAKE TOMATO SLICES IN SEASONED FLOUR. FRY TOMATO SLICES IN OLIVE OIL UNTIL BROWNED AND CRISP. DRAIN PASTA, TOSS WITH BUTTER AND A LITTLE FRESHLY GROUND BLACK PEPPER, CHOP THE FRIED TOMATOES, ADD TO AND TOSS WITH THE BUTTERED PASTA, SERVE.

OR, ARRANGE TOMATO SLICES OVER THE PASTA, SERVE, AND ALLOW THE DINER TO CUT HIS OWN.

RECOMMENDED PASTA: CURLY STRINGS.

TOMATO AND BRANDY SAUCE

AS WITH ANY SAUCE THAT HAS AN ALCOHOL ADDED, MAKE SURE YOU REALLY LIKE THE TASTE OF WHATEVER YOU ADD. ALCOHOL IS GENERALLY ADDED DURING THE LAST MOMENT OR TWO TO GIVE A PERVASIVE FLAVOR AND BOUQUET TO THE SAUCE. IN MOST CASES THAT'S BARELY ENOUGH TIME TO EVAPORATE THE ALCOHOL, SO THE FULL FLAVOR COMES THROUGH. IF YOU HAVE COGNAC IN YOUR LIQUOR CABINET, USE THAT.

INGREDIENTS:

1	ONION, CHOPPED
1	CLOVE GARLIC, CRUSHED
3	TABLESPOONS OLIVE OIL
3	TABLESPOONS BUTTER
1	8 OUNCE CAN TOMATO SAUCE
1/3	CUP BRANDY
2	CUPS WHIPPING CREAM (ROOM TEMPERATURE OR WARMED)
PINCH	GROUND NUTMEG

METHOD: SAUTE THE ONION AND GARLIC IN THE OLIVE OIL/BUTTER FOR 3 MINUTES. ADD THE TOMATO SAUCE, COVER AND SIMMER FOR 15 MINUTES. REMOVE AND DISCARD THE GARLIC, ADD BRANDY, CONTINUE TO SIMMER FOR 3 MINUTES. REMOVE SAUCE FROM HEAT. TOSS YOUR HOT DRAINED PASTA WITH THE WHIPPING CREAM AND NUTMEG. ADD THE TOMATO SAUCE, TOSS AGAIN, SERVE.

RECOMMENDED PASTA: STRING TYPES.

ONION AND TOMATO SAUCE

THIS SAUCE HAS AN UNUSUAL BLENDING OF FLAVORS. IT IS EITHER AN INTERESTING PRODUCT OF "MAKE DO" OR CREATIVE EFFORT. IT ALSO COULD BE A CASE OF SOMEONE WANTING A VERY SWEET AND MILD SAUCE FOR THEIR PASTA.

INGREDIENTS:

1/4	CUP OLIVE OIL
3	SWEET ONIONS, WEDGED TOP TO BOTTOM, OR CHOPPED
1/4	CUP MILK
1/2	TEASPOON SALT
4	PEAR TOMATOES PEELED AND PUREED, OR
1	8 OUNCE CAN TOMATO SAUCE
2	TABLESPOONS CHOPPED PARSLEY
	GRATED PARMESAN CHEESE

METHOD: SAUTE ONIONS IN OIL UNTIL THEY ARE TRANSPARENT, ADD THE MILK, CONTINUE COOKING FOR 5 MINUTES. ADD TOMATOES AND PARSLEY, COVER AND SIMMER FOR 15 MINUTES. POUR SAUCE OVER PASTA. TOSS AND SERVE WITH GRATED CHEESE ON THE SIDE.

RECOMMENDED PASTA: CURLY STRING TYPES.

WE TRIED THIS SAUCE . . . AND

LOVED IT ( )
HATED IT ( )
MAYBE WE'LL TRY IT AGAIN ( )
WE'LL USE IT FOR UNWELCOME GUESTS ( )

TOMATO SAUCE #1

SIMPLE WITH A SHORT COOKING TIME THIS NEAPOLITAN SAUCE MAY JUST BECOME ONE OF YOUR FAVORITES. WHILE IT'S NICE TO HAVE A WIDE SELECTION OF SAUCES TO CHOOSE FROM, WE ALL TEND TO FALL BACK ON A SIMPLE ONE THAT'S EASY AND QUICK AND USES ONLY A FEW INGREDIENTS. THIS IS ONE OF THEM, BUT ONLY WITH FRESH TOMATOES. IF YOU CHOOSE TO USE CANNED, REDUCE THE OREGANO TO 1/4 TEASPOON OR LESS.

INGREDIENTS:

10	PEAR TOMATOES (B/P/C)
3	TABLESPOONS BUTTER
3	TABLESPOONS OLIVE OIL
1/2	TEASPOON DRY OREGANO
1	TABLESPOON PARSLEY, CHOPPED
1	SCANT TEASPOON SALT

METHOD: PLACE ALL INGREDIENTS INTO A SAUCE PAN. BRING SAUCE TO A BOIL, REDUCE HEAT TO LOW, COOK PARTIALLY COVERED FOR 20 MINUTES. REMOVE SAUCE FROM HEAT. POUR SAUCE OVER PASTA, TOSS AND SERVE.

RECOMMENDED PASTA: RIBBON TYPES.

TOMATO SAUCE #2

(LONG AND LOW)

SIMPLE AND UNCOMPLICATED, IT JUST TAKES FOREVER TO COOK AND I DON'T KNOW WHY. SOMETIMES STRANGE THINGS HAPPEN TO TOMATOES WHEN COOKED FOR A VERY LONG TIME, BUT THERE ARE THOSE WHO SUPPORT LONG, SLOW COOKING OF A SAUCE AS THE ONLY VALID WAY TO DO IT. IF YOU HAVE THE TIME, TRY IT! IT MAY HAVE THERAPEUTIC VALUE TO THE COOK TO HAVE A SIMMERING SAUCE ON WHILE YOU PUTTER AROUND WITH OTHER CHORES. TRY THIS ONE ON A BLUSTERY OR RAINY DAY.

INGREDIENTS:

4	POUNDS TOMATOES (B/P/C)
1/4	CUP OLIVE OIL
1	ONION, CHOPPED (SWEETER THE BETTER)
3	CLOVES GARLIC, MINCED
1/3	CUP TOMATO PASTE
1	TEASPOON DRY OREGANO (FRESH IF YOU HAVE IT)
1	CUP WATER
1	CUP WINE
1	TEASPOON SALT
1/4	TEASPOON FRESHLY GROUND BLACK PEPPER

METHOD: PREPARE TOMATOES, SET ASIDE. SAUTE ONION AND GARLIC IN OLIVE OIL UNTIL ONION IS TRANSPARENT. ADD ALL REMAINING INGREDIENTS. BRING SAUCE TO A BOIL, REDUCE HEAT, COVER AND SIMMER FOR ABOUT 3 TO 4 HOURS. POUR SAUCE OVER PASTA, TOSS AND SERVE.

RECOMMENDED PASTA: MEDIUM TUBE TYPES, STRAIGHT EDGED OR DIAGONAL CUT.

TOMATO SAUCE #3

THIS SAUCE IS A TOMATO SAUCE WITH A BLENDING OF CHEESES, A LITTLE LIKE THE MIXTURE FOR A LASAGNA, BUT USE IT OVER MEDIUM TUBE TYPES. IF YOU'RE, LIKE GARFIELD THE CAT, CRAVE LASAGNA, YOU'LL PROBABLY LOVE THIS ONE.

INGREDIENTS:

2	TABLESPOONS OLIVE OIL
1	CLOVE GARLIC, MINCED
1	TABLESPOON CHOPPED ONION
1	TABLESPOON SHREDDED CARROT
1	16 OUNCE CAN PEAR TOMATOES, BLENDERIZED
1	CUP RICOTTA CHEESE
2	TABLESPOONS FRESH BASIL, CHOPPED
1/4	CUP GRATED PECORINO OR PARMESAN CHEESE

METHOD: SAUTE GARLIC, ONION AND CARROT IN OLIVE OIL UNTIL OIL IS ORANGE COLORED. ADD TOMATOES. BRING SAUCE TO A BOIL, PARTIALLY COVER, REDUCE HEAT TO SIMMER AND COOK FOR 25 MINUTES. REMOVE FROM HEAT. ADD RICOTTA AND BASIL. POUR SAUCE OVER PASTA, MIX WELL AND SERVE WITH GRATED CHEESE ON THE SIDE.

RECOMMENDED PASTA: MEDIUM TUBE TYPES.

TOMATO SAUCE #4

(THIS SAUCE COMES WITH COMPLETE INSTRUCTIONS ON HOW TO ROAST PEPPERS)

THIS SAUCE REQUIRES ROASTED PEPPERS. YOU CAN BUY THEM, GENERALLY IN SMALL BOTTLES, IF YOU DON'T WANT TO MAKE THEM. IF YOU'D LIKE TO TRY YOUR HAND AT MAKING THEM, READ ON. THIS IS A NEAPOLITAN STYLE SAUCE AND IT TAKES ON A PLEASANT SWEETNESS FROM THE SKINNED PEPPERS. THERE ARE HISTORIC REFERENCES THAT SUGGEST THIS SAUCE ORIGINATED IN PUGLIA, THAT PUTS IN IN THE SOUTHEASTERN ITALY, MORE SPECIFICALLY, BETWEEN THE APENNINES AND THE ADRIATIC SEA.

INGREDIENTS:

3	GREEN OR RED BELL PEPPERS*, OR LONG MILDLY HOT ONES
2	TABLESPOONS OLIVE OIL
1	CLOVE GARLIC
4	PEAR TOMATOES (B/P/C)
PINCH	CRUSHED RED PEPPER
1/3	TEASPOON SALT
2	TABLESPOONS FRESH BASIL, CHOPPED

METHOD: IF YOU WISH TO TRY SKINNING THE PEPPERS, THERE ARE SEVERAL METHODS YOU MAY USE, THEY WILL ALL SUBSTANTIALLY BLACKEN THE SKIN AND PREPARE THE PEPPER FOR THE NEXT STEP.

1. PLACE THEM UNDER A BROILER, MONITOR AND TURN UNTIL BLACKENED.

2. PLACE PEPPERS INTO A PREHEATED 450 DEGREE OVEN UNTIL BLACKENED, ABOUT 10 TO 15 MINUTES.

3. ON AN ELECTRIC STOVE, ROLL THEM OVER AND OVER ON THE A RED HOT ELEMENT UNTIL BLACKENED.

226

4.   DITTO FOR A GAS STOVE.

ONCE THE SKIN HAS BEEN BLACKENED ON ALL SIDES, PEEL THEM UNDER COLD RUNNING WATER. SLICE THE PEPPER INTO THIN STRIPS.

SAUTE THE GARLIC IN THE OLIVE OIL UNTIL GOLDEN. REMOVE AND DISCARD. ADD TOMATOES, PEPPER STRIPS, CRUSHED PEPPER AND SALT. BRING SAUCE TO A BOIL, REDUCE HEAT AND SIMMER FOR 25 MINUTES. REMOVE FROM HEAT, ADD BASIL, POUR SAUCE OVER PASTA, BLEND AND SERVE.

RECOMMENDED PASTA: MEDIUM TUBE TYPES.

*   SINCE WE'VE ADDRESSED THE METHOD OF SKINNING PEPPERS, LET ME PROPOSE THAT YOU CONSIDER SERVING SKINNED PEPPERS AS A VEGETABLE (A SOUTHERN FAVORITE) OR AS PART OF AN ANTIPASTO. YOU MAY EXTEND THE COOKING TIME BY PLACING THE HOT AND BLACKENED PEPPERS INTO A PLASTIC BAG, SEAL IT AND LET THE PEPPERS COOK FROM THEIR OWN HEAT FOR ABOUT 20 MINUTES. NOW PEEL THEM (UNDER COLD WATER IF YOU WISH), PLACE IN A SERVING DISH, SPRINKLE WITH OLIVE OIL, SEASON WITH SALT AND POSSIBLY A LITTLE BLACK PEPPER OR A FEW DROPS OF BALSAMIC VINEGAR.

WE TRIED THIS SAUCE . . . AND

LOVED IT ( )
HATED IT ( )
MAYBE WE'LL TRY IT AGAIN ( )
WE'LL USE IT FOR UNWELCOME GUESTS ( )

TOMATO SAUCE #5

THIS SAUCE COOKS QUICKLY. THAT HAPPENS BECAUSE YOU'LL BE COOKING OVER A MEDIUM HIGH FLAME AND IT WILL THICKEN YOUR SAUCE IN ABOUT 15 MINUTES. ITALIAN CHEF'S WHEN COOKING OVER A MEDIUM HIGH TO HIGH FLAME REFER TO THAT PROCESS AS COOKING OVER A "LIVELY FLAME". BEAR IN MIND THAT THE FASTER, HIGHER OR HOTTER A COOKING FLAME, THE GREATER YOUR NEED TO KEEP YOUR HAND UPON THE PAN AND AN EYE ON YOUR SAUCE. DON'T WALK AWAY FROM THE STOVE.

INGREDIENTS:
1/3 CUP OLIVE OIL
2 CLOVES GARLIC, MINCED
3 TABLESPOONS PARSLEY, CHOPPED
1 TABLESPOON FRESH BASIL, CHOPPED
1 16 OUNCE CAN TOMATOES, BLENDERIZED
1/2 TEASPOON FRESHLY GROUND BLACK PEPPER
1/4 CUP FRESHLY GRATED PECORINO OR PARMESAN CHEESE

METHOD: SAUTE GARLIC, PARSLEY AND BASIL FOR 3 MINUTES. ADD TOMATOES AND BLACK PEPPER. BRING TO A BOIL, REDUCE HEAT TO MEDIUM HIGH, COOK FOR 15 MINUTES. REMOVE SAUCE FROM HEAT, POUR OVER PASTA, TOSS AND SERVE.

RECOMMENDED PASTA: STRING TYPES.

TOMATO SAUCE #6

(HERE YOU'RE OFFERED TWO RECIPES IN ONE!)

A GREAT DEAL OF MINT MUST GROW ON THE ADRIATIC SIDE OF THE APENNINES, THE SAUCE RECIPES FROM THAT REGION (ESPECIALLY ABRUZZO-MOLISE) CALL FOR MINT ON A REGULAR BASIS.

INGREDIENTS:

1/2	CUP OLIVE OIL
1	CLOVE GARLIC MINCED
1	TABLESPOON FRESH BASIL, CHOPPED
1	TEASPOON FRESH MINT, CHOPPED
2	TABLESPOONS PARSLEY, CHOPPED
1	16 OUNCE CAN PEAR TOMATOES, BLENDERIZED
1/4	TEASPOON FRESHLY GROUND BLACK PEPPER
1/4	LONG GREEN MILDLY HOT PEPPER, MINCED
1/2	CUP GRATED PECORINO CHEESE

METHOD: SAUTE GARLIC, BASIL, MINT AND PARSLEY FOR 3 MINUTES. ADD TOMATOES, BLACK AND FRESH GREEN PEPPER. BRING SAUCE TO A BOIL, DROP HEAT TO LOW AND COOK FOR 20 MINUTES. POUR SAUCE OVER PASTA. TOSS AND SERVE WITH GRATED CHEESE ON THE SIDE.

ALTERNATE: THIS SAUCE IS ALSO RECOMMENDED FOR USE IN A BAKED PASTA DISH. IF YOU CHOOSE TO DO SO, PLACE PASTA IN A BAKING DISH, COVER WITH SAUCE AND GRATED CHEESE. COVER THE WHOLE PLATE WITH A LAYER OF THINLY SLICED MOZZARELLA AND BAKE IN A 425 DEGREE OVEN UNTIL THE CHEESE MELTS AND BUBBLES. REMOVE AND SERVE.

RECOMMENDED PASTA: RIBBON TYPES FOR EITHER METHOD.

WE TRIED THIS SAUCE . . . AND

LOVED IT ( )
HATED IT ( )
MAYBE WE'LL TRY IT AGAIN ( )
WE'LL USE IT FOR UNWELCOME GUESTS ( )

TOMATO SAUCE #7

THIS IS A VERY LIGHT SAUCE FROM THE ISLAND OF SARDINIA, TRY IT YOU'LL LIKE IT.

INGREDIENTS:

1/3	CUP OLIVE OIL
2	CLOVES GARLIC, CRUSHED
12	FRESH PEAR TOMATOES (B/P/C)
1/4	TEASPOON FRESHLY GRATED BLACK PEPPER
3/4	TEASPOON SALT
1	TABLESPOON PARSLEY, CHOPPED

YOU MAY SUBSTITUTE 1-28 OUNCE CAN PEAR TOMATOES FOR THE FRESH TOMATOES, IF YOU DO, OMIT THE SALT.

METHOD: SAUTE GARLIC IN OLIVE OIL UNTIL LIGHTLY GOLDEN. ADD TOMATOES, SALT AND PEPPER. BRING TO A BOIL. REDUCE HEAT, COVER AND SIMMER FOR 30 MINUTES. POUR SAUCE OVER PASTA. ADD PARSLEY, TOSS AND SERVE.

RECOMMENDED PASTA: MEDIUM TUBE TYPES.

TOMATO SAUCE #8

AS WITH SO MANY TOMATO SAUCES, THIS ONE IS FROM THE HAPPY COUNTRY. THE ROMANS CALLED IT THAT BECAUSE THEY BELIEVED THE GODS HAD BLESSED THE AREA AND THAT IT WAS A HAPPY PLACE TO LIVE, THUSLY DID THEY CALL IT: CAMPANIA FELIX. WE KNOW IT AS THE REGION OF CAMPANIA WITH ITS VIBRANCE CENTERED IN NAPLES. ENOUGH TOUR GUIDE TRIVIA, BACK TO THE SAUCE. THIS SAUCE COMES OFF QUITE LIGHT, KEEP IT THAT WAY, DON'T OVER COOK IT.

INGREDIENTS:

1/3	CUP OLIVE OIL
1	ONION, CHOPPED
1	POUND PEAR TOMATOES (B/P/C)
1	TABLESPOON BASIL, CHOPPED
2/3	TEASPOON SALT
PINCH	FRESHLY GROUND BLACK PEPPER

METHOD: SAUTE ONION IN OLIVE OIL UNTIL TRANSPARENT. ADD TOMATOES, BASIL, SALT AND PEPPER. BRING TO A BOIL, REDUCE HEAT TO SIMMER, PARTIALLY COVER AND SIMMER FOR 30 MINUTES. POUR SAUCE OVER PASTA, TOSS AND SERVE.

RECOMMENDED PASTA: STRING TYPES.

TOMATO SAUCE #9

THIS ONE COMES FROM AROUND ROME. IT'S A NICE BLEND OF PEPPERS, TOMATOES AND OLIVES.

INGREDIENTS:

2/3	CUP OLIVE OIL
1	PEPPER, SEEDED AND SLICED (GREEN OR YELLOW BELL OR LONG MILDLY HOT)
3	FRESH PEAR TOMATOES (B/P/C)
	SALT AND FRESHLY GROUND BLACK PEPPER TO TASTE
3/4	CUP RIPE OLIVES, PITTED AND SLICED
1/2	CUP PECORINO CHEESE

METHOD: HEAT THE OIL, ADD PEPPER, TOMATOES, SALT AND PEPPER. BRING SAUCE TO A BOIL, REDUCE HEAT TO SIMMER, COVER AND COOK FOR 20 MINUTES. ADD OLIVES, COOK AN ADDITIONAL 5 MINUTES. POUR SAUCE OVER PASTA, TOSS, SPRINKLE WITH CHEESE AND SERVE.

RECOMMENDED PASTA: STRING TYPES.

TOMATO SAUCE #10

(ANOTHER QUICKIE)

THIS IS A SAUCE YOU COULD LOVE. IT IS VERY FAST, BUT REQUIRES CONSTANT WATCHING. RESTAURANTS OFTEN HAVE A REDUCING FLAME ON THEIR RANGES. IT IS A VERY HOT, INTENSE FLAME. AND ALLOWS THE CHEF TO REDUCE THE LIQUID IN A SAUCE IN JUST A FEW MOMENTS. YOU CAN DO IT AT HOME, JUST DON'T WALK AWAY FROM THE STOVE.

INGREDIENTS:

3	POUNDS FRESH TOMATOES (B/P/C)
6	TABLESPOONS BUTTER
6 TO 8	CHIVES, INCLUDING STEMS, MINCED
3	TABLESPOONS FRESH BASIL, CHOPPED
3	TABLESPOONS PARSLEY, CHOPPED
1/2	TEASPOON SALT
PINCH	FRESHLY GROUND BLACK PEPPER
	GRATED PARMESAN

METHOD: SAUTE CHIVES IN THE BUTTER UNTIL WHITE PORTION IS TRANSPARENT. ADD BASIL AND PARSLEY, STIR TO COAT. ADD TOMATOES. BRING SAUCE TO A RAPID BOIL AND KEEP IT THERE UNTIL MOST OF THE LIQUID HAS EVAPORATED AND SAUCE HAS THICKENED. REMOVE FROM HEAT, ADD SALT AND PEPPER. POUR SAUCE OVER PASTA, TOSS AND SERVE WITH CHEESE ON THE SIDE.

RECOMMENDED PASTA: STRING AND THIN STRING TYPES.

TOMATO SAUCE #11

(THINK PASTA PIE!)

I'M SURE THAT YOU'VE OCCASIONALLY SEEN PICTURES OF A BAKED SPAGHETTI WITH A WEDGE CUT OUT OF IT, IT COMES OFF LOOKING LIKE A DEEP DISH PASTA PIE. THIS IS THE SAUCE TO ONE OF THEM.

INGREDIENTS:
1/2	CUP OLIVE OIL
1/2	POUND MUSHROOMS, SLICED
1	ONION, CHOPPED
2	CLOVES GARLIC, SLICED INTO ROUNDS
1	CARROT, SHREDDED
1	STALK CELERY, MINCED
1	BELL PEPPER, SEEDED AND FINELY CHOPPED
4	8 OUNCE CANS TOMATO SAUCE

METHOD: SAUTE EVERYTHING EXCEPT TOMATO SAUCE IN OLIVE OIL FOR ABOUT 15 MINUTES. ADD TOMATO SAUCE TO WARM THROUGH. REMOVE FROM HEAT.

TO MAKE A PASTA PIE: COOK PASTA, DRAIN IT, PLACE IT IN A BAKING DISH AND SET IT ASIDE. MEANWHILE, PREHEAT OVEN TO 350 DEGREES. COOK YOUR SAUCE AS ABOVE. WHEN DONE, LAY SAUCE OVER PASTA, COVER LOOSELY WITH FOIL OR A LID LAID ASKEW, BAKE FOR 30 MINUTES.

RECOMMENDED PASTA: STRING TYPES

TOMATO SAUCE #12

SOME OF THE INGREDIENTS IN THIS SAUCE MIGHT MAKE YOU THINK YOU WERE PREPARING A STUFFING FOR ROAST CHICKEN, BUT IT AIN'T SO. THIS IS AN OLD ITALIAN RECIPE AND CAN BE REFERRED TO AS AN AROMATIC SAUCE (ITALIAN: AROMATICI) ALSO KNOWN AS AN HERB SAUCE.

INGREDIENTS:

2	TABLESPOON OLIVE OIL
3	ONIONS, CHOPPED
1	SMALL CAN ANCHOVIES OR 8 FILETS
1	STALK CELERY
1	TEASPOON FRESH ROSEMARY (HALF IF DRY)
1	TEASPOON FRESH SAGE (DITTO)
2	TABLESPOONS PARSLEY, CHOPPED
1	POUND FRESH TOMATOES (B/P/C)
1/2	TEASPOON SALT
PINCH	FRESHLY GROUND BLACK PEPPER
2	TABLESPOONS FRESHLY GRATED PARMESAN
2	TABLESPOONS FRESHLY GRATED ROMANO

METHOD: SAUTE THE ONIONS IN THE OLIVE OIL UNTIL ONION IS TRANSPARENT. ADD ANCHOVIES, CELERY, ROSEMARY, SAGE AND PARSLEY, COOK 5 ADDITIONAL MINUTES. ADD TOMATOES, BRING TO A BOIL, REDUCE HEAT TO SIMMER, LOOSELY COVER AND COOK 30 MINUTES. POUR SAUCE OVER PASTA. ADD CHEESE, TOSS AND SERVE.

RECOMMENDED PASTA: STRING TYPES, SOLID OR HOLLOW.

WE TRIED THIS SAUCE . . . AND

TOMATO SAUCE #13

IF YOU'VE EVER HAD FRESH MINT GROWING IN YOUR YARD, YOU'LL KNOW THAT IT SEEMS TO SPREAD LIKE AN UNWANTED WEED. AND THAT MOST OF IT JUST GOES TO WASTE. I'VE ALWAYS FELT THERE SHOULD BE SOME OTHER USE FOR IT BESIDE PUTTING IT INTO MINT JULEPS OR MAKING TEA. I REALIZE IT ALSO GOES INTO JELLY, CANDY, GUM AND SAUCES FOR LAMB AND FISH. I DON'T KNOW WHERE THIS PARTICULAR SAUCE ORIGINATED, BUT I SUSPECT IT IS NORTHERN, ALTHOUGH I KNOW THAT THE FOLKS IN ABBRUZZO-MOLISE USE MINT IN QUITE A NUMBER OF THEIR PASTA SAUCES. WELL, THAT'S WHAT WE'VE GOT HERE, TOMATOES AND FRESH MINT, WE'LL EVEN ADD SOME WALNUTS FOR A NUTTY TEXTURE. SO, IF YOU LIKE MINT, YOU'LL WANT TO TRY THIS ONE.

INGREDIENTS:
1	TABLESPOON BUTTER
1/2	CUP WALNUTS, COARSELY CHOPPED
1/4	CUP OLIVE OIL
1	CLOVE GARLIC, MINCED
1	ONION, CHOPPED
2	LARGE TOMATOES, OR 5 PEAR TOMATOES (B/P/C)
3/4	TEASPOON SALT
1/4	CUP FRESH MINT LEAVES, CHOPPED
	SEVERAL FRESH BASIL LEAVES, CHOPPED

METHOD: SAUTE THE WALNUTS IN THE BUTTER FOR 3 MINUTES REMOVE THEM FROM THE PAN AND SET ASIDE. NOW SAUTE THE ONION IN OLIVE OIL, UNTIL IT IS TRANSPARENT. ADD GARLIC, TOMATOES, SALT, MINT AND BASIL. BRING SAUCE TO A BOIL. REDUCE HEAT TO LOW, COOK PARTIALLY COVERED FOR 10 MINUTES. POUR OVER PASTA, TOSS AND SERVE.

RECOMMENDED PASTA: RIBBON TYPES OR STRING TYPES.

WE TRIED THIS SAUCE . . . AND

TOMATO SAUCE #14

WHEN I READ A RECIPE, THOUGHTS JUMP INTO MY HEAD ABOUT OTHER POSSIBLE USES. THE UNUSUAL SPICE BLEND IN THIS SAUCE SEEMS TO SUGGEST THAT IT COULD READILY BE A CHICKEN STEW MERELY BY TOSSING SEVERAL PIECES OF SKINNED CHICKEN INTO IT AND COOKING UNTIL TENDER. THE FACT IS, THAT IT IS A PASTA SAUCE. BUT SINCE YOU'RE DOING THE COOKING, DO WHAT YOU LIKE.

INGREDIENTS:

3	TABLESPOONS OLIVE OIL
2	CLOVES GARLIC, MINCED OR SLICED
1	ONION, CHOPPED
1/2	CUP WATER OR WINE
3/4	TEASPOON SALT
1/4	TEASPOON FRESHLY GROUND BLACK PEPPER
1/2	TEASPOON PAPRIKA
1/4	TEASPOON ANISE SEED; CRUSH WITH ROLLING PIN
1 1/2	TEASPOONS OREGANO,
1/2	TEASPOON DRIED ROSEMARY, CRUSHED
3	WHOLE CHIVES, SLICED INTO ROUNDS
1/2	BELL PEPPER, SEEDED AND CHOPPED
2	POUNDS FRESH TOMATOES, PEELED AND CHOPPED*
	GRATED PARMESAN CHEESE

METHOD: SAUTE ONION AND GARLIC IN OLIVE OIL UNTIL ONION IS TRANSPARENT. ADD WATER OR WINE, SALT, PEPPER, PAPRIKA, ANISE, OREGANO AND ROSEMARY. COVER AND SIMMER FOR ABOUT 15 MINUTES. ADD BELL PEPPER, CHIVES AND TOMATOES COOK TO HEAT THROUGH ONLY, 2 MINUTES OR LESS. POUR OVER PASTA. TOSS AND SERVE. HAVE CHEESE ON THE SIDE.

* AN INTERESTING OPTION IF YOU ARE USING FRESH ITALIAN STYLE TOMATOES, IS TO CUT THEM INTO ROUNDS AFTER PEELING, THEN ADD THEM TO THE SAUCE JUST BEFORE SERVING. DO NOT ALLOW THEM TO COOK.

RECOMMENDED PASTA: CURLY TYPES.

TOMATO SAUCE #15

IF YOU SUSPECT THAT SOME OF THE SAUCES IN THIS CHAPTER ARE VARIATIONS, YOU'RE RIGHT. THEY ARE, AND THEY ARE OFFERED BECAUSE MANY COOKS WILL LOOK FOR A SAUCE THAT MATCHES WHAT THEY HAVE ON HAND. AND ALSO BECAUSE SOME COOKS WILL NOT VARY A RECIPE ON THEIR OWN. THEY'D RATHER GO WITH THE TRIED AND TRUE, RATHER THAN EXPERIMENT AND GO AWRY.

INGREDIENTS:

1/4	CUP OLIVE OIL OR BUTTER
3	CLOVES GARLIC, BRUISED
1	ONION CHOPPED OR SLICED
5	WHOLE TOMATOES OR 8 PEAR TOMATOES (B/P/C)
1 1/2	TEASPOONS SALT
PINCH	FRESHLY GROUND BLACK PEPPER
1	TEASPOON DRIED OREGANO

METHOD: SAUTE ONION AND GARLIC IN OIL. WHEN ONION IS TRANSPARENT, REMOVE GARLIC AND DISCARD. ADD TOMATOES, SALT, PEPPER AND OREGANO. BRING TO A QUICK BOIL, REDUCE HEAT TO SIMMER, PARTIALLY COVER AND COOK FOR 45 MINUTES. POUR SAUCE OVER PASTA, TOSS AND SERVE WITH PARMESAN CHEESE.

RECOMMENDED PASTA: CURLY TYPES AND MEDIUM TUBE TYPES.

WE TRIED THIS SAUCE . . . AND

LOVED IT ( )
HATED IT ( )
MAYBE WE'LL TRY IT AGAIN ( )
WE'LL USE IT FOR UNWELCOME GUESTS ( )

TOMATO SAUCE #16

THIS SAUCE COMES OFF BOTH FRESH LOOKING AND LIGHTLY SWEET.   TO CREATE A SMOOTHER SAUCE AND POSSIBLY ENHANCE ITS APPEARANCE, YOU MAY BLENDERIZE SOME OR ALL OF THE SAUCE AFTER IT IS COOKED.   THEN SERVE IT.

INGREDIENTS: 1/4   CUP OLIVE OIL
                1   ONION, FINELY CHOPPED
                1   CLOVE GARLIC, MINCED
                1   CARROT, SHREDDED
                1   STALK CELERY, FINELY CHOPPED

(YOU COULD JUST MINCE THE WHOLE LOT IN A FOOD PROCESSOR)

                1   28 OUNCE CAN TOMATOES
                1   TABLESPOON CHOPPED FRESH BASIL OR 1 TEASPOON DRIED
PINCH   WHITE PEPPER

METHOD: SAUTE ONION, GARLIC, CARROT AND CELERY UNTIL OIL TURNS ORANGE FROM THE CARROT.   ADD BLENDERIZED TOMATOES, PEPPER AND DRIED BASIL (IF USING FRESH BASIL, HOLD UNTIL YOU REMOVE SAUCE FROM HEAT, THEN ADD.) BRING SAUCE TO A BOIL, REDUCE HEAT TO SIMMER, COOK ALMOST FULLY COVERED FOR 30 MINUTES.   REMOVE FROM HEAT. POUR OVER PASTA, TOSS AND SERVE.

RECOMMENDED PASTA: RIBBON OR OVAL TYPES.

TOMATO SAUCE #17

VERY FEW INGREDIENTS IN THIS SAUCE, BUT THEY ARE THE INGREDIENTS NEEDED TO GIVE YOU A SWEET, LIGHT SAUCE. FEEL FREE TO OMIT THE WINE.

INGREDIENTS:

3	TABLESPOONS BUTTER
1	ONION, CHOPPED
1	BELL PEPPER, SEEDED AND CHOPPED
1	28 OUNCE CAN TOMATOES
1	CUP DRY WHITE WINE

(YOU MAY SUBSTITUTE 1 MILDLY HOT LONG GREEN PEPPER FOR THE BELL PEPPER, IT WILL GIVE YOU A SURPRISINGLY DIFFERENT TASTE).

METHOD: SAUTE ONIONS AND GREEN PEPPER UNTIL ONION IS TRANSPARENT. ADD BLENDERIZED TOMATOES AND WINE. BRING SAUCE TO A BOIL, REDUCE HEAT TO LOW, COOK PARTIALLY COVERED FOR 30 MINUTES, OR UNTIL SAUCE IS SOMEWHAT THICKENED. POUR OVER PASTA, TOSS AND SERVE.

ON THE WINE: THE ALCOHOL WILL HAVE EVAPORATED BY THE TIME THE SAUCE COMES TO A BOIL. ALL THAT WILL BE LEFT IS THE TASTE OF THE WINE. MAKE SURE IT IS A WINE WHOSE TASTE YOU ENJOY OR ELSE OMIT THE WINE.

RECOMMENDED PASTA: STRING TYPES, SOLID OR HOLLOW.

TOMATO SAUCE #18

ANOTHER SWEET, LIGHT, SAUCE. DON'T BE GENEROUS WITH DRY BASIL IF YOU CHOOSE TO USE IT INSTEAD OF FRESH BASIL.

INGREDIENTS:

2	TABLESPOONS BUTTER
1	ONION, CHOPPED
1	CARROT, SHREDDED
1	28 OUNCE CAN ITALIAN STYLE TOMATOES
1/4	CUP FRESH PARSLEY, CHOPPED
1	TABLESPOON FRESH BASIL (OR, 1 TEASPOON DRY)

METHOD: SAUTE ONION AND CARROT IN BUTTER UNTIL ONION COLORS SLIGHTLY. ADD TOMATOES, PARSLEY AND BASIL. BARELY COVER AND SIMMER FOR 30 MINUTES. SERVE.

RECOMMENDED PASTA: USE THIS SAUCE OVER A STUFFED PASTA, SUCH AS GIANT SEA SHELLS, CANNELLONI OR MANICOTTI.

241

TOMATO SAUCE #19

(PUNGENT)

IF YOU'RE A GARLIC LOVER, THIS ONE IS FOR YOU! IF YOU'RE NOT, STEER A WIDE COURSE AROUND THIS RECIPE.

INGREDIENTS:

1/3	CUP OLIVE OIL
6 TO 8	CLOVES GARLIC, MINCED
1	16 OUNCE CAN ITALIAN STYLE TOMATOES
1	TEASPOON DRIED BASIL
1/2	TEASPOON FRESHLY GROUND BLACK PEPPER
1/2	TEASPOON CRUSHED RED PEPPER (THOSE OF DELICATE PALATE MAY USE LESS OR NONE)
	PARMESAN CHEESE

METHOD: BLENDERIZE TOMATOES, ADD BASIL AND PEPPERS. STIR AND SET ASIDE. SAUTE GARLIC IN OLIVE OIL UNTIL LIGHTLY GOLDEN, ADD TOMATO MIXTURE. BRING SAUCE TO A BOIL, REDUCE HEAT TO LOW, COOK FOR 10 TO 15 MINUTES. POUR OVER PASTA. TOSS AND SERVE WITH GRATED CHEESE ON THE SIDE.

RECOMMENDED PASTA: RIBBON TYPES.

TOMATO SAUCE #20

AN INTERESTING ADDITION TO THIS SAUCE IS THE ALLSPICE, IT WILL ADD A CHARACTER TO THE SAUCES BOUQUET THAT WILL MAKE YOUR GUEST ASK WHAT YOU'VE DONE TO BE SO CREATIVE. YOU MAY EITHER TELL THEM, OR SMILE SEDUCTIVELY AND SAY IT'S AN OLD FAMILY SECRET RECIPE.

INGREDIENTS:
1	28 OUNCE CAN PEAR TOMATOES
1	CLOVE GARLIC (YOUR CHOICE)
1/3	CUP BUTTER
3/4	TEASPOON SALT
1/2	TEASPOON GROUND ALLSPICE
1/2	TEASPOON BASIL
1/2	TEASPOON ROSEMARY, CRUMBLED
PINCH	WHITE PEPPER

METHOD: CHOP TOMATOES IN BLENDER, ADD TO MELTED BUTTER ALONG WITH REMAINING INGREDIENTS. BRING SAUCE TO A BOIL, REDUCE HEAT TO SIMMER AND COOK PARTIALLY COVERED FOR 30 MINUTES. POUR SAUCE OVER PASTA AND SERVE.

YOU MAY WISH TO COOK SAUCE FOR A FEW ADDITIONAL MINUTES IF YOU WANT IT SLIGHTLY THICKER.

RECOMMENDED PASTA: FILLED PILLOW TYPES.

WE TRIED THIS SAUCE . . . AND

LOVED IT ( )
HATED IT ( )
MAYBE WE'LL TRY IT AGAIN ( )
WE'LL USE IT FOR UNWELCOME GUESTS ( )

TOMATO SAUCE #21

SHALLOTS AND GINGER ARE THE STARS IN THIS SAUCE. SHALLOTS ARE SWEET, BUT GINGER, THE LITTLE TART, IS HOT! MOST OF YOUR DINERS MAY NOT BE ABLE TO IDENTIFY FRESH GINGER AS AN INGREDIENT, LET THEM THINK YOU'VE BEEN CREATIVE.

INGREDIENTS:

4	TABLESPOONS OLIVE OIL
1/4	CUP MINCED SHALLOTS
1/4	CUP MINCED GINGER
1	CLOVE GARLIC, MINCED
1	POUND FRESH TOMATOES (B/P/C)
1/4	CUP DRY WHITE WINE
1/2	TEASPOON SALT
1/2	TEASPOON SUGAR
PINCH	WHITE PEPPER
1/4	CUP FRESH BASIL, CHOPPED

METHOD: HEAT OIL, ADD SHALLOTS, GINGER AND GARLIC, SAUTE ABOUT 5 MINUTES. ADD TOMATOES COOK AN ADDITIONAL 5 MINUTES. ADD WINE, SALT, SUGAR AND WHITE PEPPER. COOK OVER MEDIUM HEAT UNTIL SAUCE HAS SOMEWHAT THICKENED, 15 TO 20 MINUTES. TOSS SAUCE WITH COOKED PASTA AND THE FRESH BASIL.

RECOMMENDED PASTA: FANCY SHAPES LIKE RADIATORE, OR MEDIUM TUBE TYPES.

TOMATO SAUCE #22

(LONG AND LOW)

THIS SAUCE HAS ALL THE NECESSARY INGREDIENTS TO BE A MARINARA, AND I'M COMFORTABLE WITH THE FACT THAT MANY COOKS WOULD CALL IT THAT. THE SLIGHT VARIATIONS ARE THE TOMATO MIXTURE AND THE BAY LEAF. WINE AND SUGAR COULD BE ADDED TO ALMOST ANY TOMATO SAUCE.

INGREDIENTS:

2	TABLESPOONS OLIVE OIL
1/2	CUP ONION, CHOPPED
1	CLOVE GARLIC (YOUR CHOICE)
1	16 OUNCE CAN ITALIAN STYLE TOMATOES
1	16 OUNCE CAN WHOLE TOMATOES
2	TABLESPOONS TOMATO PASTE
1/2	TEASPOON DRIED BASIL
1/2	TEASPOON DRIED OREGANO LEAVES
PINCH	BLACK PEPPER
1	BAY LEAF
1/4	CUP RED WINE
1	TABLESPOON SUGAR

METHOD: SAUTE ONION AND GARLIC UNTIL ONION IS TRANSPARENT. CRUSH TOMATOES IN BLENDER AND ADD TO PAN. ADD REMAINING INGREDIENTS. BRING SAUCE TO A BOIL, REDUCE HEAT TO LOWEST POSSIBLE AND SIMMER FOR ABOUT 1 1/2 HOURS. REMOVE BAY LEAF PRIOR TO SERVING.

RECOMMENDED PASTA: STRING OR MEDIUM TUBE TYPES.

TOMATO SAUCE #23

THIS SAUCE REQUIRES FURTHER COOKING, GENERALLY TO BE USED IN BAKED PASTAS, AT THIS STAGE IT IS ONLY PARTIALLY COOKED.

INGREDIENTS:

1	LARGE ONION, CHOPPED
1	CLOVE GARLIC
1	TABLESPOON OLIVE OIL
1	16 OUNCE CAN TOMATOES
2	TABLESPOONS TOMATO PASTE
1/4	TEASPOON SALT
1/4	TEASPOON DRIED THYME (CRUMBLED)
1/4	TEASPOON DRIED ROSEMARY (CRUMBLED)
PINCH	BLACK PEPPER

METHOD: SAUTE ONION AND GARLIC UNTIL LIGHTLY COLORED. ADD TOMATOES AND REMAINING INGREDIENTS. BRING SAUCE TO A BOIL, REDUCE HEAT TO LOW AND COOK UNCOVERED FOR 10 MINUTES. REMOVE FROM HEAT.

THIS SAUCE IS NOW READY TO BE USE IN DISH THAT REQUIRES FURTHER COOKING. IT IS BEST USED IN A DISH TO BE BAKED.

RECOMMENDED PASTA: STUFFABLE TUBES, SHELLS, STRINGS OR BROAD RIBBONS.

TOMATO SAUCE #24

THIS IS NOT A QUICKIE, BUT IT IS AN UNCOMPLICATED TOMATO SAUCE. AMONG OTHER FEATURES, IT CAN BE EASILY REMEMBERED, THAT MAKES IT A CANDIDATE TO BECOME ONE OF YOUR FAVORITES.

INGREDIENTS:

2	TABLESPOON OLIVE OIL
2	CLOVES GARLIC, MINCED
1	TABLESPOON CHOPPED PARSLEY
6 TO 8	PEAR TOMATOES (B/P/C)
1/2	TEASPOON SALT
	FRESHLY GRATED ASIAGO CHEESE

METHOD: SAUTE GARLIC AND PARSLEY IN OLIVE OIL FOR 3 MINUTES. ADD TOMATOES AND SALT. BRING SAUCE TO A BOIL, REDUCE HEAT AND SIMMER FOR 35 MINUTES. POUR SAUCE OVER PASTA. TOSS AND SERVE WITH CHEESE ON THE SIDE.

RECOMMENDED PASTA: FANCY TYPES.

TOMATO SAUCE #25

(SIMPLE SAUCE)

THIS TOMATO SAUCE IS AN "ADD TO" PRODUCT. THAT IS YOU WILL ADD IT TO MANY OTHER RECIPES CALLING FOR TOMATO SAUCE. I REALLY DON'T KNOW WHY YOU'D WANT TO MAKE THIS ONE UNLESS YOU JUST HAPPEN TO HAVE AN EXTRA CASE OF CANNED TOMATOES AROUND THE HOUSE. THE SMALL 8 OUNCE CAN OF "TOMATO SAUCE" IS THE SAME THING, LESS WORK AND A LOT CHEAPER.

INGREDIENTS: 1   28 OUNCE CAN OF ITALIAN STYLE TOMATOES
                1   TABLESPOON OLIVE OIL
                      FRESHLY GROUND BLACK PEPPER TO TASTE
                      OR
                      USE A SMALL PIECE OF A MILDLY HOT LONG GREEN PEPPER

METHOD: SIEVE THE TOMATOES, ADD THE OLIVE OIL, PEPPER. BRING TO A BOIL, LOWER HEAT, SIMMER UNCOVERED ABOUT 20 MINUTES. REMOVE PIECE OF PEPPER AND USE THE SAUCE AS NEEDED.

             YOU MAY SUBSTITUTE FRESH TOMATOES FOR THE CANNED. USE 2 POUNDS OF TOMATOES, BLANCH, PEEL AND SEED. PREPARE AS ABOVE, COOK UNTIL FAIRLY THICK. ABOUT 30 TO 45 MINUTES.

RECOMMENDED PASTA: IF YOU ENJOY A VERY LIGHTLY SEASONED TOMATO SAUCE, YOU MIGHT TRY THIS ON A STRING TYPE, OR YOUR FAVORITE PASTA SHAPE.

CHAPTER 9

SAUCES MADE FROM TOMATOES AND MEAT

OCCASIONALLY YOU'LL FIND A RECIPE THAT USES CANNED TOMATO SAUCE AND/OR TOMATO PASTE AS THE SOLE SOURCE OF TOMATOES. THAT'S OK BECAUSE THE SAUCE WAS MEANT TO BE VERY SMOOTH, AND YOU'LL GET A VERY TASTY SAUCE. YOU'LL ALSO GET A HEAVINESS THAT IS CHARACTERISTIC OF TOMATO PASTE AND CANNED TOMATO SAUCE. IF YOUR TASTE PREFERENCE IN SAUCES RUN TO THE FRESHER AND LIGHTER SIDE, AVOID USING THOSE SAUCES CALLING FOR ONLY TOMATO PASTE OR CANNED TOMATO SAUCE. OF COURSE YOU DO HAVE THE OPTION OF SUBSTITUTING FRESH TOMATOES OR CANNED WHOLE TOMATOES THAT HAVE BEEN SIEVED. I DON'T BELIEVE A SUBSTITUTION WILL SERIOUSLY AFFECT THE END RESULT. IF I'M WRONG, YOU CAN SHRUG YOUR SHOULDERS IN THE ITALIAN FASHION AND SAY IN ENGLISH, "NOTHING VENTURED, NOTHING GAINED!" I SUGGEST ENGLISH BECAUSE I DON'T KNOW THE ITALIAN EQUIVALENT.

IN THE COOKING OF ANY SAUCE WITH MEAT, NO MATTER HOW LEAN THE BUTCHER TELLS YOU IT IS, IT WILL RELEASE FAT IN THE FORM OF OIL INTO YOUR SAUCE. IF YOU ARE PREPARING A SAUCE FOR TODAY'S DINNER, YOU'LL NEED TO SCOOP IT OFF! THE BEST METHOD I'VE FOUND, IS TO SCOOP IT AFTER THE SAUCE HAS SIMMERED FOR A WHILE, THE OIL WILL RISE TO THE TOP, REMOVE IT, THEN STIR YOUR SAUCE. YOU'LL NEED TO REPEAT THIS OPERATION SEVERAL TIMES DURING THE COOKING OF YOUR SAUCE. MANY COOKS I'VE KNOWN BELIEVE THAT ALL THE SAUCE'S FLAVOR LIES IN THE OIL. MAYBE. IT ALSO GIVES YOU AN OILY SAUCE.

MEAT JUICES HAVE AN ADDED EFFECT. IT'S NOT WHAT THEY DO, IT'S WHAT THEY CREATE. BY MOST DEFINITIONS, THE REDUCED OR THICKENED JUICES OF MEAT ARE GRAVY. SOME PEOPLE THEREFORE CALL A SAUCE MADE BY COOKING THE MEAT IN THE SAUCE UNTIL SOMEWHAT THICKENED, A GRAVY. YOU MAY IF YOU WISH TOO, I'M STICKING WITH SAUCE. PERHAPS IT'S ONLY SEMANTICS, OR IT'S THE AMERICAN IN ME. I LIKE MY GRAVY OVER MASHED POTATOES, NOT ON PASTA.

Continued on next page

THERE IS ANOTHER SIDE TO COOKING MEAT AND VEGETABLES TOGETHER THAT WE NEED TO EXPLORE. AT SOME POINT THEY BECOME A STEW. KNOWN AS RAGU IN ITALIAN (THERE ARE THOSE WHO WOULD ARGUE THE POINT, MAINTAINING THERE IS NO SIMILARITY BETWEEN RAGU AND STEW; THE ITALIAN WORD FOR STEW IS STUFATO) AND RAGOUT IN FRENCH, I DON'T KNOW WHEN THAT HAPPENS, AND I'M NOT SO SURE I CARE. IT WOULD SEEM TO ME THAT IF IT WAS MY INTENTION TO EAT THE VEGETABLES AND THE MEAT IN THE RESULTING GRAVY, IT IS AT THAT POINT I WOULD CALL IT STEW, OR RAGOUT. IF I WISH TO USE THE MIXTURE AS A DRESSING FOR ANOTHER FOOD, IT BECOMES A RAGU OR SAUCE. AND WE WILL HANG OUR HAT ON THAT ASSUMPTION.

WE TRIED THIS SAUCE . . . AND

BOLOGNESE MEAT SAUCE #1

(LONG AND LOW)

FROM AMONG MANY MEAT SAUCES, ONE HAS FOUND ITS WAY INTO THE AMERICAN MAINSTREAM. THAT IS THE "BOLOGNESE" MEAT SAUCE. I'M SURE IT IS DUE TO THE SAUCES ABILITY TO BE A SINGLE DISH MEAL. VERY SUBSTANTIAL, TASTY AND MEETS THE NUTRITIONAL REQUIREMENTS OF THE FOUR BASIC FOOD GROUPS ALL IN ONE DISH.

HOW DID WE ACCOMPLISH THAT ONE?   MEAT, VEGETABLES, GRAINS AND DAIRY PRODUCTS!

LETS TAKE A LOOK: 1. GROUND MEAT; (BEEF, VEAL, PORK, OR ALL THREE)
2. TOMATOES, ONIONS, CARROTS, CELERY;
3. MILK AND CHEESE;
4. GRAINS (PASTA)

BOLOGNESE MEAT SAUCE IS NOT ALONE HERE, ACTUALLY MOST PASTA SAUCES WITH MEAT, FOWL OR SEAFOOD PROBABLY QUALIFY. BOLOGNESE MEAT SAUCE IS SO VERSATILE THAT IT COMES CLOSE TO BEING A UNIVERSAL PASTA SAUCE. I'VE HAD IT SERVED TO ME IN AND ON LASAGNE AS WELL AS ALMOST ANY PASTA TYPE YOU CAN NAME.

ONCE AGAIN, WHEN A SAUCE HAS A HIGH DEGREE OF POPULARITY, IN ITALY, (AS WELL AS AMERICA) THERE ARE MANY VERSIONS AVAILABLE. ITALIANS DO NOT MAKE A SCIENCE OF MAINTAINING A SAUCE'S FORMULA. UNLIKE FRENCH SAUCES WHERE THERE IS ONE RIGID FORMULA FOR A SAUCE OF A PARTICULAR NAME, PERIOD. ITALIANS ADD OR DROP INGREDIENTS AS THEY FEEL LIKE IT. THERE ARE THOSE WHO INSIST THAT MILK IS AN ESSENTIAL INGREDIENT IN A BOLOGNESE MEAT SAUCE AND THAT IT MUST BE ABSORBED BY THE GROUND BEEF BEFORE ADDING TOMATOES BECAUSE THE MILK WILL MAKE THE GROUND BEEF CREAMIER AND SWEETER, MAYBE. THE BOLOGNESE RECIPE FOLLOWING THIS

Continued on next page

ONE, DOESN'T USE MILK. THERE IS ALSO THE GROUP THAT MAINTAINS NO MILK IS REQUIRED, BUT, THEY ADD CREAM AT THE END TO COMPLETE THE COOKING. MANY OF THE RECIPES ALSO REQUIRE A WINE BE ADDED TO THE MEAT AND EVAPORATED PRIOR TO ADDING THE MILK. I'VE TRIED IT THAT WAY AND DIDN'T LIKE IT, YOU MAY.

THE FOLLOWING "BOLOGNESE" SAUCES ARE A COUPLE FROM AMONG TOO MANY TO COUNT.

INGREDIENTS:

2	TABLESPOONS OLIVE OIL
1	MEDIUM ONION, CHOPPED
1	POUND GROUND MEAT (BEEF, VEAL, PORK, OR ALL THREE)
1/2	CARROT, PEELED AND MINCED
1	STALK CELERY, FINELY CHOPPED
1/2	CUP MILK OR CREAM
PINCH	GROUND NUTMEG
1	28 OUNCE CAN WHOLE TOMATOES, CHOPPED OR SIEVED
3	TABLESPOONS TOMATO PASTE
1	TEASPOON SALT
1	TEASPOON DRIED BASIL
1/2	TEASPOON THYME
PINCH	BLACK PEPPER
1	BAY LEAF
1	CUP GRATED CHEESE

METHOD: SAUTE ONIONS IN OLIVE OIL UNTIL SOFT. ADD GROUND MEAT, COOK UNTIL GREY. ADD CARROTS AND CELERY, COOK AN ADDITIONAL 2 MINUTES. ADD MILK AND NUTMEG, COOK UNTIL MILK HAS EVAPORATED. ADD TOMATOES, TOMATO PASTE, SALT, BASIL, THYME, PEPPER AND BAY LEAF. BRING SAUCE TO A BOIL, REDUCE HEAT TO SIMMER AND COOK PARTIALLY COVERED UNTIL SAUCE IS THICK. 1 TO 1 1/2 HOURS. DISCARD BAY LEAF BEFORE ADDING SAUCE TO PASTA. SPRINKLE CHEESE ON THE SAUCED PASTA.

THERE ARE THOSE WHO ADVANCE THE ARGUMENT THAT A PROPER RAGU (BOLOGNESE MEAT SAUCE) CANNOT BE SIMMERED FOR FEWER THAN 3 1/2 TO 5 HOURS. IF YOU'VE GOT THE TIME, TRY IT. THEY MAY BE RIGHT.

RECOMMENDED PASTA: STRINGS, MEDIUM TUBES, LARGE SHELLS, OR USE IT AS THE FILLER IN A LASAGNE.

BOLOGNESE MEAT SAUCE #2

(LONG AND LOW)

THIS IS A VERSION FROM THE "MILK IS NOT REQUIRED GROUP". BOTH THIS SAUCE AND THE PRECEDING BOLOGNESE SAUCE ARE OFTEN REFERRED BY ITALIANS AS A RAGU. RAGU IS A MEAT AND VEGETABLE STEW (WITH NO CHUNKS OF ANYTHING). SEMANTICS COME INTO PLAY HERE BECAUSE I HAVE A REAL PROBLEM WITH THE NAME, NOT THE SAUCE. IT MUST BE THE AMERICAN IN ME, I DON'T WANT TO PUT STEW ON MY PASTA.

INGREDIENTS:

4	TABLESPOONS BUTTER
4	TABLESPOONS OLIVE OIL
1	ONION, CHOPPED
1	CARROT, SHREDDED
1	STALK CELERY, FINELY CHOPPED
4	SLICES BACON, MINCED
6	OUNCES GROUND PORK
6	OUNCES GROUND BEEF
4	OUNCES ITALIAN SAUSAGE, SKINNED AND CRUMBLED
2 TO 3	CHICKEN LIVERS, MINCED
1/2	CUP DRY WHITE WINE
1/2	TEASPOON SALT
1/4	TEASPOON FRESHLY GROUND BLACK PEPPER
1	HEAPING TABLESPOON TOMATO PASTE
1	CUP WATER OR BEEF BROTH
1/3	CUP HALF AND HALF
1/4	POUND MUSHROOMS, SLICED

Continued on next page

METHOD: USING 2 TABLESPOONS BUTTER AND ALL THE OLIVE OIL, SAUTE THE ONION, CARROT, CELERY AND BACON, 3 MINUTES.   ADD GROUND PORK, GROUND BEEF, ITALIAN SAUSAGE AND CHICKEN LIVER, COOK 5 MINUTES. USE WINE TO PREVENT THE MEAT FROM FRYING.   ADD SALT, PEPPER, TOMATO PASTE AND WATER.   COVER AND SIMMER FOR 1 1/2 HOURS.   ADD REMAINING BUTTER, HALF AND HALF, COOK 5 ADDITIONAL MINUTES.   ADD MUSHROOMS, CONTINUE COOKING FOR 5 MORE MINUTES.   POUR SAUCE OVER PASTA. TOSS AND SERVE.

RECOMMENDED PASTA: STRING TYPES.

WE TRIED THIS SAUCE . . . AND

LOVED IT ( )
HATED IT ( )
MAYBE WE'LL TRY IT AGAIN ( )
WE'LL USE IT FOR UNWELCOME GUESTS ( )

NEAPOLITAN MEAT SAUCE

(LONG AND LOW)

THE TITLE LEAVES YOU WITHOUT DOUBT AS TO THE ORIGIN OF THIS PASTA SAUCE. AS IN THE ITALIAN MANNER, YOU MAY USE THE SAUCE ON A PASTA, THEN SERVE THE MEAT SEPARATELY WITH FRESH VEGETABLES, FOLLOWED BY A SALAD. OR DO AS I DO, SERVE THE MEAT AND PASTA TOGETHER, FOLLOWED BY FRESH FRUIT OR MELON.

INGREDIENTS:

2	POUND BONELESS PIECE OF PORK OR BEEF
2	GARLIC CLOVES, QUARTERED
1/2	TEASPOON SALT
2	OUNCES LARD OR OLIVE OIL
3	ONIONS, CHOPPED
2	CARROTS, SHREDDED
1	STALK CELERY, CHOPPED
1/2	CUP RED WINE
1/2	CUP WATER
1	TABLESPOON TOMATO PASTE
1	8 OUNCE CAN TOMATO SAUCE

METHOD: MAKE SMALL INCISIONS IN THE MEAT AND INSERT A PIECE OF GARLIC INTO EACH INCISION. SALT THE MEAT, THEN BROWN IT ON ALL SIDES IN THE LARD OR OIL. ADD ONION, CARROTS AND CELERY, COOK FOR AN ADDITIONAL 5 MINUTES. BLEND WINE, WATER AND TOMATO PASTE, ADD TO THE MEAT AND VEGETABLES. BRING SAUCE TO A BOIL, REDUCE HEAT, COVER AND SIMMER FOR 30 MINUTES, ADD TOMATO SAUCE. CONTINUE SIMMERING FOR AN ADDITIONAL 2 HOURS. IF IT BECOMES NECESSARY, ADD ADDITIONAL WATER OR BEEF BROTH.

RECOMMENDED PASTA: STRINGS, SOLID OR HOLLOW, MEDIUM TUBE TYPES.

TOMATO AND SAUSAGE SAUCE

(LONG AND LOW)

ITALIAN SAUSAGE ADDS A MARVELOUS TASTE TO A TOMATO SAUCE, AS DOES ANY CUT OF FRESH PORK. THE SAUSAGE HOWEVER, GIVES YOU PORK PLUS IT'S SEASONING, IN PARTICULAR, FENNEL (KISSIN' KIN TO ANISE), THE COMBINATION IS ONE DESIGNED TO PLEASE.

INGREDIENTS:
2	POUNDS SWEET ITALIAN SAUSAGE (A.K.A. MILD)
1	POUND HOT ITALIAN SAUSAGE (A.K.A. SPICY)
1	SWEET ONION, CHOPPED
2	BELL PEPPERS, SEEDED AND CHOPPED
2	28 OUNCE CANS PEAR TOMATOES
2	6 OUNCE CANS TOMATO PASTE
1	CUP WATER OR WINE
1	TEASPOON FENNEL SEED

METHOD: DECISIONS, DECISIONS, YOU'VE GOT TO MAKE ONE NOW. IF YOU WANT A GROUND MEAT EFFECT IN YOUR SAUCE, STRIP THE SAUSAGE OF ITS CASING, CRUMBLE AND FRY UNTIL PINK COLOR IS GONE.

OR,

BROWN THE SAUSAGES WHOLE, OR CUT INTO 2 INCH CHUNKS. OR, DO IT MY WAY, DROP THE SAUSAGE, WHOLE OR IN CHUNKS INTO THE SAUCE A'BLANC.

NOW THAT WE'VE GOT THAT OUT OF THE WAY, LET'S MOVE ON:

SAUTE THE ONION AND BELL PEPPER IN OIL UNTIL THE ONION IS TRANSPARENT. ADD TOMATOES, TOMATO PASTE, WATER AND FENNEL SEED. BRING SAUCE TO A BOIL, REDUCE TO A SIMMER AND COOK LIGHTLY COVERED FOR ONE AND ONE HALF TO TWO HOURS.

RECOMMENDED PASTA: MEDIUM TUBES, OR SHELL TYPES.

MILANESE CREAMY FRESH TOMATO SAUCE

WHIPPING CREAM AND GREEN PEAS WILL ADD AN INTERESTING CHARACTER TO THIS SAUCE. SO, IF YOU DON'T LIKE PINK SAUCES, DON'T MAKE THIS ONE.

INGREDIENTS:

1	LINK OF ITALIAN SAUSAGE (OR ABOUT 4 OUNCES)
1	ONION, CHOPPED
1	CLOVE GARLIC, MINCED
4	FRESH PEAR TOMATOES (B/P/C)
1	CUP TOMATO SAUCE OR TOMATO JUICE OR V8 JUICE
1/2	TEASPOON SALT
1/3	CUP PEAS, FRESH OR FROZEN
1/2	CUP WHIPPING CREAM
	GRATED PARMESAN CHEESE

METHOD: STRIP SAUSAGE OF CASING, CRUMBLE AND SAUTE UNTIL SAUSAGE RELEASES ITS OIL. ADD ONION AND GARLIC, CONTINUE COOKING UNTIL SAUSAGE LIGHTLY BROWNS. ADD TOMATOES, JUICE AND SALT. BRING SAUCE TO A BOIL, PARTIALLY COVER, REDUCE HEAT AND SIMMER FOR 15 MINUTES. ADD CREAM AND PEAS. COOK AN ADDITIONAL 5 TO 10 MINUTES. POUR SAUCE OVER PASTA. TOSS AND SERVE WITH CHEESE ON THE SIDE.

RECOMMENDED PASTA: MEDIUM TUBE TYPES.

Marsala Ragu Sauce

NO, THE SAUCE DIDN'T ORIGINATE IN SICILY, ONLY THE WINE. THIS IS A NORTHERN SAUCE WITH A VERY INTERESTING MIX OF FLAVORS. AND, IN TOTAL DEFIANCE OF THE THE NORTHERN SCHOOL THAT STOUTLY MAINTAINS A RAGU MUST USE MILK TO SWEETEN THE MEAT, AND THEN COOK FROM BREAKFAST 'TIL DINNER. THIS SAUCE IS READY IN UNDER AN HOUR.

INGREDIENTS:

1/4	CUP OLIVE OIL
1/4	CUP BUTTER
2	CLOVES GARLIC, MINCED
1/2	TEASPOON DRY ROSEMARY, CRUSHED
1/2	POUND GROUND BEEF (VEAL OR PORK)
	SALT AND PEPPER TO TASTE
PINCH	GROUND CINNAMON
1/2	CUP MARSALA WINE
1/2	CUP TOMATO CANNED SAUCE, OR
1	TABLESPOON TOMATO PASTE AND 7 TABLESPOONS WATER
1/2	CUP GRATED PARMESAN CHEESE

METHOD: SAUTE GARLIC AND ROSEMARY IN OIL/BUTTER UNTIL GARLIC TURNS LIGHTLY GOLDEN, ADD THE GROUND MEAT, STIRRING CONSTANTLY UNTIL MEAT HAS LOST ITS PINK COLOR AND IS SEPARATED. SEASON WITH SALT AND PEPPER. ADD CINNAMON AND MARSALA, SIMMER FOR 10 MINUTES. ADD TOMATO SAUCE, COVER AND CONTINUE SIMMERING FOR 40 ADDITIONAL MINUTES. TOSS HOT, DRAINED PASTA WITH GRATED CHEESE. POUR SAUCE OVER PASTA, TOSS AGAIN, SERVE.

RECOMMENDED PASTA: RIBBON TYPES.

GROUND BEEF AND TOMATO SAUCE

WHY ISN'T THIS A RAGU? I DON'T KNOW, MAYBE IT IS. FOR STARTERS, IT COOKS IN ABOUT 20 MINUTES. RAGU SUPPORTER'S INSIST THAT A GENUINE RAGU TAKES HOURS OF SIMMERING, THEY MAY BE RIGHT. THIS SAUCE HAS THE RIGHT INGREDIENTS TO BE A RAGU BUT ISN'T. THEREFORE, AS I'VE SUSPECTED, THE REAL DIFFERENCE MUST BE TIME. A RAGU, AS IN BOLOGNESE MEAT SAUCE, IS THE VERY SLOW SIMMERING OF MINCED MEAT WITH VEGETABLES AND TOMATOES, THE END RESULT IS ESSENCE. THIS SAUCE WON'T GIVE YOU THAT, BUT IT WILL PUT DINNER ON THE TABLE IN UNDER THIRTY MINUTES.

INGREDIENTS:

1	POUND GROUND BEEF
1	ONION, CHOPPED
1	CARROT, SHREDDED
1	CUP PARSLEY
1	28 OUNCE CAN ITALIAN STYLE TOMATOES
1	6 OUNCE CAN TOMATO PASTE
1	CUP WATER OR BROTH
1	TEASPOON DRY BASIL
3/4	TEASPOON SALT
1/2	TEASPOON FRESHLY GROUND BLACK PEPPER

SUBSTITUTIONS: INSTEAD OF GROUND BEEF, YOU MAY USE SKINNED AND CRUMBLED ITALIAN SAUSAGE

METHOD: UNLESS YOUR GROUND BEEF IS EXTRAORDINARILY LEAN, YOU WON'T NEED ANY ADDED OIL; HOWEVER, IF IT APPEARS THAT YOU'LL NEED OIL, ADD EQUAL AMOUNTS OF OLIVE OIL AND BUTTER (1 OR 2 TABLESPOONS EACH) COOK THE BEEF UNTIL GREY. ADD ONION, CARROT AND PARSLEY UNTIL ONION IS TRANSPARENT. ADD TOMATOES, TOMATO PASTE, WATER, BASIL, SALT AND PEPPER. BRING SAUCE TO A BOIL, COOK AT FAST SIMMER FOR ABOUT 20 MINUTES. SEE BELOW.

Continued on next page

RECOMMENDED PASTA: ANY SHAPE YOU LIKE.

YOU MAY ALSO USE THE ABOVE SAUCE AS A GOOD GO TOGETHER WITH STUFFED PASTAS, SUCH AS STUFFED SEA SHELLS, CANNELLONI OR MANICOTTI. TO DO SO, COOK SAUCE FOR ABOUT 10 MINUTES, SAUCE THE BAKING PAN, PLACE STUFFED PASTA IN THE PAN.   SAUCE PASTA AND BAKE AS PER RECIPE. GENERALLY ABOUT 30 TO 45 MINUTES AT 325 DEGREES.

GROUND BEEF AND TOMATO SAUCE TOO!

THIS SAUCE SEEMS TO BE A REAL FAVORITE OF CHILDREN. IT IS VERY HARDY AND VERY SIMILAR TO THE PRECEDING SAUCE, IT WILL BE A LITTLE SWEETER BECAUSE OF THE ADDED ONION AND OMISSION OF A SALTY BROTH. THIS SAUCE IS OCCASIONALLY REFERRED TO BY SOME COOKS AS A RAGU. THEY SEEM TO HAVE DIFFICULTY IN DEFINING THE TERM ALSO.

INGREDIENTS:

3	TABLESPOONS OLIVE OIL
3	TABLESPOONS BUTTER
2	CLOVES GARLIC, MINCED
1	CUP CHOPPED ONION
1	STALK CELERY, FINELY CHOPPED
1	CARROT, SHREDDED
1	POUND GROUND BEEF (LEAN AS POSSIBLE)
1/4	TEASPOON ROSEMARY, CRUSHED
1	TEASPOON SALT
1/2	TEASPOON FRESHLY GROUND BLACK PEPPER
1	28 OUNCE CAN PEAR TOMATOES (BLENDERIZED)
	CHOPPED PARSLEY GARNISH

METHOD: SAUTE THE GARLIC, ONION, CELERY AND CARROT IN THE OIL/BUTTER UNTIL ONIONS ARE TRANSPARENT. ADD GROUND BEEF, CRUMBLE AND STIR UNTIL IT SEPARATES. ADD ROSEMARY, SALT AND PEPPER, COVER AND SIMMER MEAT MIXTURE FOR 15 MINUTES. ADD TOMATOES, BRING SAUCE TO A BOIL, REDUCE HEAT TO SIMMER AND COOK FOR 1 HOUR. POUR SAUCE OVER PASTA. TOSS, GARNISH WITH PARSLEY, SERVE.

RECOMMENDED PASTA: STRINGS, CURLY TYPES, SHELLS OR MEDIUM TUBES.

GROUND BEEF AND TOMATO SAUCE III

AS IN THE PRECEDING RECIPE, THIS SAUCE IS ALSO A FAIRLY FAST SAUCE TO PREPARE. IT'S DIFFERENCE LIES NOT ONLY IN THE SPICE THAT IS ADDED, BUT HOW THAT SPICE IS TREATED. SOME SAUCE RECIPES USING CINNAMON ARE REFERRED TO AS "ARGENTINIAN", ALTHOUGH I HAVEN'T THE FAINTEST UNDER-STANDING AS TO WHY (ASIDE FROM THE FACT THAT THERE ARE MILLIONS OF ITALIANS IN ARGENTINA), THERE ARE AT LEAST A DOZEN OTHER RECIPES USING CINNAMON IN THIS BOOK, THREE OF THEM HAVE NO IDENTITY APPLICATION, ONE IS REFERRED TO AS "SARDINIAN" AND ONE OF THEM IS REFERRED TO AS A "GREEK STYLE" SAUCE. THE LATTER TWO SAUCES ARE IN THIS CHAPTER.

INGREDIENTS:

1/3	CUP OLIVE OIL
1	ONION, CHOPPED
1	CLOVE GARLIC, MINCED
1/2	POUND GROUND BEEF
1/2	TEASPOON SALT
1 1/2	CUPS CANNED TOMATO SAUCE
PINCH	GROUND CINNAMON
	GRATED PARMESAN CHEESE

METHOD: SAUTE ONION AND GARLIC AND CINNAMON IN OLIVE OIL FOR 3 MINUTES. ADD GROUND BEEF AND STIR CONSTANTLY TO CRUMBLE, WHEN ALL THE PINK COLOR IS GONE AND THE MEAT WELL SEPARATED, ADD THE TOMATO SAUCE. BRING SAUCE TO A BOIL, REDUCE HEAT, COVER AND SIMMER FOR 20 MINUTES.

RECOMMENDED PASTA: STRING TYPES.

STEAK AND TOMATO SAUCE

MOST AMERICAN'S LOVE MEAT AND POTATOES, WELL THIS IS AS CLOSE AS WE GET, STEAK AND TOMATOES! THE TREATMENT OF THE STEAK HERE IS SIMILAR TO THE WAY STEAK IS GENERALLY CUT FOR A BEEF STROGANOFF. THIN STRIPS, ABOUT 1/4" INCH BY 2" INCHES.

INGREDIENTS:

1	POUND BEEF LOIN OR TOP SIRLOIN
4	TABLESPOONS OLIVE OIL
2	CLOVES GARLIC, CRUSHED
1	28 OUNCE CAN PEAR TOMATOES, BLENDERIZED
1	TEASPOON SALT
1/2	TEASPOON FRESHLY GROUND BLACK PEPPER
1	TABLESPOON CHOPPED PARSLEY
PINCH	DRY OREGANO

METHOD: SAUTE GARLIC IN OLIVE OIL UNTIL LIGHTLY GOLDEN. REMOVE GARLIC AND DISCARD. ADD STEAK AND SAUTE FOR 5 MINUTES. REMOVE STEAK AND SET ASIDE. ADD TOMATOES, SALT, PEPPER, PARSLEY AND OREGANO. BRING SAUCE TO A BOIL, REDUCE HEAT AND SIMMER, WHILE PARTIALLY COVERED FOR 20 MINUTES. RETURN STEAK TO THE SAUCE AND HEAT THROUGH, ABOUT 5 MINUTES, REMOVE FROM HEAT, POUR SAUCE OVER PASTA, TOSS AND SERVE.

RECOMMENDED PASTA: NARROW RIBBONS, STRINGS OR MEDIUM TUBE TYPES.

MEAT AND TOMATO SAUCE #1

(LONG AND LOW)

A GOOD HEARTY MEAT SAUCE, SLOWLY SIMMERED AND LIGHTLY SEASONED, A SAUCE YOUR FAMILY WILL LOVE.

INGREDIENTS:

1/4	CUP OLIVE OIL
1	MEDIUM ONION, CHOPPED
1	POUND MEAT (ANY CUT OF BEEF, VEAL OR PORK)*
2	28 OUNCE CANS OF WHOLE OR DICED TOMATOES
1	TEASPOON SALT
PINCH	FRESHLY GROUND BLACK PEPPER
1	6 OUNCE CAN TOMATO PASTE

METHOD: SAUTE ONION IN OIL UNTIL TRANSPARENT. ADD TOMATOES, MEAT, SALT AND PEPPER, BRING TO A BOIL, REDUCE HEAT TO SIMMER. COVER TIGHTLY AND COOK FOR 1 HOUR. ADD THE TOMATO PASTE, COOK PARTIALLY COVERED FOR 1 ADDITIONAL HOUR OR LONGER. COOK MEAT TO YOUR PREFERENCE OF DONENESS. REMOVE MEAT TO A SEPARATE SERVING DISH. POUR SAUCE OVER PASTA. TOSS AND SERVE. (IT MAY BE NECESSARY TO ADD A LITTLE WATER OR TOMATO JUICE TO THIS SAUCE IF IT GETS TOO THICK.)

* WITH THIS SAUCE YOU HAVE AN OPPORTUNITY TO USE YOUR CHOICE OF MEAT; BEEF, VEAL, PORK, ITALIAN SAUSAGE, GROUND MEAT SEASONED AND MADE INTO MEATBALLS. WHICH EVER ONE YOU CHOOSE, THE MEAT SHOULD BE PLACED INTO THE SAUCE "A'BLANC". I KNOW THAT'S A FRENCH TERM, BUT THAT DOESN'T CHANGE ITS MEANING OF "UNCOOKED".

RECOMMENDED PASTA: STRING, TUBE OR SHELL TYPES.

MEAT AND TOMATO SAUCE #2

(LONG AND LOW)

WHEN I PREPARE A SAUCE AND MEAT IN THIS FASHION, I SERVE PASTA, THE MEAT AND ONE OR MORE VEGETABLES AT THE SAME TIME. THIS OBVIOUSLY DIFFERS FROM THE ITALIAN METHOD OF SERVING THE PASTA, AND THEN THE MEAT AND VEGETABLES. THAT MANNER OF SERVING IS WONDERFUL WHEN YOU WISH TO SERVE A MULTI-COURSE MEAL.

INGREDIENTS:

3	TABLESPOONS OLIVE OIL
3 +/-	POUND ROAST (BEEF, PORK OR VEAL)
3	ONIONS, SLICE TOP TO BOTTOM
3	CLOVES GARLIC
3	6 OUNCE CANS TOMATO PASTE
6	CUPS WATER
1/2	POUND MUSHROOMS, SLICED
1	CUP FRESH PARSLEY, CHOPPED
1	TABLESPOON DRY ROSEMARY, CRUSH OR CRUMBLE SPIKES
1 1/2	TEASPOONS MARJORAM
1	TEASPOON SALT
1/2	TEASPOON BLACK PEPPER

METHOD: HEAT THE OIL IN A DUTCH OVEN, BROWN YOUR ROAST WELL ON ALL SIDES, REMOVE THE ROAST, ADD ONIONS AND GARLIC*, SAUTE UNTIL EDGES LIGHTLY COLOR. ADD WATER, TOMATO PASTE, MUSHROOMS, PARSLEY, ROSEMARY, MARJORAM, SALT AND PEPPER. RETURN ROAST TO THE PAN, COVER TIGHTLY, REDUCE HEAT AND SIMMER FOR 1 1/2 TO 2 HOURS. REMOVE ROAST, SLICE AND SERVE, USE SAUCE OVER PASTA.

* IF YOU PREFER, INSERT SLIVERS OF GARLIC INTO THE ROAST AS OPPOSED TO SAUTEING THEM WITH THE ONION. OR YOU COULD DOUBLE UP AND DO BOTH.

Continued on next page

RECOMMENDED PASTA: MEDIUM TUBE TYPES, STRING TYPES, SOLID OR HOLLOW.

GREAT SUBSTITUTIONS!! TRY THE ABOVE RECIPE USING A LARGE ROUND STEAK OR FLANK STEAK INSTEAD OF A SMALL ROAST. PREPARE THE STEAK IN THE MANNER OF A SICILIAN BRACIOLA, THAT'S A BEEF ROLL. FLATTEN THE STEAK SOMEWHAT BY POUNDING, LAY OVER THE ENTIRE STEAK, A LAYER OF MINCED GARLIC, PARSLEY AND POSSIBLY A LITTLE OREGANO AND/OR CHEESE, SALT AND PEPPER, ROLL AND TIE WITH STRING. COOK AS DIRECTED. THERE ARE RECIPES THAT ALSO USE RAISINS, PRUNES AND/OR DATES. IF YOU PREFER A SWEET FILLING, GO FOR IT.

WE TRIED THIS SAUCE . . . AND

LOVED IT ( )
HATED IT ( )
MAYBE WE'LL TRY IT AGAIN ( )
WE'LL USE IT FOR UNWELCOME GUESTS ( )

MEAT AND TOMATO SAUCE #3

(LONG AND LOW)

I DON'T KNOW WHY THIS SAUCE NEEDS A FOUR PLUS HOUR COOKING TIME, BUT THAT'S THE RECOMMENDATION. IF YOU WANT TO TRY IT YOU'LL AT LEAST HAVE BEEN FOREWARNED.

INGREDIENTS:

3	TABLESPOONS OLIVE OIL
3	TABLESPOONS BUTTER
1	POUND BEEF, TRY DICING IT BY HAND OR WITH A FOOD PROCESSOR.
1/4	CUP ONION, CHOPPED
1/2	SMALL CLOVE GARLIC
1	STALK CELERY, FINELY CHOPPED
1	CARROT, MINCED
PINCH	CRUSHED ROSEMARY
1 OR 2	MUSHROOMS, MINCED
1	CUP RED WINE
6	PEAR TOMATOES (B/P/C)
1	CUP BEEF BROTH
3/4	TEASPOON SALT
1/4	TEASPOON FRESHLY GROUND BLACK PEPPER

METHOD: BROWN MEAT IN THE OLIVE OIL AND BUTTER. ADD ONION, GARLIC, CELERY, CARROT, ROSEMARY AND MUSHROOMS. COOK FOR SEVERAL MINUTES. ADD WINE, COOK ON MEDIUM HEAT FOR 15 MINUTES. ADD TOMATOES, SALT AND PEPPER. REDUCE HEAT TO SIMMER, COVER AND COOK FOR 4 HOURS. ADD SMALL AMOUNTS OF THE BROTH TO PREVENT THE SAUCE FROM GETTING TOO THICK.

RECOMMENDED PASTA: FANCIES OR MEDIUM TUBE TYPES.

MEAT SAUCE MARINARA

(LONG AND LOW)

NOT WITHSTANDING THE FACT THAT THIS NAME IS A CONTRADICTION IN TERMS WITH THE FOLLOWING INGREDIENTS, IT IS A VERY GOOD MEAT SAUCE WITH THE MARVELOUS FLAVOR OF SLOWLY SIMMERED PORK. IT IS ONE OF THE FIVE MARINARA SAUCES AVAILABLE IN THIS BOOK. CHECK OUT THE SEAFOOD VERSIONS AND THE MEATLESS TOMATO VERSION. ITALIAN RELUCTANCE TO OBEY THE FORMULA REALLY SHOWS UP IN A MARINARA SAUCE.

INGREDIENTS:
2	TABLESPOONS OLIVE OIL
1	ONION, CHOPPED
1	CARROT, SHREDDED OR CHOPPED
1	BELL PEPPER, SEEDED AND CHOPPED
4	CLOVES GARLIC, MINCED
1	28 OUNCE CAN PEAR TOMATOES, BLENDERIZED
2	8 OUNCE CANS TOMATO SAUCE
2	TEASPOONS SALT
1/2	TEASPOON FRESHLY GROUND BLACK PEPPER
PINCH	FENNEL SEED, CRUSHED
1	TEASPOON ROSEMARY, CRUSHED
1	TEASPOON OREGANO
1	TEASPOON DRY BASIL
2	POUNDS LEAN BONELESS PORK (CUT INTO 1/2" CUBES)
1/2	CUP MUSHROOMS, SLICED
	GRATED PARMESAN OR ROMANO CHEESE

METHOD: SAUTE ONION, CARROT, BELL PEPPER AND GARLIC IN THE OLIVE OIL UNTIL OIL TURNS ORANGE. ADD TOMATOES, TOMATO SAUCE, SALT, BLACK PEPPER, FENNEL SEED, ROSEMARY, OREGANO, BASIL AND PORK. BRING SAUCE TO A BOIL, REDUCE HEAT, COVER AND SIMMER FOR ABOUT 2 HOURS. 15 MINUTES BEFORE SAUCE IS DONE, ADD MUSHROOMS.

TO SERVE; REMOVE MEAT FROM THE SAUCE AND PLACE IN A SEPARATE SERVING DISH. POUR SAUCE OVER PASTA, TOSS, SPRINKLE CHEESE OVER PASTA AND THE PORK.

RECOMMENDED PASTA: STRING TYPES.

GROUND VEAL AND MUSHROOM SAUCE

(LONG AND LOW)

VEAL IS TO THE NORTHERN ITALIAN COOK, WHAT BEEF IS TO AN AMERICAN COOK. THEY HAVE MANY CALVES FROM THE MILK HERDS AND THEY'RE NOT WILLING TO SHARE MILK THAT'S SCHEDULED FOR CHEESE PRODUCTION WITH THE CALVES, HENCE, VEAL ON THE TABLE. THEY DO HAVE BEEF, BUT OVERALL AND WITH LIMITED EXCEPTIONS, IT DOES NOT MATCH THE QUALITY OF AMERICAN BEEF.

INGREDIENTS:

6	SLICES BACON, COOKED, BUT NOT CRISP, DRAIN
1/2	CUP SLICED MUSHROOMS
3	TABLESPOONS OLIVE OIL
1	POUND GROUND VEAL
1	ONION, CHOPPED
1	CARROT, SHREDDED OR CHOPPED
1	16 OUNCE CAN TOMATOES, BLENDERIZED
2	8 OUNCE CANS TOMATO SAUCE
1	TEASPOON SALT
1/4	TEASPOON FRESHLY GROUND BLACK PEPPER
1/4	TEASPOON GROUND ALLSPICE

METHOD: CRUMBLE GROUND VEAL AND SAUTE IN THE OLIVE OIL UNTIL PINK COLOR IS GONE. ADD MUSHROOMS, ONION, CARROT, TOMATOES, TOMATO SAUCE, SALT, PEPPER AND ALLSPICE. BRING SAUCE TO A BOIL, REDUCE HEAT, COVER AND SIMMER FOR ABOUT 2 HOURS. OCCASIONALLY SKIM OF THE FLOATING OIL. SERVE OVER FAVORITE PASTA.

RECOMMENDED PASTA: TRY A GNOCCHI OR CAVATELLI OR OTHER FANCIES.

SARDINIAN LAMB AND TOMATO SAUCE

(LONG AND LOW)

FROM THE ISLAND OF SARDINIA OFF ITALY'S WESTERN COAST AND JUST A LITTLE SOUTH OF WHERE THE CORSICAN BROTHERS MAY STILL BE FIGHTING OFF THE BAD GUYS, COMES THIS SAUCE OF LAMB KISSED WITH CINNAMON.

INGREDIENTS:

1	POUND OF BONELESS LAMB OR 2 POUNDS OF LAMB RIBS
2	TABLESPOONS OLIVE OIL
	SALT
2	CLOVES GARLIC, MINCED
1	ONION, CHOPPED
3/4	TEASPOON GROUND CINNAMON
1/4	TEASPOON CRUSHED RED PEPPER
1	28 OUNCE CAN PEAR TOMATOES, BLENDERIZED
1/4	CUP PARSLEY, CHOPPED
	GRATED PARMESAN CHEESE

METHOD: CUT LAMB INTO SMALL BITE SIZED PIECES AND BROWN IN OLIVE OIL. REMOVE LAMB, POUR OFF ALL BUT 1 TABLESPOON PAN DRIPPINGS. REPLACE PAN DRIPPINGS AND SAUTE ONION AND GARLIC UNTIL ONION IS TRANSPARENT. RETURN LAMB. ADD CINNAMON, CRUSHED PEPPER, PARSLEY AND TOMATOES. BRING SAUCE TO A BOIL, COVER AND REDUCE HEAT TO SIMMER. COOK FOR 1 1/2 HOURS. SKIM ANY EXCESS OIL. POUR SAUCE OVER PASTA, TOSS AND SERVE WITH CHEESE ON THE SIDE.

RECOMMENDED PASTA: CAVATELLI OR OTHER MEDIUM SHELLS.

GREEK STYLE SAUCE

(LONG AND LOW)

A BRIEF NOTE ON SICILIAN HISTORY MIGHT HELP HERE. SICILY WAS ORIGINALLY SETTLED BY THE GREEKS, AND THEY ESTABLISHED SEVERAL MAJOR GREEK CITIES DURING THEIR CLASSICAL PERIOD, AMONG THEM WAS SYRACUSE, THE APPARENT HOME OF THIS SAUCE. AGAIN, ONE OF THE MANY PEOPLES WHO CONQUERED AND RULED SICILY WERE THE ARABS WHO ALSO LEFT AN INDELIBLE MARK ON SICILIAN COOKERY, IN PARTICULAR REINFORCING THE LEFTOVER, BUT WELL ESTABLISHED MEAT PREFERENCE OF SICILY FOR LAMB, OVER THE SOUTHERN ITALIAN PREFERENCE FOR PORK. NOW ON WITH THE SAUCE:

INGREDIENTS:

2	TABLESPOONS OLIVE OIL OR BUTTER
2	ONIONS, CHOPPED
2	POUNDS GROUND LAMB
	(IF YOU DON'T LIKE LAMB, USE BEEF)
2	CLOVES GARLIC, UNCUT
2	6 OUNCE CANS TOMATO PASTE
2	TEASPOONS SALT
2	CUPS WATER
1	STICK CINNAMON
1	TEASPOON GROUND MIXED PICKLING SPICE, OR WHOLE SPICE PLACED IN A REMOVABLE CHEESE CLOTH BAG.

METHOD: SAUTE ONIONS IN THE BUTTER UNTIL TRANSPARENT. REMOVE THE ONIONS, ADD THE GROUND MEAT AND COOK UNTIL NO LONGER PINK. RETURN ONIONS. ADD GARLIC, TOMATO PASTE, SALT, WATER AND SPICE. COVER LOOSELY AND SIMMER FOR 1 1/2 TO 2 HOURS. IF SPICE IS BAGGED, REMOVE IT, ALONG WITH THE CINNAMON STICK AND GARLIC. POUR SAUCE OVER YOUR PASTA. TOSS AND SERVE.

RECOMMENDED PASTA: ANY ONE YOU LIKE.

HOME STYLE SAUCE

THIS SAUCE IS ONE OF THE VERY FEW, BUT NOT THE ONLY SAUCE IN THIS BOOK WHERE THE OIL OF PREFERENCE IS LARD, BACON OIL COMES IN SECOND.

INGREDIENTS:

1	TABLESPOON LARD
1	SMALL ONION, CHOPPED
1	CLOVE GARLIC
1	STALK CELERY, FINELY CHOPPED
1	CARROT, SHREDDED
3	SLICES BACON OR 2 OUNCES SALT PORK
1	TABLESPOON FRESH PARSLEY, CHOPPED
1/2	CAN TOMATO PASTE (3 OUNCES)
1	CUP WATER
PINCH	FRESHLY GROUND BLACK PEPPER

METHOD: BLEND THE TOMATO PASTE WITH THE WATER, SET ASIDE. SAUTE OVER MEDIUM HEAT, THE ONION, GARLIC, CELERY, CARROT, PARSLEY AND BACON IN THE LARD UNTIL BACON CRISPS. ADD THINNED TOMATO PASTE AND PEPPER. BRING SAUCE TO A BOIL, LOWER HEAT, SIMMER FOR 20 TO 30 MINUTES. POUR OVER PASTA. TOSS AND SERVE.

RECOMMENDED PASTA: STRING TYPES.

AMATRICE STYLE SAUCE

FROM A VILLAGE IN WEST CENTRAL ITALY, IN THE REGION OF LAZIO (ROME) WE GET THIS SAUCE. HERE WE'LL USE PANCETTA OR BACON AS THE FLAVORING MEAT. I SAY FLAVORING BECAUSE THERE'S NOT ENOUGH OF IT TO GIVE YOU ANY MEAT SATISFACTION, JUST ENOUGH FOR GOOD FLAVORING.

INGREDIENTS:

1/4	POUND PANCETTA OR BACON, CUT INTO 1" PIECES, OLIVE OIL
1	ONION, CHOPPED
1/2	TEASPOON CRUSHED RED PEPPER
1	28 OUNCE CAN PEAR TOMATOES, BLENDERIZED
2	TABLESPOONS PARSLEY, CHOPPED
	GRATED PARMESAN CHEESE

METHOD: FRY PANCETTA OR BACON UNTIL COOKED TO YOUR PREFERENCE. REMOVE MEAT AND SET ASIDE. ADD ENOUGH OLIVE OIL TO GIVE YOU ABOUT 1/4 CUP OF OIL AND BACON FAT. SAUTE THE ONION AND CRUSHED RED PEPPER IN THE OIL UNTIL ONION IS TRANSPARENT. ADD PARSLEY AND TOMATOES, BRING SAUCE TO A BOIL, LOOSELY COVER AND SIMMER FOR 30 MINUTES. REMOVE FROM HEAT, POUR OVER PASTA. TOSS AND SERVE WITH GRATED CHEESE ON THE SIDE.

RECOMMENDED PASTA: HOLLOW STRING TYPES.

MEATBALLS AND SPAGHETTI SAUCE

IF YOU PREFER, SPAGHETTI AND MEATBALL(S) SAUCE

(LONG AND LOW)

I'M UNCERTAIN AS TO PROPER ETIQUETTE AND PROTOCOL HERE. IS IT COMPLEX CARBOHYDRATES FIRST FOLLOWED BY PROTEIN OR THE OTHER WAY AROUND? DO YOU CARE? IN EITHER CASE, THE TASTE AND THE DISH REMAIN THE SAME, THE FIRST IS EXCELLENT AND THE LATTER IS ONE OF AMERICAS GREAT FAVORITES.

AN UNCOMPLICATED TOMATO SAUCE IS USED HERE. ACTUALLY MEATBALLS CAN BE COOKED IN ANY TOMATO SAUCE, BUT TO FILL THE NEEDS OF COOKS WHO KNOW IN THEIR HEART'S THAT ITALIAN STYLE FOOD IS "MEATBALLS AND SPAGHETTI", I OFFER YOU THE FOLLOWING RECIPE.

I INCLUDE ONE CAVEAT, THERE ARE ALMOST AS MANY RECIPES FOR MEAT BALLS AS THERE ARE RECIPES FOR PASTA SAUCE. I AM ONLY OFFERING ONE.

INGREDIENTS: FOR THE MEATBALLS:

2	POUNDS GROUND BEEF OR 1 BEEF & 1 GROUND PORK
5	SLICES BREAD, FRESH OR STALE
1/2	CUP WATER, MILK OR WINE
3	CLOVES GARLIC, MINCED
1	ONION, CHOPPED
1	CUP GRATED PARMESAN CHEESE
1/2	CUP PARSLEY, CHOPPED
1	EGG (USE UP TO 3, BUT LOOK OUT FOR STICKINESS)
1	TEASPOON SALT
1/2	TEASPOON FRESHLY GRATED BLACK PEPPER
1	TEASPOON DRIED OREGANO
PINCH	DRIED BASIL
	OLIVE OIL; MAYBE?

Continued on next page

METHOD: IF USING FRESH BREAD, SOAK THE FRESH BREAD SLICES IN THE MILK, WATER OR WINE, SQUEEZE TO DISCARD THE SURPLUS LIQUID.

IF YOU ARE USING DRY, STALE BREAD, MAKE CRUMBS BY WHIRLING THEM IN A BLENDER OR PROCESSOR. ADD MORE BREAD IF NECESSARY, YOU'LL NEED ABOUT 1-1/2 TO 2 CUPS OF CRUMBS. (DON'T TURN THE DRY BREAD TO FLOUR).

PLACE ALL INGREDIENTS INTO A LARGE BOWL AND BLEND WELL. ROLL THE MEATBALLS INTO ANY SIZE YOU LIKE. LARGER MEATBALLS ARE JUICIER YOU MIGHT TRY THEM AT ABOUT 2 INCHES IN DIAMETER.

NOW COMES A REAL PERSONAL CHOICE; I DO NOT PRECOOK MY MEATBALLS, I PREFER TO DROP THEM "A'BLANC" DIRECTLY IN A SIMMERING SAUCE. THIS PROCEDURE DOES REQUIRE THE YOU SCOOP THE EXCESS OIL FROM THE SAUCE, IT'S EASY TO DO.

IF YOU WISH TO PRECOOK THEM, YOU MAY BAKE THEM AT 325 DEGREES FOR ABOUT 20 MINUTES. OR BROIL THEM, TURNING FREQUENTLY OR FRY THEM UNTIL GOLDEN BROWN ALL AROUND.

INGREDIENTS: FOR THE SAUCE:

2	TABLESPOONS OLIVE OIL
2	28 OUNCE CANS OF "TOMATO SAUCE"
2	CUPS WATER OR WINE
2	CLOVES GARLIC, SLICED
1/2	CUP PARSLEY, CHOPPED
1/2	POUND MUSHROOMS, SLICED
1	TABLESPOON DRIED BASIL
1	TABLESPOON DRIED OREGANO
1/2	TEASPOON FRESHLY GRATED BLACK PEPPER.

METHOD: I WOULD SUGGEST YOU DO NOT USE PUREE OR EVEN TOMATO PASTE, TO DO SO WILL REQUIRE THE ADDITION OF SUGAR.

IF YOU USE THE A'BLANC METHOD, USE THE OLIVE OIL AND VERY BRIEFLY SAUTE THE GARLIC, ADD ALL OTHER INGREDIENTS. BRING SAUCE TO A BOIL, STIR WHILE REDUCING HEAT TO SIMMER. ADD ALL THE MEATBALLS, PARTIALLY COVER AND SIMMER FOR A LEAST 15 MINUTES BEFORE STIRRING AGAIN. CONTINUE COOKING FOR AN ADDITIONAL 30 TO 45 MINUTES.

IF YOU FRY, BAKE OR BROIL THE MEATBALLS; FRY THEM IN THE OLIVE OIL, THEN DRAIN OFF MOST OF THE OIL. ADD ALL THE SAUCE INGREDIENTS, COOK AS DIRECTED ABOVE.

REMOVE MEATBALLS FROM SAUCE. POUR SAUCE OVER PASTA. TOSS AND SERVE WITH MEATBALLS AND EXTRA CHEESE ON THE SIDE.

RECOMMENDED PASTA: WHAT ELSE? SPAGHETTI!

TOMATO AND CHICKEN LIVER SAUCE

I KNOW THAT THERE MUST BE OTHER USES FOR CHICKEN LIVER ASIDE FROM PATE AND HORS D'OEUVRES WRAPPED IN BACON. CHICKEN LIVER LOVERS, LOVE CHICKEN LIVER, THEREFORE FOR MY WIFE AND YOU ALONE, I OFFER THIS RECIPE, BECAUSE I WON'T EAT IT. ALSO SEE CHAPTER 19 FOR A LIVER SAUCE WITHOUT TOMATOES.

INGREDIENTS:

1	POUND CHICKEN LIVERS
2	TABLESPOONS OLIVE OIL
1	ONION, MINCED
1	6 OUNCE CAN TOMATO PASTE
1 1/2	CUPS WATER
1/2	TEASPOON SALT
1/4	TEASPOON FRESHLY GROUND BLACK PEPPER
1/2	CUP FRESHLY GRATED PARMESAN CHEESE
1/2	POUND MUSHROOMS, SLICED
8	TABLESPOONS BUTTER

METHOD: SAUTE ONION IN THE OLIVE OIL UNTIL ONION BEGINS TO BROWN, IMMEDIATELY ADD TOMATO PASTE, WATER, SALT AND PEPPER AND WHISK TO BLEND. SLOWLY WHISK IN THE CHEESE UNTIL THOROUGHLY BLENDED, ALLOW TO REMAIN ON VERY LOW HEAT WHILE IN A SECOND SKILLET, YOU'LL SAUTE THE MUSHROOM AND CHICKEN LIVERS TOGETHER IN THE BUTTER. WHEN DONE, POUR THE SAUCE OVER THE PASTA AND TOSS. NOW LAY THE LIVER AND MUSHROOMS OVER THE PASTA, SERVE.

RECOMMENDED PASTA: STRING TYPES.

MEAT AND VEGETABLE SAUCE #1

FROM NORTH CENTRAL ITALY COMES THIS HEARTY SAUCE. IT HAS A LONG INGREDIENT LIST, BUT IS EASY TO MAKE. ALL THE VEGETABLES WILL BE FINELY CHOPPED IN YOUR PROCESSOR, YOU MAY ALSO DO THIS WITH A BLENDER. TO GET THE VEGETABLES TO TURNOVER IN A BLENDER PUT 2 CUPS OF WATER IN WITH THE VEGETABLES, THEN USING THE PULSE BUTTON, PROCESS UNTIL WELL CHOPPED, DRAIN.

INGREDIENTS:

1/4	CUP MUSHROOMS
1	ONION, QUARTERED
1	CARROT, PEELED AND QUARTERED
1	CELERY STALK, QUARTERED
2	OUNCES HAM OR BACON (DICED)
5	TABLESPOONS BUTTER
1/4	CUP OLIVE OIL
4	OUNCES GROUND BEEF
4	OUNCES GROUND PORK
1/4	CUP RED WINE
1	16 OUNCE CAN PEAR TOMATOES (BLENDERIZED)
1/2	TEASPOON SALT
1/4	TEASPOON FRESHLY GROUND BLACK PEPPER
1	CUP FROZEN PEAS
3/4	CUP PARMESAN CHEESE

METHOD: PROCESS TOGETHER; MUSHROOMS, ONION, CARROT, CELERY AND HAM. SAUTE THE MIX IN THE 1/2 THE BUTTER AND ALL THE OLIVE OIL. COOK OVER MEDIUM HEAT FOR 10 MINUTES, ADD THE GROUND BEEF, PORK, SALT AND PEPPER, COOK 5 ADDITIONAL MINUTES. ADD WINE, COVER AND SIMMER FOR 15 MINUTES, ADD TOMATOES AND SIMMER AN ADDITIONAL 30 MINUTES. IN A SEPARATE PAN. SAUTE THE FROZEN PEAS IN THE REMAINING 1/2 BUTTER FOR 5 MINUTES. ADD PEAS TO SAUCE AND CONTINUE COOKING FOR 5 ADDITIONAL MINUTES. POUR SAUCE OVER PASTA. TOSS AND SERVE WITH CHEESE ON THE SIDE.

RECOMMENDED PASTA: HOLLOW STRING TYPES.

MEAT AND VEGETABLE SAUCE #2
(MAY BE USED AS A BAKING SAUCE)

FROM WAY DOWN YONDER IN SICILY COMES THIS SAUCE, THE SICILIANS REFER TO THIS AS A RAGU. MY RECIPE FILES SHOW THIS SAUCE TO BE USED IN TWO WAYS, AS A PASTA SAUCE OR AS A BAKING SAUCE, TRY IT BOTH WAYS.

INGREDIENTS:

1/4	CUP OLIVE OIL
1	ONION, CHOPPED
1	CARROT SHREDDED
1	CELERY STALK, CHOPPED
1	CLOVE GARLIC, CHOPPED
12	FRESH PEAR TOMATOES (B/P/C)
	OR
1	28 OUNCE CAN PEAR TOMATOES, BLENDERIZED
1/2	POUND GROUND VEAL
1/4	POUND CHICKEN LIVERS, CHOPPED
1/4	TEASPOON FRESHLY GROUND BLACK PEPPER
1/3	TEASPOON SALT
2	HARD COOKED EGGS, SLICED
1/4	POUND MOZZARELLA CHEESE, SHREDDED
1/4	CUP GRATED ROMANO CHEESE

IF YOU CHOOSE TO USE FRESH TOMATOES, ADD 3/4 TEASPOON SALT

METHOD: SAUTE ONION, CARROT, CELERY AND GARLIC IN THE OLIVE OIL FOR ABOUT 5 MINUTES. ADD TOMATOES, VEAL, CHICKEN LIVERS, SALT AND PEPPER, COVER AND SIMMER FOR 30 MINUTES. NOW YOU MAY USE THIS AS A PASTA SAUCE AS IS, OR, BAKE WITH IT, USING ALTERNATING LAYERS OF PASTA, EGG AND MOZZARELLA, SPRINKLING THE ROMANO OVER THE FINAL LAYER. BAKE IN A PREHEATED OVEN AT 350 DEGREES FOR 20 MINUTES. SERVE.

RECOMMENDED PASTA: RIBBON TYPES, FOR EITHER METHOD.

ROMAN STYLE TOMATO SAUCE

THIS SAUCE AND MANY SIMILAR TO IT ARE REFERRED TO AS A (SUGO FINITO ALLA ROMANA). I HAVE NO LESS THAN FOURTEEN VERSIONS OF THIS RECIPE. THIS ONE APPEARS TO BE THE BEST COMPROMISE.

INGREDIENTS:

8	TABLESPOONS BUTTER
4	SLICES SUGAR CURED BACON, MINCED
1	ONION, CHOPPED
1	CLOVE GARLIC, CRUSHED
1	16 OUNCE CAN PEAR TOMATOES (BLENDERIZED)
1/2	CUP MUSHROOMS, SLICED
12	OUNCES CHICKEN GIBLETS, CHOPPED
1/3	CUP WHITE WINE
1/2	TEASPOON SALT
1/4	TEASPOON FRESHLY GROUND BLACK PEPPER

METHOD: SAUTE BACON, ONION AND GARLIC IN 4 TABLESPOONS BUTTER UNTIL GARLIC TURNS GOLDEN. REMOVE AND DISCARD GARLIC. ADD TOMATOES AND MUSHROOMS, BRING TO A BOIL, REDUCE HEAT AND SIMMER FOR 20 MINUTES WHILE LOOSELY COVERED. IN A SEPARATE PAN, USE REMAINING BUTTER TO SAUTE GIBLETS FOR 3 MINUTES. ADD SALT, PEPPER AND WINE, CONTINUE COOKING UNTIL WINE EVAPORATES AND THE GIBLETS ARE TENDER. ADD GIBLETS TO SAUCE, MIX WELL, POUR SAUCE OVER PASTA. TOSS AND SERVE.

RECOMMENDED PASTA: RIBBON TYPES.

CART DRIVER'S SAUCE TOO!

WHILE VERY SIMILAR TO THE PRECEDING SAUCE, THIS CART DRIVER STYLE SAUCE IS OUR THIRD OFFERING OF A SAUCE WITH THIS NAME. SEE CHAPTERS 8 AND 11 FOR FURTHER VARIATIONS. MORE TO THE POINT HOWEVER, IS THAT I FIND IT DIFFICULT TO BELIEVE THAT A CART DRIVER HAD EITHER THE TIME TO MAKE THIS SAUCE, OR EVEN THE ABILITY TO CARRY ALL THE INGREDIENTS, MUCH LESS START A FIRE, PREPARE COOK AND EAT THE MEAL. UNLESS OF COURSE, HE HAD MADE HIS DELIVERY AND WAS ON THE RETURN TRIP. WHATEVER THE CASE, THIS IS A SOUTHERN STYLE SAUCE.

INGREDIENTS:

3	TABLESPOONS OLIVE OIL
1	CLOVE GARLIC, CRUSHED
2	ONIONS, CHOPPED
1/2	LONG GREEN MILDLY HOT PEPPER, MINCED
4	SLICES OF BACON, CURED OR FRESH, DICED
4	PEAR TOMATOES (B/P/C)
1/2	TEASPOON SALT
1/2	CAN TUNA, (OIL PACK) DRAINED IF YOU WISH
2	MUSHROOMS, SLICED
1/4	CUP GRATED ROMANO CHEESE

METHOD: SAUTE GARLIC, ONIONS, GREEN PEPPER AND BACON, IN THE OLIVE OIL, WHEN GARLIC IS LIGHTLY GOLDEN, REMOVE AND DISCARD. ADD THE TOMATOES AND SALT, BRING SAUCE TO A BOIL, REDUCE HEAT, COVER AND SIMMER FOR 25 MINUTES. ADD TUNA, MUSHROOMS AND A LARGE PINCH OF THE GRATED CHEESE. COOK FOR 10 ADDITIONAL MINUTES. REMOVE SAUCE FROM HEAT, SPRINKLE GRATED CHEESE OVER PASTA, TOSS, ADD SAUCE, TOSS AGAIN, SERVE.

RECOMMENDED PASTA: HOLLOW STRING TYPES.

FRESH TOMATOES AND MINT SAUCE

FROM THE MOUNTAINS OF CENTRAL ITALY COMES THIS TOMATO SAUCE WITH A HINT OF MINT AND A LITTLE ADDED ZIP.

INGREDIENTS:

1/2	CUP OLIVE OIL
3	SLICES PANCETTA OR SALT PORK, DICED
1	ONION, CHOPPED OR THINLY SLICED
2	CLOVES GARLIC, HALVED
2	POUNDS FRESH PEAR TOMATOES (B/P/C) OR PUREE THEM IN BLENDER
1/2	TEASPOON SALT
1/4	LONG GREEN MILDLY HOT PEPPER (WHOLE)
5	MINT LEAVES, CHOPPED

METHOD: SAUTE PANCETTA, ONION AND GARLIC IN OLIVE OIL. WHEN GARLIC TURNS GOLDEN, REMOVE AND DISCARD. ADD TOMATOES, SALT, HOT PEPPER AND MINT. BRING SAUCE TO A BOIL, REDUCE HEAT, LOOSELY COVER AND SIMMER FOR 30 MINUTES. REMOVE HOT PEPPER AND DISCARD. POUR SAUCE OVER PASTA. TOSS AND SERVE.

RECOMMENDED PASTA: STRING TYPES.

LAMB AND SWEET PEPPER SAUCE

(LONG AND LOW)

FROM THE ADRIATIC PROVINCE OF ABRUZZI WE GET THIS SLOW SIMMERED INTERESTING SAUCE. WHILE THE NAME CERTAINLY CALLS FOR SWEET PEPPERS, IT IS NOT OUT OF LINE TO SWAP THOSE FOR 1 TEASPOON OF CRUSHED RED PEPPER FLAKES, OR EVEN A FRESH LONG GREEN MILDLY HOT PEPPER. IF YOU HAVE A FEW MUSHROOMS, YOU MAY TOSS THEM IN TOO.

INGREDIENTS:

1	POUND LAMB MEAT, DICED
1/2	TEASPOON SALT
1/2	TEASPOON FRESHLY GROUND BLACK PEPPER
1/2	CUP OLIVE OIL
2	CLOVES GARLIC, HALVED
2	BAY LEAVES
6	PEAR TOMATOES (B/P/C)
3	BELL PEPPERS, SLICED OR CHOPPED
1	CUP WATER, BROTH, OR WINE

METHOD: SALT AND PEPPER THE DICED MEAT, SET ASIDE FOR 1 HOUR. SAUTE THE GARLIC AND BAY LEAVES IN THE OLIVE OIL. WHEN GARLIC TURNS GOLDEN, REMOVE AND DISCARD GARLIC AND BAY LEAVES. SAUTE LAMB IN SEASONED OIL FOR 10 MINUTES. ADD TOMATOES AND BELL PEPPERS. COVER, REDUCE HEAT TO SIMMER AND COOK FOR 1 1/2 HOURS. ADD LIQUID AS NEEDED. POUR SAUCE OVER PASTA. TOSS AND SERVE.

RECOMMENDED PASTA: STRING TYPES, SOLID OR HOLLOW.

WE TRIED THIS SAUCE . . . AND

LOVED IT ( )
HATED IT ( )
MAYBE WE'LL TRY IT AGAIN ( )
WE'LL USE IT FOR UNWELCOME GUESTS ( )

CALABRIAN STYLE SAUCE

THIS SAUCE USES PARMA HAM (PROSCIUTTO) AND CACIOCAVALLO CHEESE. AMERICAN OR DANISH HAM JUST DOESN'T DO IT. A GERMAN STYLE WESTPHALIAN HAM MAY COME CLOSE. SINCE WE'RE ONLY USING 4 OUNCES, IT MIGHT BE WORTH SPLURGING TO BUY THE ITALIAN OR GERMAN STYLE HAM. CACIOCAVALLO IS A DIFFERENT MATTER, FINDING SOMETHING BY THAT NAME MAY BE QUITE DIFFICULT, PROVOLONE IS A MEMBER OF THE SAME FAMILY AND READILY AVAILABLE. THIS DISH WILL BE LAYERED BEFORE SERVING.

INGREDIENTS:
2 1/2	POUNDS PEAR TOMATOES (B/P/C)
1/2	CUP OLIVE OIL
1	CLOVE GARLIC, CRUSHED
1/4	MILDLY HOT GREEN PEPPER, MINCED
1	ONION, CHOPPED
4	OUNCES PROSCUITTO, MINCED
1/2	TEASPOON SALT
1	CUP SHREDDED PROVOLONE

METHOD: SAUTE GARLIC AND PEPPER IN OLIVE OIL. DISCARD GARLIC WHEN IT HAS BROWNED. ADD ONION AND COOK UNTIL IT BECOMES TRANSPARENT. ADD PROSCIUTTO, COOK FOR 2 MINUTES. ADD TOMATOES, BRING SAUCE TO A BOIL, REDUCE HEAT, LOOSELY COVER AND SIMMER FOR 30 MINUTES.

USE A CASSEROLE SERVING DISH FOR THE TABLE PREPARATION. START WITH A LAYER OF SAUCE AND THEN USE ALTERNATING LAYERS OF PASTA, SAUCE AND CHEESE, ETC., SERVE.

RECOMMENDED PASTA: HOLLOW STRING TYPES, BROKEN INTO 3 INCH LENGTHS BEFORE COOKING.

APULIA STYLE TOMATO SAUCE

(LONG AND LOW)

THIS RECIPE CALLS FOR A HARD RICOTTA CHEESE. UNLESS YOU LIVE IN A COMMUNITY WITH A LARGE ITALIAN POPULATION, IT MAY BE DIFFICULT TO COME BY. I'M NOT SURE WHAT COULD BE USED AS A REPLACEMENT. POSSIBLY A DRY JACK OR A DRY "FARMER" TYPE AMERICAN CHEESE, OR USE THAT OLD STANDBY, PARMESAN.

INGREDIENTS:

1/2	CUP OLIVE OIL
1	CLOVE GARLIC, CRUSHED OR MINCED
1/2	POUND GROUND LAMB OR PORK
1	ONION, SLICED
1	POUND PEAR TOMATOES (B/P/C)
1/2	TEASPOON SALT
1/4	TEASPOON FRESHLY GROUND BLACK PEPPER
2	TABLESPOONS PARSLEY, CHOPPED
2	TABLESPOONS BASIL, CHOPPED
1	CUP GRATED DRY RICOTTA

METHOD: SAUTE THE GARLIC IN THE OLIVE OIL, ADD MEAT AND ONION, COOK UNTIL MEAT CHANGES COLOR. ADD TOMATOES, SALT AND PEPPER. BRING SAUCE TO A BOIL, LOWER HEAT, COVER AND SIMMER FOR 1 HOUR. REMOVE FROM HEAT. ADD PARSLEY AND BASIL. POUR SAUCE OVER PASTA, MIX WELL, SERVE WITH CHEESE ON THE SIDE.

RECOMMENDED PASTA: FANCY TYPES SUCH AS "PRIESTS' HATS".

WE TRIED THIS SAUCE . . . AND

LOVED IT ( )
HATED IT ( )
MAYBE WE'LL TRY IT AGAIN ( )
WE'LL USE IT FOR UNWELCOME GUESTS ( )

SAUSAGE AND EGGPLANT SAUCE

LOTS OF VEGETABLES IN THIS SAUCE, BUT THE USE OF SAUSAGE PLACES IT IN THIS CHAPTER. SOME RECIPES COMBINING THESE INGREDIENTS CALL FOR UNPEELED EGGPLANT. YOU MAY DO IT THAT WAY IF YOU WISH, BUT UNLESS YOU'RE USING THE TINY JAPANESE EGGPLANT, THE SKIN IS TOO TOUGH TO LEAVE ON.

THIS RECIPE CALLS FOR BELL PEPPERS, YOU MAY SUBSTITUTE MILDLY HOT GREEN PEPPERS FOR THE SWEET VARIETY.

INGREDIENTS:
1	POUND SWEET ITALIAN SAUSAGE, (SKINNED AND CRUMBLED)
1	MEDIUM EGGPLANT, PARED AND DICED
3	TABLESPOONS OLIVE OIL
4	TABLESPOONS BUTTER
2	CLOVES GARLIC, CRUSHED
2	TABLESPOONS CHOPPED PARSLEY
1	ONION, CHOPPED
1	TEASPOON SALT
1/2	TEASPOON FRESHLY GROUND BLACK PEPPER
3	BELL PEPPERS, SEEDED AND THINLY SLICED
1	16 OUNCE CAN PEAR TOMATOES, BLENDERIZED AND
4	FRESH PEAR TOMATOES (B/P/C)
	CUP GRATED PARMESAN CHEESE

METHOD: COOK SAUSAGE IN IT'S OWN FAT UNTIL BROWNED. DRAIN AND DISCARD OIL, SET SAUSAGE ASIDE. SAUTE ONION, GARLIC AND PARSLEY IN OLIVE OIL AND BUTTER UNTIL ONION IS TRANSPARENT. REMOVE AND DISCARD GARLIC. ADD SALT AND PEPPER, SAUSAGE, BELL PEPPERS AND EGGPLANT. COOK FOR ABOUT 5 MINUTES, ADD CANNED AND FRESH TOMATOES. LOWER HEAT, COVER AND SIMMER FOR 30 MINUTES. POUR SAUCE OVER PASTA. TOSS AND SERVE WITH GRATED CHEESE ON THE SIDE.

RECOMMENDED PASTA: STRING TYPES.

287

HOT RED PEPPER SAUCE

THIS ROMAN SAUCE IS FOR THOSE WHO LOVE A GOOD FIRE ..., ON THEIR PLATE AND IT WILL CERTAINLY GET ALL OF YOUR ATTENTION WITH YOUR FIRST BITE. THE SAUCE FALLS INTO THIS CHAPTER BECAUSE IT USES SALT PORK, OR IF YOU WISH, USE BACON. YOU MAY EVEN BYPASS THOSE TWO IN FAVOR OF OLIVE OIL.

IF YOU ARE UNABLE TO FIND FRESH, LITTLE (1 TO 2 INCHES LONG) HOT PEPPERS. YOU MAY SUBSTITUTE ONE TEASPOON CRUSHED DRY RED PEPPER.

INGREDIENTS:
- 1/2 POUND SALT PORK, DICED
- 1 ONION, CHOPPED
- 2 CLOVES GARLIC, CRUSHED
- 4 TO 6 FRESH HOT RED PEPPERS, SEEDED AND MINCED
- 1 16 OUNCE CAN PEAR TOMATOES, BLENDERIZED
- 1/2 CUP GRATED PARMESAN CHEESE

METHOD: SAUTE SALT PORK, ONION AND GARLIC, UNTIL GARLIC IS LIGHTLY GOLDEN. REMOVE AND DISCARD GARLIC. ADD PEPPERS AND TOMATOES. BRING SAUCE TO A BOIL, REDUCE HEAT AND COOK AT LOW FOR 20 MINUTES, OR UNTIL SAUCE HAS THICKENED. POUR SAUCE OVER PASTA. MIX. ADD PARMESAN CHEESE, MIX AGAIN AND SERVE.

RECOMMENDED PASTA: MEDIUM TUBE TYPES.

HOT GREEN PEPPER SAUCE

THIS IS VERY SIMILAR TO THE PRECEDING AND ALSO A ROMAN FAVORITE. THE DIFFERENCES ARE BACON OVER SALT PORK AND HOT GREEN PEPPERS VERSUS HOT RED PEPPERS.

INGREDIENTS:

6	SLICES SUGAR CURED BACON, DICED
1	28 OUNCE CAN PEAR TOMATOES (BLENDERIZED)
1/4	TEASPOON FRESHLY GROUND BLACK PEPPER
2	GREEN HOT PEPPERS (YOUR CHOICE OF VARIETY) DICED
2	TABLESPOONS BUTTER
1/2	CUP FRESHLY GRATED ASIAGO OR ROMANO CHEESE

METHOD: COOK BACON UNTIL IT JUST BEGINS TO CRISP. (IF BACON WAS NOT LEAN, YOU MAY WISH TO DRAW OFF SOME OF THE OIL, IF BACON IS LEAN AND THERE IS ALMOST NONE, ADD A LITTLE OLIVE OIL), ADD TOMATOES, BLACK PEPPER AND GREEN PEPPERS. BRING SAUCE TO A BOIL, LOWER HEAT TO LOW AND COOK FOR 25 MINUTES. TOSS HOT, DRAINED PASTA WITH THE BUTTER. ADD GRATED CHEESE, TOSS AGAIN. POUR SAUCE OVER PASTA, TOSS A THIRD TIME, SERVE.

RECOMMENDED PASTA: MEDIUM TUBE TYPES.

ROMAN STYLE TRIPE SAUCE

(LONG AND LOW)

THIS IS A SAUCE SIMILAR TO WHAT MY DEAR OLD GRANNY USED TO MAKE. IF NOT THIS EXACT RECIPE, IT WAS SOMETHING VERY NEAR TO IT. MY GRAND-MOTHER CAME FROM ROCCA d'ASPIDE IN CAMPANIA. THIS SAUCE IS A ROMAN VERSION, SO THERE IS PROBABLY AN INGREDIENT OR TWO THAT WOULD BE DIFFERENT. I REMEMBER THE TRIPE AND THE PASTA AND HOW TASTY IT WAS, BUT I NEVER GOT THE RECIPE. ONE OF THE FEW I DIDN'T. AND . . . , THIS SAUCE IS AN ALL DAY JOB, WAIT UNTIL YOU'VE GOT THE TIME.

INGREDIENTS:

3	POUNDS HONEYCOMB TRIPE (VEAL TRIPE IF POSSIBLE)
3	TABLESPOONS OLIVE OIL
1	OUNCE SALT PORK, MINCED
1	LEMON, QUARTERED
1/2	TEASPOON DRY OREGANO
1/2	TEASPOON SALT
1/4	TEASPOON CRUSHED RED PEPPER
1	28 OUNCE CAN PEAR TOMATOES, BLENDERIZED
1/2	CUP FROZEN PEAS

METHOD: RINSE THE TRIPE. PLACE INTO 4 QUARTS SALTED WATER, BRING TO A BOIL, COVER AND SIMMER FOR 1 HOUR, DRAIN AND REPEAT, DRAIN AND REPEAT AGAIN. AT THIS POINT TRIPE SHOULD BE FORK TENDER, IF NOT CONTINUE COOKING. WHEN IT IS FORK TENDER, CUT THE TRIPE INTO STRIPS OF 1/4" BY 2" INCHES, OR 1" SQUARES.

SAUTE THE TRIPE IN OLIVE OIL WITH THE SALT PORK, LEMON, OREGANO, SALT AND PEPPER FOR 5 MINUTES. ADD TOMATOES. BRING SAUCE TO A BOIL, REDUCE HEAT, COVER AND SIMMER FOR 30 MINUTES, ADD PEAS, COOK AN ADDITIONAL 10 MINUTES. REMOVE SAUCE FROM HEAT. REMOVE LEMON AND DISCARD. POUR OVER PASTA, TOSS AND SERVE. PLACE A PEPPER MILL ON THE TABLE FOR ADDING FRESHLY GROUND BLACK PEPPER TO TASTE.

RECOMMENDED PASTA: NARROW RIBBON TYPES.

VARIATION: ACTUALLY AS I REMEMBER MY GRANDMOTHERS TRIPE DISH, IT WAS MORE OF A THICK, HEARTY BOWL OF PASTA AND TRIPE. TO MAKE IT THAT WAY, COOK 2 CUPS OF DITALINI (SALAD MAC) OR SHELLS. ADD THE PASTA AND 1 OR MORE CUPS OF LIQUID (WATER, BROTH OR PASTA WATER) TO THE SAUCE. ADJUST SEASONING. SERVE WITH BLACK PEPPER OR GRATED CHEESE ON THE SIDE. YOU MAY ALSO CUT THE TRIPE INTO SMALLER, BITE SIZE PIECES.

TOMATOES AND BACON SAUCE

THIS IS REALLY A LIGHT TOMATO SAUCE WITH BACON ADDED. A LEAN BACON WILL KEEP THE OIL LEVEL DOWN. IN ITALY THIS SAUCE IS REFERRED TO AS A SPRINGTIME SAUCE, BUT THAT NAME HAS ALREADY BEEN APPLIED TO SEVERAL SAUCES WITH CREAM AND VEGETABLES.

INGREDIENTS:

2	TABLESPOONS OLIVE OIL
1/2	CLOVE GARLIC
8	SLICES SUGAR CURED BACON, DICED
10	PEAR TOMATOES (B/P/C)
1/2	CUP FRESH CHOPPED BASIL LEAF
	FRESHLY GROUND BLACK PEPPER TO TASTE

METHOD: SAUTE THE BACON AND GARLIC IN OLIVE OIL. WHEN THE BACON IS JUST BEGINNING TO CRISP, ADD THE TOMATOES, BASIL AND BLACK PEPPER. BRING SAUCE TO A BOIL, REDUCE HEAT, SIMMER UNCOVERED FOR 25 MINUTES. POUR SAUCE OVER PASTA. TOSS AND SERVE.

RECOMMENDED PASTA: THIN STRINGS.

TOMATOES AND BACON SAUCE TOO!

NOT ONLY DOES THIS SAUCE HAVE FEWER INGREDIENTS THAN THE PRECEDING SAUCE, BUT IT USES SMALLER AMOUNTS OF THEM, EXCEPT FOR THE BACON.

INGREDIENTS:

2	TABLESPOONS BUTTER
8	OUNCES OF LEAN, SUGAR CURED BACON, DICED
1/2	CUP WHITE WINE
4	PEAR TOMATOES (B/P/C)
1/4	CUP CHOPPED PARSLEY
1/4	CUP PARMESAN CHEESE

METHOD: SAUTE THE BACON IN THE BUTTER UNTIL BACON IS CRISP, ADD WINE AND CONTINUE COOKING FOR 5 MINUTES, WHILE STIRRING CONSTANTLY, ADD THE TOMATOES, SIMMER FOR 15 MINUTES, REMOVE FROM HEAT. ADD AND STIR IN THE PARSLEY, BRIEFLY SET ASIDE. TOSS THE COOKED PASTA WITH THE GRATED CHEESE. POUR SAUCE OVER PASTA. TOSS AGAIN AND SERVE.

RECOMMENDED PASTA: MEDIUM STRAIGHT EDGED TUBE TYPES.

ROMAN STYLE TOMATO SAUCE II

FOR REASONS THAT PROBABLY NO ONE CAN EXPLAIN, ROMANS CALL THIS SAUCE A "MOCK SAUCE", AND IT CAN BE SERVED AS COOKED, OR SIEVED TO CREATE A SMOOTH SAUCE.

INGREDIENTS:

2	POUNDS FRESH PEAR TOMATOES (B/C/P)
	OR
1	28 OUNCE CAN PEAR TOMATOES AND
1	8 OUNCE CAN TOMATO SAUCE
3	TABLESPOONS OLIVE OIL
2	TABLESPOONS BUTTER
4	SLICES BACON, MINCED
1	ONION, CHOPPED
1	STALK CELERY, MINCED
1	CARROT, MINCED
1/2	CLOVE GARLIC, MINCED
2	TABLESPOONS PARSLEY, CHOPPED
1/2	CUP BEEF BROTH
1/2	TEASPOON SALT (USE 1 TSP FOR FRESH TOMATOES)
1/4	TEASPOON FRESHLY GROUND BLACK PEPPER

METHOD: COOK BACON IN OLIVE OIL AND BUTTER FOR 2 MINUTES. ADD ONION, CELERY, CARROT, GARLIC AND PARSLEY, SAUTE FOR 5 MINUTES. ADD BEEF BROTH AS NEED TO ALLOW BROWNING AND PREVENT BURNING. WHEN VEGETABLES BEGIN TO BROWN, ADD TOMATOES, SALT AND PEPPER. BRING TO A BOIL, REDUCE HEAT TO SIMMER, LOOSELY COVER AND COOK FOR 45 MINUTES.

RECOMMENDED PASTA: LONG RIBBON TYPES, STRING TYPES.

CHAPTER 10

SAUCES MADE FROM TOMATOES AND VEGETABLES

SEVERAL OF THE SAUCES IN THIS CHAPTER USE ANCHOVY AS AN INGREDIENT, AND BECAUSE ANCHOVY DISSOLVES IN THE SAUCE, YOU'RE NOT EATING FISH, BUT GETTING A SEASONING. THAT'S WHY, THEY ARE HERE, AND NOT IN SEAFOOD SAUCES.

MANY OF THE RECIPES IN THIS CHAPTER ARE CENTERED AROUND EGGPLANT. TO GIVE YOU SOME OPTIONS, PLEASE READ ABOUT EGGPLANT IN THE AUTHORS NOTES.

SPRING VEGETABLE SAUCE

(PRIMAVERA #1)

IN OUR INTRODUCTION WE COMMENTED ON PASTA PRIMAVERA, IS IT VEGE-TABLES WITH PASTA OR A VEGETABLE SAUCE FOR PASTA? I DON'T KNOW, BUT I AM GOING ON THE ASSUMPTION THAT IT IS A SAUCE. IF YOU CAN PREPARE THE "SAUCE" APART FROM THE PASTA AND THEN DRESS THE PASTA WITH YOUR PREPARATION, THAT'S A SAUCE. AND THAT'S THE SUBJECT OF THIS BOOK! PASTA SAUCES. AS YOU PROBABLY KNOW "PRIMAVERA" IS ITALIAN FOR SPRING AND THAT GIVES US A WIDE RANGE OF EARLY VEGETABLES TO CHOOSE FROM. YOU MAY USE THE FOLLOWING INGREDIENT AMOUNTS AS A GUIDE AND USE THE SPRINGTIME VEGETABLES YOU HAVE HANDY.

INGREDIENTS:

1/3	CUP OLIVE OIL
1 OR 2	CLOVES GARLIC, MINCED
1	ONION, SLICED TOP TO BOTTOM
6	SMALL TOMATOES (B/P/C)
1/4	POUND ASPARAGUS
1	ZUCCHINI, SLICED INTO ROUNDS OR JULIENNED
1/4	POUND MUSHROOMS, SLICED
1	BELL PEPPER (RED, GREEN OR YELLOW)
1/4	CUP PARSLEY, CHOPPED
1/2	TEASPOON SALT +/-

METHOD: PREPARE THE VEGETABLES BY CUTTING THE WHOLE TIP OFF THE ASPAR-AGUS, CUT THE STALKS INTO THIN ROUNDS.

SLICE THE PEPPER INTO THIN STRIPS OR DICE. SAUTE THE PEPPER FOR ABOUT 5 MINUTES, THEN ADD THE MUSHROOMS, ZUCCHINI AND ONION COOK AN ADDITIONAL 5 MINUTES. ADD SALT, TOMATOES AND ASPARAGUS, BRING TO A BOIL, REDUCE HEAT TO MEDIUM AND COOK 10 ADDITIONAL MINUTES. REMOVE FROM HEAT, ADD THE PARSLEY.

HERE WE'RE GOING TO ADD A ZINGER. THE GARLIC MAY BE ADDED WITH THE PARSLEY. IT HASN'T BEEN COOKED SO IT WILL GIVE A LIGHT FRESH GARLICKY TASTE TO YOUR SAUCE. IF YOU DON'T THINK YOU'LL LIKE IT THERE, SAUTE THE GARLIC WITH THE ONION. TOSS AND SERVE.

RECOMMENDED PASTA: STRING TYPES.

WE TRIED THIS SAUCE . . . AND

LOVED IT ( )
HATED IT ( )
MAYBE WE'LL TRY IT AGAIN ( )
WE'LL USE IT FOR UNWELCOME GUESTS ( )

ROMAGNA STYLE SPINACH SAUCE

FRESH SPINACH COATED WITH GARLIC FLAVORED OIL AND THEN SIMMERED WITH TOMATOES! DOESN'T THAT SOUND INVITING? IF YOU LIKE SPINACH IT DOES.   YOU MAY USE FROZEN SPINACH IF FRESH IS NOT AVAILABLE WHEN YOUR TASTE BUDS TELL YOU IT'S TIME TO TRY THIS SAUCE. (SQUEEZE THAWED, FROZEN SPINACH DRY BEFORE USING).

INGREDIENTS: 1   BUNCH FRESH SPINACH, WASHED, DRIED AND CHOPPED
1   POUND PEAR TOMATOES (B/P/C)
1/2   CUP OLIVE OIL
2   CLOVES GARLIC, MINCED
1/2   TEASPOON SALT
1/4   TEASPOON FRESHLY GROUND BLACK PEPPER
       PARMESAN CHEESE

METHOD: SAUTE GARLIC IN THE OLIVE OIL UNTIL LIGHTLY GOLDEN. ADD SPINACH, SALT AND PEPPER, COOK UNTIL SPINACH IS WELL COATED.   ADD TOMATOES, BRING SAUCE TO A BOIL, REDUCE HEAT AND SIMMER, LOOSELY COVERED FOR 25 MINUTES. POUR SAUCE OVER PASTA. TOSS AND SERVE WITH CHEESE ON THE SIDE.

RECOMMENDED PASTA: NARROW RIBBON TYPES.

SQUASH SAUCE

(ARE YOU KIDDING, THAT'S A GAME! OR POSSIBLY THE LOSER.)

THERE IS NO QUESTION THAT ZUCCHINI IS ONE OF AMERICA'S FAVORITE SQUASH, OR CERTAINLY IT IS AMONG THE TOP SUMMER SQUASHES. YOU NEED NOT USE ZUCCHINI IN THIS SAUCE IF YOU HAVE ANOTHER SUMMER VARIETY AVAILABLE. WHATEVER YOUR CHOICE, YOU'LL BE HAPPY WITH THE RESULTS.

INGREDIENTS:

3	TABLESPOONS OLIVE OIL
1	ONION, CHOPPED
1	BELL PEPPER, CHOPPED AND SEEDED (GREEN, RED OR YELLOW)
1	CLOVE GARLIC, MINCED
1	16 OUNCE CAN ITALIAN STYLE TOMATOES
3	TABLESPOONS FRESH PARSLEY, CHOPPED
1	TABLESPOON FRESH BASIL, CHOPPED
1/2	TEASPOON DRY MARJORAM LEAVES
1/2	TEASPOON SALT
PINCH	BLACK PEPPER
4	ZUCCHINI OR OTHER SUMMER SQUASH, SLICED INTO THIN ROUNDS GRATED PARMESAN CHEESE

METHOD: SAUTE IN THE OLIVE OIL, ONION, BELL PEPPER AND GARLIC, UNTIL ONIONS ARE TRANSPARENT. ADD BLENDERIZED TOMATOES, PARSLEY, BASIL, MARJORAM, SALT AND PEPPER. BRING SAUCE TO A BOIL, REDUCE HEAT, COVER AND SIMMER FOR 30 MINUTES. ADD THE SQUASH AND COOK AN ADDITIONAL 5 MINUTES, OR UNTIL SQUASH IS DONE TO YOUR LIKING. ADJUST SALT IF NEEDED. POUR SAUCE OVER PASTA. TOSS AND SERVE WITH CHEESE ON THE SIDE.

A SPLASH OF A LIGHT RED OR PINK WINE MAY BE ADDED TO THE SAUCE ALONG WITH THE SQUASH.

RECOMMENDED PASTA: RIBBON TYPES.

EGGPLANT SAUCE #1

IF THIS DISH IS NOT SICILIAN, IT CERTAINLY IS FROM THE DEEP SOUTH, THAT'S CALABRIA, NOT ALABAMA.

INGREDIENTS:

1	SMALL EGGPLANT
2	TEASPOONS SALT
1	CAN (28 OUNCE) ITALIAN PLUM TOMATOES
7	SICILIAN OR GREEK STYLE BLACK OLIVES
6	ANCHOVY FILLETS
2	TEASPOONS OF DRAINED CAPERS
1	LARGE GREEN BELL PEPPER
1	MEDIUM ONION
2	CLOVES GARLIC
1/3	CUP OLIVE OIL
2	TEASPOONS CHOPPED FRESH BASIL (OR 3/4 TEASPOON IF DRIED)
1/4	CUP FRESH PARSLEY (CHOPPED) GRATED PARMESAN OR ROMANO CHEESE (OPTIONAL)

METHOD: BEGIN COOKING YOUR PASTA WHEN THE SAUCE IS ALMOST COMPLETE.

PARE EGGPLANT AND CUT INTO SMALL CUBES. SALT THE EGGPLANT, TOSS. PLACE SALTED EGGPLANT INTO A COLANDER AND LET DRAIN FOR 1 HOUR.

CHOP YOUR TOMATOES, OR USE A BLENDER/PROCESSOR. PIT THE OLIVES (OR WAGER YOUR TEETH AGAINST THE OUTCOME). RINSE OIL OFF THE ANCHOVIES, PAT DRY, CHOP ANCHOVIES, OLIVES AND CAPERS. SET ASIDE.

RINSE THE EGGPLANT, DRAIN AND SQUEEZE DRY. CORE, SEED AND CHOP THE GREEN PEPPER. CHOP OR MINCE ONION AND GARLIC.

HEAT OIL, ADD EGGPLANT, GARLIC, ONION AND GREEN PEPPER SAUTE FOR 5 MINUTES. ADD TOMATOES AND BASIL.

BRING SAUCE TO A BOIL, COVER AND SIMMER FOR 20 MINUTES. REMOVE COVER AND REDUCE LIQUID FOR 10 MINUTES TO THICKEN SAUCE. ADD ANCHOVIES/OLIVE/CAPER MIX AND PARSLEY. REPLACE COVER AND SIMMER 5 ADDITIONAL MINUTES. REMOVE FROM HEAT. BLEND WITH PASTA AND SERVE.

RECOMMENDED PASTA: STRINGS, OVAL OR LONG HOLLOW TYPES.

EGGPLANT SAUCE #2

ANOTHER SAUCE FROM THE HEEL AND TOE OF ITALY. THEY SURE LOVE EGGPLANT DOWN THAT WAY.

INGREDIENTS:

1	LARGE EGGPLANT, PARED AND DICED
1/4	CUP OLIVE OIL
2	POUNDS FRESH TOMATOES (B/P/C)
3	CLOVES GARLIC
1	6 OUNCE CAN TOMATO PASTE
1/2	CUP WATER
1	ONION, CHOPPED
1	TEASPOON SALT
1/4	TEASPOON FRESHLY GROUND BLACK PEPPER
1/2	TEASPOON DRY OREGANO
1/4	CUP PARSLEY, CHOPPED
	GRATED PARMESAN CHEESE

METHOD:

1. SAUTE EGGPLANT IN 1/2 THE OLIVE OIL UNTIL IT BEGINS TO BROWN. REMOVE EGGPLANT FROM THE PAN, SET ASIDE.

2. ADD REMAINING OIL, SAUTE THE FRESH TOMATOES AND GARLIC FOR ABOUT 5 MINUTES. ADD TOMATO PASTE, WATER, ONION, SALT AND PEPPER. BRING SAUCE TO A BOIL, PARTIALLY COVER AND SIMMER FOR 1 HOUR. ADD EGGPLANT AND PARSLEY. RETURN TO A BOIL, REDUCE HEAT AND SIMMER FOR 45 MINUTES. REMOVE FROM HEAT. POUR SAUCE OVER PASTA, TOSS AND SERVE WITH CHEESE ON THE SIDE.

RECOMMENDED PASTA: STRING TYPES.

SYRACUSE STYLE EGGPLANT SAUCE

IN CASE YOU FAILED GEOGRAPHY, THIS IS NOT THE ONE IN UP STATE NEW YORK, IT'S THE ORIGINAL GREEK CITY OF SYRACUSE, IN SICILY.

INGREDIENTS:

1/2	CUP OLIVE OIL
2	CLOVES GARLIC, BRUISED OR CRUSHED
2	LONG GREEN MILDLY HOT PEPPERS, SEEDED AND CHOPPED
8	FRESH PEAR TOMATOES (B/P/C)
1	SMALL EGGPLANT, PARED AND DICED
10	SICILIAN OR GREEK STYLE OILED OLIVES, PITTED
1	TEASPOON CAPERS
1	TABLESPOON FRESH BASIL, MINCED
3	ANCHOVY FILETS, MINCED
1/2	TEASPOON SALT
1	TEASPOON FRESHLY GROUND BLACK PEPPER
1/3	CUP FRESHLY GRATED ROMANO CHEESE

METHOD: SAUTE THE GARLIC AND GREEN PEPPER IN OLIVE OIL. WHEN GARLIC HAS TURNED LIGHTLY GOLDEN, DISCARD GARLIC ONLY, ADD TOMATOES AND EGGPLANT TO THE OIL, PARTIALLY COVER AND COOK ON LOW HEAT FOR 30 MINUTES. ADD OLIVES, CAPERS, BASIL, ANCHOVIES, SALT AND PEPPER, REDUCE HEAT TO SIMMER AND COOK FOR AN ADDITIONAL 15 MINUTES. POUR SAUCE OVER PASTA. TOSS AND SERVE WITH GRATED CHEESE ON THE SIDE

(YOU MAY SWAP SWEET PEPPERS FOR THE HOT VARIETY.)

RECOMMENDED PASTA: STRING TYPES.

NORTHERN STYLE EGGPLANT SAUCE

EGGPLANT IS A POPULAR VEGETABLE THROUGHOUT ITALY, MOST OF THE SAUCES AND ANTIPASTO'S USING EGGPLANT ARE SOUTHERN. THIS NORTHERN TREATMENT USES FEWER INGREDIENTS AND IN EFFECT IS A LIGHTER SAUCE.

INGREDIENTS:

1	MEDIUM EGGPLANT, PARED, JULIENNED, SALTED AND FRIED (SET ASIDE TO DRAIN ON PAPER TOWELS)
2	CLOVES GARLIC, MINCED
1/3	CUP OLIVE OIL
1/4	CUP CHOPPED PARSLEY
1	16 OUNCE CAN PEAR TOMATOES, BLENDERIZED
PINCH	CRUSHED RED PEPPER

METHOD: AFTER FRYING EGGPLANT, SAUTE GARLIC IN REMAINING OLIVE OIL UNTIL LIGHTLY GOLDEN. ADD PARSLEY, TOMATOES AND CRUSHED RED PEPPER. BRING SAUCE TO A BOIL, LOWER HEAT AND SIMMER FOR 25 MINUTES, ADD FRIED EGGPLANT TO HEAT THROUGH. POUR SAUCE OVER PASTA. TOSS AND SERVE.

RECOMMENDED PASTA: THIN STRING TYPES.

SICILIAN CAPONATA SAUCE

CAPONATA IS ONE OF MY FAVORITE APPETIZERS, AS A RESULT I MAKE IT QUITE OFTEN. HOWEVER, I NEVER CONSIDERED USING IT AS A PASTA SAUCE, AND STILL HAVEN'T. THE CAPONATA I MAKE IS A CLASSIC VERSION (OCCASIONALLY CALLED "PALERMO STYLE") AND USES A SWEET AND SOUR RECIPE (SUGAR AND VINEGAR), AND I CAN SAY WITH ABSOLUTE AUTHORITY, THAT THERE ARE PROBABLY AS MANY CAPONATA RECIPES AS THERE ARE SICILIAN COOKS. THIS PASTA SAUCE SUGGESTION HOWEVER COMES FROM CAMPANIA, NOT SICILY. AS FAR AS SICILIANS ARE CONCERNED, THEY ARE NORTHERNERS AND NEVER GET ANYTHING RIGHT. I DON'T KNOW IF ITS RIGHT EITHER, HOWEVER THAT DOESN'T MEAN YOU WOULDN'T LIKE IT.

LET'S MAKE A COMPARISON CLOSER TO HOME, AMERICAN SOUTHERNERS USE GRITS AS A VEGETABLE, (IT'S CEREAL SEED!) ESPECIALLY AT BREAKFAST WHEN IT MIGHT BE SEASONED WITH SALT AND PEPPER, OR SPRINKLED WITH A LOUISIANA HOT SAUCE, OR, WHERE THEY WOULD GLEEFULLY BLEND IT WITH ANYTHING ELSE ON THE PLATE, EGGS, HASH BROWNS, SAUSAGE, ET CETERA. IMAGINE THEIR ASTONISHMENT WHEN ON A VISIT TO THE NORTH, AND AT BREAKFAST DISCOVER THAT NORTHERNERS EAT A GRITS LOOK-A-LIKE (FARINA, ALSO A CEREAL SEED), WITH THE SAME TEXTURE, COLOR AND FLAVOR, BUT THEY (GASP) EAT IT FROM A BOWL AND PUT SUGAR AND CREAM ON IT. DO YOU SUPPOSE A FEW SOUTHERNERS THOUGHT NORTHERNERS WERE A LITTLE ODD OVER THAT.

LET'S GET BACK TO EGGPLANT. AS A THOUGHT, PERHAPS IF YOU OMIT THE SUGAR AND VINEGAR IT WOULD BE LESS OF AN APPETIZER AND MORE LIKE THE OTHER EGGPLANT SAUCES. AND SINCE THIS WILL BE A PASTA SAUCE, YOU'LL JULIENNE THE EGGPLANT. FOR AN APPETIZER, CUT THEM INTO 1 INCH CUBES.

Continued on next page

IT IS POSSIBLE THAT I DON'T UNDERSTAND THE MEANING OF THE WORD "CAPONATA". IF IT MEANS AN APPETIZER WITH EGGPLANT BEING THE DOMINANT INGREDIENT, THEN ALL THE EGGPLANT SAUCES IN THIS CHAPTER QUALIFY AS A "CAPONATA". INTERESTINGLY, THE RECIPES (ELEVEN) IN MY COLLECTION WITH THAT NAME, ONLY FOUR OF THEM USE A SWEETENER AND VINEGAR AS INGREDIENTS.

INGREDIENTS:
2	MEDIUM EGGPLANTS, PARED AND JULIENNED
1/3	CUP OLIVE OIL
1	ONION, SLICED TOP TO BOTTOM
1	POUND PEAR TOMATOES (ABOUT 8) (B/P/C)
2	STALKS CELERY, CHOPPED
1	BELL PEPPER, SEEDED AND DICED
	SALT TO TASTE
3/4	CUP RIPE OLIVES (BLACK OR GREEN)
2	TABLESPOONS HALVED OR SLIVERED ALMONDS (TOASTED IF YOU WISH)
3	TABLESPOONS SUGAR
1/2	CUP WINE VINEGAR

METHOD: PREPARE AND SOAK THE EGGPLANT IN A BRINE FOR 30 MINUTES. DRAIN, RINSE, DRAIN AGAIN, PLACE THEM ON PAPER TOWELS AND SET ASIDE.

SAUTE THE EGGPLANT IN THE OLIVE OIL UNTIL SOMEWHAT SOFTENED, ABOUT 5 MINUTES. REMOVE EGGPLANT, PLACE ON PAPER TOWELS, SET ASIDE.

SAUTE ONIONS, TOMATOES, CELERY AND BELL PEPPER UNTIL ONION BECOMES TRANSPARENT. SALT TO TASTE. ADD OLIVES, ALMONDS AND SAUTEED EGGPLANT.

DISSOLVE SUGAR IN THE WINE VINEGAR, ADD MIXTURE TO THE VEGETABLES. LOOSELY COVER AND SIMMER FOR 10 MINUTES. POUR SAUCE OVER PASTA. TOSS AND SERVE.

RECOMMENDED PASTA: STRING, RIBBON OR WIDE SHELL TYPES.

FARMER'S EGGPLANT SAUCE

CANTADINO IS ITALIAN FOR SOMEONE LIVING IN THE COUNTRY (FEMALE: CONTADINA), LIKE A FARMER, A SQUIRE OR EVEN A COUNTRY BUMPKIN. SO THIS SAUCE COULD BE CALLED "PASTA ALLA DEL CONTADINO". WELL, SO MUCH FOR THAT ASIDE. THROUGHOUT AMERICA, SMALL EGGPLANTS ARE DIFFICULT TO FIND, MOST OF THE STORES SEEM TO HAVE 1 TO 2 POUNDERS. THERE IS A NEW WHITE SKINNED EGGPLANT VARIETY NOW ENTERING AMERICAN MARKETS. THEY ARE SMALLER THAN THEIR BIG PURPLE COUSINS AND QUITE MILD. AS AN ALTERNATIVE, IF YOUR STORE OFFERS A JAPANESE STYLE EGGPLANT, TRY USING THEM. THEY ARE SMALL, GENERALLY ABOUT THE SIZE OF A MEDIUM ZUCCHINI AND EQUALLY AS TENDER. AND . . . , IF VERY FRESH, THEY DON'T NEED TO BE PARED.

INGREDIENTS:

1/4	CUP OLIVE OIL
1	CLOVE GARLIC (YOUR CHOICE)
1	ONION, CHOPPED
1	STALK CELERY, CHOPPED
1	CARROT, PEELED AND CHOPPED
2	TABLESPOONS CHOPPED FRESH BASIL
1/2	TEASPOON SALT
1/4	TEASPOON FRESHLY GROUND BLACK PEPPER
1	8 OUNCE CAN TOMATO SAUCE
1/4	CUP CHOPPED PARSLEY
2	SMALL EGGPLANTS, PARED AND DICED
	FRESHLY GRATED ROMANO CHEESE

METHOD: SAUTE THE GARLIC. ONION, CELERY, CARROT, BASIL, SALT AND PEPPER IN 1/2 THE OLIVE OIL FOR 15 MINUTES. (MEANWHILE, BACK ON THE RANGE) IN A SEPARATE PAN, SAUTE EGGPLANT IN THE REMAINING OLIVE OIL FOR ABOUT 10 MINUTES. ADD TOMATO AND EGGPLANT TO THE SAUTEED VEGETABLES, COVER AND SIMMER FOR 10 MINUTES. POUR SAUCE OVER PASTA. TOSS AND SERVE WITH GRATED CHEESE ON THE SIDE.

RECOMMENDED PASTA: CURLY STRINGS.

EGGPLANT SAUCE #3

*(MAY ALSO BE USED FOR A BAKED PASTA)

I AM REALLY GIVING YOU TWO RECIPES HERE. THE FIRST IS AS A SAUCE AND THE SECOND IS A MORE ELABORATE PREPARATION FOR A BAKED PASTA PIE WITH EGGPLANT AS THE TOP AND BOTTOM CRUST. I AM OFFERING IT TO YOU IN THIS FASHION SO AS TO KEEP TO OUR PREMISE, OF "PASTA SAUCES ONLY", AND OCCASIONALLY, SOMETHING EXTRA. (SEE VERSION TWO OF THIS SAUCE ON THE NEXT PAGE.)

INGREDIENTS:

2	MEDIUM EGGPLANTS
4	TEASPOONS SALT
3/4	CUP OLIVE OIL
1	LARGE ONION, CHOPPED
2	CLOVES GARLIC, MINCED
1	POUND GROUND BEEF
1	TABLESPOON BUTTER
1	15 OUNCE CAN TOMATOES (CHOPPED)
2	TABLESPOONS TOMATO PASTE
3/4	TEASPOON DRIED OREGANO
	PINCH OF BLACK PEPPER
1	10 OUNCE PACKAGE FROZEN PEAS
2	TABLESPOONS CHOPPED PARSLEY

METHOD: PARE AND SLICE THE EGGPLANTS CROSSWISE INTO 1/4 INCH ROUNDS, SALT THE SLICES WITH 3 TEASPOONS OF THE SALT, STAND THEM IN A COLANDER TO DRAIN FOR AN HOUR.

RINSE THE EGGPLANT, DRAIN AND PRESS DRY WITH PAPER TOWELS. SLICE THE ROUNDS INTO STRIPS, AS THOUGH YOU WERE MAKING FRENCH FRIES.

HEAT 1/4 CUP OF OLIVE OIL AND FRY THE EGGPLANT STRIPS FOR 1 TO 2 MINUTES EACH, ADD MORE OIL AS NEEDED. SET COOKED STRIPS ON PAPER TOWELS TO DRAIN.

SAUTE THE GROUND BEEF IN THE BUTTER, COOK UNTIL IT'S NO LONGER
PINK.   ADD ONION, GARLIC, TOMATOES, TOMATO PASTE, OREGANO, 1
TEASPOON SALT AND THE PEPPER.   COOK UNCOVERED 30 MINUTES.   ADD
UNCOOKED PEAS AND COOK 5 ADDITIONAL MINUTES.   ADD EGGPLANT
STRIPS, COOK 5 MORE MINUTES. REMOVE SAUCE FROM HEAT, POUR OVER
PASTA. TOSS AND SERVE.

RECOMMENDED PASTA: STRING TYPES.

EGGPLANT SAUCE #3, VERSION TWO

(FOR A BAKED PASTA DISH)

INGREDIENTS: USE THE PRECEDING RECIPE INGREDIENTS PLUS THE FOLLOWING;

1	CUP OF GRATED PARMESAN CHEESE
1	CUP SHREDDED CHEDDAR CHEESE
1/2	CUP BREAD CRUMBS
2	TABLESPOONS CHOPPED PARSLEY

METHOD: PARE AND SLICE THE EGGPLANTS CROSSWISE INTO 1/4 INCH ROUNDS, SALT THE SLICES WITH 3 TEASPOONS SALT, STAND THEM IN A COLANDER AND LET DRAIN FOR AN HOUR.

COOK YOUR PASTA CHOICE, DRAIN AND SET ASIDE.

COOK GROUND BEEF UNTIL IT'S NO LONGER PINK. ADD ONION, GARLIC, TOMATOES, TOMATO PASTE, OREGANO, 1 TEASPOON SALT AND THE PEPPER. COOK UNCOVERED 15 TO 20 MINUTES.

TOSS SAUCE, PASTA, AND THE UNCOOKED PEAS TOGETHER. SET ASIDE.

RINSE THE EGGPLANT, DRAIN AND PRESS DRY WITH PAPER TOWELS. HEAT THE OLIVE OIL AND FRY THE EGGPLANT SLICES FOR 1 TO 2 MINUTES EACH. SET COOKED SLICES ON PAPER TOWELS TO DRAIN.

TOSS WITH YOUR PASTA, (ONE AT A TIME OR ALL TOGETHER) THE GRATED PARMESAN CHEESE AND CHEDDAR CHEESE,

HEAT OVER TO 350 DEGREES F, BUTTER THE SIDES AND BOTTOM OF A 9 INCH SPRINGFORM PAN (THIS WILL MAKE A PRETTIER ENTREE, IF YOU DON'T HAVE ONE USE A MEDIUM DEEP BAKING DISH, 3")

PLACE AN OVERLAPPING LAYER OF EGGPLANT SLICES ON THE BOTTOM AND SIDES OF YOUR PAN, FILL THE PAN WITH YOUR PASTA, LAY A FINAL LAYER OF EGGPLANT ON THE TOP. DRIZZLE THE REMAINING OLIVE OIL OVER THE EGGPLANT AND FINALLY, SPRINKLE WITH BREAD CRUMBS AND BAKE FOR ABOUT 35 MINUTES.

REMOVE FROM OVEN, LET REST A FEW MINUTES BEFORE REMOVING SPRINGFORM SIDE. SPRINKLE TOP WITH PARSLEY AND SERVE.

RECOMMENDED PASTA: STRING TYPES.

FRESH MUSHROOMS AND ANCHOVY SAUCE

A TANGY TWOSOME, THE MUSHROOMS SURRENDER TO THE ANCHOVIES AND THE INTERLOPING TOMATO MELLOWS IT OUT. THERE IS MORE TO THE SAUCE THAN THAT, BUT AT LEAST YOU GET THE IDEA.

INGREDIENTS:
1	POUND MUSHROOMS, SLICED
1/3	CUP SWEET WINE, MARSALA OR SHERRY
1/3	CUP OLIVE OIL
1	CUP CHOPPED ONION
1	CLOVE GARLIC, MINCED
1/4	TEASPOON SALT
1/4	TEASPOON FRESHLY GROUND BLACK PEPPER
4	ANCHOVY FILLETS, MINCED
1/2	CUP CHOPPED AND DRAINED, PEAR TOMATOES
1/4	CUP CHOPPED PARSLEY

METHOD: BRAISE THE MUSHROOMS IN THE WINE FOR 3 TO 4 MINUTES, SET ASIDE. SAUTE THE ONION AND GARLIC IN 1/2 THE OLIVE OIL UNTIL ONION IS TRANSPARENT. ADD THE MUSHROOMS AND ANY JUICES, SALT, PEPPER, ANCHOVIES, TOMATOES AND PARSLEY. COVER PAN AND SIMMER FOR 10 MINUTES. POUR SAUCE OVER PASTA, TOSS. ADD REMAINING OLIVE OIL, TOSS AGAIN. SERVE.

RECOMMENDED PASTA: MEDIUM TUBE OR CURLY TYPES.

FRESH GREEN BEANS WITH TOMATO SAUCE

STRING BEANS ARE CERTAINLY AN AMERICAN FAVORITE. I BELIEVE EVERY GARDEN I'VE EVER SEEN HAD THEM IN PROFUSION, YOU'LL ALSO FIND SEVERAL VARIETIES OF THEM AT YOUR GROCERS THROUGHOUT THE GROWING SEASON. WHY NOT MAKE USE OF THEM IN A PASTA SAUCE. HERE'S ONE THAT WILL DO IT.

INGREDIENTS:

1	POUND FRESH GREEN BEANS, TRIMMED AND CUT OR SLICED
1/3	CUP OLIVE OIL
1	ONION, CHOPPED
1	CLOVE GARLIC, MINCED
1	16 OUNCE CAN TOMATOES OR 3 FRESH TOMATOES (B/C/P)
1/2	TEASPOON SALT
1/4	TEASPOON FRESHLY GROUND BLACK PEPPER

METHOD: SAUTE ONION, GARLIC AND BEANS TOGETHER UNTIL ONION IS TRANSPARENT. ADD TOMATOES, SALT AND PEPPER. BRING TO A BOIL, REDUCE HEAT TO SIMMER, PARTIALLY COVER AND COOK FOR 30 MINUTES OR UNTIL BEANS ARE COOKED. POUR SAUCE OVER PASTA. TOSS AND SERVE.

RECOMMENDED PASTA: CURLY TYPES, SHELLS OR MEDIUM TUBE TYPES.

FRESH BROCCOLI SAUCE #2

THIS IS A CALABRIAN STYLE SAUCE, OR ALLA CALABRESE IF YOU PREFER, IT'S A GEM OF A VEGETABLE SAUCE FOR YOUR PASTA.

INGREDIENTS:

1	POUND BROCCOLI (USE THE FLORETS ONLY)
1/4	OLIVE OIL
1	ONION, SLICED
8	PEAR TOMATOES (B/P/C)
1/2	TEASPOON SALT
1/4	TEASPOON FRESHLY GROUND BLACK PEPPER
1	CLOVE GARLIC, CRUSHED
6	ANCHOVY FILLETS
4	TABLESPOONS RAISINS
4	TABLESPOONS PINENUTS
1	TEASPOON CHOPPED BASIL LEAF
3/4	CUP GRATED PECORINO CHEESE

METHOD: COOK THE BROCCOLI IN SALTED WATER OR STEAM UNTIL DONE. DRAIN AND SET ASIDE. SAUTE THE ONION IN 1/2 THE OLIVE OIL UNTIL TRANSPARENT. ADD TOMATOES, SALT AND BLACK PEPPER. COVER AND SIMMER FOR 30 MINUTES. MEANWHILE, IN THE REMAINING 1/2 OLIVE OIL, SAUTE THE GARLIC UNTIL GOLDEN. ADD ANCHOVIES, COOK FOR 2 MINUTES. ADD COOKED TOMATOES, RAISINS, BROCCOLI AND PINE NUTS, COOK AN ADDITIONAL 5 MINUTES. REMOVE FROM HEAT, POUR SAUCE OVER PASTA. ADD BASIL AND CHEESE. TOSS AND SERVE.

RECOMMENDED PASTA: LONG HOLLOW TYPES.

CAULIFLOWER AND TOMATO SAUCE

WE RETURN AGAIN TO THE PROVINCE OF APULIA (THE DEEP SOUTH) FOR A PATRIOTIC DISH. THE LAND OF THE FOLK DANCE THAT MOST AMERICAN'S ASSOCIATE WITH ITALY, THE TARANTELLA. WHERE WE GET THIS WHITE, RED AND GREEN SAUCE.

INGREDIENTS:
1	HEAD CAULIFLOWER, FLORETS ONLY
4	PEAR TOMATOES (B/P/C)
1/2	CUP OLIVE OIL
1	CLOVE GARLIC, CRUSHED
3/4	TEASPOON SALT
1/2	TEASPOON FRESHLY GROUND BLACK PEPPER
3	TABLESPOONS PARSLEY, CHOPPED
1/4	CUP GRATED PARMESAN CHEESE

METHOD: SAUTE THE GARLIC IN THE OLIVE OIL. WHEN IT HAS TURNED GOLDEN, REMOVE AND DISCARD. ADD THE TOMATOES, SALT AND PEPPER, BRING TO A BOIL.

IN THE ITALIAN FASHION YOU WOULD ADD THE CAULIFLOWER AT THIS POINT AND COOK COVERED AT LOW HEAT, UNTIL THE CAULIFLOWER DISINTEGRATES, ABOUT 40 MINUTES. IF YOU PREFER A CRISPIER VEGETABLE, REDUCE OVER ALL COOKING TIME TO 30 MINUTES. ADD CAULIFLOWER DURING THE LAST 15 MINUTES OF COOKING. POUR SAUCE OVER PASTA, TOSS, SPRINKLE WITH PARSLEY AND CHEESE, SERVE

RECOMMENDED PASTA: HOLLOW STRING TYPES.

EGGPLANT AND MOZZARELLA SAUCE

THIS SAUCE COMES FROM THE AREA OF ITALY THAT BROUGHT INTO MY LIFE, ONE LADY WHOM I LOVED WHILE SHE LIVED AND WHO'S MEMORY I HAVE CHERISHED SINCE, MY GRANDMOTHER.   THE SAUCE COMES FROM LOWER CAMPANIA, GRANDMOTHER CAME FROM ROCCA d'ASPIDE, ABOUT TWENTY MILES SOUTH OF SALERNO. IT'S SIMPLE AND VERY GOOD.

INGREDIENTS:

1	SMALL EGGPLANT, PARED AND DICED (ABOUT 1 POUND)
2	TEASPOONS SALT
4	TABLESPOONS OLIVE OIL
6	PEAR TOMATOES (B/P/C) (ABOUT 2 CUPS)
2	TABLESPOONS FRESH BASIL, CHOPPED
8	OUNCES SHREDDED MOZZARELLA CHEESE
1/2	CUP GRATED ROMANO CHEESE

METHOD: SALT THE DICED EGGPLANT, SET ASIDE FOR ABOUT AN HOUR. NOW, SQUEEZE THE EGGPLANT TO REMOVE SALT AND MOISTNESS. PAT DRY WITH PAPER TOWELS. SAUTE EGGPLANT IN OLIVE OIL UNTIL LIGHTLY GOLDEN. REMOVE EGGPLANT FROM SKILLET TO DRAIN ON PAPER TOWELS. IN REMAINING OIL, PLACE TOMATOES, BASIL, EGGPLANT, COOKED AND DRAINED PASTA, BRING SAUCE TO A BOIL, REDUCE HEAT. ADD MOZZARELLA, MIX WELL, COOK UNTIL MOZZARELLA HAS MELTED, SERVE WITH GRATED CHEESE ON THE SIDE.

RECOMMENDED PASTA: MEDIUM DIAGONAL TUBES.

Asparagus Sauce

FROM SOUTH EASTERN ITALY WE GET THIS SPRINGTIME SAUCE OF ASPARAGUS, TOMATOES AND EGGS. A LITTLE FANCY FOOT WORK IS REQUIRED TO PREPARE THIS SAUCE, SO READ AND FOLLOW THE DIRECTIONS.

INGREDIENTS:

1	POUND ASPARAGUS, CLEANED AND CUT INTO 1" PIECES
2	POUNDS FRESH TOMATOES (B/P/C)
1/4	CUP OLIVE OIL
2	CLOVES GARLIC, CRUSHED
1/2	TEASPOON SALT
1/4	TEASPOON FRESHLY GROUND BLACK PEPPER
1	CUP GRATED ROMANO CHEESE
2	EGGS, BEATEN

METHOD:

1. PUT PASTA WATER ON, WHEN IT COMES TO A BOIL, ADD THE PASTA. SAVE ABOUT 1 CUP OF THE COOKING WATER.

2. STEAM THE ASPARAGUS UNTIL TENDER (4 TO 6 MINUTES), SET ASIDE.

3. SAUTE GARLIC IN OLIVE OIL UNTIL LIGHTLY GOLDEN, REMOVE AND DISCARD GARLIC. ADD TOMATOES, SALT AND PEPPER. BRING SAUCE TO A BOIL, REDUCE HEAT TO SIMMER AND COOK FOR 10 MINUTES.

4. ADD COOKED ASPARAGUS TO THE DRAINED PASTA. TOSS TO MIX, ADD CHEESE AND TOSS AGAIN. ADD EGGS AND TOSS A THIRD TIME. ADD TOMATOES, TOSS A FOURTH TIME. SERVE.

RECOMMENDED PASTA: MEDIUM TUBE TYPES, STRAIGHT OR DIAGONAL CUT ENDS.

ASPARAGUS SAUCE II

ASIDE FROM ASPARAGUS AND TOMATO, THIS RECIPE HAS NO RELATIONSHIP TO THE PRECEDING SAUCE. IT'S ALSO FASTER TO PREPARE.

INGREDIENTS:

1	POUND ASPARAGUS, COOKED AND CUT INTO 1" INCH LENGTHS
1	HALF CUP BUTTER
1/4	POUND PROSCUITTO, CUT INTO THIS STRIPS
3	PEAR TOMATOES (B/P/C) AND DRAINED
1/2	TEASPOON SALT
1/2	TEASPOON FRESHLY GROUND BLACK PEPPER
1/2	CUP FRESHLY GRATED PARMESAN CHEESE

METHOD: STEAM THE ASPARAGUS UNTIL TENDER, RINSE AND SET ASIDE. SAUTE THE PROSCUITTO IN 1/4 CUP BUTTER FOR 2 MINUTES, ADD TOMATOES, SALT AND PEPPER, COOK FOR 5 ADDITIONAL MINUTES. DURING THE LAST MINUTE, ADD ASPARAGUS, STIR TO MIX. REMOVE FROM HEAT. TOSS THE COOKED PASTA WITH THE REMAINING 1/4 CUP BUTTER. TOSS AGAIN WITH THE GRATED CHEESE. POUR SAUCE OVER PASTA, TOSS A THIRD TIME. SERVE.

RECOMMENDED PASTA: RIBBONS OR STRINGS.

ARTICHOKE SAUCE

THIS SAUCE RECIPE CALLS FOR FRESH ARTICHOKES, TRIMMED, THINLY SLICED AND THEN SIMMERED WITH THE TOMATOES UNTIL TENDER. THAT'S ONE WAY, THE ALTERNATIVES ARE TO USE CANNED WATER PACKED ARTICHOKES, OR MARINATED ARTICHOKES. ANY OF THE ABOVE ALTERNATIVES WILL MAKE A GOOD SAUCE. THE MARINATED CHOKES WILL SHOW A LITTLE TARTNESS FROM THE VINEGAR. IF YOU CHOOSE ONE OF THE CANNED VERSIONS, DRAIN, THEN ADD THE CHOKES DURING FINAL 15 MINUTES.

INGREDIENTS:

3	SMALL TO MEDIUM FRESH ARTICHOKES, TRIMMED AND THINLY SLICED.
4	TABLESPOONS OLIVE OIL
1	ONION, SLICED TOP TO BOTTOM
1	CLOVE GARLIC, MINCED
1	16 OUNCE CAN PEAR TOMATOES
1/2	TEASPOON DRY BASIL

METHOD: PREPARE CHOKES BY CUTTING ABOUT 1" FROM THE TOPS. REMOVE TOUGH OUTER LEAVES AND STEMS, SLICE OR QUARTER. REMOVE CHOKE AND DISCARD. (THAT'S THE FUZZY PART IN THE CENTER).

SAUTE ARTICHOKES, ONION AND GARLIC IN OLIVE OIL UNTIL ONION IS TRANSPARENT, ADD TOMATOES AND BASIL. BRING SAUCE TO A BOIL, REDUCE HEAT TO SIMMER, COVER AND COOK FOR 30 TO 40 MINUTES, OR UNTIL ARTICHOKES ARE DONE.

RECOMMENDED PASTA: STRING TYPES.

UMBRIAN STYLE MUSHROOM SAUCE

UMBRIA IN THE VERY CENTER OF ITALY SEEMS TO STRADDLE THE APENNINE MOUNTAINS AND IS THE BIRTH PLACE OF SAINT FRANCIS OF ASSISI. PUTTING THAT ASIDE, THE UMBRIAN'S SEEM TO LIKE MUSHROOMS BECAUSE FROM THERE WE GET THIS SIMPLE SAUCE OF MOSTLY MUSHROOMS. THE SAUCE CALLS FOR AN EQUAL MIXTURE OF LARD AND OLIVE OIL. IF YOU DON'T WANT TO USE LARD, GO WITH BUTTER OR OLIVE OIL. THERE WILL OBVIOUSLY BE A TASTE DIFFERENCE. BUT, IF YOU GENUINELY LIKE THIS STYLE OF SAUCE, THEN TRY IT WITH ALL THE ABOVE.

INGREDIENTS:
1	POUND MUSHROOMS, SLICED
2	PEAR TOMATOES (B/P/C) AND DRAINED
3	TABLESPOONS LARD
3	TABLESPOONS OLIVE OIL
4	CLOVES GARLIC, CRUSHED
1	TABLESPOON CHOPPED PARSLEY
	SALT TO TASTE
PINCH	CRUSHED RED PEPPER OR BLACK PEPPER

METHOD: SAUTE GARLIC IN LARD/OIL UNTIL LIGHTLY GOLDEN, REMOVE AND DISCARD. ADD MUSHROOMS, PARSLEY, SALT AND PEPPER. COOK OVER MODERATE HEAT UNTIL LIQUID HAS EVAPORATED. ADD THE TOMATOES, COOK ADDITIONAL 10 MINUTES. POUR SAUCE OVER PASTA. TOSS AND SERVE.

RECOMMENDED PASTA: STRING OF RIBBON TYPES.

PEPPERS AND ANCHOVY SAUCE

THIS IS PROBABLY A CENTRAL REGION ITALIAN SAUCE AND WHILE ON THE SURFACE IT SOUNDS AS THOUGH IT SHOULD BE IN A DIFFERENT CATEGORY, IT'S HERE BECAUSE OF THE NATURE OF CANNED ANCHOVIES, THEY DISSOLVE DURING COOKING, THEREFORE ANCHOVY BECOMES A SEASONING. FOR THIS RECIPE CHOOSE ANY COLOR SWEET PEPPER YOU LIKE.

INGREDIENTS:	4	TABLESPOONS OLIVE OIL
	3	SWEET PEPPERS SEEDED AND JULIENNED
	2	TABLESPOONS WATER
	2	GARLIC CLOVES, CRUSHED
	4	FILLETS OF ANCHOVY
	6	PEAR TOMATOES (B/P/C)
	1/4	TEASPOON FRESHLY GROUND BLACK PEPPER

METHOD: SAUTE THE PEPPERS IN OLIVE OIL FOR ABOUT 5 MINUTES. ADD WATER, COVER PAN, REDUCE HEAT AND SIMMER FOR 10 MINUTES. ADD GARLIC, ANCHOVIES, TOMATOES AND BLACK PEPPER. SIMMER WHILE LOOSELY COVERED FOR 20 MINUTES. REMOVE AND DISCARD GARLIC, POUR SAUCE OVER PASTA. TOSS AND SERVE.

RECOMMENDED PASTA: RIBBON TYPES.

BELL PEPPER AND TOMATO SAUCE

YOU MAY USE ANY COLOR PEPPERS YOU LIKE. YOU'LL ALSO USE ONE BELL PEPPER TO A POUND OF TOMATOES, THAT CREATES A GOOD TASTING AND BALANCED BLENDING. HOWEVER, IF THAT'S TOO MUCH PEPPER FOR YOU REDUCE THE AMOUNT BY ONE OR DON'T USE GREEN PEPPERS, THEY ARE FAR AND AWAY THE MOST DYNAMIC IN ADDING THEIR FLAVOR. THE RED AND YELLOW BELL PEPPERS ARE THE MILDEST.

INGREDIENTS:

3	POUNDS PEAR TOMATOES (B/P/C)
1/2	TEASPOON SALT
PINCH	GROUND CLOVE, OR 2 WHOLE CLOVES
2	TABLESPOONS BUTTER
2	TABLESPOONS OLIVE OIL
1	CLOVE GARLIC, CRUSHED
1	ONION, SLICED TOP TO BOTTOM
3	BELL PEPPERS, SEEDED AND JULIENNED
1/2	TEASPOON FRESHLY GROUND BLACK PEPPER

METHOD: PLACE TOMATOES, SALT, CLOVES AND BUTTER IN A SAUCE PAN. BRING TO A BOIL, REDUCE HEAT TO SIMMER, COOK FOR 25 MINUTES. IN A SEPARATE PAN, SAUTE THE GARLIC, ONIONS, BELL PEPPERS AND BLACK PEPPER IN THE OLIVE OIL, UNTIL ONIONS ARE TRANSPARENT. REMOVE THE GARLIC AND WHOLE CLOVES IF USED. BLEND TOGETHER THE TOMATOES AND PEPPERS MIX. POUR OVER PASTA. TOSS AND SERVE.

RECOMMENDED PASTA: MEDIUM TUBE TYPES, STRAIGHT OR DIAGONAL CUT.

CHAPTER 11

SAUCES MADE FROM CHEESE

THIS IS NOT A MACARONI AND CHEESE CHAPTER, ALTHOUGH I'VE INCLUDED A FEW RECIPES BECAUSE I LIKE MACARONI AND CHEESE AND SO DOES AMERICA.

FOUR CHEESE SAUCE #1

IT IS OBVIOUS TO ANY EXPERIENCED COOK THAT WHOLESALE SUBSTITUTIONS CAN TAKE PLACE WITH THIS RECIPE. I SAY DO IT, FEEL FREE TO USE WHATEVER IS IN YOUR PANTRY. THERE IS NOTHING SACRED ABOUT THE LISTED CHEESES. IN FACT I'LL OFFER YOU A LIST OF POSSIBLE SUBSTITUTES FOLLOWING THE PREPARATION METHOD.

INGREDIENTS:

3	TABLESPOONS BUTTER
1 1/2	TABLESPOONS FLOUR
2	CUPS HALF AND HALF
1/2	CUP FONTINA CHEESE, SHREDDED
1/2	CUP BEL PAESE CHEESE, DICED OR SHREDDED
1/2	CUP GORGONZOLA, CRUMBLED
1/2	CUP FRESHLY GRATED PARMESAN
PINCH	NUTMEG
PINCH	WHITE PEPPER

METHOD: MAKE A ROUX BY MELTING THE BUTTER, ADD THE FLOUR AND COOK OVER LOW HEAT FOR SEVERAL MINUTES. REMOVE FROM HEAT, STIR IN THE HALF AND HALF, NUTMEG AND WHITE PEPPER. RETURN TO HEAT AND COOK UNTIL SAUCE THICKENS SLIGHTLY. ADD ALL FOUR CHEESES AND CONTINUE COOKING UNTIL SMOOTH AND CREAMY. POUR HOT SAUCE OVER YOUR PASTA. TOSS AND SERVE.

RECOMMENDED PASTA: RIBBON TYPES OR HOLLOW STRINGS.

HERE ARE A FEW RECOMMENDATIONS FOR POSSIBLE CHEESE SUBSTITUTES:

FOR THE FONTINA, USE:
JACK, CHEDDAR, COLBY, AMERICAN, SWISS, JARLSBERG, BRICK, MUENSTER, PROVOLONE, GOUDA, EDAM OR MOZZARELLA

FOR THE BEL PAESE, USE:
    LIEDERKRANZ, CAMEMBERT OR BRIE

FOR THE GORGONZOLA, USE:
    BLUE, ROQUEFORT, STILTON. OR FETA.

FOR THE PARMESAN, USE:
    ASIAGO, ROMANO, DRY PROVOLONE, DRY JACK OR DRY
    RICOTTA.

FOUR CHEESE SAUCE #2

(ANOTHER QUICKIE)

THIS IS THE FOUR CHEESE RECIPE THAT MOST PROBABLY QUALIFIES AS THE CLASSIC RECIPE. THIS IS AN ITALIAN RECIPE, SO THAT MAKES IT AS AUTHENTIC AS I CAN GET IT TO BE. SINCE YOU'RE REALLY JUST MELTING THE CHEESE AND NOT COOKING IT, YOU MAY START THIS SAUCE AFTER YOU'VE STARTED YOUR PASTA ON A MERRY BOIL.

INGREDIENTS:
3 TABLESPOONS BUTTER
4 OUNCES SWISS CHEESE
4 OUNCES MOZZARELLA
4 OUNCES RICOTTA
4 OUNCES PARMESAN, FRESHLY GRATED
1/2 CUP WHIPPING CREAM
1/2 TEASPOON SALT
1/4 TEASPOON FRESHLY GROUND BLACK PEPPER

METHOD: MELT THE BUTTER IN A SAUCE PAN. KEEP HEAT LOW, ADD THE SWISS, MOZZARELLA AND RICOTTA CHEESES. WHEN THEY HAVE MELTED, ADD THE CREAM AND THE PARMESAN, SALT AND PEPPER. SIMMER UNTIL WELL BLENDED. POUR CHEESE SAUCE OVER PASTA. TOSS AND SERVE.

NOTE: THE PASTA SHOULD NOT BE DRAINED DRY, SAUCE AND TOSS WHILE IT IS STILL DRIPPING AND QUITE MOIST OR, YOU MAY NEED TO ADD SOME ADDITIONAL CREAM OR MILK. WITH THIS SAUCE YOU'VE GOT TO GO BY ITS FEEL.

RECOMMENDED PASTA: STRING TYPES.

RICOTTA AND BUTTER SAUCE

(ANOTHER QUICKIE)

DON'T YOU JUST LOVE FAST AND SIMPLE SAUCES? IF YOU LOVE AND EAT SMALL SIDE DISHES OF PASTA EVERY DAY, THIS IS YOUR KIND OF SAUCE.

INGREDIENTS:
4 OUNCES BUTTER
8 OUNCES RICOTTA CHEESE
4 OUNCES HAM (ANY KIND), FINELY CHOPPED

METHOD: HEAT THE HAM IN THE BUTTER, REMOVE FROM HEAT. ON INDIVIDUAL PLATES, PLACE A SERVING OF DRAINED PASTA, LAY A DOLLOP OF RICOTTA CHEESE ON YOUR STEAMING PASTA, SPOON SOME OF THE HAM/BUTTER MIX OVER THE CHEESE, TOSS AND EAT.

RECOMMENDED PASTA: MEDIUM TUBE TYPES.

RICOTTA AND CREAM SAUCE

(ANOTHER QUICKIE)

RICOTTA IS SUCH A VERSATILE CHEESE, ITS VERY MILDNESS ALLOWS IT TO BE PAIRED WITH MANY SEASONINGS. LOOK AT OUR OWN COTTAGE CHEESE FOR INSTANCE, IT'S SALTED, BUT YOU CAN PAIR IT WITH SWEET THINGS LIKE PINEAPPLE AND/OR MIXED FRUITS, OR MILD ONIONS (CHIVES) AND IT'S VERY GOOD WITH ANY OF THEM.

INGREDIENTS:

1/4	CUP BUTTER
1	CUP RICOTTA CHEESE
1/2	CUP WHIPPING CREAM
PINCH	GROUND NUTMEG
1/4	CUP CHOPPED FRESH BASIL
1/4	FRESHLY GRATED PARMESAN CHEESE

METHOD: MIX AND BLEND THE RICOTTA CHEESE, WHIPPING CREAM, NUTMEG AND BASIL. MELT THE BUTTER AND POUR IT INTO THE RICOTTA MIXTURE, STIR IN UNTIL WELL BLENDED. POUR SAUCE OVER YOUR PASTA, TOSS, ADD GRATED CHEESE AND TOSS AGAIN. SERVE.

RECOMMENDED PASTA: MEDIUM STRAIGHT EDGED TUBES, OR SHELL TYPES.

SHEPHERD'S SAUCE

FROM THE HILL COUNTRY OF CALABRIA COMES THIS TASTY AND INTERESTING SAUCE OF RICOTTA CHEESE AND PORK SAUSAGE.

INGREDIENTS:

1/2	POUND FRESH ITALIAN SAUSAGE (ALMOST ANY VARIETY OF FRESH ITALIAN STYLE SAUSAGE MAY BE USED.)
1	POUND RICOTTA CHEESE
1/2	CUP GRATED ROMANO CHEESE
1/2	TEASPOON FRESHLY GROUND BLACK PEPPER
2 OR 3	TABLESPOONS PASTA WATER
	SALT TO TASTE

METHOD: SKIN, CRUMBLE AND FRY THE ITALIAN SAUSAGE UNTIL IT BROWNS. DRAIN ITS OIL AND SET ASIDE. ADD THE PASTA WATER TO THE RICOTTA, BLEND TO MAKE A THICK SAUCE. ADD SAUSAGE, GRATED CHEESE, PEPPER AND SALT. POUR SAUCE OVER PASTA. TOSS AND SERVE.

RECOMMENDED PASTA: HOLLOW STRING TYPES.

CREAM CHEESE SAUCE

(ANOTHER QUICKIE)

THIS SAUCE REQUIRES AN ITALIAN CREAM CHEESE THAT MAY BE DIFFICULT, BUT NOT IMPOSSIBLE TO FIND OUTSIDE OF CITIES WITH LARGE ITALIAN POPULATIONS. IT'S CALLED MASCARPONE. IF YOU CAN'T FIND IT, LET'S JUST PRETEND, AND GO WITH ANY BRAND OF AMERICAN CREAM CHEESE THAT'S AVAILABLE IN YOUR NEIGHBORHOOD.

INGREDIENTS:

4	OUNCES CREAM CHEESE
1/2	CUP WHIPPING CREAM OR BUTTERMILK
1/4	CUP SWEET BUTTER
1/2	CUP PINE NUTS
1	CLOVE GARLIC (YOUR CHOICE)
2	TABLESPOONS FRESH BASIL LEAF, CHOPPED
	FRESHLY GRATED PARMESAN CHEESE

METHOD: THIN CREAM CHEESE WITH CREAM OR BUTTERMILK, SET ASIDE. SAUTE PINE NUTS AND GARLIC IN THE BUTTER UNTIL NUTS COLOR SLIGHTLY, REMOVE FROM HEAT, ADD THE BASIL. POUR THE HOT NUT MIXTURE OVER YOU PASTA. ADD THE THINNED ROOM TEMPERATURE CREAM CHEESE. TOSS AND SERVE.

RECOMMENDED PASTA: LONG RIBBON TYPES.

CREAM CHEESE SAUCE TOO!

(ANOTHER QUICKIE)

THE NAME OF THIS SAUCE MIGHT SUGGEST TO YOU THAT IT IS SIMILAR TO THE PRECEDING SAUCE. YOU'RE RIGHT! BUT, IT DOES HAVE A MORE EXTENSIVE INGREDIENT LIST, PLUS A HEFTY MEASURE OF BRANDY. YOU MAY USE A HEAT PROOF CASSEROLE DISH TO PREPARE THIS SAUCE.

INGREDIENTS:

1/4	POUND BUTTER
2	OUNCES CREAM CHEESE (MASCARPONE IF POSSIBLE)
2	OUNCES GORGONZOLA CHEESE (CRUMBLED)
1/2	CUP WHIPPING CREAM
1 1/2	OUNCES BRANDY
1	TEASPOON TOMATO PASTE, OR
2	TABLESPOONS TOMATO SAUCE (CANNED VARIETY)
1/4	CUP CHOPPED WALNUTS
1/2	CUP FRESHLY GRATED ASIAGO CHEESE
	SALT AND PEPPER TO TASTE
2	TABLESPOONS CHOPPED PARSLEY

METHOD: OVER LOW HEAT MELT THE BUTTER. DISSOLVE IN THE MELTED BUTTER THE CREAM CHEESE AND GORGONZOLA. ADD THE WHIPPING CREAM, BRANDY, TOMATO PASTE AND WALNUTS, BLEND WELL. ADD YOUR HOT, DRAINED PASTA TO THE SAUCE, TOSS WELL, ADD GRATED CHEESE. TOSS AGAIN, ADJUST SEASONING, GARNISH WITH PARSLEY, SERVE.

RECOMMENDED PASTA: MEDIUM TUBES, DIAGONAL CUT.

MOZZARELLA AND TOMATO SAUCE

FROM ITALY'S PASSIONATE FOOD CENTER, THE HAPPY COUNTRY, AND THE ANCESTRAL HOME OF MY FATHERS PARENTS, IN THE REGION OF CAMPANIA, COMES THIS BLEND OF TOMATOES TOGETHER WITH ITALY'S FAMOUS STRINGY CHEESE. I SUPPOSE WE COULD HAVE PLACED THIS ONE UNDER MEATLESS TOMATO SAUCES, BUT BECAUSE OF THE QUANTITY OF MOZZARELLA CHEESE AND THE STRINGY QUALITY OF THE FINISHED SAUCE, I'VE DECIDED TO PUT IT HERE, WITH THE CHEESE SAUCES.

AS A REFERENCE POINT, ITALIAN'S CALL A NUMBER OF THE DISHES PREPARED WITH MOZZARELLA CHEESE, "ALLA SORRENTINA". AS IN THE MANNER OF SPINACH IN A DISH GETTING THE TAG "FLORENTINE". MOZZARELLA CHEESE WAS CREATED IN THE REGION OF CAMPANIA NEAR SORRENTO AND CONSEQUENTLY GETS OCCASIONAL ACKNOWLEDGMENT.

INGREDIENTS:

1/4	CUP OLIVE OIL
3	CLOVES GARLIC, CRUSHED
1	28 OUNCE CAN PEAR TOMATOES, BLENDERIZED
1/2	TEASPOON OREGANO
1/2	CUP FRESH BASIL, CHOPPED OR 1 TABLESPOON DRIED
2	CUPS SHREDDED MOZZARELLA CHEESE
	GRATED PARMESAN CHEESE

METHOD: SAUTE ONION AND GARLIC IN THE OLIVE OIL. WHEN GARLIC HAS LIGHTLY COLORED, REMOVE AND DISCARD. ADD TOMATOES AND OREGANO. BRING TO A BOIL, REDUCE HEAT TO LOW, PARTIALLY COVER AND COOK FOR 20 TO 30 MINUTES. ADD BASIL, STIR IN, REMOVE FROM HEAT. TOSS HOT DRAINED PASTA AND MOZZARELLA CHEESE. ADD THE TOMATO SAUCE AND TOSS AGAIN. SERVE WITH PARMESAN ON THE SIDE.

RECOMMENDED PASTA: CURLY TYPES.

MOZZARELLA AND GARLIC SAUCE

IN RECENT YEARS, GARLIC SAUCES HAVE BECOME THE DARLING IN-FOOD OF THE FOODIES AND YUPPIES. AS A RESULT, BAKED GARLIC HAS RECEIVED AN UNUSUAL AMOUNT OF PRESS, SUGGESTING THAT THE METHOD WAS ONLY RECENTLY DISCOVERED. YOU AND I BOTH KNOW THE METHOD HAS BEEN AROUND FOR A LONG, LONG TIME, IN COUNTRIES LIKE FRANCE, THE BASQUE PYRENEES COMMUNITIES, SPAIN, PORTUGAL AND ITALY, AND LORD KNOWS WHERE ELSE IN THE MEDITERRANEAN. IT HAS BEEN THE ELEVATION OF GARLIC TO A NEAR FAD FOOD IN THE UNITED STATES THAT HAS MADE IT SOCIALLY ACCEPTABLE TO OFFER GARLIC SAUCES TO GUESTS. WELL, THIS IS ONE OF THEM, AND A VERY GOOD ONE.

INGREDIENTS:
2	FULL GARLIC BULBS
1	POUND SHREDDED MOZZARELLA CHEESE
	FRESHLY GROUND BLACK PEPPER TO TASTE, OR
1	TEASPOON
1/3	CUP OLIVE OIL

METHOD:

1. WRAP THE UNPEELED GARLIC BULBS INDIVIDUALLY, IN ALUMINUM FOIL. BAKE THEM IN A 300 F. DEGREE OVEN FOR 45 MINUTES.

2. PLACE THE SHREDDED MOZZARELLA CHEESE IN A FOOD PROCESSOR. WHEN THE GARLIC IS COOL ENOUGH TO HANDLE, TAKE INDIVIDUAL CLOVES AND SQUEEZE THE SOFT GARLIC ONTO THE CHEESE, DISCARD THE SKINS.

3. ADD OLIVE OIL AND BLACK PEPPER.

4. PROCESS UNTIL YOU HAVE A MEDIUM THICK, BUT POURABLE SAUCE. ADD ADDITIONAL OLIVE OIL AS NEEDED.

5. POUR SAUCE OVER YOUR PASTA, TOSS AND SERVE.

RECOMMENDED PASTA: RIBBONS OR THIN STRINGS.

PASTA WITH FOUR CHEESES

(OUR ONLY CASSEROLE OFFERING, BECAUSE IT CANNOT BE OFFERED AS A SAUCE)

IN MANY CHEESE SAUCE RECIPES, YOU'LL USE A NUMBER OF CHEESES, AND YOU CANNOT MERELY MELT THEM TOGETHER. IN ORDER TO SEPARATE THE FLAVORS YOU'LL NEED TO LAYER THE CHEESES USED IN THE RECIPE, AS IN THIS GOOD FOUR CHEESE RECIPE, WHERE IT WILL BE BAKED IN THE MANNER OF A LASAGNA, LAYERED WITH PASTA, CHEESE AND SAUCE. WE'LL START OUR PREPARATION WITH A QUICK TOMATO SAUCE. THIS GROUPING OF CHEESES IS AT NO POINT A SAUCE, WHAT WE HAVE HERE IS A RECIPE FOR A BAKED PASTA DISH. I LIST IT AS AN OFFERING TO CASSEROLE LOVERS.

INGREDIENTS:
- 3 — 8 OUNCE CANS TOMATO SAUCE OR 3 CUPS FRESH TOMATOES
- 1/2 — TEASPOON BASIL OR A FEW FRESH BASIL LEAVES
- 1/4 — CUP ONION, CHOPPED
- 1 — CUP RICOTTA CHEESE (BLENDERIZED COTTAGE CHEESE MAY BE SUBSTITUTED)
- 3 — SLICES OF JARLSBERG OR BRICK CHEESE
- 1 — CUP GRATED MOZZARELLA CHEESE OR 10 THIN SLICES
- 6 — THIN SLICES PROVOLONE CHEESE
- 1/2 — CUP FRESH PARSLEY, CHOPPED

METHOD: START YOUR PASTA COOKING. PLACE ONION AND TOMATOES INTO A SAUCE PAN, BRING IT QUICKLY TO A BOIL, REDUCE HEAT TO MEDIUM AND COOK FOR 5 MINUTES. REMOVE FROM HEAT, STIR IN BASIL, SET ASIDE. SPRAY YOUR BAKING PAN WITH PAM OR SIMILAR PRODUCT. BY NOW THE PASTA SHOULD BE DONE, DRAIN AND SET ASIDE.

BEGIN BUILDING WITH A THIN LAYER OF TOMATO SAUCE ON THE BAKING PAN BOTTOM.

PLACE A LAYER OF PASTA, ALL THE RICOTTA, A SPRINKLE OF SAUCE AND PARSLEY.

ADD THE SECOND LAYER OF PASTA, SPRINKLE WITH SAUCE AND PARSLEY, LAY ON THE JARLSBERG.

LAY A THIRD LAYER OF PASTA, SPRINKLE WITH SAUCE AND PARSLEY THEN THE MOZZARELLA.

ADD THE FOURTH LAYER OF PASTA, SPRINKLE WITH SAUCE AND PARSLEY, LAY ON THE PROVOLONE

COVER WITH FOIL, BAKE FOR 30 MINUTES AT 375 DEGREES.

RECOMMENDED PASTA: LONG OR MEDIUM TUBE TYPES.

GORGONZOLA SAUCE

WHILE GORGONZOLA IS THE PREFERRED CHEESE FOR THIS SAUCE, DON'T LET THAT STOP YOU. TRY BLUE, ROQUEFORT OR EVEN STILTON. BECAUSE YOU'LL COMPLETE THE COOKING IN THE SAUCE PAN, YOU'LL NEED A PYREX CASSEROLE DISH.

INGREDIENTS: 4   OUNCES GORGONZOLA
1/3   CUP MILK
3   TABLESPOONS BUTTER
1/4   CUP WHIPPING CREAM
1/4   CUP FRESHLY GRATED PARMESAN CHEESE
      SALT TO TASTE

METHOD: CRUMBLE THE GORGONZOLA. PLACE CHEESE, MILK AND BUTTER IN PYREX DISH, HEAT UNTIL BUTTER IS MELTED AND CHEESE IS WELL INCORPORATED INTO A LIGHT PASTE. ADD CREAM AND BLEND. ADD COOKED PASTA, TOSS TO COAT. ADD GRATED CHEESE, TOSS AGAIN, SERVE.

RECOMMENDED PASTA: MEDIUM RIBBON TYPES (ABOUT 8 OUNCES).

FONTINA CHEESE SAUCE

(ANOTHER QUICKIE)

FONTINA IS THE MELTING CHEESE OF CHOICE IN THIS SAUCE, BUT, YOU COULD PROBABLY SWAP THE FONTINA FOR A DOZEN OTHER CHEESES IN THIS SIMPLE SAUCE. IF YOU DID, WHO'S GOING TO KNOW? GO WITH WHAT YOU HAVE.

INGREDIENTS:
3	TABLESPOONS BUTTER
1	CLOVE GARLIC, LIGHTLY CRUSHED
1/2	POUND SHREDDED FONTINA CHEESE
1/4	CUP GRATED PARMESAN CHEESE

METHOD: SAUTE THE GARLIC IN THE BUTTER FOR 3 MINUTES. REMOVE AND DISCARD THE GARLIC. TOSS PASTA WITH THE GARLIC FLAVORED BUTTER. SPRINKLE BOTH CHEESES OVER THE PASTA, TOSS AGAIN. SERVE.

RECOMMENDED PASTA: MEDIUM SHELL TYPES OR DUMPLINGS.

BAKING CHEESE SAUCE

(FOR LARGE STUFFED PASTAS)

ONCE AGAIN I'VE PLAYED FAST AND LOOSE WITH THE PREMISE OF THIS BOOK, SAUCES ONLY. THIS IS A LITTLE MORE THAN A SAUCE IT IS, IN ADDITION, A PREPARATION. PRESENTLY THERE ARE A NUMBER OF PRECOOKED, LARGE, STUFFED PASTAS ON THE MARKET. THEY ONLY REQUIRE YOU TO ADD A SAUCE AND BAKE. IF YOU HAVE NOT YET TRIED ONE, YOU MAY BE SURPRISED. ASIDE FROM RELIEVING YOU OF THE LABOR INTENSIVE PREPARATION, THEY ARE TO A VERY LARGE DEGREE, EXCELLENT. SOME OF THEM HAVE SAUCE RECIPES ON THE PACKAGE. WHAT WE'RE DOING IS OFFERING YOU AN ALTERNATIVE SAUCE. THIS SAUCE IS TO BE LAID OVER AND UNDER A STUFFED PASTA, AND THEN THE COOKING IS COMPLETED BY BAKING.

IF YOU OMIT THE TOMATO PASTE, THIS SAUCE MAY ALSO BE USED WITH AN ELBOW MACARONI OR SMALL SEA SHELLS TO CREATE AN EXCELLENT BAKED "MACARONI AND CHEESE".

INGREDIENTS:

3	TABLESPOONS BUTTER
3	TABLESPOONS FLOUR
1 1/2	CUPS MILK
1	TABLESPOON TOMATO PASTE
2	TABLESPOONS SHREDDED SWISS CHEESE
2	TABLESPOONS PARMESAN CHEESE, GRATED
PINCH	NUTMEG
PINCH	CAYENNE PEPPER

METHOD: MAKE A ROUX OF THE BUTTER AND FLOUR. REMOVE FROM HEAT. WHISK IN THE MILK, RETURN TO HEAT AND COOK UNTIL SMOOTH AND THICKENED. ADD THE TOMATO PASTE, SWISS AND PARMESAN CHEESES, NUTMEG AND CAYENNE. COOK UNTIL CHEESE IS MELTED.

USE THIS SAUCE BOTH UNDER AND OVER A STUFFED PASTA. BAKE FOR 30 MINUTES AT 350 DEGREES. OR AS PER PACKAGE INSTRUCTIONS.

RECOMMENDED PASTA: STUFFED MANICOTTI, CANNELLONI OR LARGE SHELLS.

FAST AND EASY CHEESE SAUCE

(ANOTHER QUICKIE)

THIS IS A WHITE SAUCE (ITALIAN; BALSAMELLA) WITH GRATED CHEESE AND PARSLEY. FAST AND SIMPLE, ALSO TASTY. THIS CAN ALSO BE USED AS A GREAT SAUCE FOR A BAKED MACARONI AND CHEESE. IF YOU WISH TO USE IT AS A CHEESE SAUCE FOR BAKED MACARONI AND CHEESE, SEE THE FOLLOWING RECIPES FOR TEMPERATURE AND TIME.

INGREDIENTS:

2	TABLESPOONS BUTTER
2	TABLESPOONS FLOUR
1	CUP MILK OR HALF AND HALF
1/4	CUP FRESHLY GRATED PARMESAN CHEESE
1	FRESH PEAR TOMATO CUT INTO ROUNDS
2	TABLESPOONS PARSLEY, CHOPPED

METHOD: OVER MEDIUM HEAT, MAKE A ROUX OF THE BUTTER AND FLOUR. ADD THE MILK, WHISK UNTIL SMOOTH AND CREAMY, WHISK IN THE GRATED CHEESE. REMOVE FROM HEAT. ADD THE PARSLEY, MIX, POUR OVER PASTA. GARNISH WITH TOMATO. SERVE.

RECOMMENDED PASTA: ELBOWS, MEDIUM SHELLS.

ALL THE MACARONI AND CHEESE RECIPES CALL FOR 2 CUPS OF DRY MEASURE PASTA (8 OUNCES), AND MUST BE COOKED PRIOR TO BAKING.

WE TRIED THIS SAUCE . . . AND

LOVED IT ( )
HATED IT ( )
MAYBE WE'LL TRY IT AGAIN ( )
WE'LL USE IT FOR UNWELCOME GUESTS ( )

MACARONI AND CHEESE #1

(WITH AMERICAN CHEESE)

I DON'T KNOW WHERE THIS DISH ORIGINATED, BUT I AM SURE IT QUALIFIES AS ONE OF AMERICA'S FAVORITE PASTA DISHES. SIMPLE AND WONDERFUL, MACARONI AND CHEESE. IT GOES BACK QUITE A WAY. WE KNOW FOR A FACT THAT PRESIDENT THOMAS JEFFERSON ATE IT AND SERVED IT. HE WAS AN EARLY AFICIONADO OF ITALIAN PASTA DISHES. HE WAS PROBABLY ONE OF THE EARLIEST AMERICANS TO OWN A PASTA MAKING MACHINE, HAVING BOUGHT ONE IN ITALY AND BRINGING IT HOME FOR HIS HOUSEHOLD USE. WE ALSO RECOGNIZE THAT THE VERSION OF MACARONI AND CHEESE HE ATE WAS SUBSTANTIALLY DIFFERENT FROM THE ONE WE USUALLY MAKE TODAY. HIS MACARONI WAS A TUBE VARIETY (MOSTACCHOLI OR PENNE) COOKED AND DRAINED, THE CHEESE HE USED WAS A HARD GRATING VARIETY (PARMESAN, ROMANO, OR ASIAGO), OR A YELLOW TYPE (POSSIBLY A CHEDDAR) ADD SOME BUTTER, AND POSSIBLY SOME MILK OR CREAM, TOSS AND BAKE IN A MODERATE OVEN FOR ABOUT 30 MINUTES. TRY IT, YOU MIGHT LIKE IT.

THE VERSIONS WE'LL OFFER HERE ARE MADE WITH THE CURRENT AMERICAN FAVORITES IN CHEESE. SUCH AS CHEDDAR CHEESE OR AMERICAN CHEESE OR GO CHEESELESS WITH A WHITE SAUCE.

THIS SAUCE USES AMERICAN CHEESE, AND MAY I RECOMMENDED YOU DO NOT USE ONE OF THE "SOUP/SAUCE" CANNED THINGS. THEY HAVE AN UNACCEPTABLE TASTE. USE THE REAL THING.

Continued on next page

INGREDIENTS: 3 TABLESPOONS BUTTER
3 TABLESPOONS FLOUR
2 1/2 CUPS MILK
8 OUNCES AMERICAN OR SIMILAR CHEESE
1/2 TEASPOON DRY MUSTARD
OR
PINCH CAYENNE PEPPER
1/2 CUP FRESH PARSLEY, CHOPPED

METHOD: MAKE A ROUX OF THE BUTTER AND FLOUR. REMOVE FROM HEAT, WHISK IN THE MILK, BRING TO A LOW BOIL. ADD CHEESE AND MUSTARD. STIR UNTIL CHEESE IS MELTED, ADD PARSLEY AND REMOVE FROM HEAT. COMBINE SAUCE AND PASTA, PLACE IN A TWO QUART BAKING DISH. COVER AND BAKE FOR 30 MINUTES AT 350 DEGREES.

RECOMMENDED PASTA: SHORT OR MEDIUM TUBES OR ELBOW SHAPES

MACARONI AND CHEESE #2

(WITH CHEDDAR CHEESE)

FROM AMERICAN CHEESE IN THE PRECEDING RECIPE, WE NOW TURN TO CHEDDAR CHEESE. THIS IS THE FIRST OF THREE CHEDDAR CHEESE RECIPES AND THE ONE THAT USES THE LEAST AMOUNT OF CHEDDAR. OUR NEXT RECIPE USES SWISS AND VERY SMALL AMOUNT OF THAT. INSTEAD OF BAKING THIS ONE, WE'RE GOING TO COMPLETE IN ON THE STOVE TOP. CONSIDER IT TO BE A HOMEMADE VERSION OF THE STORE BOUGHT PACKAGE TYPE.

INGREDIENTS:

2	TABLESPOONS BUTTER
2	TABLESPOONS FLOUR
1	CUP MILK
1/4	TEASPOON SALT
1	CUP SHREDDED CHEDDAR CHEESE (WHITE OR ORANGE)
DASH	CAYENNE OR PAPRIKA

METHOD: MAKE A ROUX OF THE BUTTER AND FLOUR, BY MELTING THE BUTTER, ADD THE FLOUR AND WHISK WHILE COOKING FOR ABOUT 3 MINUTES. ADD THE MILK, SALT, CHEESE AND CAYENNE. BRING TO A LOW BOIL, ADD THE COOKED AND DRAINED PASTA. BLEND WELL AND SERVE.

RECOMMENDED PASTA: ELBOWS, TWIST ELBOWS, CURLY TYPES, OR SHELLS.

MACARONI AND CHEESE #3

(WITH SWISS CHEESE)

SWISS CHEESE IS THE CHEESE OF CHOICE IN THIS RECIPE, AND VERY LITTLE OF IT TOO. THIS IS A DOWN RIGHT INEXPENSIVE DISH.

INGREDIENTS:

3	TABLESPOONS BUTTER
3	TABLESPOONS FLOUR
1 1/2	CUPS MILK
PINCH	NUTMEG
4	TABLESPOONS SHREDDED SWISS CHEESE
2	TABLESPOONS FRESHLY GRATED PARMESAN

METHOD: MAKE A ROUX OF THE BUTTER AND FLOUR. REMOVE FROM HEAT, WHISK IN THE MILK. RETURN TO HEAT AND COOK UNTIL SMOOTH AND THICKENED. ADD SWISS CHEESE AND NUTMEG. COOK UNTIL CHEESE HAS MELTED. BLEND SAUCE WITH YOUR COOKED PASTA, SPRINKLE WITH PARMESAN AND BAKE FOR 30 MINUTES AT 350 DEGREES.

RECOMMENDED PASTA: SHORT TUBES, ELBOWS OR SHELLS.

MACARONI AND CHEESE #4

(WITH CHEDDAR CHEESE)

THIS RECIPE IS AN OLD ONE. IT USES A LOT OF CHEDDAR CHEESE AND AT TODAY'S PRICES IT MAY BE QUITE EXPENSIVE. THERE ARE 4 OUNCES OF SHREDDED CHEESE TO THE CUP, AND 4 CUPS EQUAL ONE POUND, THAT'S A LOT OF CHEESE, BUT HERE IT IS.

INGREDIENTS:

2	CUPS SHARP CHEDDAR CHEESE, SHREDDED
2	CUPS MILD CHEDDAR CHEESE (COLBY OR LONGHORN)
2	EGGS, BEATEN
2	CUPS MILK
1	TEASPOON GRATED ONION
1/2	TEASPOON SALT
1/4	TEASPOON WHITE PEPPER
1/4	CUP CORN FLAKES, CRUSHED TO CRUMBS

METHOD: COMBINE ALL INGREDIENTS, EXCEPT CORN FLAKES, IN A BOWL AND MIX WELL. ADD COOKED MACARONI, MIX AGAIN. PLACE THE MACARONI IN A BUTTERED BAKING DISH. SPRINKLE THE CRUSHED CORN FLAKES EVENLY OVER THE MACARONI. SET THE BAKING DISH IN A LARGER PAN WITH 1 INCH OF WATER IN IT AND BAKE IN A 350 DEGREE OVEN FOR 1 HOUR. SERVE.

IF YOU DON'T HAPPEN TO HAVE ANY CORN FLAKES IN THE HOUSE, USE 1/2 CUP BREAD CRUMBS, SAUTE THEM IN BUTTER UNTIL WELL COATED. OR TOAST THE BREAD CRUMBS WITHOUT BUTTER IN A SKILLET FOR SEVERAL MINUTES. PROCEED AS DIRECTED ABOVE.

RECOMMENDED PASTA: ELBOWS, ELBOW TWISTS OR SHELLS.

MACARONI AND CHEESE #5

(WITH CHEDDAR CHEESE)

(SINGLE SERVING)

THIS IS A SMALL RECIPE USING ONLY 1 CUP OF COOKED PASTA, IT IS ENOUGH FOR ONE PERSON. TWO, IF BOTH ARE LIGHT EATERS AND THIS IS NOT THE ENTREE.

INGREDIENTS:

1	CUP COOKED MACARONI
1/2	CUP CHEDDAR CHEESE, SHREDDED (ANY VARIETY)
2	EGGS, BEATEN
1	CUP MILK
1/4	TEASPOON SALT
PINCH	BLACK OR WHITE PEPPER
2	TABLESPOONS BREAD CRUMBS
2	TABLESPOONS GRATED PARMESAN CHEESE

METHOD: BLEND MACARONI, CHEDDAR CHEESE, EGGS, MILK, SALT AND PEPPER IN A SMALL MIXING BOWL. POUR INTO A SMALL BAKING DISH, SPRINKLE BREAD CRUMBS AND PARMESAN CHEESE EVENLY OVER THE MACARONI. PLACE INTO A PREHEATED OVEN AND BAKE FOR 40 MINUTES AT 350 DEGREES.

RECOMMENDED PASTA: ELBOWS, ELBOW TWISTS OR SHELLS.

Chapter 12

Sauces made from Uncooked Cheese

These are very quick sauces, and they require more attention than just grating some cheese over the pasta. They are also in wide use throughout Italy. I think you're going to like them.

FOUR CHEESE SAUCE

(ANOTHER QUICKIE)

SHREDDED CHEESE ON HOT PASTA, NO COOKING, TOSS AND SERVE. CAN I MAKE IT ANY SIMPLER FOR YOU TO BE A GRAND GOURMET HOST(ESS)? TRY IT, YOU'LL LOVE IT AND ME FOR MAKING YOU LOOK LIKE SUCH A WONDERFUL AND CREATIVE COOK.

INGREDIENTS:

1/4	CUP MELTED BUTTER
1/4	CUP SHREDDED FONTINA
1/4	CUP SHREDDED SWISS CHEESE
1/2	CUP SHREDDED MOZZARELLA
2	TABLESPOONS FRESHLY GRATED PARMESAN
	FRESHLY GROUND BLACK PEPPER TO TASTE

METHOD: HAVE ALL CHEESES AT ROOM TEMPERATURE, POUR BUTTER OVER HOT PASTA, TOSS, SPRINKLE THE FONTINA, SWISS AND MOZZARELLA EVENLY OVER THE PASTA, TOSS AGAIN. ADD GRATED PARMESAN AND BLACK PEPPER, TOSS A THIRD TIME, SERVE.

FOR A LIST OF CHEESES YOU MAY USE AS SUBSTITUTES FOR THE ABOVE, SEE THE FOUR CHEESE SAUCE IN CHAPTER 11.

RECOMMENDED PASTA: MEDIUM SHELL TYPES OR DUMPLING TYPES.

TWO CHEESE SAUCE

(ANOTHER QUICKIE)

HERE'S ANOTHER VARIATION ON THE FORMULA OF "LET'S JUST USE A LITTLE BUTTER THIS TIME". BUTTER, FOR AS GOOD AS IT IS, GETS TIRESOME. SO IF YOU USE IT OFTEN, YOU'VE PROBABLY REACHED FOR A GRATING CHEESE AND OR A LITTLE BLACK PEPPER. WELL, THAT'S WHAT WE HAVE HERE, BUTTER, TWO CHEESES AND BLACK PEPPER.

INGREDIENTS: 1/2 CUP BUTTER, MELTED
3/4 CUP FRESHLY GRATED PARMESAN CHEESE
3/4 CUP FRESHLY GRATED ROMANO CHEESE
FRESHLY GROUND BLACK PEPPER TO TASTE

METHOD: MELT THE BUTTER. POUR OVER HOT, DRAINED PASTA, TOSS. ADD THE CHEESE, TOSS AGAIN. ADD BLACK PEPPER, TOSS AND SERVE.

RECOMMENDED PASTA: THIN STRING TYPES.

RICOTTA SAUCE

(ANOTHER QUICKIE)

RICOTTA IS PROBABLY ITALY'S FAVORITE FILLING, STUFFING, SPREADING AND BAKING CHEESE. YOU'RE APT TO FIND IT IN ANY FILLED OR STUFFED PASTA, AS WELL AS MOST LAYERED PASTA DISHES, AND MANY DESSERTS. IT IS THE SOUTHERNERS FAVORITE RAVIOLI FILLING AND THE SICILIANS FAVORITE CANNOLI FILLING. IT IS ALSO THE BREAKFAST CHAMPION. SPREAD OVER TOAST, IT CAN BE USED PLAIN, SALT AND PEPPERED OR SWEETENED WITH SUGAR AND SPICE, OR SUGAR AND GROUND COFFEE, (YOU COULD ALSO USE INSTANT COFFEE). AND, IT IS ALSO LOW IN CALORIES. TRY IT, YOU'LL LIKE IT! NOW TO THE SAUCE AT HAND, IT IS ONLY A THINNED RICOTTA USING OLIVE OIL AND SEASONING. LET'S LOOK. SEVERAL REGIONS SEEM TO LAY CLAIM TO THIS STYLE OF SAUCE, CENTRAL OR SOUTHERN, TAKE YOUR CHOICE.

INGREDIENTS:
1	POUND RICOTTA CHEESE
4	TABLESPOONS OLIVE OIL
1/2	TEASPOON SALT
1/2	TEASPOON FRESHLY GROUND BLACK PEPPER

METHOD: YOU MAY USE THE RICOTTA STRAIGHT FROM THE PACKAGE BLENDED WITH THE OIL AND SEASONING, OR PLACE RICOTTA, OIL, SALT AND PEPPER IN A FOOD PROCESSOR AND WHIRL UNTIL SMOOTH AND CREAMY. SPOON SAUCE OVER COOKED PASTA, SERVE.

RECOMMENDED PASTA: RIBBONS OR MEDIUM TUBE TYPES.

SWEET RICOTTA SAUCE I

(ANOTHER QUICKIE)

THIS SAUCE IS ONE GENERALLY LIKED BY CHILDREN. IT IS SERVED IN AND AROUND ROME, AND PROBABLY ELSEWHERE TOO. OMIT THE MILK AND YOU'LL HAVE A BREAKFAST SPREAD THAT ITALIANS LOVE ON BREAD, TOASTED OR NOT. (SEE CHAPTER 11 FOR A SIMILAR SAUCE THAT'S BARELY COOKED).

INGREDIENTS:
1	CUP RICOTTA CHEESE
1/2	CUP MILK, WARMED
2 1/2	TABLESPOONS SUGAR
PINCH	GROUND CINNAMON

METHOD: IN A BLENDER OR FOOD PROCESSOR, PLACE THE CHEESE, MILK, SUGAR AND CINNAMON AND PROCESS UNTIL QUITE SMOOTH. POUR OVER PASTA. TOSS AND SERVE.

RECOMMENDED PASTA: HOLLOW STRING TYPES.

GRATED CHEESE AND PEPPER SAUCE

(ANOTHER QUICKIE)

THIS METHOD OF SERVING PASTA IS FROM THE PROVINCE OF LAZIO, (THEY GET THE CREDIT THIS TIME) AND WHILE IT MAY SEEM THAT I'M PLAYING FAST AND LOOSE WITH THE WORD SAUCE ON THIS ONE, IT IS A LEGITIMATE AND CLASSIC PASTA DRESSING, POPULAR THROUGHOUT ITALY.

INGREDIENTS:

1	CUP FRESHLY GRATED ROMANO CHEESE
1/2	TO 1 TEASPOON FRESHLY GRATED BLACK PEPPER
1/4	CUP RESERVED PASTA WATER

METHOD: RESERVE 1/4 CUP OF THE PASTA WATER BEFORE DRAINING. PLACE COOKED BUT NOT COMPLETELY DRAINED PASTA IN A SERVING DISH, ADD THE RESERVED WATER, CHEESE AND BLACK PEPPER, TOSS AND SERVE.

RECOMMENDED PASTA: STRING TYPES.

PARMESAN AND CREAM SAUCE

(ANOTHER QUICKIE)

FITTING NICELY BETWEEN THE PRECEDING AND THE FOLLOWING SAUCES, WE OFFER A SAUCE SIMILAR TO BOTH AND YET DIFFERENT. A FEATURE OF THIS SAUCE IS THE METHOD, ONE INGREDIENT AT A TIME. PREPARE THIS IN A PREWARMED CHAFING DISH OR PYREX CASSEROLE DISH ON THE STOVE TOP AND OVER LOW HEAT.

INGREDIENTS:
1	CUP FRESHLY GRATED PARMESAN CHEESE
4	TABLESPOONS BUTTER
3	TABLESPOON WHIPPING CREAM

METHOD: COOK AND DRAIN YOUR PASTA, TRANSFER TO SERVING BOWL. ADD THE GRATED CHEESE AND TOSS. ADD THE BUTTER, TOSS AGAIN. ADD THE CREAM AND TOSS A THIRD TIME. SERVE. (IF YOU WISH, ADD SOME FRESHLY GROUND BLACK PEPPER).

RECOMMENDED PASTA: STRING OR MEDIUM TUBE TYPES.

PIEDMONT STYLE CHEESE AND BUTTER SAUCE

(ANOTHER QUICKIE)

THIS CERTAINLY IS ONE OF THE SIMPLER, CLASSIC NORTHERN PREPARATIONS. IF YOU HAPPEN TO HAVE SOME FRESH SAGE GROWING IN YOUR YARD, ADD ABOUT A DOZEN LEAVES TO THE BUTTER WHILE IT IS BEING MELTED.

INGREDIENTS: 1/2 POUND BUTTER, MELTED
1 CUP FRESHLY GRATED PARMESAN CHEESE

(OPTION): FRESHLY GROUND BLACK PEPPER TO TASTE

METHOD: MIX PASTA WITH THE MELTED BUTTER. ADD THE CHEESE, MIX AGAIN, (DITTO, IF USING BLACK PEPPER) SERVE.

RECOMMENDED PASTA: FILLED LITTLE PILLOW TYPES.

WE TRIED THIS SAUCE . . . AND

LOVED IT ( )
HATED IT ( )
MAYBE WE'LL TRY IT AGAIN ( )
WE'LL USE IT FOR UNWELCOME GUESTS ( )

PROVOLONE CHEESE SAUCE

(ANOTHER QUICKIE)

HERE AGAIN A VARIATION OF GRATED CHEESE, BUTTER AND BLACK PEPPER. ITALY, LIKE FRANCE PRODUCES IN THE NEIGHBORHOOD OF TWO HUNDRED TYPES OF CHEESE. YOU COULD PROBABLY USE MOST OF DRY ONES IN THIS FASHION.

INGREDIENTS: 1/4   POUND BUTTER, VERY SOFT TO MELTED
              1 1/2   CUPS GRATED PROVOLONE CHEESE (SHARP IF POSSIBLE)
                      FRESHLY GRATED GROUND BLACK PEPPER TO TASTE

METHOD: POUR BUTTER OVER HOT, DRAINED PASTA. TOSS. ADD CHEESE TOSS AGAIN. ADD BLACK PEPPER, TOSS AND SERVE.

RECOMMENDED PASTA: THIN STRING TYPES.

SWEET RICOTTA SAUCE II

(ANOTHER QUICKIE)

THE ROMANS WERE CREDITED FOR HAVING CREATED SAUCE I. NOW TO SHOW THAT I'M IMPARTIAL, THE SICILIANS GET THE CREDIT FOR THIS VERSION. HERE WE'LL USE AN ADDED CHEESE* AND LESS SUGAR. SINCE THIS SAUCE WILL NOT BE COOKED, HAVE THE RICOTTA CHEESE AT ROOM TEMPERATURE.

*THE SICILIANS WOULD USE A GRATED RAGUSANO CHEESE, THAT MAY BE NEAR IMPOSSIBLE TO FIND HERE. IF YOU CAN FIND IT, USE IT. IN THE MEANWHILE, I'VE SUBSTITUTED ASIAGO SO THAT YOU CAN GET ON WITH IT.

INGREDIENTS:

2	CUPS (16 OUNCE PACKAGE) RICOTTA CHEESE
1/2	CUP GRATED ASIAGO CHEESE
1/2	TEASPOON SUGAR
1/2	TEASPOON GROUND CINNAMON
2	TABLESPOONS CHOPPED PARSLEY
2	TABLESPOONS HOT WATER OR PASTA WATER (OPTION)

METHOD: MIX THE RICOTTA, ASIAGO, SUGAR AND CINNAMON, POUR MIXTURE OVER HOT, DRAINED PASTA. TOSS, GARNISH WITH PARSLEY, SERVE.

OR

PREPARE AND SET ASIDE CHEESE MIXTURE. DRAIN PASTA AND RETURN TO THE COOKING PAN. OVER LOW HEAT ADD THE CHEESE MIXTURE, TOSS TO HEAT THROUGH, ADD HOT WATER IF NEEDED. TURN OUT INTO A SERVING BOWL. GARNISH WITH PARSLEY. SERVE.

RECOMMENDED PASTA: MEDIUM TUBE TYPES.

SHREDDED SWISS CHEESE SAUCE

(ANOTHER QUICKIE)

SIMPLE AND UNCOMPLICATED, MIX AND TOSS. IT'S GREAT JUST THE WAY WE PRESENT IT, BUT, YOU MAY ADD FRESHLY GROUND BLACK PEPPER, OR SOME GRATED HARD CHEESE IF YOU WISH. THIS RECIPE IS VERY FLEXIBLE. TRY IT WITH WHATEVER CHEESE YOU HAVE HANDY.

INGREDIENTS:
2   TABLESPOONS BUTTER
1   CUP WHIPPING CREAM (MUST BE AT ROOM TEMPERATURE)*
1   CUP SHREDDED SWISS CHEESE
1   TABLESPOON CHOPPED PARSLEY

METHOD: TOSS THE HOT DRAINED PASTA WITH THE BUTTER. ADD WHIPPING CREAM AND CHEESE. TOSS UNTIL CHEESE HAS MELTED. GARNISH WITH PARSLEY, SERVE.

* ALTERNATELY, YOU MAY BRING THE CREAM TO A BOIL BEFORE ADDING IT TO THE BUTTERED PASTA.

OR ADD THE CHEESE TO THE HOT CREAM TO CREATE A SMOOTH SAUCE. IT WILL GIVE YOU A SAUCE WITH A LITTLE MORE CHARACTER.

RECOMMENDED PASTA: USE 8 OUNCES OF: NARROW RIBBONS, STRINGS OR SHELL TYPES.

Green Ricotta Cheese Sauce

(Another Quickie)

IF GREEN ISN'T ITS NATURAL COLOR, I'D BE INCLINED TO THROW IT AWAY. HOWEVER, THAT RULE DOESN'T APPLY WHEN YOU COLOR IT GREEN. THIS SAUCE OFFERS A REFRESHING CHANGE IN BOTH TASTE AND COLOR. THE DOMINANT TASTE WILL BE THAT OF PARSLEY, THE MILD FLAVOR OF RICOTTA, THE CREAM AND MILK ARE INFUSED BY THE PARSLEY.

INGREDIENTS:

1	CUP PARSLEY (RINSED AND DRIED)
10	OUNCES RICOTTA CHEESE
1	CUP WHIPPING CREAM
2/3	CUP MILK
3/4	CUP FRESHLY GRATED PARMESAN CHEESE
	SALT AND WHITE PEPPER TO TASTE

METHOD: PLACE THE PARSLEY INTO A FOOD PROCESSOR AND PROCESS UNTIL WELL CHOPPED. ADD RICOTTA, WHIPPING CREAM, MILK AND GRATED CHEESE, PROCESS AGAIN UNTIL WELL BLENDED. SEASON TO TASTE, POUR SAUCE OVER PASTA. TOSS AND SERVE.

RECOMMENDED PASTA: RIBBONS, MEDIUM TUBES, SHELLS.

CHAPTER 13

MEATLESS SAUCES MADE FROM VEGETABLES

SEVERAL OF THE SAUCES IN THIS CHAPTER USE ANCHOVY AS AN INGREDIENT, AND BECAUSE ANCHOVY DISSOLVES IN THE SAUCE, YOU'RE NOT EATING FISH, BUT, GETTING A SEASONING. THAT'S WHY, THEY ARE HERE, AND NOT IN SEAFOOD SAUCES.

WE TRIED THIS SAUCE . . . AND

LOVED IT ( )
HATED IT ( )
MAYBE WE'LL TRY IT AGAIN ( )
WE'LL USE IT FOR UNWELCOME GUESTS ( )

Summer Vegetable Sauce

DO YOU LOVE THE COMBINATION OF FRESH VEGETABLES THAT ARE PUT IN TO A GREAT VEGETABLE SOUP? IF YES, THEN I THINK YOU'RE GOING TO LIKE THIS SAUCE. YOU'LL USE A MIX OF VEGETABLES, AT LEAST THREE AND AS MANY AS SIX. USE YOUR RESOURCEFULNESS, COOKED LEFTOVERS ARE QUITE ACCEPTABLE. YOU'LL FINISH COOKING THIS SAUCE WITH THE PASTA IN THE SKILLET (COUNTRY STYLE), USE A LARGE SKILLET IF YOU HAVE ONE.

INGREDIENTS:
4	TABLESPOONS OLIVE OIL
2	CLOVES GARLIC, BRUISED
PINCH	CRUSHED RED PEPPER OR 1/4 FRESH HOT PEPPER
3	CUPS VEGETABLES (YOUR CHOICE, COOKED AND CHOPPED)

METHOD: SAUTE GARLIC AND PEPPER IN OLIVE OIL UNTIL GARLIC BEGINS TO TURN GOLDEN. REMOVE AND DISCARD. DITTO FOR THE PEPPER IF IT IS FRESH. ADD THE COOKED VEGETABLES AND CONTINUE COOKING UNTIL PASTA IS DONE. ADD DRAINED PASTA TO THE VEGETABLES. TOSS WHILE OVER HEAT FOR A MOMENT OR TWO, REMOVE FROM HEAT, SERVE.

RECOMMENDED PASTA: MEDIUM TUBE TYPES OR FANCIES.

SPRINGTIME SAUCE

(PRIMAVERA #2)

(ANOTHER QUICKIE)

FOR PRIMAVERA #1 SEE CHAPTER 10, TOMATOES AND VEGETABLE SAUCES. SPRINGTIME IN ITALY AND ELSEWHERE BRINGS FRESH ASPARAGUS TO THE MARKET PLACE AND THAT'S WHAT PASTA PRIMAVERA FEATURES, FRESH ASPARAGUS.

INGREDIENTS:
1/4	CUP BUTTER
1/2	POUND MUSHROOMS, SLICED
1/2	POUND ASPARAGUS, CUT INTO 1" PIECES
1	CARROT, THINLY SLICED
1	ZUCCHINI, SLICED OR DICED
1/2	CUP FROZEN PEAS
3	WHOLE CHIVES, CHOPPED
	SEVERAL FRESH BASIL LEAVES
1/2	TEASPOON SALT
PINCH	WHITE PEPPER
PINCH	NUTMEG
1	CUP WHIPPING CREAM
1/4	CUP FRESHLY GRATED PARMESAN CHEESE
	CHOPPED FRESH PARSLEY

METHOD: PREPARE INGREDIENTS AND SET ASIDE, GET YOUR PASTA OFF TO A ROLLING BOIL, NOW START YOUR SAUCE.

SAUTE MUSHROOMS, ASPARAGUS, CARROT, ZUCCHINI, PEAS AND CHIVES IN THE BUTTER FOR ABOUT FIVE MINUTES. ADD THE WHIPPING CREAM, SALT, PEPPER, NUTMEG AND BASIL LEAVES. BRING THE SAUCE TO A BOIL, REMOVE FROM HEAT, POUR OVER YOUR PASTA, TOSS. ADD THE CHEESE AND PARSLEY, TOSS AGAIN. SERVE.

RECOMMENDED PASTA: RIBBON OR STRING TYPES.

MARINATED EGGPLANT SAUCE

THIS SAUCE AND THE PASTA ARE SERVED AT ROOM TEMPERATURE. IT IS ANOTHER NICE SUMMER MEAL. YOU'LL TOSS THE SAUCE AND PASTA TOGETHER THEN LET THEM COOL BEFORE SERVING.

INGREDIENTS:

1	EGGPLANT
1/2	POUND MUSHROOMS, SLICED
1	CUP OLIVE OIL
3	CLOVES GARLIC, MINCED
1	ONION, FINELY CHOPPED
1	FRESH PEPPER (YOUR CHOICE) JULIENNED
1	SMALL CAN ANCHOVIES, MINCED
12	RIPE OLIVES, HALVED
1/4	CUP PARSLEY, CHOPPED

METHOD: PARE AND DICE THE EGGPLANT (YOU MAY SALT THE EGGPLANT. SET IT ASIDE FOR 30 MINUTES, RINSE AND SQUEEZE DRY). FRY THE EGGPLANT AND MUSHROOMS IN OLIVE OIL UNTIL EGGPLANT BEGINS TO BROWN. REMOVE THEM FROM PAN, SET ASIDE. SAUTE THE GARLIC, ONION AND FRESH PEPPER UNTIL PEPPER IS SOFT. ADD ANCHOVIES, OLIVES, EGGPLANT, MUSHROOMS AND PARSLEY, STIR TO BLEND WELL. REMOVE FROM HEAT. COOK PASTA WHILE THE SAUCE IS COOKING, DRAIN PASTA. POUR SAUCE OVER PASTA AND TOSS. COVER AND SET ASIDE UNTIL COOLED TO ROOM TEMPERATURE. SERVE.

RECOMMENDED PASTA: STRING TYPES OR MEDIUM TUBES.

WE TRIED THIS SAUCE . . . AND

LOVED IT ( )
HATED IT ( )
MAYBE WE'LL TRY IT AGAIN ( )
WE'LL USE IT FOR UNWELCOME GUESTS ( )

HOT AND SWEET PEPPER SAUCE, OR
SWEET AND HOT PEPPER SAUCE

(ANOTHER QUICKIE)

HERE'S ONE THAT OFFERS REAL ZIP UND ZING (IS THAT THE GERMAN CHORAL GROUP AGAIN?)

INGREDIENTS:

4	GREEN ONIONS, FINELY CHOPPED
1/2	BELL PEPPER, SEEDED AND CHOPPED
2	CLOVES GARLIC (YOUR CHOICE)
2	FRESH SMALL HOT PEPPERS (YOUR CHOICE OF COLOR)
6	TABLESPOONS OF BUTTER
1/2	CUP FRESHLY GRATED PARMESAN CHEESE
1/4	CUP FRESHLY CHOPPED PARSLEY
1/2	TEASPOON SALT
PINCH	BLACK PEPPER

METHOD: CORE, SEED AND FINELY CHOP THE HOT PEPPER. (FOR THE INEXPERIENCED COOK, I OFFER THIS SAGE ADVICE: DON'T RUB YOUR EYES OR, YOU'LL PAY DEARLY FOR IT.) IF YOU HAVE RUBBER GLOVES USE THEM FOR THIS PART OF THE PREPARATION.

MELT THE BUTTER, WHEN IT BEGINS TO BUBBLE, ADD GREEN ONIONS, GARLIC, BELL PEPPER AND HOT PEPPER. COOK WHILE STIRRING CONSTANTLY FOR ABOUT 2 MINUTES. ADD COOKED PASTA TO THE SAUCE, TOSS, ADD PARSLEY AND CHEESE, SERVE.

RECOMMENDED PASTA: LONG HOLLOW TYPES.

WE TRIED THIS SAUCE . . . AND

SAUTEED ONION SAUCE #1

IF YOU LIKE ONIONS, YOU LOVE THIS ONE, USE SWEET WALLA WALLA OR THE GEORGIA VIDALIA ONIONS YOU'LL HAVE A SAUCE WITH A LIGHT SWEET TASTE FOR A LIGHT PASTA SUPPER. SERVE WITH CRUSTY BREAD OR ROLLS.

INGREDIENTS:
2 TABLESPOONS BUTTER
2 TABLESPOONS OLIVE OIL
2 LARGE ONIONS, SLICED THIN TOP TO BOTTOM
1/2 TEASPOON SALT
1/4 TEASPOON NUTMEG (FRESHLY GRATED IF YOU CAN)

METHOD: SAUTE THE ONIONS AND SALT IN THE OIL AND BUTTER OVER LOW HEAT UNTIL SOFT AND TRANSPARENT. REMOVE FROM HEAT ADD NUTMEG, LAY OVER YOUR PASTA, TOSS AND SERVE.

RECOMMENDED PASTA: OVAL TYPES, VERY THIN STRINGS OR A SMALL FILLED PILLOW TYPES SUCH AS CAPPELLETTI, TORTELLINI OR RAVIOLINI.

WE TRIED THIS SAUCE . . . AND

LOVED IT ( )
HATED IT ( )
MAYBE WE'LL TRY IT AGAIN ( )
WE'LL USE IT FOR UNWELCOME GUESTS ( )

SAUTEED ONION SAUCE #2

SWEET ONIONS ARE THE ONION OF CHOICE FOR THIS SAUCE, BUT USE WHAT YOU HAVE.

INGREDIENTS:
4 TABLESPOONS BUTTER
4 ONIONS, CHOPPED OR SLICED
1/4 CUP FRESHLY GRATED PARMESAN CHEESE
1/2 TEASPOON SALT
1/4 TEASPOON FRESHLY GROUND BLACK PEPPER
2 TABLESPOONS LIQUID

METHOD: SAUTE THE ONIONS UNTIL TRANSPARENT. ADD SALT AND PEPPER, SPLASH IN A LITTLE LIQUID (SHERRY, MARSALA, BROTH OR WATER). COVER TIGHTLY AND STEAM THE ONIONS WHILE YOU COOK YOUR PASTA. POUR SAUCE OVER PASTA. ADD THE PARMESAN CHEESE. TOSS AND SERVE.

RECOMMENDED PASTA: RIBBON TYPES OR MEDIUM TUBE TYPES.

SALTALT

WE TRIED THIS SAUCE . . . AND

LOVED IT (   )
HATED IT (   )
MAYBE WE'LL TRY IT AGAIN (   )
WE'LL USE IT FOR UNWELCOME GUESTS (   )

SAUTEED ONION SAUCE #3

(ANOTHER QUICKIE)

HEY, AUTHOR, HOW MANY OF THESE ONION SAUCES DO YOU THINK I'M EVER GOING TO MAKE? WELL, CONSIDER THAT THE MORE WE LEARN ABOUT NUTRITION AND THE ONION'S ROLE IN OUR HEALTH, THE MORE YOU WOULD WANT TO INCLUDE ONION IN YOUR DIET, WE ALSO ARE KEENLY AWARE OF THE FACT THAT SAUCES LIKE THIS ARE LIGHT, VERY TASTY, HEALTHFUL AND BENEFICIAL. 'NUF SAID?

INGREDIENTS:
3	TABLESPOONS OLIVE OIL
3	ONIONS, SLICED TOP TO BOTTOM (SWEET VARIETY)
1	TEASPOON SALT, OR TO TASTE
3	TABLESPOONS BUTTER
1/3	CUP FRESHLY GRATED PARMESAN CHEESE
	FRESHLY GROUND BLACK PEPPER TO TASTE

METHOD: SAUTE THE ONIONS IN OLIVE OIL OVER LOW HEAT UNTIL ONIONS ARE TRANSPARENT, SALT WHILE COOKING. TOSS THE COOKED AND DRAINED PASTA WITH BUTTER. ADD CHEESE AND BLACK PEPPER, TOSS AGAIN. ADD ONIONS TOSS A THIRD TIME. SERVE.

RECOMMENDED PASTA: MEDIUM TUBE TYPES, STRINGS, SOLID OR HOLLOW.

SAUTEED ONION SAUCE #4

SAUTEED ONION SAUCE #4

THIS SAUCE IS REALLY A NEAR DRY ONION SOUP. IF YOU WERE TO REDUCE THE COOKING TIME TO 15 MINUTES AFTER SAUTEING THE ONIONS, ADD A SMALL AMOUNT OF GRAVY MASTER OR WORCHESTERSHIRE SAUCE TO GIVE IT A DARK COLORING, PLUS SEVERAL CUPS OF WATER YOU'D HAVE ONION SOUP. BUT HERE IT IS A PASTA SAUCE.

INGREDIENTS: 1/2 POUND SWEET BUTTER
6 MEDIUM ONIONS, SLICED
1 TABLESPOON SUGAR
1/4 CUP WINE (MARSALA, AMONTILLADO OR MADEIRA)
GRATED CHEESE

METHOD: SAUTE ONIONS IN THE BUTTER UNTIL TRANSPARENT, ADD SUGAR, REDUCE HEAT AND SIMMER FOR 1 HOUR. STIR IN THE WINE AND REMOVE SAUCE FROM HEAT. POUR SAUCE OVER PASTA. TOSS AND SERVE WITH GRATED CHEESE ON THE SIDE.

RECOMMENDED PASTA: RIBBON TYPES OR FANCY TYPES.

ONION AND ANCHOVY SAUCE

EXCEPT FOR THE TEARS YOU'LL SHED OVER THIS SAUCE, IT IS THE SIMPLEST OF THE ONION SAUCES.

INGREDIENTS:

1/4	POUND BUTTER
4 TO 6	SWEET ONIONS, CHOPPED OR VERY THINLY SLICED
6	ANCHOVY FILLETS, MASHED

METHOD: MELT THE BUTTER AND SAUTE THE ONIONS UNTIL THEY BEGIN TO DEVELOP A CARAMEL GLAZE (ABOUT 10 TO 15 MINUTES). STIR IN THE MASHED ANCHOVIES. REDUCE HEAT AND SIMMER FOR 5 MINUTES. POUR SAUCE OVER PASTA, TOSS AND SERVE.

RECOMMENDED PASTA: THIN STRINGS.

CREAMY ONION SAUCE

THIS SAUCE IS SO TASTY IN ITS OWN RIGHT, THAT ON OCCASION I HAVE EATEN THE SAUCE FOR A LIGHT SUPPER ACCOMPANIED BY SOME CRISP FRIED POTATOES AND A LOAF OF CRUSTY BREAD. IF YOU WISH TO TRY IT THAT WAY, USE THE OPTIONAL EGGS; ADD 2 EXTRA EGGS (FOR TOTAL OF 4 OR MORE) ALONG WITH AN EXTRA ONION, SWAP THE FRESH OREGANO LEAVES FOR A PINCH OF NUTMEG. YOU COULD ALSO SERVE IT OVER TOAST.

INGREDIENTS:	3	TABLESPOONS BUTTER, OR EXTRA LIGHT OLIVE OIL
	2	LARGE SWEET ONIONS, SLICE TO TOP BOTTOM IN 1/2" WEDGES.
	1/2	TEASPOON SALT
	1/4	SCANT TEASPOON WHITE PEPPER
	20+/-	FRESH OREGANO LEAVES, MINCED OR TORN (IF YOU HAVE 'EM, IF NOT, DON'T USE DRY LEAVES.)
	3	TABLESPOONS BUTTER OR LIGHT OLIVE OIL
	3	TABLESPOONS FLOUR
	1/2	TEASPOON SALT
	1 3/4	CUPS HALF AND HALF OR MILK

OPTION:	2	HARD BOILED EGGS (FOR THE PUREST; YOU MAY USE HARD COOKED EGGS)

METHOD: SAUTE ONIONS IN EXTRA LIGHT OLIVE OIL OR BUTTER, SEASON WITH SALT AND WHITE PEPPER, COOK UNTIL UNTIL TRANSPARENT AND QUITE SOFT. ADD OREGANO WHILE ONIONS ARE COOKING.

TO PREPARE YOUR WHITE SAUCE, REMOVE COOKED ONIONS FROM THE PAN. ADD BUTTER OR LIGHT OLIVE OIL TO THE PAN, NOW ADD THE FLOUR TO THE PAN, WHISK OVER MEDIUM HIGH HEAT FOR 2 TO 3 MINUTES, ADD HALF AND HALF AND SALT, CONTINUE TO WHISK UNTIL SAUCE BEGINS TO THICKEN, RETURN ONIONS TO THE PAN, BLEND WELL. POUR OVER PASTA. TOSS AND SERVE.

Continued on next page

EGG OPTION: SLICE THE EGGS INTO ROUNDS OR CHOP, SET ASIDE.   ADD EGGS WHEN THE ONIONS ARE BLENDED WITH THE WHITE SAUCE.

RECOMMENDED PASTA: RIBBON TYPES, SHORT MEDIUM TUBE TYPES.

SAUTEED ZUCCHINI SAUCE

(ANOTHER QUICKIE)

A VERY SIMPLE USE OF FRESH ZUCCHINI, YOU MIGHT EVEN LEAVE OUT THE BLACK PEPPER TO GET THAT FRESH MILD TASTE OF THE ZUCCHINI.

INGREDIENTS: 1   POUND ZUCCHINI, SLICED INTO ROUNDS
1/4   CUP OLIVE OIL
1/2   TEASPOON SALT
1/4   TEASPOON FRESHLY GRATED BLACK PEPPER

METHOD: SAUTE THE SLICED ZUCCHINI, SALT AND PEPPER IN THE OLIVE OIL UNTIL COOKED AND LIGHTLY GOLDEN. LAY OVER PASTA, TOSS AND SERVE.

AN ALTERNATE METHOD WILL ALLOW YOU TO LAY THE ZUCCHINI ON THE PASTA AFTER IT IS PLACED IN THE SERVING DISH. THIS VERSION MAY LOOK A LITTLE BETTER ON THE TABLE. TO DO IT, REMOVE THE COOKED ZUCCHINI FROM THE SKILLET WITH A SLOTTED SPATULA, PLACE ON PAPER TOWELS. ADD THE DRAINED PASTA TO THE OILED SKILLET AND TOSS TO COAT. PLACE PASTA IN SERVING DISH, LAY ZUCCHINI OVER THE PASTA AND SERVE WITH ADDITIONAL BLACK PEPPER.

RECOMMENDED PASTA: STRING TYPES.

FRESH BROCCOLI SAUCE #1

THIS SAUCE COULD BE EXPANDED UPON BY USING 1/2 HEAD CAULIFLOWER, (CUT INTO FLORETS) AND 1/2 BUNCH BROCCOLI, OR REPLACE THE BROCCOLI WITH CAULIFLOWER. THE METHOD IS THE SAME.

INGREDIENTS:

1	BUNCH BROCCOLI (FLORETS ONLY)
4	TABLESPOONS BUTTER
1/3	CUP OLIVE OIL
2	CLOVES GARLIC, MINCED
1/3	TEASPOON SALT
PINCH	FRESHLY GROUND BLACK PEPPER

METHOD: STEAM THE FLORETS UNTIL ALMOST DONE. NOW SAUTE THE FLORETS AND GARLIC IN THE OLIVE OIL/BUTTER UNTIL TENDER. REMOVE FROM HEAT. POUR OVER PASTA. ADD SEASONING TOSS AND SERVE.

RECOMMENDED PASTA: SMALL OR MEDIUM SHELLS OR HOLLOW STRINGS.

FRESH CAULIFLOWER SAUCE

IN MANY PASTA AND VEGETABLE DISHES IN ITALY, THE PASTA IS COOKED ALONG WITH THE VEGETABLE. TO ENCOURAGE YOU TO TRY THAT METHOD, I OFFER THE FOLLOWING RECIPE FROM SOUTH EASTERN ITALY, (PUGLIA) THAT'S THE HEEL REGION.

INGREDIENTS:

1	HEAD CAULIFLOWER, DIVIDED INTO FLORETS
1/2	OLIVE OIL
1/4	CUP COURSE BREAD CRUMBS
1/4	TEASPOON FRESHLY GROUND BLACK PEPPER

METHOD: BRING THE WATER FOR YOUR PASTA TO A BOIL, SALT IT TO YOUR PREFERENCE. ADD THE CAULIFLOWER, COOK FOR 3 MINUTES. ADD YOUR PASTA AND COOK IT UNTIL THE PASTA IS AL DENTE, ABOUT 8 MINUTES. MEANWHILE, SAUTE THE BREAD CRUMBS IN THE OLIVE OIL UNTIL THEY BROWN. DRAIN PASTA AND CAULIFLOWER. POUR OIL AND BREAD CRUMBS OVER PASTA, ADD PEPPER. TOSS AND SERVE.

IF YOU PREFER TO USE THIS AS A SAUCE, STEAM THE CAULIFLOWER UNTIL NEARLY DONE. SAUTE THE CAULIFLOWER, BLACK PEPPER AND BREAD CRUMBS TOGETHER UNTIL BREAD CRUMBS TURN BROWN AND CAULI-FLOWER BEGINS TO COLOR. POUR THIS OVER YOUR PASTA. TOSS AND SERVE.

RECOMMENDED PASTA: HOLLOW STRING TYPES.

Fresh Cauliflower Sauce II

YOU MAY, OR MAY NOT KNOW, OR POSSIBLY NOT EVEN CARE THAT THE ITALIANS DEVELOPED THE CAULIFLOWER. THAT HAS ABSOLUTELY NOTHING TO DO WITH THIS SAUCE, BUT, IT PROBABLY GOT YOUR ATTENTION. THERE IS NOT MUCH THAT IS DIFFERENT IN THIS SAUCE OVER THE PRECEDING. WELL . . . , THAT'S NOT ENTIRELY TRUE. THE ONLY SIMILARITY IS THE CAULIFLOWER AND BLACK PEPPER.

INGREDIENTS:

1	HEAD CAULIFLOWER
	OR, 1-10 OUNCE PACKAGE OF FROZEN FLORETS.
1	TEASPOON SALT
4	TABLESPOONS BUTTER
1/2	TEASPOON FRESHLY GROUND BLACK PEPPER
	FRESHLY GRATED PARMESAN CHEESE

METHOD: SEPARATE THE HEAD INTO FLORETS, STEAM THE CAULIFLOWER UNTIL COOKED. OR, IF FRESH AND TO BE SIMMERED IN SALTED WATER, COOK 15 TO 20 MINUTES. COMBINE COOKED CAULIFLOWER, COOKED PASTA, BUTTER AND BLACK PEPPER. TOSS WELL, SERVE WITH GRATED CHEESE ON THE SIDE.

RECOMMENDED PASTA: SHELL TYPES.

CAULIFLOWER SAUCE

THE FLAVOR OF CAULIFLOWER IS SO DELICATE, THAT JUST ABOUT ANYTHING YOU ADD TO IT WILL BECOME THE DOMINANT FLAVOR. AND THAT IS NO LESS TRUE IN THIS SAUCE WITH IT'S USE OF ANCHOVY.

INGREDIENTS:

1	SMALL HEAD CAULIFLOWER
	OR
	10 OUNCE PACKAGE FROZEN CAULIFLOWER
3	TABLESPOONS OLIVE OIL
2	FILLETS OF ANCHOVY
1/2	TEASPOON SALT
PINCH	WHITE PEPPER
1/2	CUP FRESHLY GRATED ROMANO CHEESE

METHOD: COOK CAULIFLOWER UNTIL SLIGHTLY FIRM, DRAIN AND ADD COOKING WATER TO YOUR PASTA WATER. CHOP CAULIFLOWER INTO SMALL PIECES, SALT AND SPRINKLE WITH WHITE PEPPER, SET ASIDE. SAUTE ANCHOVIES IN OLIVE OIL WHILE MASHING TO DISSOLVE. WHEN DISSOLVED, ADD CAULIFLOWER AND COOK FOR 3 TO 4 MINUTES. POUR SAUCE OVER PASTA, TOSS WITH CHEESE, SERVE.

RECOMMENDED PASTA: MEDIUM TUBE TYPES.

FRESH ASPARAGUS SAUCE

FRESH ASPARAGUS IN LIGHT CREAM MAKES THIS A DELIGHTFUL SPRING PASTA TREAT. MAY I SUGGEST THAT THIS SAUCE WOULD BEST BE PREPARED IN A PYREX OR CORNING WARE STOVE PROOF SERVING DISH.

INGREDIENTS:

2	CUPS CUT ASPARAGUS
1	CLOVE GARLIC, CRUSHED
1/2	CUP FRESH PARSLEY, CHOPPED
1/4	CUP FRESH BASIL, CHOPPED
2	TABLESPOONS OLIVE OIL
1	CUP HALF AND HALF
1	CUP FRESHLY GRATED PARMESAN CHEESE
	FRESHLY GROUND BLACK PEPPER

METHOD: BUY SLENDER ASPARAGUS SPEARS FOR THIS DISH; CUT ASPARAGUS INTO LENGTHS OF 1 TO 1 1/2 INCHES AND STEAM IT TO THE DEGREE OF DONENESS THAT YOU LIKE, SET ASIDE. SAUTE GARLIC, PARSLEY AND BASIL IN OLIVE OIL FOR 3 MINUTES, REMOVE GARLIC AND DISCARD. ADD HALF AND HALF, BRING SAUCE TO A NEAR BOIL, NOW, ADD THE COOKED AND DRAINED PASTA TO THE SAUCE, TOSS TO COAT. ADD CHEESE AND BLACK PEPPER, TOSS AGAIN. ADD ASPARAGUS AND TOSS A THIRD TIME. SERVE.

RECOMMENDED PASTA: RIBBON TYPES.

FRESH ASPARAGUS SAUCE II

THIS SAUCE IS THE CREAMLESS VERSION OF THE PRECEDING SAUCE, WELL, ALMOST, THERE ARE ALSO FEWER INGREDIENTS.

INGREDIENTS:
1	POUND ASPARAGUS SPEARS
1/2	TEASPOON SALT
1/4	POUND BUTTER
1/2	CUP FRESHLY GRATED PARMESAN CHEESE
	BLACK PEPPER TO TASTE

METHOD: REMOVE THE TIPS, SAVE REMAINDER OF SPEAR'S FOR ANOTHER USE.

STEAM THE TIPS UNTIL DONE TO YOUR SATISFACTION, OR SAUTE THE TIPS IN THE BUTTER FOR ABOUT FIVE MINUTES. REMOVE PAN FROM HEAT, ADD SALT AND BLACK PEPPER, TOSS TO BLEND. POUR SAUCE OVER PASTA, TOSS. ADD CHEESE, TOSS AGAIN, SERVE.

RECOMMENDED PASTA: OVAL STRING TYPES.

FENNEL SAUCE

ANOTHER VEGETABLE SAUCE FROM THE ITALIAN DEEP SOUTH, CALABRIA. FENNEL IS SO SIMILAR TO ANISE THAT I WOULD IMAGINE THEM TO BE INTERCHANGEABLE AS USED HERE.

INGREDIENTS: 1   POUND BULB FENNEL
                SALT TO TASTE
            3   TABLESPOONS OLIVE OIL
            2   TABLESPOONS GRATED PARMESAN CHEESE

METHOD: CUT THE BULBS IN HALF, STEAM OF COOK THEM IN SALTED WATER UNTIL DONE, ABOUT 15 MINUTES. IF COOKED IN WATER, SQUEEZE THEM UNTIL SOMEWHAT DRY. NOW THINLY SLICE OR MINCE THE BULBS, SAUTE FENNEL IN OLIVE OIL FOR ABOUT 3 MINUTES, DO NOT BROWN. POUR OVER PASTA. TOSS AND SERVE WITH PARMESAN CHEESE ON THE SIDE.

RECOMMENDED PASTA: STRING TYPES, SOLID OR HOLLOW.

WE TRIED THIS SAUCE . . . AND

LOVED IT ( )
HATED IT ( )
MAYBE WE'LL TRY IT AGAIN ( )
WE'LL USE IT FOR UNWELCOME GUESTS ( )

Sauteed Zucchini Sauce II

(Another Quickie)

ZUCCHINI HAS BECOME ONE OF AMERICA'S FAVORITE SQUASHES, THERE ARE WHOLE COOKBOOKS DEVOTED TO ZUCCHINI RECIPES. I'M SURE THAT MUCH OF THE ATTRACTION TO ZUCCHINI COMES FROM ITS PROLIFIC PRODUCTION RATE PLUS ITS MILD FLAVOR, A FLAVOR THAT LENDS ITSELF SO WELL TO SO MANY KINDS OF PREPARATIONS. HERE IT IS IN A SOUTHERN STYLE PASTA SAUCE.

INGREDIENTS:

1/4	CUP OLIVE OIL
2	CLOVES GARLIC, BRUISED
4	SMALL ZUCCHINI, JULIENNED
1/3	TEASPOON SALT
	FRESHLY GROUND BLACK PEPPER TO TASTE
1	CUP PECORINO CHEESE
2 OR 3	TABLESPOONS OF THE PASTA WATER

METHOD: SAUTE THE GARLIC UNTIL LIGHTLY GOLDEN, REMOVE AND DISCARD. ADD ZUCCHINI, SALT AND PEPPER, COOK FOR 3 TO 5 MINUTES OR UNTIL JUST TENDER. POUR SAUCE OVER PASTA, TOSS. ADD CHEESE, ADD PASTA WATER IF NEEDED. TOSS AGAIN AND SERVE. SERVE WITH ADDITIONAL FRESHLY GROUND BLACK PEPPER ON THE SIDE.

AS AN INTERESTING OPTION, YOU MIGHT REPLACE THE PECORINO CHEESE WITH AN EQUAL AMOUNT OF RICOTTA CHEESE.

RECOMMENDED PASTA: STRING TYPES.

379

SICILIAN STYLE BROCCOLI SAUCE

THIS SAUCE HAS SWEET/SOUR CHARACTER, IT'S A TASTE WELL LIKED IN SICILY AND SOUTHERN ITALY. AFTER ALL, AREN'T THESE THE SAME FOLKS WHO GAVE US "CAPONATA", THE DELIGHTFUL SWEET/SOUR EGGPLANT APPETIZER.

INGREDIENTS:
1	HEAD BROCCOLI (FLORETS ONLY)
	OR
1	10 OUNCE PACKAGE FROZEN CHOPPED BROCCOLI
1/4	CUP RAISINS, PLUMPED IN HOT WATER
PINCH	SAFFRON, DISSOLVED IN:
1/4	CUP WARM WATER
2	TEASPOONS TOMATO PASTE MIXED IN:
1/4	CUP WATER
3	ANCHOVY FILLETS, MASHED
1	TABLESPOON OLIVE OIL
1	CLOVE GARLIC, MINCED
4	TABLESPOONS PINE NUTS
1/4	TEASPOON SALT
	FRESHLY GROUND BLACK PEPPER TO TASTE

METHOD: STEAM THE BROCCOLI UNTIL TENDER BUT FIRM. IF USING FRESH, CHOP AND SET ASIDE. ADD SAFFRON TO 1/4 CUP WARM WATER, SET ASIDE. BLEND TOMATO PASTE IN WATER, SET ASIDE.

SAUTE GARLIC IN OLIVE OIL UNTIL LIGHTLY GOLDEN. ADD TOMATO PASTE AND ANCHOVIES, COOK OVER LOW HEAT FOR 10 MINUTES. ADD BROCCOLI, SALT AND PEPPER, COOK UNTIL BROCCOLI IS DONE TO YOUR PREFERENCE. ADD SAFFRON WATER, PINE NUTS DRAINED RAISINS. POUR SAUCE OVER PASTA. TOSS AND SERVE.

RECOMMENDED PASTA: HOLLOW STRING TYPES.

MUSTARD GREENS SAUCE

IN DEFERENCE TO Y'ALL OF ITALIAN HERITAGE LIVING IN THE SOUTH, I OFFER A SAUCE MADE WITH ONE OF THE SOUTH'S FAVORITE GREENS. THE PREPARATION OF THE GREENS IN THIS SAUCE IS A METHOD I OFTEN USE WITH OTHER GREENS (ENDIVE, ESCAROLE AND CABBAGE) OR EVEN VEGETABLES.

INGREDIENTS:

1	BUNCH MUSTARD GREENS, WASHED AND CHOPPED
1/3	CUP OLIVE OIL
1	CLOVE GARLIC, CRUSHED
1/2	TEASPOON SALT
1/2	CUP PINE NUTS

METHOD: SAUTE THE GARLIC IN THE OLIVE OIL UNTIL LIGHTLY GOLDEN, REMOVE AND DISCARD. ADD THE GREENS TO COAT AND COOK UNTIL WELL WILTED. ADD SALT AND PINE NUTS. REMOVE SAUCE FROM HEAT. POUR SAUCE OVER PASTA, TOSS AND SERVE.

RECOMMENDED PASTA: STRING TYPES.

FRESH ESCAROLE SAUCE

IF YOUR LIKE THE TARTNESS OF THE GREENS FROM THE CHICORY FAMILY, SEE CHAPTERS 2, 5, 14 AND 16 FOR OTHER RECIPES WITHIN THIS FAMILY. YOU MAY TAKE A FEW LIBERTIES WITH COOKING OF THIS RECIPE. I'LL FILL YOU IN AT METHOD.

INGREDIENTS:

1	HEAD ESCAROLE, CHOPPED, OR SLICED TO SHRED
1	TEASPOON SALT
2	TABLESPOONS OLIVE OIL
2	TABLESPOONS BUTTER
	FRESHLY GROUND BLACK PEPPER TO TASTE
	GRATED ASIAGO CHEESE

METHOD:

1. STEAM OR COOK THE ESCAROLE IN A SMALL AMOUNT OF SALTED WATER UNTIL TENDER. DRAIN AND SET ASIDE. HEAT OLIVE OIL AND MELT BUTTER TOGETHER. TOSS WITH THE ESCAROLE TO COAT

    OR,

2. SAUTE RAW OR PARTIALLY COOKED ESCAROLE IN THE OLIVE OIL AND BUTTER UNTIL TENDER.

    THEN,

    SEASON WITH SALT AND PEPPER TO TASTE. ADD HOT, DRAINED PASTA TO THE ESCAROLE SAUCE. TOSS AND SERVE WITH CHEESE ON THE SIDE.

RECOMMENDED PASTA: SHORT HOLLOW TUBES OR HOLLOW STRINGS, BROKEN INTO SHORT LENGTHS.

FRESH MUSHROOM SAUCE

ITALIANS SEEM TO HAVE A VARIETY OF MUSHROOMS TO CHOOSE FROM. WHILE HERE, THE FRESH MUSHROOMS APPEAR TO BE LIMITED TO A SINGLE VARIETY (ALTHOUGH CHANGES ARE COMING). THAT, SOMEWHAT LIMITS OUR TASTE EXPLORATION UNLESS YOU LIKE IMPORTED AND RECONSTITUTED MUSHROOMS. OF COURSE, AN ALTERNATIVE WOULD BE TO PICK YOUR OWN. I'D RATHER GO WITH STORE BOUGHT FRESH.

INGREDIENTS:

1	TABLESPOON OLIVE OIL
1/2	POUND MUSHROOMS, SLICED
1/2	TEASPOON SALT
1	TEASPOON LEMON JUICE
1	TABLESPOON PARSLEY, CHOPPED
1/2	CUP OLIVE OIL (EXTRA VIRGIN IF YOU HAVE IT)
1	TEASPOON FRESHLY GROUND BLACK PEPPER

METHOD: SAUTE MUSHROOMS, PARSLEY AND SALT IN THE OLIVE OIL FOR 5 MINUTES. REMOVE FROM HEAT. ADD LEMON JUICE, SET ASIDE. POUR 1/2 CUP OLIVE OIL AND THE BLACK PEPPER OVER DRAINED PASTA AND TOSS. ADD THE MUSHROOMS, TOSS AGAIN. SERVE.

RECOMMENDED PASTA: STRING TYPES.

FRESH MUSHROOM SAUCE TOO!

THIS SAUCE WILL COME OFF WITH A VERY LIGHT TOUCH OF SWEETNESS THAT WILL LEAVE YOUR DINERS GUESSING. IT APPEARS TO BE A SAUCE FROM CENTRAL ITALY AND ONE YOU'LL LIKE.

INGREDIENTS:

1	TABLESPOON AMARETTO
1	POUND MUSHROOMS, SLICED
1/4	CUP OLIVE OIL
1/2	CLOVE GARLIC
PINCH	CRUSHED RED PEPPER
1	TABLESPOON CHOPPED PARSLEY
	SALT TO TASTE

METHOD: SAUTE THE MUSHROOMS WITH THE AMARETTO OVER LOW HEAT FOR 10 MINUTES. DRAIN ANY REMAINING LIQUID FROM THE MUSHROOMS. ADD OIL, GARLIC AND RED PEPPER, SAUTE AN ADDITIONAL 5 MINUTES. COVER AND COOK AND ADDITIONAL 10 MINUTES. REMOVE FROM HEAT. ADD PARSLEY, ADJUST SEASONING, POUR SAUCE OVER PASTA. TOSS AND SERVE.

IF YOU'D PREFER NOT USING AMARETTO, USE NOTHING OR 1 TABLESPOON WATER, THEN ADD SOME FRESHLY GROUND BLACK PEPPER ALONG WITH THE SALT.

RECOMMENDED PASTA: OVAL STRINGS (8 OUNCES).

Fresh Button Mushroom Sauce

(Another Quickie)

OCCASIONALLY YOU'LL GET TO THE GROCERY STORE WHEN THEY JUST BROUGHT OUT THE LOOSE, FRESH MUSHROOMS. THIS IS THE TIME YOU MAY BE VERY SELECTIVE AND PICK JUST THE SMALLEST BUTTONS. IF YOU CANNOT GET BUTTON MUSHROOMS, BUY LARGE ONES AND QUARTER THEM. THIS IS A VERY SIMPLE SAUCE AND VERY TASTY.

A WONDERFUL ADDITION TO THIS SAUCE WOULD BE A SPLASH OF MARSALA OR A SHERRY. AS A POINT IN FACT, YOUR MAY USE 1/4 CUP OF THE ABOVE WINES TO SAUTE YOUR MUSHROOMS AND OMIT THE BUTTER. IT WORKS VERY WELL AND AT THE SAME TIME GIVES YOU A LOWER CALORIE SAUCE.

INGREDIENTS: 4 TO 6 OUNCES OF BUTTON MUSHROOMS (ABOUT 30)
1/4 POUND BUTTER
FRESHLY GROUND BLACK PEPPER TO TASTE
2 TABLESPOONS GRATED PARMESAN CHEESE

METHOD: WASH AND STEM THE MUSHROOMS. SAUTE MUSHROOMS IN THE BUTTER UNTIL COOKED, ABOUT 5 TO 6 MINUTES. ADD BLACK PEPPER TO TASTE. POUR THE SAUCE OVER YOUR PASTA, TOSS. ADD GRATED CHEESE, TOSS AGAIN AND SERVE.

RECOMMENDED PASTA: THIN STRINGS.

MUSHROOMS AND ANCHOVY SAUCE

THIS SAUCE IS INTERESTING IN THAT THE MUSHROOMS ARE TO BE FINELY CHOPPED IN A FOOD PROCESSOR, OR BY HAND, AFTER COOKING. YOU'RE NOT GOING TO MAKE A PASTE OF IT, BUT RATHER FINELY MINCED. THE ANCHOVIES WILL DISSOLVE AND BECOME ONLY A SEASONING.

INGREDIENTS:
6	OUNCES OF MUSHROOM, WASHED
6	ANCHOVY FILLETS
3	TABLESPOONS OLIVE OIL
1/4	CUP BREAD CRUMBS
2	TABLESPOONS WATER
1	CLOVE GARLIC
1	TABLESPOON CHOPPED PARSLEY

METHOD: MASH THE ANCHOVIES, SET ASIDE. PLACE THE MUSHROOMS, 1 TABLE-SPOON OLIVE OIL AND THE WATER INTO A SAUCE PAN. BRING TO A BOIL, COVER AND SIMMER FOR 10 MINUTES. REMOVE FROM HEAT. PLACE IN A FOOD PROCESSOR OR BLENDER AND USING THE PULSE BUTTON, PROCESS UNTIL THE MUSHROOMS ARE FINELY CHOPPED, SET ASIDE. SAUTE THE GARLIC IN THE OLIVE OIL UNTIL LIGHTLY GOLDEN. REMOVE AND DISCARD THE GARLIC. ADD THE BREAD CRUMBS SAUTE UNTIL BROWN, ADD THE ANCHOVIES, MUSHROOMS AND THEIR LIQUID, SIMMER FOR 5 MINUTES, POUR SAUCE OVER PASTA, TOSS. ADD PARSLEY, TOSS AGAIN AND SERVE.

RECOMMENDED PASTA: HOLLOW STRINGS, BROKEN IN TO 3" INCH LENGTHS.

CREAMY ZUCCHINI SAUCE

THIS SAUCE APPEARS TO BE NORTHERN BECAUSE OF ITS CREAMY FINISH. IT IS A GREAT VEGETABLE SAUCE, USING JULIENNED ZUCCHINI WITH THE ADDED BOUQUET OF BASIL.

IN THIS RECIPE YOU'RE GOING TO SAUTE THE ZUCCHINI IN BUTTER AND OLIVE OIL. AN ALTERNATE METHOD LETS YOU FRY THEM IN ABOUT 1/2" OF OIL. IF YOU WANT TO TRY IT, GO FOR IT! FRY THEM UNTIL LIGHTLY GOLDEN, DRAIN ON PAPER TOWELS, SET ASIDE.

INGREDIENTS:
1   POUND ZUCCHINI, JULIENNE IN 3" STICKS
3   TABLESPOONS BUTTER
3   TABLESPOONS OLIVE OIL
1/3   CUP MILK
1   TEASPOON FLOUR
1/4   TEASPOON SALT
1/2   CUP BASIL LEAVES, CHOPPED
1   EGG YOLK, BEATEN
1/2   CUP FRESHLY GRATED PARMESAN CHEESE

METHOD: DISSOLVE FLOUR AND SALT IN MILK, SET ASIDE. SAUTE THE ZUCCHINI IN THE BUTTER UNTIL DONE. REMOVE FROM PAN. ADD OIL TO ANY BUTTER REMAINING IN THE PAN, ALLOW OIL/BUTTER TO GET HOT. ADD MILK, FLOUR AND SALT. BRING SAUCE TO A BOIL, REDUCE HEAT. ADD ZUCCHINI STIR TO COAT, ADD EGG YOLK AND CHEESE, BLEND WELL. POUR SAUCE OVER PASTA, TOSS AND SERVE.

RECOMMENDED PASTA: CURLY TYPES.

CREAMY ZUCCHINI SAUCE TOO!

(ANOTHER QUICKIE)

THIS IS THE EASY VERSION OF A CREAMY ZUCCHINI SAUCE. MOST OF THE WORK WILL BE IN THE CUTTING OF THE ZUCCHINI. IF YOU DON'T MIND HAVING A CURVE IN YOUR JULIENNED ZUCCHINI, YOU CAN WHIP IT OUT IN A SECOND BY USING A FOOD PROCESSOR.

INGREDIENTS:

4	MEDIUM ZUCCHINI, JULIENNED
1	CLOVE GARLIC, MINCED
1/4	CUP FRESHLY GRATED PARMESAN CHEESE
1/4	CUP GRATED MOZZARELLA CHEESE
3/4	CUP HALF AND HALF
1	TABLESPOON CHOPPED FRESH BASIL
1	CUP CHICKEN BROTH/STOCK

OPTION: 1 CARROT, JULIENNED

METHOD: BRING STOCK TO A BOIL. ADD (CARROT IF USED, COOK FOR 3 MINUTES), ADD ZUCCHINI AND GARLIC, COOK FOR 2 ADDITIONAL MINUTES. DRAIN OFF AND DISCARD BROTH. TOSS VEGETABLES WITH REMAINING IN-GREDIENTS IN YOUR SERVING DISH. ADD HOT DRAINED PASTA TO THE SAUCE, TOSS EASILY, SERVE.

RECOMMENDED PASTA: STRINGS OR MEDIUM TUBE TYPES.

BELL PEPPER SAUCE

MORE OFTEN THAN NOT, FRIED OR ROASTED BELL PEPPERS ARE USED AS A SALAD, IN A SALAD, AS A VEGETABLE, AN ANTIPASTO OR SANDWICH FILLING. HERE THEY BEING OFFERED AS A PASTA SAUCE.

INGREDIENTS:

1	ONION, FINELY CHOPPED
1	CLOVE GARLIC, MINCED
2	TABLESPOONS OLIVE OIL
2	TABLESPOONS BUTTER
3	MEDIUM BELL PEPPERS, SEEDED AND DICED
3	TABLESPOONS WATER
1	TEASPOON SALT
PINCH	FRESHLY GROUND BLACK PEPPER

METHOD: SAUTE ONION AND GARLIC IN THE OLIVE OIL AND BUTTER UNTIL THE ONION IS TRANSPARENT. ADD BELL PEPPERS AND COOK FOR AN ADDITIONAL 10 MINUTES. ADD WATER, SALT AND PEPPER. COVER AND SIMMER FOR 15 ADDITIONAL MINUTES. POUR SAUCE OVER PASTA, TOSS AND SERVE.

RECOMMENDED PASTA: THIN STRINGS.

LOMBARD STYLE GARLIC AND POTATO SAUCE

(ANOTHER QUICKIE)

THIS IS A GREAT SAUCE THAT WILL ALLOW YOU TO USE LEFT OVER BAKED OR BOILED POTATOES. BOILED ARE BETTER, AND OVEN BAKED ARE BETTER THAN MICROWAVE BAKED. YOU COULD ALSO START WITH FRESH POTATOES, JUST BOIL OFF A FEW SMALL ONES. YOU'RE GOING TO FINISH THIS OFF IN "COUNTRY STYLE".

INGREDIENTS:
3	SMALL BOILED POTATOES (ENOUGH TO GIVE YOU 1 CUP OF COOKED AND DICED POTATO)
1/3	CUP BUTTER
1/3	CUP OLIVE OIL
2	CLOVES GARLIC, MINCED
1/4	TEASPOON CRUSHED RED PEPPER
1/2	TEASPOON SALT
1/4	CUP CHOPPED PARSLEY
	FRESHLY GROUND BLACK PEPPER TO TASTE

METHOD: SAUTE POTATO AND GARLIC IN THE BUTTER/OIL UNTIL THEY TURN LIGHTLY GOLDEN. ADD CRUSHED RED PEPPER AND SALT. NOW, ADD HOT DRAINED PASTA TO THE POTATO SAUCE, TOSS WHILE UNDER HEAT. REMOVE FROM HEAT. GARNISH WITH PARSLEY. SERVE WITH GROUND BLACK PEPPER ON THE SIDE.

RECOMMENDED PASTA: RIBBON OR STRING TYPES.

MOUNTAIN STYLE MUSHROOM SAUCE

I'M NOT SURE WHAT WE'VE GOT HERE. IT'S A NORTHERN ITALIAN SAUCE MADE WITH ITEMS THAT ARE GENERALLY AVAILABLE IN ANY KITCHEN. IT'S AN INTERESTING EXAMPLE OF "MAKE DO". HE PROBABLY PICKED HIS OWN MUSH-ROOMS TOO.

INGREDIENTS:

1/4	CUP BUTTER
1	CUP CHOPPED MUSHROOMS
1	TABLESPOON FLOUR (NORTHERNERS USE POTATO FLOUR)
1	CUP CHICKEN BROTH
PINCH	DRY SAGE
2	TABLESPOONS CHOPPED PARSLEY
	SALT AND PEPPER TO TASTE
1/2	CUP FRESHLY GRATED PARMESAN CHEESE

METHOD: SAUTE THE MUSHROOMS IN BUTTER FOR 3 TO 5 MINUTES. REMOVE MUSHROOMS FROM THE PAN, RESERVING THE BUTTER AND MUSHROOM JUICES. ADD THE FLOUR, STIRRING TO MAKE A ROUX. SLOWLY ADD AND WHIP IN THE CHICKEN BROTH. ADD SAGE AND PARSLEY, SEASON WITH SALT AND PEPPER. COVER AND SIMMER SAUCE FOR 20 MINUTES. TOSS HOT, DRAINED PASTA WITH THE GRATED CHEESE. POUR SAUCE OVER PASTA. TOSS AGAIN, SERVE.

RECOMMENDED PASTA: OVAL STRINGS.

SPINACH AND RICOTTA SAUCE

I SUPPOSE THIS COULD GET THE DESIGNATION "FLORENTINE", BUT IT'S NOT FROM THERE, WHEREVER ITS ORIGINS, IT'S A GOOD BLENDING OF CHEESE AND SPINACH. YOU COULD, IF NEEDED, SUBSTITUTE THE RICOTTA FOR A CREAMED COTTAGE CHEESE. START OUT WITH A GOOD SIZED SAUCE PAN, YOU'RE GOING TO FINISH THIS COUNTRY STYLE, I.E., YOUR DRAINED PASTA IS ADDED TO AND TOSSED IN THE SAUCE PAN.

INGREDIENTS:
1	10 OUNCE PACKAGE, FROZEN CHOPPED SPINACH
3	TABLESPOONS OLIVE OIL
1	CLOVE GARLIC, MINCED
1	CUP RICOTTA CHEESE
2	TABLESPOONS GRATED PARMESAN CHEESE
1/4	CUP CHOPPED PARSLEY
PINCH	FRESHLY GROUND BLACK PEPPER
1/2	CUP HALF AND HALF

METHOD: COOK SPINACH ACCORDING TO PACKAGE DIRECTIONS. PLACE IN A STRAINER, SET ASIDE TO DRAIN. MEANWHILE, BACK ON THE RANGE, SAUTE YOUR GARLIC IN THE OLIVE OIL UNTIL LIGHTLY GOLDEN. SQUEEZE SPINACH UNTIL QUITE DRY, THEN ADD IT TO THE GARLIC/OIL, STIR TO MIX. ADD RICOTTA, PARMESAN, PARSLEY, BLACK PEPPER AND HALF AND HALF. MIX WELL, ADD DRAINED PASTA TO THE SAUCE PAN. TOSS WELL, SERVE.

RECOMMENDED PASTA: 8 OUNCES OF ANY RIBBON TYPE.

ZUCCHINI AND FRESH HERBS SAUCE

THIS IS ALMOST AN UNCOOKED SAUCE, THE ONLY COOKING REQUIRED WILL BE FRYING THE ZUCCHINI. AND OF COURSE COOKING THE PASTA.

INGREDIENTS:

8	MEDIUM ZUCCHINI CUT INTO 1/4 INCH THICK WHEELS OR 1/4 X 2 INCH STRIPS
1/2	CUP OLIVE OIL
1/2	CUP VEGETABLE OIL
3	TABLESPOONS BUTTER MELTED
1/4	CUP CHOPPED PARSLEY
1/4	CUP CHOPPED FRESH BASIL LEAVES
1/2	CUP FRESHLY GRATED PARMESAN CHEESE

METHOD: FRY THE ZUCCHINI IN THE OILS UNTIL LIGHTLY GOLDEN, DRAIN ON PAPER TOWELS, SET ASIDE. MELT THE BUTTER (MICROWAVE IS OK), PLACE MELTED BUTTER IN THE SERVING BOWL, ADD PARSLEY AND BASIL, BLEND WITH MELTED BUTTER, (RESERVE 1/2 CUP PASTA WATER BEFORE DRAINING) ADD HOT, LIGHTLY DRAINED PASTA, TOSS. ADD THE GRATED CHEESE, TOSS AGAIN (IF THE PASTA SEEMS DRY ADD SOME OF THE RESERVED WATER). ADD MOST OF THE ZUCCHINI, TOSS A THIRD TIME. ADD REMAINING ZUCCHINI AS A GARNISH, SERVE.

RECOMMENDED PASTA: STRINGS.

Chapter 14

Sauces made from Vegetables and Meat

CABBAGE AND SAUSAGE SAUCE #1

YOU KNOW THIS MUST BE A FAR NORTHERN SAUCE, MOST LIKELY FROM ONE OF THE NORTHWESTERN REGIONS BORDERING THE AUSTRIAN ALPS OR YUGO-SLAVIA. THERE ARE SEVEN REGIONS OF ITALY THAT COMPRISE HER NORTHERN BORDER. SEVERAL OF THEM ARE CONTIGUOUS TO ITALIAN SPEAKING CANTONS OF SWITZERLAND, OR FRANCE, BOTH DOUBTFUL SOURCES FOR A CABBAGE SAUCE RECIPE.

INGREDIENTS:

1	POUND ITALIAN SAUSAGE (YOUR CHOICE, SWEET OR HOT)
1	HEAD SAVOY OR NAPA CABBAGE, CORED AND SHREDDED
1/2	TEASPOON SALT
PINCH	FRESHLY GROUND BLACK PEPPER
1/2	CUP WATER

METHOD: SKIN AND CRUMBLE THE SAUSAGE. SAUTE THE SAUSAGE IN ITS OWN FAT UNTIL WELL BROWNED. ADD THE CABBAGE AND SAUTE FOR SEVERAL MINUTES TO COAT. ADD SALT, PEPPER AND WATER. COVER, REDUCE HEAT TO SIMMER AND COOK FOR 20 MINUTES. POUR SAUCE OVER PASTA, TOSS AND SERVE.

RECOMMENDED PASTA: WIDE OR NARROW RIBBON TYPES.

CABBAGE AND SAUSAGE SAUCE #2

CLOSE, BUT DIFFERENT FROM THE PRECEDING SAUCE IN BOTH PREPARATION AND INGREDIENTS. A LITTLE HISTORY HERE WOULDN'T HURT. CABBAGE IS NOT A TRADITIONAL ITALIAN VEGETABLE AND SUBSEQUENTLY HAS FEW USES IN ITALIAN COOKERY. BUT, GERMANIC INFLUENCES COME ACROSS THE BORDER FROM AUSTRIA AND SWITZERLAND, PLUS THE FACT THAT LOMBARDY WAS NAMED FOR THE TEUTONIC TRIBE WHO NOT ONLY OCCUPIED THAT FAR NORTHERN PORTION OF ITALY, BUT STAYED. SO, WHILE CABBAGE MAY NOT BE A TRADITIONAL VEGETABLE, IT IS NOT OUT OF CHARACTER IN NORTH ITALIAN COOKERY.

INGREDIENTS:

2	LINKS ITALIAN SAUSAGE, SWEET (MILD) OR HOT OR, AN 8 INCH PIECE OF ROPE STYLE
1/2	CUP OLIVE OIL
1	SWEET ONION, SLICED TOP TO BOTTOM
1	CLOVE GARLIC, MINCED
1	HEAD SAVOY OR NAPA, CABBAGE, CORED AND SHREDDED
1/4	TEASPOON ROSEMARY, CRUSHED
1/2	TEASPOON SALT
1	CUP HOT WATER

METHOD: SKIN AND CRUMBLE THE SAUSAGES, SAUTE THEM IN THEIR OWN FAT UNTIL MEAT IS SOMEWHAT BROWNED. REMOVE SAUSAGE FROM THE PAN AND PLACE ON PAPER TOWELS. DRAIN THE SAUSAGE OIL AND DISCARD. ADD OLIVE OIL TO THE PAN, SAUTE THE ONION AND GARLIC UNTIL ONION IS TRANSPARENT, RETURN SAUSAGE TO THE PAN. ADD CABBAGE, ROSEMARY, SALT AND HOT WATER. MIX WELL, REDUCE HEAT, COVER AND SIMMER FOR 20 MINUTES. POUR SAUCE OVER YOUR PASTA, TOSS AND SERVE.

RECOMMENDED PASTA: THIN STRINGS OR RIBBON TYPES.

WE TRIED THIS SAUCE . . . AND

LOMBARD STYLE CABBAGE SAUCE

AGAIN FROM THE FAR NORTH WE GET A SAUCE EXHIBITING THE GERMANIC AND/OR SLAVIC INFLUENCES OF THE BORDER REGION. ACTUALLY THE ASSOCIATION IS STRONGER THAN THAT. THE LOMBARD'S WERE ONE OF THE TEUTONIC TRIBES THAT INVADED AND SETTLED IN CENTRAL EUROPE. IN THIS CASE, NORTHERN ITALY. HENCE, LOMBARDY.

INGREDIENTS:
4	TABLESPOONS BUTTER
4	SLICES BACON, MINCED
4	FRESH TOMATOES (B/P/C)
1	ONION, FINELY CHOPPED
1	CLOVE GARLIC, CRUSHED
1	TABLESPOON, CHOPPED PARSLEY
1 1/2	TEASPOONS SALT
1/2	TEASPOONS FRESHLY GROUND BLACK PEPPER
1/2	CUP BEEF BROTH OR WATER
1	HEAD SAVOY OR NAPA CABBAGE, SHREDDED OR DICED
1/4	CUP GRATED PARMESAN CHEESE

METHOD: SAUTE BACON IN BUTTER UNTIL IT BEGINS TO BROWN. ADD TOMATOES, ONION, GARLIC, SALT AND PEPPER, BRING SAUCE TO A BOIL, COVER AND REDUCE HEAT TO SIMMER FOR 15 MINUTES. REMOVE AND DISCARD GARLIC, ADD BROTH AND CABBAGE, COVER AND CONTINUE SIMMERING FOR 45 MINUTES. POUR SAUCE OVER PASTA, TOSS AND SERVE WITH GRATED CHEESE ON THE SIDE.

TO PREPARE THIS "COUNTRY STYLE", FOLLOWING THE 45 MINUTE COOKING PERIOD. ADD AN ADDITIONAL 3 1/2 CUPS OF BEEF BROTH, FOR A TOTAL OF 4 CUPS OF LIQUID. BRING SAUCE AND BROTH TO A BOIL. ADD 1/2 POUND OF PASTA AND COOK PASTA IN THE SAUCE FOR 15 MINUTES, SERVE.

RECOMMENDED PASTA: STRING TYPES.

Fresh Carrot Sauce

FRESH CARROTS ARE WONDERFUL ANYTIME, HAVING THEM WITH PASTA CREATES A VERY INTERESTING COMBINATION. CARROTS ARE GENERALLY USED IN TOMATO BASED PASTA SAUCES AS A SWEETENER, THEREFORE, THIS SAUCE WOULD BE ON THE SWEET SIDE IF THE SWEETNESS WERE NOT TEMPERED BY THE SALTINESS OF THE PROSCUITTO. I HAVE NO KNOWLEDGE OF THE ORIGIN OF THIS SAUCE, BUT I SUSPECT IT IS A NORTHERN PREPARATION, AND ONE OF THE ONLY RECIPES I'VE FOUND THAT USES CARROTS AS THE DOMINANT INGREDIENT.

INGREDIENTS:	5	CARROTS, PEELED AND DICED, SLICED OR JULIENNED
	3	TABLESPOONS OLIVE OIL
	3	TABLESPOONS BUTTER
	8	SMALL MUSHROOMS, SLICED
	3	OUNCES OF PROSCUITTO, JULIENNED
		GRATED ASIAGO CHEESE
	1/4	CUP RESERVED PASTA WATER

METHOD: STEAM THE CARROTS FOR 5 MINUTES, OR SAUTE THEM IN THE BUTTER UNTIL COOKED, BUT SLIGHTLY CRISP. ADD OLIVE OIL TO THE BUTTER. SAUTE THE CARROTS, MUSHROOMS AND PROSCUITTO FOR 5 MINUTES. RESERVE 1/4 CUP OF THE PASTA WATER, SET ASIDE. POUR SAUCE OVER PASTA. ADD RESERVED WATER. TOSS AND SERVE WITH CHEESE ON THE SIDE.

RECOMMENDED PASTA: A: NARROW RIBBON TYPES (PREFERABLY EGG VARIETIES).

BACON AND ONION SAUCE

THIS SAUCE APPEARS TO BE SOMEWHAT OF A FAVORITE QUICKIE IN AND AROUND ROME. WHILE THE SAUCE MAY NOT HAVE ORIGINATED THERE, THAT'S WHERE WE GET THE RECIPE. TRY TO USE SWEET ONIONS, IT WILL MAKE A SUBSTANTIAL DIFFERENCE TO THE END RESULT.

INGREDIENTS:

8	SLICES SUGAR CURED BACON, CUT INTO THIN PIECES
2	ONIONS, CHOPPED
1	CLOVE GARLIC, CRUSHED
	FRESHLY GRATED ASIAGO CHEESE

METHOD: COOK BACON PIECES UNTIL CRISP, ADD GARLIC AND ONION, SAUTE UNTIL ONIONS ARE TRANSPARENT. REMOVE AND DISCARD GARLIC. POUR SAUCE OVER PASTA. TOSS AND SERVE WITH GRATED CHEESE ON THE SIDE.

RECOMMENDED PASTA: THIN STRINGS.

SPINACH SAUCE

HERE IS A SAUCE WITH COLOR AND ZIP. IT IS ALSO A SAUCE THAT COULD ALLOW YOU TO SERVE THIS DISH AS A SALAD. IF YOU CHOOSE TO DO SO, MAKE IT EARLY AND LET IT COOL DOWN TO ROOM TEMPERATURE.

INGREDIENTS:

1/2	POUND FRESH SPINACH (CHOPPED OR SHREDDED)
1/4	POUND OF COPPA (MINCED)
1	SMALL RED OR GREEN CHILI PEPPER (MINCED)
1	SMALL BELL PEPPER (ANY COLOR) (DICED)
1	SMALL ONION (SWEET, IF POSSIBLE) FINELY CHOPPED
1	CLOVE GARLIC (MINCED)
6	TABLESPOONS OLIVE OIL
1/2	TEASPOON SALT
PINCH	BLACK PEPPER
1	TABLESPOON GRATED PARMESAN CHEESE

METHOD: PREPARE YOUR INGREDIENTS AND SET ASIDE. GET YOUR PASTA OFF TO A ROLLING BOIL. THEN START YOUR SAUCE.

SAUTE THE COPPA, BELL PEPPER, ONION, GARLIC AND CHILI PEPPER IN THE OLIVE OIL FOR ABOUT 3 MINUTES. ADD SPINACH AND COOK FOR AN ADDITIONAL 2 MINUTES. REMOVE FROM HEAT. BLEND IN CHEESE, SALT AND PEPPER.

POUR SAUCE OVER PASTA, TOSS AND SERVE, OR LET COOL AND USE AS A PASTA SALAD.

RECOMMENDED PASTA: ROTELLE, ROTINI OR OTHER CURLY TYPES.

FRESH ENDIVE SAUCE

ENDIVE IS A SLIGHTLY TART TASTING GREEN, NOT QUITE AS TART AS THE DANDELION PLANT, BUT NONE THE LESS TART. IT TOO IS A MEMBER OF THE CHICORY FAMILY, AND, IT HAS A TASTE YOU'LL EITHER LOVE OR NOT. IF IT IS ONE THAT YOU DO ENJOY, SEE CHAPTERS 2 AND 5 FOR OTHER SAUCES OF ENDIVE. IF YOU DON'T LIKE ENDIVE, BUT WANT A GREENS SAUCE, YOU MAY CHOOSE FROM THE SAME FAMILY, THE MILDER ESCAROLE OR CHICORY.

INGREDIENTS:
1	HEAD ENDIVE, WASHED AND CHOPPED
1/2	POUND SUGAR CURED BACON, CUT INTO 1/2" STRIPS
1/2	TEASPOON SALT
	FRESHLY GROUND BLACK PEPPER TO TASTE
1/2	CUP WHIPPING CREAM
1/3	CUP GRATED PARMESAN CHEESE

METHOD: COOK BACON UNTIL MOST OF IT IS CRISP. ADD THE ENDIVE, SAUTE WITH THE BACON UNTIL THE ENDIVE IS WELL COATED WITH BACON OIL. COVER AND SIMMER FOR ABOUT 15 MINUTES. ADD CREAM, COOK UNCOVERED AN ADDITIONAL 5 MINUTES. POUR SAUCE OVER PASTA, TOSS, ADD CHEESE, TOSS AGAIN, SERVE.

RECOMMENDED PASTA: STRINGS, STRAIGHT OR CURLY, MEDIUM TUBES, OR NARROW RIBBON TYPES.

ESCAROLE AND SAUSAGE

(CAN BE MEATLESS)

I LOVE THESE GREENS AND PASTA SAUCES AND I BELIEVE YOU WILL TOO. IN THIS ONE, ESCAROLE, ENDIVE, CHICORY, DANDELION, NAPA CABBAGE AND SAVOY CABBAGE ARE INTERCHANGEABLE. THE SINGLE FACTOR THAT SETS THIS SAUCE APART FROM OTHERS IN THIS CHAPTER, IS THAT THE SELECTED GREEN IS PAR BOILED IN SALTED WATER BEFORE IT IS SAUTEED IN THE GARLIC, OIL AND SAUSAGE. TO MAKE THIS A MEATLESS OFFERING, SIMPLY OMIT THE SAUSAGE.

INGREDIENTS:

1	POUND ITALIAN SAUSAGE (SWEET/MILD OR HOT)
1	HEAD ESCAROLE, WASHED, LEAVES CUT INTO 1 INCH LENGTHS.
1/2	CUP OLIVE OIL
2	CLOVES GARLIC (YOUR CHOICE)
1	TEASPOON SALT (FOR THE GREENS WATER)
	FRESHLY GRATED PARMESAN CHEESE, OR
1/2	CUP TOASTED BREAD CRUMBS (TO TOAST BREAD CRUMBS, COOK IN A DRY SKILLET OVER MEDIUM UNTIL BROWNED.)

METHOD: FRY SAUSAGE OVER MEDIUM HEAT UNTIL WELL BROWNED, (ABOUT 15 MINUTES) PUNCTURE SKINS WHILE COOKING. REMOVE SAUSAGES FROM HEAT, SLICE INTO 1/4 INCH ROUNDS. SET ASIDE.

COOK ESCAROLE IN 1 OR 2 QUARTS OF BOILING SALTED WATER UNTIL JUST TENDER, (1 TO 3 MINUTES). DRAIN AND SET ASIDE.

DRAIN AND DISCARD SAUSAGE OIL, SAUTE THE GARLIC IN OLIVE OIL UNTIL LIGHTLY GOLDEN. ADD SAUSAGE AND ESCAROLE, COOK SEVERAL MINUTES TOGETHER (IF SAUCE IS TOO DRY FOR YOUR TASTE, ADD UP TO 1/2 CUP PASTA WATER) WHEN ALL INGREDIENTS ARE HOT, POUR OVER DRAINED PASTA. TOSS AND SERVE WITH CHEESE OR BREAD CRUMBS ON THE SIDE.

RECOMMENDED PASTA: MEDIUM TUBE OR SHELL TYPES.

CHAPTER 15

SAUCES MADE FROM SEAFOOD

PROBABLY A DOZEN ADDITIONAL AND UNCOUNTED RECIPES
OR
PERSONAL OBSERVATIONS ON AN OYSTER

OF THE EXTENSIVE LIST OF SEAFOOD ITEMS USED IN PASTA SAUCES, OYSTERS SEEM TO HAVE BEEN NEGLECTED OR ARE PREFERRED IN OTHER PREPARATIONS. YOU CAN USE OYSTERS INTERCHANGEABLY WITH CLAMS. SO, IF YOU LOVE OYSTERS, FRESH OR BOTTLE PACKED, SUBSTITUTE THEM FOR CLAMS IN ANY RECIPE. A PERSONAL CHOICE IS THAT THE WHITE CLAM SAUCES OFFER YOU THE BEST VEHICLE FOR THAT USE. IF YOU CHOOSE TO USE OYSTERS, BOTH THE FRESH OR BOTTLED WILL REQUIRE STEAMING TO PRECOOK THEM. OYSTERS MAY BE STEAMED IN A LITTLE WHITE WINE AND THEIR OWN JUICES. IF YOU'RE USING FRESH OYSTERS, WASH 'EM, STEAM 'EM, SHUCK 'EM, CHOP OR MINCE 'EM. THEN ADD AS DIRECTED BY THE RECIPE. IF YOU ARE USING BOTTLED OYSTERS, JUST STEAM THEM IN THEIR OWN JUICES PLUS A LITTLE WINE. IN EITHER CASE, RESERVE AND USE THE POT LIQUOR AS DIRECTED BY THE RECIPE.

RED CLAM SAUCE #1

OF THE MANY SEAFOOD SAUCES, WHITE AND RED CLAM SAUCES SEEM TO BE AMERICAN FAVORITES, WHILE THAT MAY BE TRUE, I BELIEVE WE WOULD PREFER TO BYPASS THE PREPARATION OF FRESH CLAMS AND OPT OUT FOR CANNED MINCED OR CHOPPED CLAMS. IF YOU WANT FRESH CLAMS, BUY ABOUT 4 POUNDS OF STEAMERS, WASH 'EM, STEAM 'EM, STRAIN 'EM, SAVE THE CLAMS AND JUICES, ADD WHEN CALLED FOR.

THIS IS THE FIRST OF SIX CLAM SAUCES OFFERED IN THIS CHAPTER OF THE RED OR WHITE VARIETY. MOST OF THE RECIPES CALL FOR ONE 6 1/2 OUNCE CAN OF CLAMS. YOU WOULD NOT NEED TO CHANGE ANYTHING IF YOU CHOSE TO USE 2 CANS OF CLAMS. I WOULD ONLY DRAIN THE SECOND CAN, AND RESERVE THE JUICE JUST IN CASE. YOU MAY WISH TO USE IT IF YOUR PASTA ABSORBS SAUCE LIQUID TOO QUICKLY.

INGREDIENTS: 1   6 1/2 OUNCE CAN CHOPPED OR MINCED CLAMS
1/3   CUP OLIVE OIL
3   TABLESPOONS FRESH PARSLEY, CHOPPED
3   TABLESPOONS FRESH BASIL, CHOPPED
1   CLOVE GARLIC, MINCED
2   TABLESPOONS TOMATO PASTE
SALT AND FRESHLY GROUND BLACK PEPPER

METHOD: SAUTE GARLIC IN OLIVE OIL UNTIL LIGHTLY GOLDEN, ADD PARSLEY AND BASIL JUST A FEW SECONDS BEFORE ADDING CLAM JUICE AND TOMATO PASTE, STIR TO BLEND, SEASON WITH SALT AND PEPPER. SIMMER FOR ABOUT TEN MINUTES. ADD CLAMS AND JUST HEAT THROUGH. POUR OVER PASTA, TOSS AND SERVE.

RECOMMENDED PASTA: STRING TYPES OR RIBBON TYPES.

RED CLAM SAUCE #2

WITH THIS SAUCE YOU'LL USE FRESH TOMATOES AND A LITTLE ADDED PEPPER ZIP.

INGREDIENTS:
- 1/4 CUP OLIVE OIL
- 4 TABLESPOONS BUTTER
- 1 CLOVE GARLIC, MINCED
- 3 MEDIUM TOMATOES OR 6 PEAR TOMATOES (B/P/C)
- 1/2 TEASPOON SALT
- PINCH FRESHLY GROUND BLACK PEPPER
- PINCH DRIED OREGANO
- 2 OR 3 DROPS OF A LIQUID PEPPER SAUCE
- 1 6 1/2 CAN CLAMS, CHOPPED OR MINCED

METHOD: BRIEFLY SAUTE THE GARLIC AND PARSLEY IN THE BUTTER AND OIL. ADD TOMATOES, SALT, PEPPER, OREGANO, PEPPER SAUCE. SIMMER FOR ABOUT TEN MINUTES. ADD CLAMS TO HEAT THROUGH. POUR SAUCE OVER PASTA, TOSS AND SERVE.

RECOMMENDED PASTA: STRING TYPES.

RED CLAM SAUCE #3

THIS SAUCE IS CLOSE TO THE #1 SAUCE, IT OMITS THE BASIL, AND CHUCKS OUT THE GARLIC, WHILE KEEPING THE GARLIC FLAVORING.

INGREDIENTS:

1	6 1/2 OUNCE CAN CHOPPED OR MINCED CLAMS
1/2	CUP OLIVE OIL
1	CLOVE GARLIC, BRUISED OR HALVED
4	TABLESPOONS TOMATO PASTE
1/2	CUP WATER
1	TEASPOON SALT
1/2	TEASPOON FRESHLY GROUND BLACK PEPPER
2	TABLESPOONS PARSLEY, CHOPPED

METHOD: SAUTE GARLIC IN OLIVE OIL UNTIL LIGHTLY GOLDEN, DISCARD GARLIC. ADD TOMATO PASTE, WATER, SALT AND PEPPER, WHISK TILL SMOOTH. COVER AND SIMMER FOR ABOUT 15 MINUTES. ADD UNDRAINED CLAMS TO HEAT THROUGH, ADD PARSLEY, REMOVE FROM HEAT. POUR OVER PASTA. TOSS AND SERVE.

RECOMMENDED PASTA: THIN STRING TYPES.

WHITE CLAM SAUCE #1

(ANOTHER QUICKIE)

SIMPLE, FAST AND UNCOMPLICATED, THAT'S PROBABLY WHAT MAKES WHITE CLAM SAUCES SO POPULAR.

INGREDIENTS:

1/4	CUP OLIVE OIL
1 OR 2	CLOVES GARLIC, MINCED
1/4	CUP WATER OR BOTTLED CLAM JUICE
1	TABLESPOON FRESH PARSLEY, CHOPPED
1/2	TEASPOON SALT
1/4	TEASPOON WHITE PEPPER
1/4	TEASPOON OREGANO, DRIED
1	6 1/2 OUNCE CAN CLAMS, MINCED OR CHOPPED

METHOD: SAUTE GARLIC IN OIL UNTIL LIGHTLY GOLDEN, ADD ALL OTHER IN-GREDIENTS, HEAT CLAMS THROUGH. POUR OVER PASTA. TOSS AND SERVE.

RECOMMENDED PASTA: STRING TYPES, OVAL OR ROUND.

WHITE CLAM SAUCE #2

(ANOTHER QUICKIE)

WITH THIS SAUCE YOU GET A VARIATION OF THE HERBS AND SOME ADDED ZIP COMES ALONG WITH THE RED PEPPER.

INGREDIENTS:

1/4	CUP OLIVE OIL
4	TABLESPOONS BUTTER
3	CLOVES GARLIC, MINCED
2	6 1/2 OUNCE CLAMS CLAMS, CHOPPED OR MINCED
1	PACKED CUP FRESH PARSLEY, CHOPPED
1/2	TEASPOON DRIED OREGANO
1	TEASPOON DRIED BASIL OR 1 TABLESPOON FRESH
1/4	TEASPOON CRUSHED RED PEPPER

METHOD: BRIEFLY SAUTE GARLIC IN THE BUTTER AND OIL, DON'T COLOR IT, DRAIN AND ADD THE CLAM JUICE, PARSLEY, OREGANO, BASIL AND RED PEPPER, SIMMER FOR 5 MINUTES. ADD CLAMS TO HEAT THROUGH, POUR OVER PASTA. TOSS AND SERVE.

RECOMMENDED PASTA: STRING TYPES, ROUND AND OVAL.

WE TRIED THIS SAUCE . . . AND

WHITE CLAM SAUCE #3

(ANOTHER QUICKIE)

FEWER INGREDIENTS THAN EITHER OF THE PRECEDING WHITE CLAM SAUCES, GIVES YOU THE OPPORTUNITY TO GO INTO A NEARLY BARE CUPBOARD AND CREATE AN EXCELLENT PASTA SAUCE.

INGREDIENTS:
1	6 1/2 OUNCE CAN MINCED CLAMS
1/2	CUP OLIVE OIL
2	CLOVES GARLIC, SLICED
1/2	TEASPOON SALT
1	TEASPOON FRESHLY GROUND BLACK PEPPER
1	TABLESPOON PARSLEY, CHOPPED

METHOD: SAUTE THE GARLIC IN OLIVE OIL UNTIL JUST GOLDEN IN COLOR, ADD CLAMS AND THEIR JUICE, SALT, PEPPER. COOK UNTIL CLAMS ARE HEATED THROUGH; ABOUT 2 MINUTES, ADD PARSLEY. POUR SAUCE OVER PASTA. TOSS AND SERVE.

RECOMMENDED PASTA: THIN STRING TYPES.

WE TRIED THIS SAUCE . . . AND

LOVED IT ( )
HATED IT ( )
MAYBE WE'LL TRY IT AGAIN ( )
WE'LL USE IT FOR UNWELCOME GUESTS ( )

TUSCAN STYLE CLAM SAUCE

THIS IS REFERRED TO IN ITALY AS "ALLA VIAREGGINA", MEANING IN THE STYLE OF VIAREGGINA, A COASTAL FISHING VILLAGE. QUITE SIMILAR TO THE RED CLAMS SAUCES, BUT A LITTLE SWEETER, THE ONION DOES IT.

INGREDIENTS:
1 CUP OLIVE OIL
1 SMALL ONION, THINLY SLICED
1/2 CUP DRY WHITE WINE
2 CLOVES GARLIC
10 PEAR TOMATOES (B/P/C)
1/2 TEASPOON SALT
1/4 TEASPOON FRESHLY GROUND BLACK PEPPER
1/4 MILDLY HOT PEPPER, MINCED
1/4 CUP PARSLEY, CHOPPED
1 6 1/2 OUNCE CAN CHOPPED CLAMS

METHOD: SAUTE ONIONS IN THE OLIVE OIL UNTIL TRANSPARENT. ADD WINE, GARLIC, TOMATOES, HOT PEPPER, DRAINED CLAM JUICE, SALT AND PEPPER. BRING SAUCE TO A BOIL, REDUCE HEAT TO MEDIUM LOW, LOOSELY COVER AND COOK FOR 20 MINUTES. ADD CLAMS AND PARSLEY TO HEAT THROUGH. POUR SAUCE OVER PASTA. TOSS AND SERVE.

RECOMMENDED PASTA: STRING TYPES.

DOWN EAST CLAM SAUCE

(ANOTHER QUICKIE)

THERE IS SOMETHING ABOUT DILL THAT MAKES ME TREAT THIS DISH AS A SUMMER REFRESHER, ANYTHING WITH FRESH DILL WEED JUST SEEMS TO BE A COOL AND LIGHT SUMMER PLATE. TRY IT SERVED AT ROOM TEMPERATURE, YOU MAY LIKE IT.

INGREDIENTS:
2	TABLESPOONS OLIVE OIL
1	CLOVE GARLIC, MINCED
1	6 1/2 OUNCE CAN CLAMS, MINCED OR CHOPPED
1	8 OUNCE BOTTLE CLAM JUICE
2	TABLESPOONS FRESH DILL WEED, MINCED
	OR
	(1 SCANT TEASPOON DRIED DILL WEED)
2	TEASPOONS LEMON JUICE
	LEMON AND PARSLEY FOR GARNISH

METHOD: SAUTE THE GARLIC UNTIL LIGHTLY GOLDEN. STRAIN THE CLAMS AND SET ASIDE. ADD LEMON JUICE, STRAINED CLAM JUICE AND BOTTLE JUICE TO GARLIC ALONG WITH FRESH DILL. COVER AND SIMMER FOR ABOUT 5 MINUTES.

IF YOU'RE USING DRIED DILL, OMIT THE FIVE MINUTE COOKING TIME. ADD LEMON JUICE, CLAMS AND CLAM JUICE ALONG WITH THE DRIED DILL. HEAT CLAMS THROUGH. POUR OVER PASTA. TOSS AND SERVE.

RECOMMENDED PASTA: STRING TYPES.

WE TRIED THIS SAUCE . . . AND

LOVED IT ( )
HATED IT ( )
MAYBE WE'LL TRY IT AGAIN ( )
WE'LL USE IT FOR UNWELCOME GUESTS ( )

CREAMY CLAM SAUCE

THIS IS ONE OF THOSE SAUCES THAT REQUIRE A LITTLE FANCY FOOTWORK, IT PROBABLY IS NOT A SAUCE FOR A BEGINNING COOK TO TRY. BUT DON'T LET THAT STOP YOU, IF THE INGREDIENT LIST READS LIKE SOMETHING YOU'D ENJOY, GO FOR IT!

INGREDIENTS:

6	TABLESPOONS BUTTER
1/2	POUND MUSHROOMS, SLICED
3	WHOLE CHIVES, THINLY CHOPPED
1	TABLESPOON FLOUR
2	6 1/2 OUNCE CANS CLAMS, CHOPPED OR MINCED
1/2	CUP WHIPPING CREAM
3	EGG YOLKS, BEATEN
3	TABLESPOONS FRESHLY GRATED PARMESAN
1	TEASPOON LEMON JUICE

METHOD: IN THE BUTTER, SAUTE MUSHROOMS AND ONIONS. WHEN MUSHROOMS ARE NICELY COLORED, EITHER REMOVE MUSHROOM/ONION MIX FROM THE PAN, OR DRAIN THE JUICES FROM YOUR COOKING PAN INTO ANOTHER PREHEATED PAN. NOW ADD FLOUR AND WHISK TO MAKE A SMOOTH ROUX. ADD WHIPPING CREAM AND STRAINED CLAM JUICE, WHISK IN. ADD PARMESAN CHEESE AND WHISK IN, VERY SLOWLY ADD THE BEATEN EGG YOLKS WHILE WHISKING. CONTINUE COOKING WHILE STIRRING CONSTANTLY UNTIL SAUCE THICKENS, DO NOT ALLOW SAUCE TO BOIL. RETURN THE MUSHROOM AND ONIONS TO THE SAUCE. ADD THE CLAMS TO HEAT THROUGH. REMOVE SAUCE FROM HEAT, ADD THE LEMON JUICE, BLEND IN WELL. POUR SAUCE OVER PASTA. TOSS AND SERVE.

AFTER THE EGG YOLKS ARE ADDED, IF THE SAUCE IS TO THICK, ADD SOME CREAM OR MILK TO THIN.

RECOMMENDED PASTA: MEDIUM TUBE TYPES OR STRING TYPES.

CLAMS AND ZUCCHINI SAUCE

THIS CLAM AND VEGETABLE SAUCE IS APPARENTLY OF NORTHERN ORIGIN. YOU MAY USE FRESH CLAMS IF YOU WISH, CANNED CLAMS ARE QUICKER AND CERTAINLY EASIER TO COME BY IF YOU DON'T HAPPEN TO LIVE IN A COASTAL AREA. ON THE ASSUMPTION THAT YOU MAY OPT OUT FOR FRESH CLAMS, AND YOU LIVE INLAND. YOUR SOURCE OF CLAMS IS LIKELY TO BE A SUPERMARKET WHERE CLAMS MAY BE SOLD PREPACKAGED. REMOVE AND DISCARD ANY OPEN CLAMS BEFORE COOKING. IF CLAMS ARE OFFERED TO YOU FROM A LOOSE SELECTION IN THE REFRIGERATED CASE, DON'T ACCEPT OPEN CLAMS. THEY'RE DEAD. (YOU MOST LIKELY WON'T HAVE A PROBLEM IF YOU'RE BEING HELPED BY A BUTCHER. BUT IF A YOUNG CLERK IS ASSISTING, SHE/HE MAY NOT BE AWARE OF THE CONDITION OF OPEN CLAMS).

INGREDIENTS:

1/2	CUP OLIVE OIL
1	1 MEDIUM ONION, CHOPPED
2	CLOVES GARLIC, CRUSHED OR MINCED
1	POUND ZUCCHINI, DICED
1/2	TEASPOON SALT
1/4	TEASPOON FRESHLY GROUND BLACK PEPPER
1/2	CUP WHITE WINE
1	6 1/2 OUNCE CAN CHOPPED CLAMS
2	TABLESPOONS CHOPPED BASIL OR ITALIAN PARSLEY

METHOD: SAUTE ONION AND GARLIC IN OLIVE OIL UNTIL ONION IS TRANSPARENT. ADD ZUCCHINI, SALT, PEPPER AND WINE, BRING SAUCE TO A BOIL, COOK FOR 5 MINUTES OR UNTIL ZUCCHINI IS JUST FORK TENDER. ADD CLAMS, JUICE AND BASIL. CONTINUE COOKING UNTIL ZUCCHINI IS DONE TO YOUR SATISFACTION. POUR SAUCE OVER PASTA. TOSS AND SERVE.

IF GARLIC WAS ONLY CRUSHED, REMOVE BEFORE ADDING ZUCCHINI.

RECOMMENDED PASTA: NARROW RIBBON TYPES OR OVAL STRINGS.

WE TRIED THIS SAUCE . . . AND

LOVED IT ( )
HATED IT ( )
MAYBE WE'LL TRY IT AGAIN ( )
WE'LL USE IT FOR UNWELCOME GUESTS ( )

TYRRHENIAN FISHERMAN'S SAUCE

THIS SAUCE IS A FAIRLY EXPENSIVE ONE TO PREPARE, UNLESS YOU HAPPEN TO LIVE IN A COASTAL AREA WHERE OYSTERS, SCALLOPS AND SHRIMP ARE THE LEADING CATCH.

INGREDIENTS:

8	OYSTERS (CANNED OR FRESH), RESERVE LIQUOR
1/2	POUND SCALLOPS, FRESH
6	ANCHOVY FILLETS
1/3	CUP ONION, CHOPPED
2	TABLESPOONS OLIVE OIL
1	CLOVE GARLIC, SLICED
1/2	CUP WHITE WINE
6	LARGE RIPE TOMATOES (B/P/S)
1	TABLESPOON TOMATO PASTE
1/2	TEASPOON DRIED BASIL
1/2	TEASPOON DRIED OREGANO
1	TEASPOON SALT
PINCH	WHITE PEPPER
1	POUND SHRIMP (ANY SIZE)
1/4	CUP PARSLEY, CHOPPED

METHOD: SAUTE ONIONS AND GARLIC IN OLIVE OIL UNTIL ONION IS SOFT. ADD WINE, TOMATOES, OYSTER LIQUOR, ANCHOVIES, TOMATO PASTE, BASIL, OREGANO, SALT AND PEPPER. BRING INGREDIENTS TO A BOIL, REDUCE HEAT TO LOW, COOK SAUCE FOR 30 MINUTES. ADD SEAFOOD, COOK 2 TO 3 ADDITIONAL MINUTES. POUR OVER COOKED PASTA, ADD PARSLEY, TOSS AND SERVE.

RECOMMENDED PASTA: STRING TYPES.

CAPRI STYLE SAUCE

FROM THE ISLE OF CAPRI WE GET THIS TUNA/ANCHOVY PASTA SAUCE, IT IS SOMEWHAT DIFFERENT FROM THE FOLLOWING SAUCES IN THAT A PASTE IS MADE FROM THE FISH, AND THE INGREDIENTS ARE NOT COOKED TOGETHER, BUT BLENDED WITH THE PASTA IN THE SERVING DISH.

INGREDIENTS:

1	POUND PEAR TOMATOES (B/P/C)
1/2	TEASPOON SALT
1/2	CUP OLIVE OIL
1	OUNCE OF ANCHOVY
1/2	CAN OF TUNA (3 TO 4 OUNCES)
8	RIPE PITTED OLIVES
3/4	CUP DICED OR SHREDDED MOZZARELLA CHEESE
	FRESHLY GROUND BLACK PEPPER TO TASTE

METHOD:

1. PLACE THE TOMATOES, SALT AND 1/4 CUP OLIVE OIL INTO A SAUCE PAN. BRING TOMATOES TO A BOIL, AND COOK BRISKLY FOR ABOUT 15 MINUTES.

2. PLACE ANCHOVY, TUNA AND OLIVES WITH 1/4 CUP OLIVE OIL INTO A BLENDER AND PROCESS UNTIL SMOOTH.

3. POUR TOMATO SAUCE OVER HOT PASTA AND TOSS. ADD THE FISH PASTE AND TOSS. ADD MOZZARELLA AND BLACK PEPPER, TOSS AND SERVE.

RECOMMENDED PASTA: STRING TYPES.

TUNA AND TOMATO SAUCE

IF YOU LIKE TUNA CASSEROLES, THEN YOU'RE SURE TO LIKE THIS SAUCE OF TUNA, KISSED WITH ANCHOVY.

INGREDIENTS:

1/4	CUP OLIVE OIL
2	CLOVES GARLIC, MINCED
4	ANCHOVY FILLETS, MINCED
1	28 OUNCE CAN ITALIAN STYLE TOMATOES (BLENDERIZED)
1	6 1/2 OUNCE CAN OF TUNA (PREFERABLY IN OIL)
4	TABLESPOONS FRESH PARSLEY, CHOPPED
1	TEASPOON FRESHLY GROUND BLACK PEPPER

METHOD: SAUTE GARLIC AND ANCHOVIES UNTIL GARLIC TURNS LIGHTLY GOLDEN AND ANCHOVIES FALL APART. ADD TOMATOES. BRING TO A BOIL, REDUCE HEAT, PARTIALLY COVER AND SIMMER FOR 30 MINUTES. STIR IN TUNA, PARSLEY AND BLACK PEPPER. REMOVE FROM HEAT. POUR OVER HOT PASTA. TOSS AND SERVE.

RECOMMENDED PASTA: STRING TYPES.

TUNA SAUCE

(ANOTHER QUICKIE)

IN THIS SAUCE YOU'LL USE NO OIL BUT YOU WILL SIMMER THE TOMATOES AND TUNA TOGETHER, AS OPPOSED TO THE PRECEDING RECIPE IN WHICH THE TUNA WAS ADDED AT THE LAST MOMENT AND MERELY WARMED.

INGREDIENTS:
1	16 OUNCE CAN PEAR TOMATOES, DRAINED AND BLENDERIZED
1	6 1/2 OUNCE CAN TUNA (DRAINED)
1/4	MILDLY HOT GREEN PEPPER, MINCED OR DASH OF TABASCO
1/2	CUP PARSLEY, CHOPPED

METHOD: START THIS SAUCE AFTER YOU'VE PLACED YOUR PASTA INTO THE COOKING WATER. BRING TOMATOES TO A BOIL. ADD PARSLEY PEPPER AND TUNA. COOK OVER MEDIUM HEAT UNTIL PASTA IS COOKED. POUR SAUCE OVER PASTA. TOSS AND SERVE.

RECOMMENDED PASTA: STRING TYPES.

Tuna Sauce II

(Another Quickie)

THIS IS A TOMATOLESS SAUCE WITH A GREAT DEAL OF FLAVOR. TUNA PACKED IN OIL WILL ADD SUBSTANTIALLY MORE TO THIS RECIPE THAN WATER PACKED. THIS SAUCE ALSO HAS THE ABILITY TO BE SERVED AS A PASTA/TUNA SALAD. IF YOU DON'T LIKE YOUR TUNA HOT, TOSS THE PASTA WITH A LITTLE OIL TO PREVENT STICKING, LET THE PASTA COOL, THEN MIX AND SERVE AT ROOM TEMPERATURE, OR CHILLED.

INGREDIENTS:

1/4	CUP OLIVE OIL
1	ONION, CHOPPED
1	6 1/2 OUNCE CAN TUNA FISH, DRAINED.
2	TABLESPOONS FRESH BASIL, CHOPPED
1/2	TEASPOON FRESHLY GROUND BLACK PEPPER

METHOD: SAUTE THE ONION IN THE OLIVE OIL UNTIL TRANSPARENT. ADD TUNA AND HEAT THROUGH, ABOUT 2 OR 3 MINUTES, REMOVE FROM HEAT. ADD BASIL AND BLACK PEPPER, POUR SAUCE OVER PASTA, MIX WELL AND SERVE.

RECOMMENDED PASTA: CURLY TYPES.

420

CREAMED TUNA SAUCE

(ANOTHER QUICKIE)

NICE TOUCH HERE, THE CANNED TUNA AND ITS INGREDIENTS ARE BLENDED INTO A PASTE, BY HAND OR PROCESSOR. THE FIRST WILL HAVE A MORE INTERESTING TEXTURE, THE SECOND, VERY SMOOTH. YOUR CHOICE.

INGREDIENTS:

1	6 1/2 OUNCE CAN TUNA, DRAINED (OIL PACK IS PREFERRED)
1/4	POUND BUTTER
1	TABLESPOON CAPERS (MINCED, IF YOU HAND BLEND)
1	CLOVE GARLIC, MINCED
1	EGG
1	CUP WHIPPING CREAM
1	TABLESPOON CHOPPED PARSLEY

METHOD:

1. PLACE ALL INGREDIENTS INTO A PROCESSOR AND PROCESS UNTIL SMOOTH, OR,

2. ADD TUNA, AND BLEND BY HAND AFTER PROCESSING ALL OTHER INGREDIENTS, OR,

3. MINCE GARLIC, CAPERS AND PARSLEY, ADD ALL REMAINING INGREDIENTS AND BLEND UNTIL TEXTURE IS PLEASING TO YOU.

RECOMMENDED PASTA: RIBBON TYPES.

TUNA AND ROASTED PEPPERS SAUCE

(ALSO INCLUDES THE RECIPE FOR ROASTING PEPPERS)

SEVERAL RECIPES IN THIS BOOK CALL FOR ROASTED PEPPERS, SO IF YOU LIKE ROASTED PEPPERS WITH YOUR PASTA, YOU MAY MAKE YOUR OWN. I'LL TELL YOU HOW, OR YOU MAY BUY THEM. HOMEMADE IS BETTER.

INGREDIENTS:

2	BELL PEPPERS, USE DIFFERENT COLORS IF YOU CAN
2	TABLESPOONS BREAD CRUMBS, DRY TOASTED IN A SKILLET
1/3	CUP OLIVE OIL
2	CLOVES GARLIC, MINCED
1/4	CUP CHOPPED PARSLEY
2	TABLESPOONS CAPERS
1/2	TEASPOON SALT
1/4	TEASPOON FRESHLY GROUND BLACK PEPPER
1	6 1/2 OUNCE CAN OIL PACK TUNA, DRAINED AND CRUMBLED

METHOD:

1. ROAST THE PEPPERS IN A 500 DEGREE OVEN, OR ON YOUR STOVE TOP BURNER, GAS OR ELECTRIC, UNTIL THE OUTER SKIN IS THOROUGHLY CHARRED. PLACE PEPPERS IN A PLASTIC BAG, SEAL AND SET ASIDE FOR 15 TO 20 MINUTES. PEEL, CORE AND SEED THE PEPPERS. CUT THE FLESH INTO NARROW STRIPS. SET ASIDE.

2. SAUTE THE GARLIC IN OLIVE OIL UNTIL LIGHTLY GOLDEN. ADD THE PEPPERS, SAUTE FOR ABOUT 3 MINUTES. ADD PARSLEY, CAPERS, SALT AND PEPPER, COOK 1 ADDITIONAL MINUTE. REMOVE FROM HEAT. ADD THE TUNA, MIX THOROUGHLY. POUR SAUCE OVER PASTA. ADD TOASTED BREAD CRUMBS. TOSS AND SERVE.

RECOMMENDED PASTA: MEDIUM TUBE TYPES.

FEAST OF THE ASSUMPTION SAUCE

(LONG AND LOW)

THE FEAST OF THE ASSUMPTION IS ONE OF THE TRULY LARGE FEAST DAYS IN ITALIAN CATHOLICISM. SINCE THIS EVENT OCCURS ON AUGUST 15TH, THIS SAUCE IS ALSO REFERRED TO AS "15TH OF AUGUST" PASTA. ALL COUNTRIES HAVE SPECIAL DISHES THEY PREPARE FOR THEIR VARIOUS HOLIDAYS. SO DO WE. OUR THANKSGIVING DAY DISHES ARE SUBSTANTIALLY DIFFERENT FROM THE FOODS WE'LL PREPARE ON THE 4TH OF JULY. SO, IF THE LADY OF THE HOUSE WANTS TO SPEND THE DAY IN THE KITCHEN FOLLOWING HER ATTENDANCE AT MASS, SHE PICKED THE RIGHT SAUCE. NO QUICKIE HERE, THIS IS PROBABLY A COUPLE OF HOURS IN THE MAKING.

INGREDIENTS:

6	TABLESPOON OLIVE OIL
1	16 OUNCE CAN PEAR TOMATOES, BLENDERIZED
1	TABLESPOON CHOPPED FRESH BASIL
1	CLOVE GARLIC, MINCED
2	SHALLOTS, MINCED
1	CARROT, SHREDDED
1	STALK CELERY, CHOPPED
1/2	TEASPOON SALT
1	SMALL EGGPLANT, PARED AND DICED INTO 1/2" CUBES
12	GREEN OLIVES, SLICED OR HALVED (RIPE VARIETY)
1	TEASPOON MINCED CAPERS
1/2	CAN TUNA FISH, (GRATED) WELL DRAINED

METHOD: PLACE 3 TABLESPOONS OLIVE OIL IN A SAUCE PAN ALONG WITH THE TOMATOES, BASIL, GARLIC, SHALLOTS, CARROT, CELERY AND SALT. BRING TO A BOIL, REDUCE HEAT TO SIMMER, COVER AND COOK FOR 1 HOUR. MEANWHILE, FRY EGGPLANT IN REMAINING OIL FOR 8 TO 10 MINUTES. REMOVE FROM HEAT AND DRAIN ON PAPER TOWELS. WHEN TOMATOES AND VEGETABLES ARE COOKED, PUREE. OVER LOW HEAT, BLEND PUREED VEGETABLES, EGGPLANT, OLIVES, CAPERS AND TUNA, ADJUST SEASONING. POUR SAUCE OVER PASTA. TOSS AND SERVE.

RECOMMENDED PASTA: STRING TYPES.

CRAB MEAT SAUCE #1

THE DUNGENESS CRAB OF THE WEST COAST AND THE GIANT KING CRAB LEGS FROM ALASKA ARE PROBABLY THE MEAT FOR THIS PASTA SAUCE. SINCE THE CRABMEAT IS PRE-COOKED, AND THEN ONLY HEATED THROUGH, THE TASTY, SIMULATED CRAB MEAT MADE FROM VARIOUS FISH WILL WORK ALMOST AS WELL.

INGREDIENTS:

3	TABLESPOONS OLIVE OIL
1	CLOVE GARLIC (YOUR CHOICE)
1	28 OUNCE CAN ITALIAN STYLE TOMATOES
1/2	BELL PEPPER, MINCED
PINCH	FRESHLY GROUND BLACK PEPPER
1	POUND CRABMEAT
1	EGG, WELL BEATEN

METHOD: SAUTE THE GARLIC UNTIL LIGHTLY GOLDEN. ADD THE BLENDERIZED TOMATOES, BELL PEPPER AND BLACK PEPPER. BRING SAUCE TO A BOIL, REDUCE HEAT TO SIMMER FOR ABOUT 30 MINUTES. ADD THE CRAB MEAT TO HEAT THROUGH. FINALLY, DRIZZLE IN THE BEATEN EGG, COOK 1 ADDITIONAL MINUTE. POUR SAUCE OVER PASTA. TOSS AND SERVE.

RECOMMENDED PASTA: STRING TYPES.

CRAB MEAT SAUCE #2

(ANOTHER QUICKIE)

IF REAL CRAB IS NOT IN SEASON WHEN THIS SAUCE WHETS YOUR APPETITE, USE IMITATION CRAB MEAT. IT REALLY IS QUITE ACCEPTABLE FOR OCCASIONAL USE.

INGREDIENTS:

2	TABLESPOONS BUTTER
2	TABLESPOONS OLIVE OIL
1	SMALL ONION, SLICED
1	CLOVE GARLIC, MINCED
2	TOMATOES, OR 4 PEAR TOMATOES, (B/P/C)
1	TABLESPOON LEMON JUICE
8	OUNCES FLAKED CRAB MEAT
1/4	CUP FRESH PARSLEY, CHOPPED
1/2	TEASPOON SALT
PINCH	WHITE PEPPER

METHOD: MELT BUTTER IN OLIVE OIL, ADD ONION AND GARLIC. SAUTE UNTIL ONION IS TRANSPARENT. ADD TOMATOES, SALT AND PEPPER, BRING TO A BOIL, COOK FOR 2 MINUTES. ADD LEMON JUICE, CRABMEAT AND PARSLEY, COOK 1 ADDITIONAL MINUTE. POUR SAUCE OVER PASTA. TOSS AND SERVE.

RECOMMENDED PASTA: VERY THIN STRINGS (USE NO MORE THAN 4 TO 6 OUNCES). IF ANGEL HAIR IS CHOSEN, USE NO MORE THAN 2 TO 3 OUNCES.

ANCHOVY SAUCE

(ANOTHER QUICKIE)

IF YOU'RE NOT AN AVOWED ANCHOVY FAN, KEEP ON GOING, THIS ONE IS NOT FOR YOU.

INGREDIENTS:
4	TABLESPOONS OLIVE OIL
20	FILLETS OF ANCHOVY
2	TABLESPOONS PARSLEY (ITALIAN)
1/4	CUP RESERVED PASTA WATER
	FRESHLY GROUND BLACK PEPPER

METHOD: JUST BEFORE YOUR PASTA IS DONE, HEAT THE OLIVE OIL IN A WIDE SKILLET. REMOVE SKILLET FROM HEAT. ADD ANCHOVIES TO WARMED OIL, WHISK AND CRUSH TO DISSOLVE. ADD HOT DRAINED PASTA TO SKILLET. ADD RESERVED LIQUID. TOSS WHILE ON HEAT TO COAT. REMOVE FROM HEAT. ADD PARSLEY AND BLACK PEPPER TO TASTE, TOSS AGAIN. SERVE.

RECOMMENDED PASTA: HOLLOW STRINGS OR LONG TUBE TYPES.

WE TRIED THIS SAUCE . . . AND

Sicilian Anchovy Sauce

(Another Quickie)

SIMPLE YET WITH STYLE, THE VEGETABLES WILL BE SAUTEED IN THE ANCHOVY OIL.

Ingredients:
1	4 OUNCE CAN ANCHOVIES IN OIL
1	TABLESPOON ONION, MINCED
1	TABLESPOON BELL PEPPER, MINCED OR, LONG GREEN AND MILDLY HOT
2 OR 3	FRESH BASIL LEAVES, MINCED
PINCH	FRESHLY GROUND BLACK PEPPER
1/4	CUP PARSLEY, CHOPPED

Method: MASH WHILE HEATING THE ANCHOVIES IN THEIR OIL. ADD ONION AND GREEN PEPPER. SAUTE UNTIL ONION BEGINS TO COLOR. REMOVE FROM HEAT. ADD PARSLEY, POUR OVER PASTA. ADD GRATED CHEESE, TOSS AND SERVE.

Recommended Pasta: THIN STRING TYPES.

SEAFOOD MEDLEY SAUCE

THIS IS ONE OF SEVERAL SAUCES WITH AN APPLIED NAME OF "TUTTO MARE", AND MEANING "ALL SEA", I REALLY DON'T UNDERSTAND THE TERM. WHILE THE SAUCE HAS SEVERAL SEAFOOD ITEMS, IT'S A LONG WAY FROM INCORPORATING ALL THE EDIBLE ITEMS AVAILABLE FROM THE SEA. ALTHOUGH, IF THE SAUCE CONTAINED AT LEAST A DOZEN TYPES OF SEAFOOD, GIVE OR TAKE A COUPLE, I COULD LIVE MORE EASILY WITH THE TERM. AN ADDED POINT IS THE SERVING TOUCH USED WITH THIS SAUCE. YOU'LL SAUCE THE PASTA AFTER IT IS ON AN INDIVIDUAL PLATE. RESTAURANTS GENERALLY SERVE PASTA THAT WAY.

A SIMILAR SAUCE MAY BE FOUND IN CHAPTER 4, THAT ONE WILL BE IN A CREAM BASE.

INGREDIENTS:
- 1/4 CUP OLIVE OIL
- 2 POUNDS FRESH TOMATOES (B/P/C)
- 1 TEASPOON SALT
- 2 CLOVES GARLIC, CRUSHED OR BRUISED
- 1 MILDLY HOT GREEN PEPPER
- 1 SMALL OCTOPUS, CUT INTO THIN STRIPS
- 1/4 POUND SHRIMP, SMALL OR MEDIUM SHELLED
- 2 POUNDS MUSSELS, WASHED, STEAMED AND SHUCKED
- 2 POUNDS FRESH TOMATOES
- CHOPPED FRESH PARSLEY

METHOD: PREPARE THE TOMATOES AND MUSSELS, SET ASIDE. SAUTE THE GARLIC, GREEN PEPPER AND OCTOPUS IN THE OIL UNTIL GARLIC IS GOLDEN, REMOVE GARLIC. ADD TOMATOES AND SALT. COOK PARTIALLY COVERED AT MEDIUM FOR 40 MINUTES. ADD SHRIMP AND MUSSELS TO HEAT THROUGH. SET A PORTION OF PASTA ON INDIVIDUAL PLATES, SPOON SAUCE OVER PASTA. GARNISH WITH CHOPPED PARSLEY. ENJOY.

RECOMMENDED PASTA: STRING TYPES.

TINY SHRIMP SAUCE

FROM THE EAST COAST OF ITALY, ALONG THE ADRIATIC SEA COMES THIS SHRIMPLY GOOD SAUCE. THESE TINY SHRIMP ARE AVAILABLE FRESH OR FROZEN ALL YEAR FROM YOUR LOCAL GROCER OR FISH MARKET. THEY ARE ALSO AVAILABLE IN 4 1/4 OUNCE CANS. YOU'LL NEED TWO CANS FOR THIS SAUCE.

INGREDIENTS:
1/3	CUP OLIVE OIL
1	ONION , CHOPPED
1	CLOVE GARLIC, MINCED
1	16 OUNCE CAN ITALIAN STYLE TOMATOES, BLENDERIZED
PINCH	CRUSHED RED PEPPER
1/4	CUP FRESH PARSLEY, CHOPPED
8	OUNCES COOKED SMALL SHRIMP

METHOD: SAUTE ONIONS IN OLIVE OIL UNTIL TRANSPARENT. ADD GARLIC, TOMATOES AND RED PEPPER. BRING TO A BOIL, PARTIALLY COVER AND COOK AT LOW HEAT FOR 15 MINUTES. ADD PARSLEY AND SHRIMP, TO HEAT THROUGH. REMOVE FROM HEAT. POUR SAUCE OVER PASTA. TOSS AND SERVE.

IF YOU CHOOSE TO, YOU MAY REPLACE THE CRUSHED RED PEPPER WITH A PINCH OF GINGER. SHOULD YOU ELECT TO DO SO, THE SAUCE WOULD THEN BE KNOWN AS "TORCELLO STYLE", AND I HAVE NO IDEA WHAT IT MEANS.

RECOMMENDED PASTA: NARROW RIBBON TYPES OR HOLLOW STRINGS.

SEAFOOD MARINARA SAUCE

THERE ARE OTHER MARINARA RECIPES IN THIS BOOK; WITHOUT SEAFOOD, AND SINCE MARINARA MEANS "SAILOR", "SAILOR STYLE" OR "SEAMAN" OR ONE OF THE MANY NAUTICAL TERMS USED TO DESCRIBE MEN WHO SAIL THE SEAS, WE SHOULD CERTAINLY OFFER A "MARINARA" WITH SOME SEAFOOD IN IT, AND HERE IT IS.

INGREDIENTS:

1/2	POUND SHRIMP, FRESH OR FROZEN, CLEANED AND PEELED
1	6 1/2 OUNCE CAN CHOPPED CLAMS, DRAINED.
1	TABLESPOONS OLIVE OIL
1/2	ONION, CHOPPED
1	CLOVE GARLIC, MINCED
1	SMALL GREEN PEPPER, SWEET OR MILDLY HOT, CHOPPED
1	8 OUNCE CAN TOMATO SAUCE
1	6 1/2 OUNCE CAN TOMATO PASTE
1 1/2	CUPS WATER
1/2	TEASPOON DRY BASIL
1/2	TEASPOON OREGANO

METHOD: SAUTE ONION, GARLIC AND GREEN PEPPER IN THE OLIVE OIL FOR 3 MINUTES. ADD TOMATO SAUCE, TOMATO PASTE, WATER, BASIL AND OREGANO. BRING TO A BOIL, REDUCE HEAT TO SIMMER, COVER AND COOK FOR 15 MINUTES. ADD CLAMS AND SHRIMP TO HEAT THROUGH. REMOVE FROM HEAT. POUR SAUCE OVER PASTA, TOSS AND SERVE.

IF YOU FIND THAT YOU HAVE EXTRA FISH OR OTHER SEAFOOD ITEMS IN THE REFRIGERATOR, ADD THEM WITH THE SHRIMP AND CLAMS. IT WON'T HURT ANYTHING TO HAVE EXTRA SEAFOOD IN THIS SAUCE. IN FACT THERE IS AN OUTSTANDING SEAFOOD DISH ON THE WEST COAST CALLED "CIOPPINO", IT IS AN ASSORTMENT OF CRAB, SHRIMP, CLAMS AND FISH. LOBSTER TOO, IF YOU HAVE ONE. IT'S SERVED UP IN A TOMATO SAUCE NEARLY IDENTICAL TO THIS ONE. CIOPPINO IS EATEN AS A STEW AND SERVED WITH CRUSTY BREAD. SAN FRANCISCO AND SEATTLE BOTH LAY CLAIM TO THIS DISH. IT IS AMERICA'S EQUIVALENT OF A LIGURIAN FISHERMEN'S SEAFOOD STEW, OR A MARSEILLAIS BOUILLABAISSE (MARSEILLE HAS A HUGE ITALIAN POPULATION).

RECOMMENDED PASTA: STRINGS, OVAL TYPES.

SALMON AND CREAM SAUCE

(ANOTHER QUICKIE)

I SUPPOSE THIS COULD HAVE BEEN CLASSIFIED UNDER CREAM SAUCES, BUT SINCE YOU'LL BE USING MORE SALMON THAN CREAM, SEAFOOD WINS THE TOSS.

INGREDIENTS:
1	10 OUNCE PACKAGE FROZEN, CHOPPED SPINACH
1	16+/- OUNCE CAN SALMON
2	TABLESPOONS OLIVE OIL
2	TABLESPOONS SHALLOTS, MINCED
1	CUP WHIPPING CREAM
1	TEASPOON DIJON MUSTARD
	SALT AND PEPPER TO TASTE
	GRATED PARMESAN CHEESE

METHOD: COMPLETELY THAW AND SQUEEZE DRY THE SPINACH, SET ASIDE. DRAIN SALMON AND RESERVE THE LIQUID. FLAKE OR CRUMBLE THE SALMON, SET ASIDE. SAUTE THE SHALLOTS IN OLIVE OIL FOR ABOUT 3 MINUTES. ADD CREAM, RESERVED SALMON LIQUID AND MUSTARD, COOK AN ADDITIONAL 2 MINUTES. ADD SPINACH, SALT AND PEPPER, COOK AN ADDITIONAL 2 MINUTES. REMOVE FROM HEAT. POUR SAUCE OVER PASTA. ADD CRUMBLED SALMON. TOSS AND SERVE WITH GRATED CHEESE ON THE SIDE.

RECOMMENDED PASTA: CURLY TYPES.

FRESH SMELT SAUCE

IN AND AROUND NAPLES WHERE THIS SAUCE APPEARS TO BE FROM, THEY MAKE MANY SAUCES INCORPORATING SEAFOOD. THIS SAUCE CALLS FOR FRESH ANCHOVIES, BUT THAT IS A DIFFICULT ITEM TO FIND IN THE U.S., SMELT IS AN ACCEPTABLE ALTERNATE AND A WHOLE LOT EASIER TO FIND IN AMERICAN MARKETS.

INGREDIENTS:

1	POUND FRESH SMELTS
1/2	TEASPOON SALT
6	PEAR TOMATOES (B/P/C)
1/2	CUP OLIVE OIL
2	CLOVES GARLIC, CRUSHED
PINCH	FRESHLY GROUND BLACK PEPPER
3	TABLESPOONS PARSLEY, CHOPPED

METHOD: REMOVE HEADS AND TAILS, CUT SMELT LENGTHWISE IN HALF, REMOVE BACKBONE, SALT AND SET ASIDE. SAUTE GARLIC IN OLIVE OIL UNTIL IT TURNS GOLDEN. REMOVE AND DISCARD GARLIC. ADD TOMATOES, SMELTS AND BLACK PEPPER. RAISE HEAT AND COOK FOR 5 MINUTES. ADD PARSLEY AND CONTINUE COOKING FOR 5 ADDITIONAL MINUTES. POUR SAUCE OVER PASTA. MIX WELL AND SERVE.

RECOMMENDED PASTA: MEDIUM TUBE TYPES OR HOLLOW STRINGS BROKEN INTO 3" LENGTHS.

RUSTIC STYLE SAUCE

(ISN'T THAT ANOTHER WORD FOR COUNTRY?)

(ANOTHER QUICKIE)

THIS SAUCE COMES FROM SARDINIA AND USES FRESH OREGANO. IF YOU DON'T HAVE FRESH, I'M SURE DRY WILL DO, ESPECIALLY SINCE THE QUANTITY IS SO SMALL.

INGREDIENTS:

1/2	CUP OLIVE OIL
2	CLOVES GARLIC, MINCED OR CRUSHED
5	FILLETS OF ANCHOVY
1	TEASPOON FRESH OREGANO
	OR
1/3	TEASPOON DRY OREGANO
2	TABLESPOON PARSLEY, CHOPPED
	GRATED PARMESAN CHEESE TO TASTE

METHOD: SAUTE GARLIC IN OLIVE OIL UNTIL LIGHTLY GOLDEN (REMOVE AND DISCARD IF CRUSHED). ADD ANCHOVIES AND COOK TO DISSOLVE. ADD OREGANO. COOK ONE ADDITIONAL MINUTE. POUR SAUCE OVER PASTA. ADD PARSLEY. TOSS AND SERVE WITH CHEESE ON THE SIDE.

RECOMMENDED PASTA: STRING TYPES.

SMELT SAUCE WITH BREAD CRUMBS

SMELT ARE BEING USED IN THIS RECIPE TO REPLACE THE FRESH SARDINES CALLED FOR IN THIS DISH OF OBVIOUS SOUTHERN ORIGIN. IF YOU CAN FIND FRESH SARDINES, USE 'EM. THE BREAD CRUMBS ARE A SOUTHERN REPLACEMENT FOR GRATED CHEESE.

INGREDIENTS:

2	CUPS BREADCRUMBS, TOASTED
1/4	CUP WATER
2	TABLESPOONS TOMATO PASTE
2	ANCHOVY FILLETS
1/2	POUND SMELT, CLEANED
1/2	CUP OLIVE OIL
2 OR 3	CLOVES GARLIC, MINCED

METHOD: TOAST THE BREAD CRUMBS IN A DRY SKILLET UNTIL THEY COLOR SLIGHTLY OR SAUTE THEM WITH 1/2 THE OLIVE OIL UNTIL COLORED. SET ASIDE.

BLEND THE TOMATO PASTE IN THE WATER, SET ASIDE.

MASH ANCHOVIES IN 1 TABLESPOON OLIVE OIL, SET ASIDE.

REMOVE HEADS, TAILS AND DEBONE SMELT, SET ASIDE.

SAUTE GARLIC IN THE OLIVE OIL UNTIL LIGHTLY GOLDEN. ADD MASHED ANCHOVIES, COOK FOR 1 MINUTE. ADD SMELT, COOK FOR 2 MINUTES. ADD TOMATO, BRING SAUCE TO A BOIL, REMOVE FROM HEAT. POUR SAUCE OVER PASTA, TOSS. ADD BREAD CRUMBS, TOSS AGAIN. SERVE.

RECOMMENDED PASTA: HOLLOW STRINGS.

FRESH SMELT SAUCE II

ONCE AGAIN A RECIPE THAT CALLS FOR FRESH SARDINES, BUT SMELT ARE EASIER TO FIND. THIS SAUCE HAS SOME INTERESTING INGREDIENT BLENDING. FISH, RAISINS, SAFFRON AND FRESH DILL. I SUSPECT THAT THIS IS ONE OF THOSE SAUCES YOU MAY WANT TO TRY, IF ONLY ONCE IN YOUR LIFETIME.

INGREDIENTS:

2	TABLESPOONS RAISINS (ANY COLOR)
1/2	CUP WARM WATER
PINCH	SAFFRON
1/4	CUP WARM WATER
2	POUNDS SMELT
2	CUPS BREAD CRUMBS
2	ONIONS, SLICED
1/4	CUP OLIVE OIL
4	ANCHOVY FILLETS, MASHED
3	TABLESPOONS PINE NUTS
3	TABLESPOONS FRESH DILL, MINCED

METHOD: SOAK RAISINS IN 1/2 CUP WARM WATER, SET ASIDE. PLACE SAFFRON IN 1/4 CUP WARM WATER TO DISSOLVE, SET ASIDE. TOAST BREAD CRUMBS IN DRY SKILLET WHILE STIRRING UNTIL LIGHTLY COLORED, SET ASIDE. REMOVE HEADS, TAILS AND DEBONE SMELT, SET ASIDE.

SAUTE ONIONS IN OLIVE OIL UNTIL TRANSPARENT. ADD ANCHOVIES AND COOK FOR 2 MINUTES. ADD DRAINED RAISINS, PINE NUTS, ADD DISSOLVED SAFFRON IN WATER, ADD DILL AND SMELT, COOK 1 ADDITIONAL MINUTE. REMOVE FROM HEAT. COVER ALLOW TO STEAM FOR 15 MINUTES. PLACE SAUCE OVER PASTA. ADD BREAD CRUMBS. TOSS AND SERVE.

OR

INSTEAD OF STEAMING FISH IN IT'S OWN HEAT, BLEND SAUCE WITH PASTA, COVER AND ALLOW TO STEAM FOR 15 MINUTES. NOW USE BREAD CRUMBS AS YOU WOULD GRATED CHEESE.

EAT AS IS, OR WARM UP IN A HOT OVEN FOR 5 MINUTES.

RECOMMENDED PASTA: HOLLOW STRINGS.

WE TRIED THIS SAUCE . . . AND

LOVED IT ( )
HATED IT ( )
MAYBE WE'LL TRY IT AGAIN ( )
WE'LL USE IT FOR UNWELCOME GUESTS ( )

FISHERMAN'S STYLE SAUCE

IN A COUNTRY SURROUNDED BY WATER, IT SHOULDN'T BE UNUSUAL TO FIND MANY SAUCES CALLED FISHERMAN'S SAUCE, AND INDEED HERE IS ANOTHER. IF YOU DON'T LIKE SQUID, JUST MOVE ON OVER TO ANOTHER RECIPE, OR YOU COULD USE CALAMARI STEAKS CUT INTO STRIPS.

INGREDIENTS: 1/4   CUP OLIVE OIL
1   CLOVE GARLIC, MINCED
1   16 OUNCE CAN TOMATOES, BLENDERIZED
1   POUND SQUID, CLEANED AND CHOPPED
1   DOZEN MUSSELS, SHUCKED AND CHOPPED
1   DOZEN CLAMS, SHUCKED AND CHOPPED

METHOD: SAUTE GARLIC IN OLIVE OIL FOR 2 MINUTES. ADD TOMATOES AND SQUID. COVER AND SIMMER FOR ONE HOUR, OR UNTIL SQUID IS DONE TO YOUR PREFERENCE. ADD MUSSELS AND CLAMS DURING THE FINAL 5 MINUTES OF COOKING. POUR SAUCE OVER PASTA. TOSS AND SERVE.

RECOMMENDED PASTA: OVAL STRING TYPES.

SCALLOPS SAUCE

(ANOTHER QUICKIE)

BAY SCALLOPS (YOUR MARKETS MAY USE A DIFFERENT TERM, IT REALLY MEANS VERY SMALL SCALLOPS) ARE READILY AVAILABLE AND CONSIDERABLY LESS EXPENSIVE THAN THEIR MUCH LARGER COUSINS. THE BASIC RECIPE HERE IS NEARLY IDENTICAL TO AN ANCHOVY SAUCE, WITH THE SCALLOPS BEING AN ADDED INGREDIENT. SCALLOPS NEED FAST COOKING, THEY BECOME RUBBERY WHEN OVER COOKED.

INGREDIENTS:

1	POUND BAY SCALLOPS
1/3	CUP OLIVE OIL
2	CLOVES GARLIC, YOUR CHOICE
3	ANCHOVY FILLETS
1	TABLESPOON CHOPPED PARSLEY

METHOD: PUT SCALLOPS ON PAPER TOWELS TO DRAIN. NORMALLY BAY SCALLOPS ARE QUITE SMALL, IF YOURS ARE LARGER THAN YOU'RE COMFORTABLE WITH, HALVE OR QUARTER THEM.

SAUTE GARLIC AND ANCHOVIES UNTIL ANCHOVIES DISSOLVE. ADD SCALLOPS, COOK FOR 2 MINUTES. REMOVE FROM HEAT. REMOVE GARLIC IF USING IT CRUSHED. POUR SAUCE OVER PASTA. ADD PARSLEY, TOSS AND SERVE.

RECOMMENDED PASTA: THIN STRING OR OVAL STRING TYPES.

SCALLOPS SAUCE TOO!

THE ATTENTION GETTER IN THIS SAUCE IS DIRECTLY PROPORTIONAL TO THE AMOUNT OF CRUSHED RED PEPPER YOU USE. SCALLOPS ARE VERY MILD AND CAN BE OVERWHELMED BY ALMOST ANYTHING. IF YOU'RE A REAL (I MEAN REAL!) HOT PEPPER FAN, START WITH A TABLESPOONFUL. IF YOU DON'T LIKE THE STUFF, LEAVE IT OUT. IT YOU ONLY WANT A VERY LIGHT PEPPER FLAVOR, USE 1/4 TEASPOON OF THE CRUSHED RED PEPPER, OR A FEW SHAKES OF TABASCO, OR A FEW DROPS OF A LOUISIANA HOT SAUCE.

INGREDIENTS:

2	TABLESPOONS OLIVE OIL
2	TABLESPOONS BUTTER
1	CLOVE GARLIC, CRUSHED
	CRUSHED HOT RED PEPPER TO TASTE
1	POUND BAY SCALLOPS
2	TABLESPOONS PESTO MIXED WITH;
2	TABLESPOONS WATER
2	TABLESPOONS FRESHLY GRATED PARMESAN CHEESE

METHOD: SAUTE THE GARLIC IN THE OIL/BUTTER UNTIL LIGHTLY GOLDEN, REMOVE AND DISCARD GARLIC. ADD CRUSHED RED PEPPER AND COOK FOR ONE MINUTE. ADD SCALLOPS, SAUTE FOR 3 TO 4 MINUTES. REMOVE FROM HEAT, ADD PESTO AND MIX TO COAT. TOSS PASTA WITH GRATED CHEESE. ADD SCALLOP SAUCE. TOSS AGAIN, SERVE.

RECOMMENDED PASTA: THIN STRINGS OR MEDIUM TUBES.

FLORENTINE ANCHOVY SAUCE

FLORENTINE AS YOU PROBABLY KNOW MEANS THAT SPINACH IS A PRIME INGREDIENT, I UNDERSTAND THAT THE FLORENTINE'S ARE CONFUSED BY THAT APPLICATION, BUT NONE THE LESS, HERE IN THE USA, THAT'S WHAT IT MEANS.

INGREDIENTS:

4	TABLESPOONS BUTTER
2	CLOVES GARLIC, MINCED
1	28 OUNCE CAN PEAR TOMATOES, BLENDERIZED
1	ONION, CHOPPED
1	TEASPOON DRY BASIL
1	BUNCH SPINACH, COOKED AND DRAINED
	OR
1	10 OUNCE PACKAGE FROZEN SPINACH, THAWED AND DRAINED
4	ANCHOVY FILLETS, CHOPPED
2	TABLESPOONS PINE NUTS, TOASTED

METHOD: SAUTE THE GARLIC IN THE BUTTER FOR 3 MINUTES. ADD TOMATOES, ONION AND BASIL. BRING SAUCE TO A BOIL, REDUCE HEAT, COVER AND COOK OVER MEDIUM HEAT FOR 20 MINUTES. UNCOVER, ADD SPINACH AND ANCHOVIES TO HEAT THROUGH. POUR SAUCE OVER PASTA, TOSS. ADD PINE NUTS, TOSS AGAIN AND SERVE.

RECOMMENDED PASTA: THIN STRING TYPES.

SEAFOOD AND CAULIFLOWER SAUCE

I BELIEVE THIS RECIPE IS SOUTHERN, ITS USE OF SPICE AND FRESH SARDINES SUGGEST THAT. FRESH SARDINES MAY BE DIFFICULT TO COME BY, BUT SMELT IS A VERY ACCEPTABLE SUBSTITUTE.

INGREDIENTS:

1	HEAD CAULIFLOWER, FLORETS ONLY
4	OUNCES FRESH SMELT
2	ANCHOVY FILLETS
3	PEAR TOMATOES (B/P/C)
4	TABLESPOONS OLIVE OIL
1	CLOVE GARLIC, MINCED
1	TABLESPOON CHOPPED ONION
1/8	TEASPOON GROUND CLOVES
PINCH	GROUND CINNAMON
	FRESHLY GROUND BLACK PEPPER TO TASTE

METHOD: STEAM OR COOK THE CAULIFLOWER IN WATER FOR 5 TO 10 MINUTES, LEAVE SLIGHTLY FIRM. DRAIN AND SET ASIDE. REMOVE HEADS AND TAILS OF SMELT, DEBONE IF DESIRED, SET ASIDE. MASH ANCHOVIES, BLEND WITH TOMATOES, SET ASIDE.

SAUTE THE GARLIC, ONION, SMELT, CLOVES, CINNAMON AND CAULI-FLOWER IN THE OLIVE OIL FOR ONE MINUTE TO COAT. ADD THE TOMATO/ANCHOVY MIXTURE, COOK AT MEDIUM HEAT FOR 5 MINUTES. MIX SAUCE AND PASTA THOROUGHLY. SERVE WITH BLACK PEPPER ON THE SIDE.

RECOMMENDED PASTA: SHORT TUBE TYPES OR LONG HOLLOW TUBES, BROKEN INTO 3 OR 4 INCH LENGTHS.

LEMON AND TUNA SAUCE

(ANOTHER QUICKIE)

THIS IS AN UNCOOKED SAUCE, AND ONE OF MANY IN THIS BOOK. IT'S A BLENDING OF TUNA, ANCHOVY AND LEMON, AN HONEST CHARACTER FLAVOR THAT COULD FIT BEAUTIFULLY INTO A SUMMERS EVE MENU. IT'S THE TYPE OF SAUCE THAT YOU'LL FIND THROUGHOUT THE COASTAL AREAS OF SOUTHERN ITALY AND SICILY.

IF YOU DON'T LIKE HOT TUNA, TRY THIS SAUCE AS A PASTA/TUNA SALAD. TOSS THE COOKED PASTA WITH A LITTLE OLIVE OIL TO PREVENT STICKING, THEN LET COOL. ADD THE TUNA SAUCE. TOSS AND SERVE AT ROOM TEMPERATURE, OR CHILLED.

INGREDIENTS:

1/4	CUP OLIVE OIL
1/2	CLOVE GARLIC OR LESS
1	LEMON, JUICED
3	TABLESPOONS PARSLEY
2	ANCHOVY FILLETS
1 OR 2	DROPS TABASCO
1	6 1/2 OUNCE CAN WATER PACKED TUNA, DRAINED

METHOD: PLACE ALL INGREDIENTS EXCEPT TUNA INTO A FOOD PROCESSOR AND PROCESS UNTIL WELL CHOPPED (DON'T PUREE), POUR MIXTURE INTO A SMALL BOWL, MASH THE TUNA INTO THE SAUCE WITH A FORK. WHEN WELL BLENDED, POUR SAUCE OVER PASTA. TOSS AND SERVE.

RECOMMENDED PASTA: HOLLOW STRING TYPES.

WE TRIED THIS SAUCE . . . AND

LOVED IT ( )
HATED IT ( )
MAYBE WE'LL TRY IT AGAIN ( )
WE'LL USE IT FOR UNWELCOME GUESTS ( )

ANCHOVY AND OLIVE SAUCE

(ANOTHER QUICKIE)

THERE IS AN UNCOOKED VERSION OF THIS SAUCE IN CHAPTER 7, SO, IF YOU LIKE THE COMBINATION, GIVE THAT ONE A TRY ON A WARM SUMMER DAY.

INGREDIENTS: 1/4   CUP OLIVE OIL
1/2   CUP CHOPPED RIPE OLIVES (BLACK OR GREEN)
1   TABLESPOON CAPERS
5   ANCHOVY FILLETS, MINCED
3   TABLESPOONS CHOPPED PARSLEY
1/2   CUP ITALIAN OR FRENCH BREAD CRUMBS

METHOD: USING 1/2 THE OLIVE OIL, SAUTE THE OLIVES, CAPERS, AND ANCHOVIES FOR 5 MINUTES. USING A SEPARATE PAN, SAUTE THE BREAD CRUMBS IN THE REMAINING OIL UNTIL GOLDEN. TOSS COOKED PASTA WITH THE BREAD CRUMBS. POUR SAUCE OVER PASTA AND TOSS AGAIN, SERVE.

RECOMMENDED PASTA: MEDIUM, DIAGONAL CUT, TUBE TYPES.

CHAPTER 16

SAUCES MADE FROM LEGUMES

I HAVE GIVEN LEGUMES SEPARATE CHAPTER'S BECAUSE OF THEIR FOOD VALUE AND PROTEIN. A SAUCE WITH LEGUMES CAN PROVIDE MOST OF THE ESSENTIAL AMINO ACIDS, AND WHEN YOU ADD THE COMPLEX CARBOHYDRATES OF PASTA YOU HAVE A MEATLESS, YET SATISFYING MEAL (FOR LEGUMES WITH MEAT, SEE CHAPTER 17). COMPLIMENT YOUR OFFERING WITH A LOAF OF CRUSTY BREAD TO CREATE A ONE DISH MEAL THAT WILL TAME THE HUNGRIEST APPETITE.

IF YOU WISH TO USE A SUBSTITUTE FOR ONE OF THE VARIETIES USED HERE, YOU COULD DO SO QUITE SUCCESSFULLY. THE BLACK EYED PEA MAY BE SUBSTITUTED FOR THE CHICK PEA, SOYBEANS MAY BE SUBSTITUTED FOR THE LIMA BEANS.

HERE-A-CHICK, THERE-A-CHICK, EVERYWHERE-A-CHICK(PEA)!

SEVERAL OF THE RECIPES IN THIS CHAPTER USE CHICK PEAS, SO MAY I SUGGEST THAT YOU BUY A VERY GOOD BRAND WHEN BUYING CANNED CHICK PEAS, THERE IS A REAL QUALITY DIFFERENCE AMONG CANNERS AND IT WILL SHOW UP IN YOUR SAUCE.

NEAPOLITAN CHICK PEA SAUCE

LET'S CONSIDER THE NAME "CHICK PEA", THAT'S ENGLISH, THE LATIN WORD IS "CICERO", THE ITALIAN WORD IS 'CECI' (PRONOUNCED SHAY-SHE) AND THE SPANISH WORD IS "GARBANZO". USE ANYONE YOU LIKE. I DON'T LIKE GARBANZO, IT SOUNDS LIKE THE NAME OF A CHIMPANZIE. I DON'T BELIEVE THERE IS A SINGLE COUNTRY BORDERING THE MEDITERRANEAN THAT DOESN'T MAKE VERY GOOD USE OF THE CHICK PEA IN THEIR CUISINE. I HAVEN'T PROVIDED THIS INFORMATION TO SHOW YOU THAT I'M A FORMIDABLE TRIVIA PLAYER, BUT RATHER TO SHOW YOU THAT THE CHICK PEA HAS BEEN AROUND FOR THOUSANDS OF YEARS AND THAT IT IS A MAINSTAY STAPLE IN MEDITERRANEAN COOKING. IT IS ALSO WIDELY USED IN THE WESTERN HEMISPHERE AND ON THE INDIAN SUBCONTINENT. THE ITALIANS USE THE CHICK PEA AS VEGETABLE, A SNACK FOOD AND AS AN INGREDIENT IN MANY SOUPS AND SALADS. HERE, AND IN A NUMBER OF THE FOLLOWING RECIPES WE'LL BE USING CHICK PEAS IN A PASTA SAUCE.

IF YOU WISH TO USE DRY CHICK PEAS FOR THIS DISH, FOLLOW THE PACKERS DIRECTIONS FOR RECONSTITUTING THEM. IT'S AN OVERNIGHT PROCESS, SO PLAN IN ADVANCE. IT'S EASY ENOUGH TO DO, BUT SO'S OPENING A CAN.

IF YOU CHOOSE TO RECONSTITUTE DRY CHICK PEAS, DRAIN THEM AFTER SOAKING. PLACE THEM IN 4 CUPS FRESH WATER COOK FOR ONE HOUR BEFORE USING AS DIRECTED BELOW.

INGREDIENTS:

2	CUPS CHICK PEAS (IF CANNED DON'T DRAIN)
1/3	CUP OLIVE OIL
4	FRESH PEAR TOMATOES (B/P/C)
2	CLOVES GARLIC, BRUISED OR CRUSHED
1/2	TEASPOON SALT
1/4	TEASPOON FRESHLY GROUND BLACK PEPPER
1	TABLESPOON PARSLEY, CHOPPED
1	TEASPOON FRESH BASIL, CHOPPED

METHOD: PLACE 1/2 THE OLIVE OIL, CHICK PEAS, TOMATOES, 1 CLOVE GARLIC, SALT AND PEPPER IN A SAUCE PAN TOGETHER. BRING TO A BOIL, REDUCE HEAT TO SIMMER, PARTIALLY COVER AND COOK FOR 20 MINUTES. ADD PARSLEY, BASIL, REMAINING OIL, AND GARLIC CLOVE TO SAUCE, REMOVE FROM HEAT. POUR OVER PASTA. TOSS AND SERVE.

RECOMMENDED PASTA: RIBBON TYPES.

CREAM OF CHICK PEA SAUCE #1

(USING DRY CHICK PEAS)

AGAIN FROM DEEP SOUTH WE GET A VERY GOOD AND EARTHY SAUCE. THIS RECIPE IS MADE FROM DRY CHICK PEAS, IF YOU WISH TO USE CANNED CHICK PEAS, SEE NEXT PAGE FOR RECIPE #2. THE PASTA WILL BE COOKED COUNTRY STYLE, THAT IS, WITH THE SAUCE.

INGREDIENTS:

1	POUND DRY CHICK PEAS
1	SPRIG FRESH ROSEMARY
2	STALKS CELERY
1	SMALL ONION, PEELED
4	BAY LEAVES
1	LEVEL TEASPOON SALT
1/2	CUP OLIVE OIL
1	CLOVE GARLIC, CRUSHED
3	TABLESPOONS TOMATO PASTE

METHOD: SOAK THE CHICK PEAS AS DIRECTED BY THE PACKER. DRAIN, ADD 2 1/2 QUARTS FRESH WATER, ROSEMARY, CELERY, ONION AND BAY LEAVES. BRING TO A BOIL, REDUCE HEAT TO LOW AND COOK COVERED FOR 1 HOUR OR UNTIL CHICK PEAS ARE TENDER. DISCARD, ROSEMARY, CELERY, ONION AND BAY LEAVES. ADD SALT THEN PLACE THE CHICK PEAS AND REMAINING LIQUID IN A BLENDER. PROCESS UNTIL SMOOTH.

ABOUT 20 MINUTES BEFORE CHICK PEAS ARE DONE, SAUTE THE GARLIC IN OLIVE OIL, WHEN IT TURNS COLOR, REMOVE GARLIC AND DISCARD. ADD THE TOMATO PASTE TO THE OIL WITH ABOUT 1/3 CUP WATER FROM THE COOKING CHICK PEAS. COOK TOMATO PASTE ABOUT 15 MINUTES. ADD THE PUREED CHICK PEAS AND BRING TO A BOIL. MOVE TO THE NEXT STEP.

ONE OF THE FEATURES THAT MAKE THIS RECIPE A LITTLE DIFFERENT IS THE NEXT STEP. BREAK YOUR PASTA INTO SHORT PIECES (ABOUT 3 INCHES). ADD PASTA TO THE SAUCE. ALLOW IT TO COOK THERE. WHEN PASTA IS DONE, SERVE.

RECOMMENDED PASTA: RIBBON TYPES.

CREAM OF CHICK PEA SAUCE #2

(USING CANNED CHICK PEAS)

INGREDIENTS:

1/2	CUP OLIVE OIL
1	CLOVE GARLIC MINCED
3	TABLESPOONS TOMATO PASTE
1/2	CUP VEGETABLE BROTH OR WATER
2	15 OUNCE CANS CHICK PEAS
1/4	TEASPOON DRY ROSEMARY, CRUSHED OR GROUND
1	STALK CELERY, FINELY CHOPPED
1/2	CUP ONION, CHOPPED

METHOD: SAUTE GARLIC IN OLIVE OIL UNTIL LIGHTLY GOLDEN. ADD TOMATO PASTE AND BROTH. BLEND WELL, COOK FOR ABOUT 5 MINUTES. ADD CHICK PEAS, ROSEMARY, CELERY AND ONION, COOK FOR ABOUT 20 MINUTES. REMOVE SAUCE FROM HEAT. SIEVE OR PROCESS THROUGH A BLENDER TO CREAM THE SAUCE. POUR SAUCE OVER PASTA. TOSS AND SERVE.

RECOMMENDED PASTA: RIBBON TYPES.

TUSCAN CHICK PEA SAUCE

THE TUSCANS USUALLY EAT THIS SAUCE WITH WIDE NOODLES, AND THEY COOK THE NOODLES WITH THE CHICK PEAS, IF YOU CHOOSE TO TRY IT THIS WAY, FOLLOWING THE COOKING OF THE SAUCE, ADD SEVERAL CUPS OF WATER AND THE NOODLES, COOK THE ADDITIONAL TIME NEEDED FOR THE NOODLES.

NOODLE IS A WORD NORTHERNERS USE TO DESCRIBE A MEMBER OF THE PASTA FAMILY THAT IS FLAT AND HAS A WIDTH OF BETWEEN 3/16" INCH AND 1" INCH, AND NORMALLY AS LONG AS SPAGHETTI. THAT TAKES IN TRENETTINE TO FETTUCCINE UP TO LASAGNE (LASAGNE STARTS AT 1 INCH AND GENERALLY HAS RIPPLED SIDES). A SECOND RIBBON FAMILY OF "NOODLES" IS THE TAGLIATELLE GROUP. I REALLY DON'T KNOW THE DIFFERENCE BETWEEN THE FAMILIES AND I'M NOT VERY SURE ANYONE ELSE DOES EITHER. IN THIS CASE HOWEVER, THEY ARE CALLING FOR A MEDIUM TO WIDE PASTA EGG NOODLE. IN THE UNITED STATES, THERE ARE VERY FEW PASTAS MADE WITH EGG. IF THEY HAVE AN EGG CONTENT, IT WILL CLEARLY STATE SO ON THE LABEL. YOU COULD OPT OUT FOR PLAIN EGG NOODLES, IF YOU CHOOSE TO DO SO, GO WITH A MEDIUM OR WIDE NOODLE.

INGREDIENTS:

1	16 OUNCE CAN CHICK PEAS
1/2	CUP OLIVE OIL
1	ONION, THINLY SLICED
1	CLOVE GARLIC, MINCED
2	TABLESPOONS PARSLEY, CHOPPED
1/4	TEASPOON ROSEMARY, CRUSHED
1	CUP WATER (USE PASTA WATER IF YOU WISH)
1	TEASPOON TOMATO PASTE
	SALT AND FRESHLY GROUND BLACK PEPPER TO TASTE
	GRATED PARMESAN CHEESE

METHOD: PUREE HALF THE CHICK PEAS WITH THE CAN LIQUOR, SET ASIDE. SAUTE THE ONION AND GARLIC IN OLIVE OIL UNTIL THEY BEGIN TO COLOR. ADD THE PARSLEY, ROSEMARY, WATER, TOMATO PASTE WHOLE AND PUREED CHICK PEAS. ADJUST SEASONING TO TASTE. COVER AND SIMMER FOR 30 MINUTES. POUR SAUCE OVER PASTA. TOSS, SERVE WITH CHEESE ON THE SIDE.

RECOMMENDED PASTA: RIBBON TYPES.

CHICK PEA SAUCE

THIS SAUCE COULD BE CREAMED, MASHED, RICED OR SIEVED, PICK THE TEXTURE YOU LIKE AND GO FOR IT.

INGREDIENTS:

2	15 OUNCE CANS CHICK PEAS
1	TABLESPOON DRY OREGANO
1	TABLESPOON PARSLEY, CHOPPED
1/4	TEASPOON FRESHLY GROUND BLACK PEPPER
3/4	CUP OLIVE OIL (EXTRA VIRGIN IF YOU HAVE IT)

METHOD: PLACE THE UNDRAINED CHICK PEAS IN A SAUCE PAN, MASH, ADD OREGANO, PARSLEY, AND BLACK PEPPER. BLEND WELL. ADD OLIVE OIL. BRING SAUCE TO A BOIL, REDUCE HEAT TO SIMMER AND COOK FOR 8 MINUTES. POUR SAUCE OVER PASTA. TOSS AND SERVE.

RECOMMENDED PASTA: NARROW RIBBON TYPES OR MEDIUM TUBES, STRAIGHT EDGE OR DIAGONAL CUT.

LIMA BEAN SAUCE

(ANOTHER QUICKIE)

THIS RECIPE IS FOR CANNED OR FROZEN BEANS AND YOU MAY USE EITHER THE GREEN LIMA BEAN FOR THIS SAUCE OR THE YELLOW BUTTER BEAN. IF YOU WISH TO TAKE THE TIME, YOU MAY PREPARE DRY LIMAS. YOU MAY ALSO USE THE ITALIAN FRESH BROAD BEAN IF THEY'RE AVAILABLE IN YOUR NEIGHBORHOOD. YOU'LL NEED TO SHELL 'EM AND COOK THEM IN WATER UNTIL TENDER, THEN USE SOME OF THE COOKING WATER IN THE SAUCE.

INGREDIENTS:

3	TABLESPOON OLIVE OIL
1	ONION, CHOPPED
1	16 OUNCE CAN LIMA OR BUTTER BEANS
2	TABLESPOON PARSLEY, CHOPPED
3/4	CUP FRESHLY GROUND PARMESAN CHEESE

METHOD: SAUTE THE ONION IN THE OLIVE OIL UNTIL ONION IS TRANSPARENT. ADD UNDRAINED BEANS TO HEAT THROUGH. ADD PARSLEY. POUR SAUCE OVER PASTA. TOSS, ADD CHEESE, TOSS AGAIN, SERVE.

RECOMMENDED PASTA: NARROW RIBBON TYPES.

PUREED GREEN PEA SAUCE

LIKE OTHER LEGUMES, FRESH OR FROZEN GREEN PEAS AND SPLIT PEAS MAY ALSO BE PUREED TO MAKE A VERY TASTY PASTA SAUCE, DITTO TOO FOR BLACK EYED PEAS. I THREW THAT IN FOR ALL YOU SOUTHERNERS WITH AN ITALIAN HERITAGE. THIS RECIPE IS OF ITALIAN ORIGIN, MOST LIKELY FROM THE FAR NORTH, BUT THAT'S A GUESS, I DON'T KNOW WHERE IT ORIGINATED.

INGREDIENTS:

1	POUND FRESH PEAS, SHELLED, OR
	1-10 OUNCE PACKAGE FROZEN PEAS
24	BUTTON MUSHROOMS
2	TABLESPOONS BUTTER
	FRESHLY GROUND BLACK PEPPER TO TASTE
1/4	CUP FRESHLY GRATED PARMESAN OR ASIAGO CHEESE

METHOD: COOK PEAS UNTIL TENDER AND PUREE IN BLENDER OR FOOD PROCESSOR, SET ASIDE. SAUTE MUSHROOMS IN BUTTER FOR 3 MINUTES. ADD PUREED PEAS AND BLACK PEPPER, BLEND WELL. POUR SAUCE OVER PASTA. TOSS, ADD CHEESE, TOSS AGAIN, SERVE.

(RESERVE SOME OF THE LIQUID IF PEAS WERE COOKED IN WATER, IF THEY WERE STEAMED RESERVE A LITTLE PASTA WATER, ADD IF NEEDED TO THE PUREE).

RECOMMENDED PASTA: STRING TYPES, SQUARE, ROUND OR OVAL.

WE TRIED THIS SAUCE . . . AND

LOVED IT ( )
HATED IT ( )
MAYBE WE'LL TRY IT AGAIN ( )
WE'LL USE IT FOR UNWELCOME GUESTS ( )

PEAS AND EGG SAUCE

(ANOTHER QUICKIE)

THIS SAUCE IS A VERY PLEASANT COMBINATION OF FRESH OR FROZEN GREEN PEAS AND EGGS. THE EGGS WILL BE COOKED BY THE PASTA, AND THE OVER ALL PLATE APPEAL WILL BE DELIGHTFUL. IT WILL TASTE AS PRETTY AS IT LOOKS. (IS THAT POSSIBLE?) USE A STOVE PROOF CASSEROLE OR A CHAFING DISH TO PREPARE THIS DISH.

INGREDIENTS:
1   10 OUNCE PACKAGE FROZEN PEAS,
OR
2   CUPS FRESH SHELLED PEAS, COOKED.
1/3   CUP RESERVED WATER FROM PASTA OR PEAS
1/3   CUP FRESHLY GRATED PARMESAN CHEESE
3   EGGS, WELL BEATEN
SALT TO TASTE
FRESHLY GROUND BLACK PEPPER TO TASTE

METHOD: COOK YOUR PASTA; DRAIN IT AND PLACE INTO A HEAT PROOF SERVING DISH. PLACE THE PASTA ALONG WITH THE RESERVED WATER OVER LOW HEAT, TOSS. ADD CHEESE, PEAS AND EGGS. TOSS SEVERAL TIMES UNTIL VERY WELL MIXED. ADD SALT AND PEPPER. TOSS AGAIN SERVE.

RECOMMENDED PASTA: THIN STRINGS.

Pasta with Beans

THIS DISH ALMOST DOESN'T BELONG HERE, EITHER IN THIS CHAPTER OR EVEN THIS BOOK. BUT, BECAUSE IT'S A NEAR UNIVERSAL FAVORITE AMONG PEOPLE WHO ENJOY PASTA, I'VE ELECTED TO INCLUDE IT. IT IS CERTAINLY ONE OF THE BETTER KNOWN PASTA DISHES. IT'S PASTA E FAGIOLI, OR PASTA AND BEANS. AND WHILE IT'S POSSIBLE THAT YOU HAVE NEVER TASTED IT, YOU'VE MOST LIKELY HEARD OF IT. PART OF THIS DISHES FAME AMONG NON-ITALIANS MAY BE RELATED TO THE SOUND OF THE ITALIAN WORD FOR BEANS; FAGIOLI, IT'S EASILY MISSPELLED. FREQUENTLY MISPRONOUNCED AND GENERALLY DELIB-ERATELY SO, TO "FAZOOL". THEREBY GIVING US "PASTA FAZOOL". IT'S ACTUALLY VERY TASTY AND GOOD. IF YOU COMPLIMENT THIS DISH WITH A GREEN SALAD, AND FINISH WITH SOME FRUIT, YOU'LL HAVE A WONDERFUL MEATLESS MEAL. A FRESH LOAF OF CRUSTY BREAD WOULDN'T HURT EITHER. A POINT WORTH REMEMBERING; THIS DISH IS NOT A SOUP, ALTHOUGH THERE ARE AREAS OF ITALY WHERE IT MAY BE CONSIDERED A SOUP, PARTICULARLY TUSCANY. IN MY FAMILY AND ELSEWHERE WHEN I'VE BEEN SERVED THIS DISH, IT WAS ALWAYS THICK TO THE POINT OF BEING A STEW. IT SHOULD NOT BE DRY. HERE'S HOW TO DO IT:

INGREDIENTS:

1/2	POUND (1 1/4 CUPS) SMALL WHITE BEANS
4	CUPS WATER
1	TEASPOON SALT
2	CUPS PASTA (8 OUNCES)
1/4	CUP FINELY CHOPPED TOMATOES, OR 1 TABLESPOON TOMATO PASTE
1	TABLESPOON OLIVE OIL
1/4	TEASPOON BLACK PEPPER
1/2	TEASPOON OREGANO
	GRATED PARMESAN CHEESE

METHOD: PLACE DRY BEANS INTO BOILING WATER. COVER AND SIMMER FOR TWO MINUTES. REMOVE FROM HEAT, SET ASIDE FOR ONE HOUR. DRAIN, ADD 4 CUPS FRESH WATER. BRING TO A BOIL AND SIMMER FOR TWO HOURS OR UNTIL BEANS ARE TENDER. ADD SALT WHEN BEANS ARE DONE. STIR OCCASIONALLY.

COOK YOUR PASTA IN SALTED WATER UNTIL NEAR DONE. RESERVE 1/2 CUP PASTA WATER AND 1 CUP PLAIN HOT WATER. DRAIN PASTA. SET ASIDE.

ADD TO THE BEANS: TOMATOES, OLIVE OIL, BLACK PEPPER AND OREGANO. SIMMER FOR TEN MINUTES, TASTE AND ADJUST SEASONING. ADD PASTA, SIMMER FOR 2 MINUTES MORE, OR UNTIL PASTA IS COOKED TO YOUR LIKING. SERVE WITH GRATED CHEESE ON THE SIDE.

VARIATIONS: IF YOU WISH TO USE COOKED BEANS, AND THEREBY SHORTEN THE PREPARATION TIME CONSIDERABLY, USE THE ITALIAN VARIETY OF WHITE KIDNEY BEANS (CANNELLINI) OR, ANY SMALL WHITE OR PINK BEAN. YOU'LL NEED TO RESERVE MORE OF THE WATER YOU PREPARED THE PASTA IN, POSSIBLY TWO CUPS.

RECOMMENDED PASTA: SHORT TUBES OR SMALL SEA SHELLS.

CHAPTER 17

SAUCES MADE FROM LEGUMES AND MEAT

BEAN AND TOMATO SAUCE

A SAUCE OF PEASANT ROOTS, AND ONE, I BELIEVE, THAT MAY COMFORTABLY BE REFERRED TO AS "RIB STICKING" GOOD. IF THAT'S A PHRASE THAT HAS APPEAL TO YOU, THEN YOU'RE SURE TO ENJOY THIS ONE, GO FOR IT.

INGREDIENTS:

1	16 OUNCE CAN OF PINK BEANS OR WHITE BEANS
1	28 OUNCE CAN PEAR TOMATOES
4	TABLESPOONS OLIVE OIL
1	ONION, CHOPPED
1	CARROT, CHOPPED
1	CELERY STALK, MINCED
1	CLOVE GARLIC (YOUR CHOICE)
6	SLICES BACON (PANCETTA IF YOU HAVE IT) DICED SPRINKLE OF GROUND SAGE
	FRESHLY GROUND BLACK PEPPER

METHOD: SAUTE ONION, CARROT, CELERY, GARLIC AND BACON IN THE OLIVE OIL UNTIL THE ONION IS SOFT. BLENDERIZE THE SAUTED VEGETABLES, SAGE, TOMATOES AND BEANS TOGETHER UNTIL SMOOTH. RETURN TO PAN, BRING TO A BOIL, PARTIALLY COVER, COOK AT A FAST SIMMER FOR ABOUT 20 MINUTES. MIX SAUCE WITH PASTA BY TOSSING LIGHTLY, SERVE. GENEROUSLY ADD FRESHLY GROUND BLACK PEPPER AND SOME GRATED PARMESAN CHEESE TO EACH SERVING.

RECOMMENDED PASTA: NARROW RIBBON TYPES OR SHORT WIDE NOODLES.

LIMA BEAN AND BACON SAUCE

THIS SAUCE HAS FEWER INGREDIENTS THAN OTHER LIMA BEAN SAUCES IN THIS BOOK, IT WILL TAKE A FEW MINUTES LONGER, AND MAY, ACCORDING TO YOUR TASTE BE MORE FLAVORFUL. YOU ALSO GET A LOT OF LATITUDE. YOU MAY USE ANY SIZE LIMA BEAN OR EVEN THE YELLOW TONED BUTTER BEAN. YOU MAY USE FRESH BEANS, OR DRIED BEANS IF YOU WISH, BUT FROZEN BEANS ARE EASIER, AND READILY AVAILABLE. IN A PINCH YOU MAY EVEN USE CANNED BEANS. THIS IS ONE OF THOSE SAUCES THAT FILLS AN ABSOLUTE NEED WHEN THE TASTE FOR BEANS JUST GRABS YOU OUT OF THE BLUE, AND YOU DON'T WANT SOUP . . . THIS IS THE ANSWER.

INGREDIENTS:
2	CUPS LIMA OR BUTTER BEANS (FRESH, FROZEN OR CANNED)
1/2	TEASPOON SALT
3	TABLESPOONS BUTTER
4	SLICES SUGAR CURED BACON, DICED

METHOD: STEAM OR COOK THE BEANS IN A LITTLE SALTED WATER UNTIL TENDER. ADD THE BUTTER AND SET ASIDE. SAUTE THE BACON IN IT'S OWN FAT UNTIL CRISP. DRAIN OFF ABOUT HALF THE OIL AND DISCARD. MIX BEANS AND BACON TOSS WELL. ADD PASTA, TOSS AGAIN AND SERVE.

RECOMMENDED PASTA: FANCY TYPES.

461

LIMA BEAN AND SAUSAGE SAUCE

ONCE AGAIN YOU'VE GOT THE OPTION OF SELECTING THE BEAN YOU LIKE, OR THE ONE YOU HAPPEN TO HAVE AVAILABLE. IF YOU HAVE A FULL SELECTION IN YOUR HOUSE TO CHOOSE FROM, GO WITH THE BABY LIMAS.

INGREDIENTS:

2	LINKS ITALIAN SAUSAGE OR AN 8" INCH PIECE OR THE ROPE TYPE
3	CUPS OF LIMA BEANS OR BUTTER BEANS (FROZEN OR PREPARED FROM DRIED BEANS)
1	ONION, DICED
1	RIB OF CELERY, CHOPPED
1	TABLESPOON CHOPPED FRESH BASIL
2	8 OUNCE CANS TOMATO SAUCE GRATED PARMESAN CHEESE

METHOD: PUNCTURE THEN FRY THE SAUSAGE FOR ABOUT 10 MINUTES, OR UNTIL COOKED ABOUT HALF WAY THROUGH. SLICE THE SAUSAGE INTO WHEELS AND SET ASIDE. TO THE SAUSAGE OIL, ADD LIMA BEANS, ONION, CELERY, BASIL AND TOMATO SAUCE. BRING SAUCE TO A BOIL, ADD SAUSAGE COVER AND SIMMER FOR 20 MINUTES. POUR SAUCE OVER PASTA. TOSS AND SERVE WITH GRATED CHEESE ON THE SIDE.

RECOMMENDED PASTA: STRING TYPES, OR MEDIUM TUBE TYPES.

PEAS AND BACON SAUCE

THIS SAUCE IS AN INTERESTING BLEND OF BACON, PROSCUITTO AND FRESH PEAS. YOU MAY CHOOSE FROZEN PEAS WHEN FRESH PEAS ARE NOT AVAILABLE. YOU'LL COOK THE PEAS IN CHICKEN BROTH, SO, TO AVOID A SOUPY SAUCE, SIMMER THE PEAS WITH YOUR PAN LID PARTIALLY OFF, THEREBY ALLOWING MOST OF THE LIQUID TO EVAPORATE.

INGREDIENTS:

6	SLICES SUGAR CURED BACON, MINCED
3	ONIONS, FINELY CHOPPED
2	CELERY RIBS, FINELY CHOPPED
4	TABLESPOONS OLIVE OIL (OR USE 1/2 BUTTER)
1	POUND FRESH PEAS (BEFORE SHELLING)
4	SLICES PROSCUITTO, JULIENNED
1	TABLESPOON CHOPPED PARSLEY
1	TEASPOON SALT
1/2	TEASPOON FRESHLY GROUND BLACK PEPPER
1	CUP CHICKEN BROTH
1/4	CUP GRATED PARMESAN CHEESE

METHOD: SAUTE THE BACON, ONIONS AND CELERY IN THE OLIVE OIL FOR FIVE MINUTES. ADD PEAS, PROSCUITTO, PARSLEY, SALT AND PEPPER. COOK FOR AN ADDITIONAL FIVE MINUTES. ADD BROTH, PARTIALLY COVER PAN AND SIMMER UNTIL PEAS ARE TENDER AND MOST OF THE BROTH HAS EVAPORATED, ABOUT 10 TO 15 MINUTES. SPRINKLE THE GRATED CHEESE OVER THE DRAINED PASTA. TOSS TO COAT. POUR SAUCE OVER PASTA. TOSS AGAIN, SERVE.

RECOMMENDED PASTA: NARROW RIBBON TYPES.

CHAPTER 18

SOUPY SAUCES

OR

PASTA IN A SEASONED LIQUID

HERE YOU MAY WISH TO TAKE EXCEPTION TO MY CLAIM THAT THIS IS A PASTA SAUCE ONLY COOKBOOK, BUT HEAR ME OUT, THEN YELL!

IN MOST OF THE FOLLOWING RECIPES, YOU'LL SAUTE SOME ONION IN OLIVE OIL AND THEN ADD THAT TO THE VEGETABLE AND PASTA. IT IS NOT STRETCHING CREDULITY TO ASK YOU TO BELIEVE THAT THIS CONSTITUTES A SAUCE, BECAUSE ELSEWHERE IN THIS BOOK YOU'LL DISCOVER ADDITIONAL CONFIRMATION OF THAT FACT.

IN DESCRIBING THE PASTA DISHES IN THIS CHAPTER, I AM AVOIDING THE USE OF THE WORD "BROTH", FOR SEVERAL REASONS, ONE IS THAT IT MAY BE CONFUSED WITH SOUP. SECONDLY, BROTH IS A LIQUID FLAVORED FROM THE COOKING OF MEAT OR VEGETABLES OR BOTH IN IT, AND THAT IS NOT TRUE HERE EITHER. SO, WE'LL ACKNOWLEDGE THAT THIS IS NOT A DISCUSSION OF SOUPS, WHILE ITALIANS CERTAINLY HAVE MANY WONDERFUL LIGHT AND FULL BODIED SOUPS, THAT IS NOT OUR CATEGORY. HERE WE WILL DEAL WITH PASTA AS SERVED IN A SOUPY SAUCE, A.K.A., SEASONED LIQUID.

NOT WANTING TO BE UPSTAGED BY A MORE KNOWLEDGEABLE PERSON ABOUT ITALIAN EATING HABITS, I THINK I'D BETTER COMMENT ON THE FACT THAT ITALIANS EAT SO MUCH PASTA IN BROTH, THAT MANY ITALIANS AS WELL AS MANY AMERICANS OF ITALIAN HERITAGE ACTUALLY REFER TO PASTA SERVED IN ANY OTHER FASHION AS "DRY DOUGH", IN ITALIAN; "PASTA ASCIUTTA"

IN THE FOLLOWING RECIPES YOU'LL BE USING SOME RESERVED LIQUID, SO I THINK A WORD IS NEEDED HERE ON THE USE OF "RESERVED LIQUID". THAT IS THE WATER YOU'VE COOKED THE PASTA IN. SOME ADDITIONAL LIQUID MAYBE NEEDED BECAUSE THE PASTA WILL CONTINUE TO ABSORB THE LIQUID AROUND IT AFTER YOU'VE COMPLETED THE COOKING, AND THAT COULD MAKE YOUR PREPARATION A VERY DRY DISH IF EXTRA LIQUID IS NOT USED. ALSO BEAR IN

Continued on next page

MIND THAT THE RESERVED LIQUID IS SALTED AND THAT MAY BE TOO MUCH FOR YOUR TASTE BUDS. YOU COULD CUT THE RESERVED LIQUID WITH WATER OR, BYPASS THE RESERVED LIQUID AND ONLY ADD PLAIN WATER IF THE DISH BEGINS TO DRY UP.

LET'S GO OVER THIS AGAIN, IF YOU HAVE SALTED YOUR PASTA WATER, MOST WILL, THAT SALTED WATER ADDED TO THE END PRODUCT MAY BE SO SALTY AS TO DESENSITIZE YOUR TONGUE. IF THAT HAPPENS, YOUR TASTE BUDS WILL BE DESENSITIZED FOR HOURS. MAY I SUGGEST IF YOU WILL BE USING SALTED PASTA WATER, THAT YOU USE PLAIN HOT WATER TO PASTA WATER IN A RATIO OF 2 TO 1. THAT MEANS IF YOU WANT TO ADD 1 CUP OF LIQUID, 1/3 OF IT WILL BE PASTA WATER, 2/3 PLAIN HOT WATER. HAVE I GOT YOU CONFUSED? IF SO USE ONLY PLAIN WATER AND ADD SALT TO YOUR TASTE SATISFACTION.

Pasta with Peas

THIS IS ONE OF THE WONDERFUL DISHES MY GRANDMOTHER MADE FOR ME WHEN I WAS A CHILD ON DAYS THAT I WAS NOT FEELING WELL. IT WAS GRANDMOTHER'S GOLDEN ELIXIR AND PLACEBO. IT ALWAYS MADE ME FEEL BETTER. PERHAPS HER SECRET INGREDIENT WAS LOVE, OR BECAUSE SHE MADE IT JUST FOR ME. SO, IF YOU'VE EVER HAD ONE OF THOSE DAYS WHEN YOUR STOMACH IS A LITTLE UNSETTLED, THEN THIS RECIPE IS FOR YOU. IT IS A GREAT STOMACH CALMER. IF THE PEAS ARE YOUNG AND SWEET, THIS DISH IS A DELIGHT TO EAT. SINCE I'M GIVING MY GRANDMOTHER'S HOME STYLE CURES AWAY, I MIGHT ADD THAT SHE HAD A SECOND CURE FOR CHILDREN WITH AN UPSET STOMACH. IT MAY HAVE NO MEDICAL VALUE AT ALL, BUT IT WORKED FOR ME. USE 1 TEASPOON OF FRESHLY GROUND COFFEE WITH A LIKE AMOUNT OF SUGAR ON TOP. CHEW TO SWALLOW, WASH IT DOWN WITH WATER. OF COURSE, I THINK GRANNY FED ME THAT POTION WHEN THERE WAS NO BRIOSCHI IN THE HOUSE.

INGREDIENTS:		
	2	CUPS PASTA
	1/4	CUP OLIVE OIL
	1/4	CUP CHOPPED ONION (WALLA WALLA OR VIDALIA VARIETIES IF POSSIBLE)
	3/4	TEASPOON SALT
	1/8	TEASPOON OREGANO (PINCH)
	1	CAN PEAS, UNDRAINED (16 +/- OUNCES)
		OR
	1	10 OUNCE PACKAGE FROZEN PEAS (IF USED, MORE LIQUID FROM THE PASTA WILL BE NEEDED)

METHOD: COOK YOUR PASTA UNTIL NEAR DONE. RESERVE 1/2 CUP OF PASTA WATER BEFORE DRAINING PASTA AND 1 1/2 CUPS OF PLAIN HOT WATER. SET ASIDE.

Continued on next page

ABOUT 5 MINUTES BEFORE THE PASTA IS COOKED, SAUTE ONION IN THE OLIVE OIL, WHEN THEIR EDGES BEGIN TO BROWN. ADD THE RESERVED LIQUID, DRAINED PASTA, PEAS, SALT, PEPPER AND OREGANO. SIMMER FOR ABOUT TEN MINUTES OR UNTIL PASTA IS DONE TO YOUR LIKING. SERVE.

RECOMMENDED PASTA: SHORT TUBES (DITALI/SALAD MAC) OR SMALL SHELLS.

PASTA WITH POTATOES

HERE'S A DOWNRIGHT YUMMY DISH, BESIDES THAT, IT CAN BE A NICE LIGHT LUNCH OR SUPPER.   THERE IS SOMETHING ABOUT POTATOES THAT WE ALL LOVE. SO, WHEN YOU COMBINE THESE TWO AMERICAN FAVORITES, PASTA AND POTATOES, YOU GET A VERY SATISFYING DISH. LETS DO IT.

INGREDIENTS:
1	POUND POTATOES, PEELED AND DICED
2	CUPS PASTA
1/4	CUP OLIVE OIL
1/2	CUP ONION, CHOPPED (WALLA WALLA OR VIDALIA)
	SALT AND PEPPER

METHOD: COOK THE PASTA IN LIGHTLY SALTED WATER . . . , MAY I REPEAT, LIGHTLY SALTED.   DRAIN AND SAVE THE WATER, SET PASTA ASIDE.   COOK THE POTATOES IN THE PASTA WATER FOR ABOUT 15 TO 20 MINUTES.   WHILE POTATOES ARE COOKING, SAUTE ONION IN THE OLIVE OIL UNTIL TRANSPARENT.   REMOVE FROM HEAT.   POUR A LITTLE PASTA/POTATO WATER INTO THE OIL TO STOP THE COOKING ACTION.   WHEN POTATOES ARE NEAR DONE, POUR OFF MOST OF THE COOKING LIQUID.   ADD COOKED PASTA AND THE OIL/ONION MIX TO THE POTATOES.   HEAT PASTA THROUGH. SERVE.

THE BALANCE YOU'RE LOOKING FOR IS GOING TO BE MOSTLY PASTA AND POTATO WITH A SMALL LIQUID AMOUNT.   LESS THAN SOUP, SOMEWHAT MORE LIKE STEW.

RECOMMENDED PASTA: SHORT TUBES, SMALL SHELLS OR FANCIES.

PASTA AND CABBAGE

HERE'S ONE THAT HAS A SURPRISINGLY GOOD TASTE. IT'S FULL OF FLAVOR AND JUST RIGHT FOR A LIGHT SUPPER. THE WAY I DO IT REQUIRES ONLY ONE PAN. BY NAME THE TWO VARIETIES OF CABBAGE RECOMMENDED ARE: NAPA OR SAVOY.

INGREDIENTS:

2	CUPS PASTA
2	TABLESPOONS OLIVE OIL
1	CLOVE GARLIC, BRUISED
4	CUPS, CURLY CABBAGE, SHREDDED AND CHOPPED
1/3	CUP PASTA WATER (BEFORE DRAINING)
2/3	CUP PLAIN HOT WATER
	A GRATING OF BLACK PEPPER TO TASTE

METHOD: BRING YOUR PASTA TO A ROLLING BOIL IN LIGHTLY SALTED WATER. ADD THE GARLIC AND 1 TABLESPOON OLIVE OIL.

5 MINUTES BEFORE PASTA IS DONE, ADD CABBAGE AND RETURN TO A BOIL. DRAIN.

ADD REMAINING OIL AND RESERVED LIQUID. SERVE.

RECOMMENDED PASTA: SHORT TUBES OR SMALL SHELLS.

PASTA AND ENDIVE

IF YOU ENJOY A MEASURE OF TARTNESS OCCASIONALLY, THEN HERE'S A PASTA AND GREENS DISH YOU'RE SURE TO ENJOY. ASIDE FROM THAT, A MEASURE OF TARTNESS IS HARD TO COME BY, SO GET IT WHILE YOU CAN.

INGREDIENTS:

2	CUPS PASTA
1/2	BUNCH ENDIVE, CHOPPED
1	CLOVE GARLIC
1/2	ONION, CHOPPED
1/4	CUP OLIVE OIL
	FRESHLY GROUND BLACK PEPPER TO TASTE

METHOD: GET YOUR PASTA OFF TO A MERRY BOIL IN A LIGHTLY SALTED WATER. IN ANOTHER SAUCE PAN, SAUTE THE ENDIVE, ONION AND GARLIC IN THE OLIVE OIL. BEFORE THE PASTA IS COMPLETELY COOKED, DRAW OFF ABOUT 1 CUP OF LIQUID AND ADD IT TO THE ENDIVE MIX. RESERVE A SECOND CUP OF PASTA WATER BEFORE YOU DRAIN THE PASTA. ADD THE DRAINED PASTA TO THE ENDIVE. BLEND WELL AND SERVE.

YOUR PASTA AND GREENS SHOULD BE IN LIQUID, THE BALANCE WE'RE LOOKING FOR IS DRIER THAN SOUP, WETTER THAN STEW.

RECOMMENDED PASTA: SHORT TUBES OR SMALL SHELLS.

PASTA WITH BROCCOLI

THIS IS JUST A NICE MIX OF VEGETABLES AND PASTA. IT WILL MAKE A LIGHT MEAL. SERVE IT WITH OVEN WARMED CRUSTY BREAD.

INGREDIENTS:

4	CUPS PASTA (1 POUND)
1	BUNCH FRESH BROCCOLI
	OR
2 -	10 OUNCES PACKAGE FROZEN CHOPPED BROCCOLI
1/4	CUP OLIVE OIL
2	CLOVES GARLIC, SLICED
1/8	TEASPOON BLACK PEPPER (PINCH)
	GRATED PARMESAN OR ROMANO CHEESE

METHOD: COOK YOUR PASTA UNTIL NEAR DONE. BEFORE DRAINING RESERVE ONE CUP OF PASTA WATER AND 2 CUPS OF PLAIN HOT WATER, DRAIN, AND SET ASIDE.

IF YOU ARE USING FRESH BROCCOLI THEN PREPARE IT BY CLEANING AND CHOPPING IT INTO BITE SIZED PIECES, OR SMALLER IF PREFERRED. THEN STEAM, OR, AND THIS IS A PERSONAL CHOICE, SAUTE UNTIL TENDER IN THE OLIVE OIL WITH THE GARLIC. I PREFER THE LATTER.

BLEND THE RESERVED LIQUID/HOT WATER, PASTA AND BROCCOLI. SIMMER FOR AN ADDITIONAL FIVE MINUTES OR UNTIL THE PASTA IS DONE, ADD A LITTLE OPTIONAL FRESHLY GROUND BLACK PEPPER, SPRINKLE WITH CHEESE AND SERVE.

RECOMMENDED PASTA: SHORT TUBES OR SMALL SHELLS.

PASTA WITH BEANS AND ESCAROLE

IF YOU LIKE ESCAROLE, YOU'LL ALSO ENJOY THE RECIPES IN CHAPTERS 5, 13 AND 14. THE CHICORY FAMILY IS WELL REPRESENTED IN ITALIAN COOKERY, WHERE YOU'LL ALSO FIND EXTENSIVE USE OF ENDIVE. THE ITALIANS LOVE THESE GREENS FOR THEIR TARTNESS, THERE ARE TIMES WHEN THAT TASTE IS A VERY SATISFYING ONE. THIS COMBINATION OF PASTA, LEGUMES AND TART GREENS IS PARTICULARLY SATISFYING.

INGREDIENTS:

1	HEAD ESCAROLE, WASHED AND SHREDDED
1	TEASPOON SALT
1/3	CUP OLIVE OIL
1	CLOVE GARLIC, CRUSHED
1/2	TEASPOON CRUSHED RED PEPPER
1	SMALL ONION, CHOPPED
1/4	CUP TOMATO SAUCE
	(SEASONED ITALIAN STYLE IF YOU WISH)
1	20 OUNCES CAN CANELLINI (WHITE KIDNEY BEANS)
2	CUPS PASTA

METHOD: FIRST, PUT ON YOUR PASTA WATER.

SECOND, ADD THE PASTA JUST AFTER YOU BEGIN COOKING THE ESCAROLE. COOK THE ESCAROLE IN 2 CUPS OF LIGHTLY SALTED WATER UNTIL TENDER (ABOUT 10 TO 15 MINUTES).

THIRD, WHILE YOUR ESCAROLE AND PASTA ARE COOKING, SAUTE THE GARLIC, CRUSHED RED PEPPER AND ONION, UNTIL EDGES OF THE ONION BEGIN TO BROWN, REMOVE AND DISCARD THE GARLIC. ADD ONION MIXTURE TO THE ESCAROLE. ALSO ADD THE TOMATO SAUCE AND UNDRAINED BEANS. BRING MIXTURE TO A BOIL. REMOVE FROM HEAT. ADD HOT DRAINED PASTA. COVER AND SET ASIDE TO STEEP AND MELD FOR 5 MINUTES, SERVE.

Continued on next page

ALTERNATE: SAUTE ENDIVE FOR 5 MINUTES IN THE OLIVE OIL.   ADD ONION, GARLIC AND PEPPER COOK UNTIL ENDIVE IS TENDER.   ADD ABOUT 1 CUP OF PASTA WATER, TOMATOES AND UNDRAINED BEANS.   COOK FOR 5 ADDITIONAL MINUTES. ADD PASTA, MIX WELL AND SERVE.

ADD MORE LIQUID IF NEEDED, BUT KEEP THE LIQUID LEVEL LOW, THIS IS NOT A SOUP. YOU MAY ADD, HOT WATER, PASTA WATER, OR WINE.

RECOMMENDED PASTA: SHORT TUBES, SHELLS OR 1/2 POUND THIN STRINGS.

PASTA IN A SOUPY SAUCE

(ANOTHER QUICKIE)

BECAUSE THERE ARE TIMES WHEN I ENJOY A LITTLE PLAIN PASTA, THAT IS WITH A SMALL AMOUNT OF SEASONED LIQUID OR BROTH, I CAN IMAGINE THAT OCCASIONALLY YOU TOO MIGHT LIKE IT THAT WAY. IF TRUE, THEN THE FOLLOWING SINGLE SERVING IS FOR YOU.

INGREDIENTS:
1 TABLESPOON OLIVE OIL OR BUTTER
1/4 CUP ONION, CHOPPED, OR
1 CLOVE GARLIC, CRUSHED
1 CUP WATER *

1 TO 2 TABLESPOONS PASTA FOR TINY VARIETIES, OR
1/2 TO 1 CUP PASTA FOR SMALL VARIETIES, OR
1 TO 2 CUPS PASTA FOR LARGE VARIETIES

OPTION: CHOPPED PARSLEY OR FRESHLY GROUND BLACK PEPPER. IF DESIRED YOU MAY USE GRATED CHEESE, BUT IT WILL MELT AND BECOME GUMMY.

METHOD: SAUTE ONION OR GARLIC IN THE OLIVE OIL/BUTTER FOR ABOUT 3 MINUTES. IF GARLIC IS USED, REMOVE AND DISCARD AT THIS POINT. ADD WATER AND HOT DRAINED PASTA, TO THE SEASONED OIL/BUTTER, BRING TO A BOIL, REMOVE FROM HEAT. ADD DESIRED OPTION, SERVE.

*SUBSTITUTIONS: BYPASS THE FIRST FOUR INGREDIENTS AND SUBSTITUTE ANY CANNED BROTH; CHICKEN, BEEF OR VEGETABLE FOR THE WATER. IF YOU ARE A SAVER OF LIQUIDS YOU'VE COOKED VEGETABLES IN, HERE'S YOUR CHANCE TO USE SOME OF THEM. ADD HOT, DRAINED PASTA TO THE BROTH OF YOUR CHOICE, SERVE. BROTH CUBES OR DRIED POWDER TYPES WILL FIRST BE ADDED TO 1 CUP WATER.

RECOMMENDED PASTA: TINY: PASTINA.
SMALL: ACINI DI PEPE, ORZO, TRIPOLINI.
LARGE: SEA SHELLS, ELBOWS, ELBOWS RIGATI, DITALINI, GNOCCHI, SHORT GEMELLI.

CHAPTER 19

FOR CARNIVORES ONLY:
SAUCES MADE MOSTLY FROM MEATS

HOT OFF THE PRESS!

INFORMATION ABOUT POSSIBLE REDUCTIONS OF SATURATED FAT FROM RED MEAT ARE OF INTEREST TO MANY PEOPLE. RECENT INFORMATION AT THE TIME THIS BOOK WAS BEING READIED FOR PRINT, WAS DETERMINED TO BE IMPORTANT ENOUGH TO BE INCLUDED FOR YOUR USE. THIS METHOD PROPOSES A SATURATED FAT REDUCTION FROM GROUND RED MEAT OF APPROXIMATELY SEVENTY PERCENT (70%). THE M.D. WHO CONDUCTED THE ACTUAL EXPERIMENTS STATED THAT THERE WAS NO APPRECIABLE LOSS OF FLAVOR WHEN USING HIS SUGGESTED METHOD. THE END RESULT IS HEALTHIER EATING, WITH NO DOWNSIDE. SO FOR WHAT IT'S WORTH, HERE IS THE SUGGESTION:

AFTER BROWNING, DRAIN AND THEN RINSE GROUND RED MEAT IN HOT WATER. USE AS DIRECTED BY THE RECIPE.

BRAISED MEAT SAUCE

AS THE CHAPTER TITLE IMPLIES, THIS IS A HIGH CALORIE SAUCE, BUT THEN AGAIN SO IS A CREAM SAUCE. THIS SAUCE WILL REQUIRE SIMMERING THE MEAT IN LIQUID; THAT'S WHAT BRAISING MEANS. AND BECAUSE OF THAT YOU HAVE GREAT OPPORTUNITIES FOR KITCHEN CREATIVITY, TRY ADDING A FAVORITE LIQUEUR, WHISKEY OR EVEN A SWEET WINE AS PART OF THE COOKING LIQUID.

INGREDIENTS:

1 1/2	POUNDS MEAT CHUNKS OR GROUND (PORK, BEEF, VEAL, LAMB, ALONE, COMBINE ONE OR MORE, OR ALL)
1/2	TEASPOON SALT
1/2	TEASPOON FRESHLY GROUND BLACK PEPPER
1/3	CUP OLIVE OIL
1	ONION, CHOPPED
2	CHIVES, MINCED
2	CUPS LIQUID (DRY WINE, OR WATER)
1/2	CUP GRATED ROMANO CHEESE

METHOD: CUT THE MEAT INTO SMALL PIECES (DON'T GRIND IT), ROLL MEAT IN SALT AND PEPPER, SET ASIDE. SAUTE THE ONION AND CHIVES IN THE OLIVE OIL FOR 2 MINUTES. ADD CHOPPED MEAT AND 1 CUP LIQUID. COVER AND SIMMER UNTIL NEARLY DRY. ADD REMAINING LIQUID AS NEEDED UNTIL MEAT IS DONE TO YOUR SATISFACTION, OR ABOUT 1 HOUR. WHEN SAUCE IS DONE, POUR SAUCE OVER PASTA. MIX WELL AND SERVE WITH GRATED CHEESE ON THE SIDE.

RECOMMENDED PASTA: MEDIUM TUBE TYPES, STRAIGHT OR DIAGONAL EDGES.

NORTHERN STYLE BEEF SAUCE

THIS SAUCE HAS MUCH OF THE SAME CHARACTER AS THE PRECEDING SAUCE, BUT THERE IS A SUBSTANTIAL DIFFERENCE AMONG INGREDIENTS, THEREFORE YOU WILL END UP WITH A SUBSTANTIAL TASTE DIFFERENCE.

INGREDIENTS:

2	TABLESPOON OLIVE OIL
2	TABLESPOONS BUTTER
2	CLOVES GARLIC, MINCED
1	POUND GROUND BEEF
1	TEASPOON SALT
1/2	TEASPOON FRESHLY GROUND BLACK PEPPER
2	CUPS BEEF BOUILLON OR STOCK
1	TABLESPOON CHOPPED PARSLEY

METHOD: SAUTE GARLIC AND GROUND BEEF TOGETHER IN THE OLIVE OIL AND BUTTER UNTIL BEEF IS WELL CRUMBLED AND LOOSE, ADD SALT AND PEPPER. COOK UNCOVERED FOR 15 MINUTES. ADD BROTH, BRING SAUCE TO A BOIL, REDUCE HEAT AND SIMMER FOR 10 MINUTES, REMOVE FROM HEAT. ADD PARSLEY. POUR SAUCE OVER PASTA. TOSS AND SERVE.

ALTERNATE: A SECOND SERVING SUGGESTION WOULD BE TO COAT THE COOKED PASTA WITH 4 TABLESPOONS OF BUTTER AND THEN COAT AGAIN WITH FRESHLY GROUND BLACK PEPPER AND 1/2 CUP GRATED ASIAGO CHEESE. SERVE WITH THE SAUCE ON THE TABLE. LET YOUR DINERS ADD A LARGE SPOONFUL OF THE SAUCE TO THEIR PASTA.

RECOMMENDED PASTA: HOLLOW STRINGS OR SHORT TUBE TYPES.

MINCED VEAL SAUCE

(ANOTHER QUICKIE)

THIS SAUCE IS SIMPLER THAN THE PRECEDING SAUCE, PARTLY BECAUSE IT HAS FEWER INGREDIENTS, BUT IT'S MAJOR ATTRIBUTE IS SPEED. IT IS NEAR READY AS SOON AS THE GROUND MEAT IS COOKED TO YOUR SATISFACTION. IF YOU'VE EVER SERVED IN THE MILITARY, I'M SURE THIS SAUCE WILL HAVE A FAMILIAR LOOK AND TASTE, SOMEWHAT AKIN TO CREAMED BEEF SERVED ON TOAST. WELL, THIS ISN'T IT, BUT IT'S CLOSE. THE REAL THING IS NEXT.

INGREDIENTS:
1 1/2   TABLESPOONS OLIVE OIL
1 1/2   TABLESPOONS BUTTER
1/2   MEDIUM ONION, CHOPPED
1   POUND GROUND VEAL
1/2   TEASPOON SALT
1/3   TEASPOON FRESHLY GROUND BLACK PEPPER
1   CUP WHIPPING CREAM
PINCH   OF SAFFRON
GRATED PARMESAN CHEESE

METHOD: SAUTE ONION FOR 2 MINUTES IN THE BUTTER AND OIL. RAISE HEAT TO MEDIUM HIGH, ADD GROUND VEAL, CRUMBLE WHILE COOKING. ADD SALT AND PEPPER, COOK 5 TO 6 ADDITIONAL MINUTES. ADD CREAM AND SAFFRON, BRING SAUCE TO A BOIL FOR 1 TO 2 ADDITIONAL MINUTES. REMOVE SAUCE FROM HEAT. POUR OVER PASTA. TOSS AND SERVE WITH GRATED CHEESE ON THE SIDE.

RECOMMENDED PASTA: NARROW RIBBON TYPES.

WE TRIED THIS SAUCE . . . AND

LOVED IT ( )
HATED IT ( )
MAYBE WE'LL TRY IT AGAIN ( )
WE'LL USE IT FOR UNWELCOME GUESTS ( )

CREAMED BEEF SAUCE

I OFFER THIS SAUCE OUT OF SHEER NOSTALGIA, BOTH FOR MYSELF AND ALL THE GUYS AND GALS WHO EVER PULLED A TOUR OF DUTY IN THE MILITARY. IT IS NOT TRULY, AT LEAST IN MY MEMORY, A PASTA SAUCE, ALTHOUGH IT COULD BE, AND THAT IS WHY IT'S HERE. IT IS THAT OLD STANDARD AND SUBSTANTIAL BREAKFAST OFFERING, CREAMED BEEF. IN THE MILITARY, IT WAS ALWAYS OFFERED ON TOAST. IT WAS A.K.A., IN IRREVERENT MILITARY SLANG AS S.O.S.

LONG BEFORE ENTERING THE MILITARY, I WAS KEENLY AWARE OF CREAMED BEEF ON TOAST AND MORE OFTEN THAN NOT IT WAS A LUNCHEON OR LIGHT DINNER OFFERING. THE BEEF USED BY MY FAMILY, WAS THE VARIETY KNOWN AS "CHIPPED BEEF", IT'S STILL AVAILABLE IN LITTLE GLASS JARS. I DIDN'T LIKE IT THEN AND I STILL DON'T. BUT, I DID COME TO ACCEPT CREAMED GROUND BEEF AS AN ACCEPTABLE SAUCE. AND, ON SOME COLD WINTER MORNINGS, I WILL STILL MAKE IT, AND SERVE IT ON BISCUITS OR TOAST. HOWEVER, WITH A LITTLE ADDED FLAVORING, IT READILY MAKES A VERY GOOD PASTA SAUCE. USE IT ON ELBOW MACARONI OR SEA SHELLS FOR A INTERESTING ENTREE. SERVE WITH SOME BRIGHT GREEN OR YELLOW VEGETABLES.

WHITE SAUCE IS USED EXTENSIVELY IN NORTHERN ITALIAN COOKERY, AND IS USED LARGELY AS A BAKING SAUCE FOR LARGE STUFFED PASTAS OR WITH SHORT TUBE TYPE MACARONI. IT FURTHER IS OFTEN USED AS A BASE FOR LOW PRICED AND LOW CALORIE CREAM SAUCES FOR FETTUCCINE (AS IN "ALFREDO"). THE LAST THREE INGREDIENTS ARE FOR THE WHITE SAUCE, IF YOU WISH TO USE A RICHER SAUCE, SEE "WHITE SAUCE" IN CHAPTER 3.

INGREDIENTS: 1 POUND GROUND BEEF
1/2 TEASPOON SALT
1/2 TEASPOON BLACK PEPPER

1 MEDIUM ONION MINCED (OMIT IF NOT FOR PASTA)
1 CLOVE GARLIC, MINCED (DITTO)

Continued on next page

481

3	TABLESPOONS BUTTER OR VEGETABLE OIL
3	TABLESPOONS FLOUR
2	CUPS MILK

METHOD: PLACE GROUND BEEF IN A SKILLET, OVER MEDIUM HEAT, ALLOWING IT TO COOK IN IT'S OWN FAT, STIR CONSTANTLY TO FULLY CRUMBLE. ADD SALT AND PEPPER (ALSO ONION AND GARLIC IF FOR PASTA). COOK FOR 10 MINUTES. REMOVE BEEF FROM HEAT. DRAIN OFF OIL AND DISCARD; SET BEEF ASIDE.

START SAUCE BY MAKING A ROUX; MELT BUTTER, WHEN HOT, ADD FLOUR AND WHISK IN. CONTINUE WHISKING WHILE COOKING THE ROUX FOR SEVERAL MINUTES. REMOVE FROM HEAT. ADD MILK SLOWLY WHILE WHISKING TO MAKE A SMOOTH SAUCE. RETURN SAUCE TO HEAT. BRING TO A NEAR BOIL, ADD COOKED GROUND BEEF, STIR CONSTANTLY WHILE BRINGING THE SAUCE TO A BOIL. REMOVE FROM HEAT, POUR SAUCE OVER PASTA. BLEND AND SERVE.

RECOMMENDED PASTA: SHORT OR MEDIUM TUBE, OR SHELL TYPES.

WE TRIED THIS SAUCE . . . AND

LOVED IT ( )
HATED IT ( )
MAYBE WE'LL TRY IT AGAIN ( )
WE'LL USE IT FOR UNWELCOME GUESTS ( )

STUFFED MEATBALL SAUCE

HERE IS AN INTERESTING APPLICATION OF THE MEATBALL. YOU'LL STUFF IT, COOK IT AND THEN CRUMBLE IT TO USE IT AS YOUR SAUCE. IN FACT, YOU MAY EVEN USE LEFT OVER MEATLOAF, IT WORKS EQUALLY AS WELL, AND IS EVEN BETTER IF YOUR MEATLOAF WAS MADE WITH ITALIAN SEASONINGS.

INGREDIENTS: 2 POUNDS LEAN GROUND BEEF
1 TEASPOON SALT
2 TABLESPOONS CHOPPED PARSLEY
1/2 POUND GORGONZOLA OR BLUE CHEESE
4 TABLESPOONS BUTTER

METHOD: MIX GROUND BEEF, SALT AND PARSLEY TOGETHER. ROLL MEATBALLS FROM THE MIX INTO 2 OUNCE MEATBALLS. PUSH INTO THE CENTER OF EACH MEATBALL ABOUT 1/2 TEASPOON OF YOUR CHEESE. COOK MEAT-BALLS IN THE BUTTER UNTIL WELL BROWNED ALL AROUND. REMOVE THE MEATBALLS AS THEY ARE COOKED, SET ASIDE.

(A SUGGESTION: TOSS YOUR PASTA WITH BUTTER OR OLIVE OIL TO COAT BEFORE TOSSING WITH THE MEAT SAUCE.)

WHEN ALL THE MEATBALLS ARE COOKED, DICE THEM OR CRUMBLE THEM WITH A FORK. RETURN MEAT TO THE PAN, COOK UNTIL HEATED THROUGH, ADD MORE BUTTER IF NEEDED. REMOVE FROM HEAT, POUR OVER PASTA, TOSS AND SERVE.

RECOMMENDED PASTA: SHELLS, THIN STRINGS, ROUND OR OVAL.

483

WE TRIED THIS SAUCE . . . AND

LOVED IT ( )
HATED IT ( )
MAYBE WE'LL TRY IT AGAIN ( )
WE'LL USE IT FOR UNWELCOME GUESTS ( )

BACON AND ROSEMARY SAUCE

BACON AND ROSEMARY MAKE A LOVELY COUPLE; ONE'S CRISP AND THE OTHER LITHE. I'M GOING TO GIVE YOU TWO CHOICES HERE TO COOK YOUR BACON (DOES THAT HAVE UNDERTONES?). COOK IT EITHER IN YOUR MICROWAVE UNTIL DONE TO YOUR SATISFACTION, OR, IN A SKILLET (IF CHOSEN, CUT INTO 1/2" STRIPS BEFORE FRYING). EITHER WAY, SAVE THE OIL, YOU'LL NEED SOME, IF NOT ALL OF IT.

INGREDIENTS:
12	OUNCES SUGAR CURED BACON
4	TABLESPOONS BUTTER
2	CLOVES GARLIC, CRUSHED
2	TEASPOONS FRESH ROSEMARY LEAVES, MINCED OR, 1 TEASPOON DRY, CRUSHED
1/2	CUP FRESHLY GRATED PARMESAN CHEESE

METHOD: COOK BACON, SAVE OIL, AND SET BOTH ASIDE. SAUTE GARLIC IN THE BUTTER, WHEN LIGHTLY GOLDEN, REMOVE AND DISCARD GARLIC. ADD ROSEMARY, AND COOK FOR 1 MINUTE. ADD BACON AND 1/2 CUP OF THE BACON OIL, BLEND WELL, REMOVE FROM HEAT. POUR SAUCE OVER PASTA. ADD GRATED CHEESE, TOSS AGAIN, SERVE.

RECOMMENDED PASTA: MEDIUM TUBE TYPES.

BACON AND BELL PEPPER SAUCE

BELL PEPPERS AND BACON SEEM TO ENJOY EACH OTHER'S COMPANY WHEN CAST TOGETHER, AND HERE'S A SAUCE THAT MAKES THAT COMBINATION SING.

INGREDIENTS:

2	RED BELL PEPPERS, SEEDED, CORED, DICED OR THINLY SLICED
1/2	POUND BACON, CUT INTO 1/2" PIECES
1/2	ONION, CHOPPED
1/4	TEASPOON SALT
1/4	TEASPOON FRESHLY GROUND BLACK PEPPER
1/3	CUP FRESHLY GRATED PARMESAN CHEESE
4	TABLESPOONS BUTTER
2	TABLESPOON CHOPPED PARSLEY

METHOD: SAUTE BACON AND ONION TOGETHER, UNTIL BACON IS COOKED TO YOUR SATISFACTION, OR SOMEWHAT CRISP AND ONION BEGINS TO BROWN AROUND THE EDGES. ADD THE DICED/SLICED PEPPERS, SALT AND BLACK PEPPER. CONTINUE COOKING FOR 6 MINUTES. REMOVE FROM HEAT. POUR SAUCE OVER PASTA. TOSS. ADD GRATED CHEESE, TOSS. ADD BUTTER AND PARSLEY. TOSS AGAIN, SERVE.

RECOMMENDED PASTA: MEDIUM TUBE OR CURLY TYPES.

485

CHICKEN LIVER SAUCE

I DON'T KNOW WHERE THIS SAUCE COMES FROM, BUT I SUSPECT THAT IT IS NORTHERN IN ORIGIN. A CHICKEN LIVER SAUCE WITH TOMATOES IS ALSO AVAILABLE IN THIS BOOK, SEE CHAPTER 9.

INGREDIENTS:

4	SLICES BACON, MINCED
1	SHALLOT, CHOPPED
2	TABLESPOONS OLIVE OIL
2	TABLESPOONS BUTTER
1/2	CLOVE GARLIC, MINCED
1/4	POUND GROUND BEEF
1	TEASPOON SALT
1/2	TEASPOON FRESHLY GROUND BLACK PEPPER
1/2	POUND CHICKEN LIVERS, CHOPPED OR MINCED
1/4	TEASPOON DRY SAGE
1	TEASPOON TOMATO PASTE
1/4	WHITE WINE (YOUR CHOICE)

METHOD: COOK BACON, DRAIN, CRUMBLE AND SET ASIDE. SAUTE SHALLOT IN OLIVE OIL AND BUTTER UNTIL TRANSPARENT. ADD GARLIC AND GROUND BEEF, COOK UNTIL COLOR IS GONE, ADD SALT, PEPPER AND LIVER, COOK UNTIL LIVER CHANGES COLOR. ADD SAGE, TOMATO PASTE, WINE AND BACON. COVER AND SIMMER FOR 10 MINUTES. POUR SAUCE OVER PASTA. TOSS AND SERVE.

RECOMMENDED PASTA: RIBBON TYPES, NARROW OR WIDE.

SNAIL SAUCE

IF YOU OCCASIONALLY EAT ESCARGOT WHEN YOU DINE OUT, THIS SAUCE IS FOR YOU. IT COMES FROM THE BASILICATA REGION, THAT'S BETWEEN THE HEEL AND THE TOE OF THE ITALIAN BOOT. I SUSPECT IT'S A HANGER-ON'ER FROM THE DAYS OF THE FRENCH OCCUPATION OF SOUTHERN ITALY AND SICILY.

INGREDIENTS:

3	DOZEN SNAILS, CANNED OR FRESH, CHOPPED
6	OYSTERS, CANNED OR FRESH, CHOPPED
1/4	CUP OLIVE OIL
3	TABLESPOONS CHOPPED PARSLEY
2	CLOVES GARLIC, MINCED
1	HOT CHILI PEPPER, SLICED
4	CHIVE ONIONS, MINCED
1	SMALL ONION, SLICED
4	PEAR TOMATOES (B/P/C)
1/2	CUP SLICED MUSHROOMS
	SALT TO TASTE
1/2	TEASPOON FRESHLY GROUND BLACK PEPPER
1/4	CUP GRATED PARMESAN CHEESE

METHOD: SAUTE THE PARSLEY, GARLIC, HOT PEPPER, CHIVES AND ONION FOR 3 MINUTES. ADD SNAILS AND OYSTERS, COOK AN ADDITIONAL 3 MINUTES. ADD TOMATOES, MUSHROOM, SALT AND PEPPER. COOK OVER LOW HEAT FOR 20 MINUTES. POUR SAUCE OVER PASTA. TOSS AND SERVE WITH GRATED CHEESE ON THE SIDE.

RECOMMENDED PASTA: THIN STRING TYPES.

ROMAN STYLE VEGETABLES AND LIVER SAUCE

IF YOU LIKE LIVER AND ONIONS, THIS SAUCE MAY REACH OUT AND TOUCH YOU. ITALIAN STYLE LIVER AND ONIONS IS FOR ALL PRACTICAL PURPOSES, AMERICAN STYLE LIVER AND ONIONS, THIS SAUCE CARRIES IT ONE STEP FURTHER.

INGREDIENTS:

1	POUND LIVER (BEEF OR CALF)
1/4	CUP BUTTER
1	CUP SLICED MUSHROOMS
1	ONION, THINLY SLICED FORM TOP TO BOTTOM
1	CARROT, COARSELY SHREDDED
1	CELERY RIB, MINCED
1/2	MARSALA WINE
1	TEASPOON SALT
1/4	TEASPOON FRESHLY GROUND BLACK PEPPER
1/2	CUP GRATED ROMANO OR ASIAGO CHEESE

METHOD: CUT THE LIVER SLICES INTO SLICES 1/8" INCH WIDE, OR, CUT INTO 1/4" INCH SLICES AND THEN DICE.

SAUTE LIVER IN BUTTER UNTIL COLOR IS CHANGED, (ABOUT 3 MINUTES) REMOVE LIVER FROM PAN AND SET ASIDE. SAUTE MUSHROOMS, ONION, CARROT AND CELERY IN REMAINING BUTTER UNTIL ONION IS TRANS-PARENT. ADD WINE, SALT AND PEPPER, COOK UNTIL LIQUID IS REDUCED BY ONE HALF. ADD LIVER TO HEAT THROUGH. REMOVE FROM HEAT. POUR SAUCE OVER PASTA. TOSS AND SERVE WITH GRATED CHEESE ON THE SIDE.

RECOMMENDED PASTA: STRINGS, ROUND, OVAL, TWISTED.

VEAL SAUCE

YOU'VE GOT SOME LATITUDE WITH THIS SAUCE, IF YOU WISH TO DO IT EXPENSIVELY, BUY A VEAL STEAK AND DICE IT INTO 1/4" CUBES.   TO DO IT INEXPENSIVELY, USE GROUND VEAL.

INGREDIENTS:

1	POUND VEAL (YOUR CHOICE)
3	TABLESPOONS OLIVE OIL
1	ONION, CHOPPED
3	TABLESPOONS FLOUR
1	TEASPOON SALT
1/4	TEASPOON FRESHLY GROUND BLACK PEPPER
1	CUP CHICKEN BROTH
PINCH	DRY OREGANO
1	TABLESPOON LEMON JUICE
1/3	CUP GRATED PARMESAN CHEESE

METHOD: IF USING VEAL STEAK, DREDGE IN FLOUR SEASONED WITH SALT AND PEPPER.   IF GROUND, MIX WITH SALT, PEPPER AND ONLY 2 TEASPOONS FLOUR, FOLLOW NEXT STEP.

COOK THE VEAL AND ONION TOGETHER UNTIL VEAL IS BROWNED.   ADD CHICKEN BROTH, OREGANO AND LEMON JUICE.   SIMMER FOR 10 MINUTES OR UNTIL SAUCE IS SLIGHTLY THICKENED.   REMOVE FROM HEAT.   POUR SAUCE OVER PASTA.   TOSS.   ADD CHEESE.   TOSS AGAIN, SERVE.

RECOMMENDED PASTA: THIN STRING TYPES.

WE TRIED THIS SAUCE . . . AND

LOVED IT ( )
HATED IT ( )
MAYBE WE'LL TRY IT AGAIN ( )
WE'LL USE IT FOR UNWELCOME GUESTS ( )

MILANESE STYLE VEAL SAUCE

THERE ARE MANY INGREDIENTS IN THIS SAUCE, BUT IT WILL COOK IN ABOUT 1/2 HOUR ONCE YOU'VE GOT THEM ALL PREPARED. LEAVE THIS ONE FOR A WHEN YOU'RE NOT RUSHED.

INGREDIENTS:
2	POUNDS VEAL (ANY MEATY CUT)
1/2	CUP FLOUR
1	TEASPOON SALT
4	TABLESPOONS BUTTER
4	TABLESPOON OLIVE OIL
1/2	TEASPOON FRESHLY GROUND BLACK PEPPER
2	ONIONS, CHOPPED
1	CARROT, PARED AND DICED
1	CELERY STALK, THINLY CHOPPED
PINCH	DRY ROSEMARY, CRUSHED
1/2	CUP TOMATO JUICE OR TOMATO SAUCE
1	CUPS CHICKEN BROTH
1/2	CUP WATER
2	ANCHOVY FILLETS, MINCED
1	CLOVE GARLIC, MINCED
1	TABLESPOON GRATED LEMON ZEST
2	TABLESPOONS CHOPPED PARSLEY

METHOD: DREDGE VEAL IN FLOUR SEASONED WITH SALT AND PEPPER. ADD VEAL TO HOT OLIVE OIL AND SAUTE UNTIL EVENLY BROWNED. ADD BUTTER, ONIONS, CARROT, CELERY, ROSEMARY, TOMATO JUICE, CHICKEN BROTH AND WATER. BRING SAUCE TO A BOIL, REDUCE HEAT, COVER AND SIMMER FOR 30 MINUTES. ADD ANCHOVY, GARLIC, LEMON ZEST AND PARSLEY. COOK AN ADDITIONAL 5 MINUTES. REMOVE FROM HEAT. POUR SAUCE OVER PASTA. TOSS AND SERVE.

RECOMMENDED PASTA: MEDIUM TUBE TYPES, SQUARE OR DIAGONAL CUT ENDS.

PORK AND EGG SAUCE

THIS ONE SOUNDS LIKE IT MIGHT BE CHINESE, BUT IT'S NOT. IF ANYTHING, IT IS NORTHERN AND PROBABLY VENETIAN. THE PORK CAN BE ROLLED INTO TINY MEATBALLS OR IN THE SHAPE OF VERY SMALL SAUSAGES, YOUR CHOICE! FIRST THINGS FIRST, SET EGGS OUT EARLY, AND ALLOW TO RISE TO ROOM TEMPERATURE.

INGREDIENTS:

1/2	POUND GROUND PORK (UNSEASONED)
2	OUNCES SALT PORK, MINCED
2	WHOLE EGGS
PINCH	CAYENNE PEPPER
1/4	CUP GRATED PARMESAN CHEESE
1	TEASPOON GRATED LEMON RIND (ZEST ONLY)
2	TABLESPOONS BUTTER
2	TABLESPOONS OLIVE OIL

METHOD: SHAPE THE GROUND PORK AND SAUTE WITH THE SALT PORK UNTIL EVENLY BROWNED. IN A SEPARATE BOWL, LIGHTLY BEAT EGGS, CAYENNE, CHEESE AND LEMON PEEL, SET ASIDE.

TOSS COOKED AND DRAINED PASTA WITH BUTTER, OLIVE OIL AND THE PORK. WHEN BUTTER IS MELTED, ADD EGG MIXTURE AND TOSS AGAIN UNTIL EGGS SET. SERVE.

RECOMMENDED PASTA: OVAL STRING TYPES.

PARMA STYLE HAM SAUCE

(ANOTHER QUICKIE)

THIS SAUCE IS FROM PARMA, ITALY, NOT PARMA, OHIO. PARMA JUST HAPPENS TO BE THE HOME OF ITALY'S GREATEST HAM (PROSCIUTTO DI PARMA), AS WELL AS, THE NEAR NATIONAL CHEESE FOR NORTHERN AND CENTRAL ITALY, (PARMIGIANO REGGIANO) PARMESAN TO YOU AND ME. THIS IS A SIMPLE HAM SAUCE, AND WHILE IT MAY BE SIMPLE, IT IS ALSO EXPENSIVE. THE PRICE OF PROSCUITTO VARIES BETWEEN $6.00 AND $25.00 DOLLARS PER POUND. IF THERE ARE NO SUPER MARKET DISCOUNT STORES IN YOUR AREA WITH LARGE DELI'S, THINK IN TERMS OF THE HIGHER PRICE. STILL, THERE MAY BE AN OCCASION WHEN YOU'LL WANT TO TRY IT.

INGREDIENTS:
4	OUNCES SWEET BUTTER
8	OUNCES PROSCUITTO, JULIENNED
	FRESHLY GROUND BLACK PEPPER

METHOD: SAUTE THE HAM IN THE BUTTER UNTIL IT BEGINS TO CRISP. REMOVE FROM HEAT. POUR SAUCE OVER YOUR PASTA. TOSS, ADD BLACK PEPPER TO TASTE. TOSS AGAIN, SERVE.

RECOMMENDED PASTA: THIN STRING TYPES OR RIBBON TYPES.

HAM AND BROCCOLI SAUCE

IN ITALY THIS SAUCE WOULD BE MADE WITH PROSCUITTO AND CALLED, "SAN MARINO STYLE". IF YOU WISH TO USE PROSCUITTO, GO FOR IT. I WILL SUGGEST THAT YOU MAY DO EQUALLY AS WELL WITH COPPACOLLA, OR COOKED COTTAGE HAM (BOTH ARE THE SAME CUT OF PORK WITH DIFFERENT PROCESSING), CANADIAN BACON, OR EVEN A WESTPHALIAN STYLE HAM. I BELIEVE AMERICAN HAM IS NOT TASTE COMPATIBLE WITH PASTA, SO, UNLESS YOU TRULY LOVE THE TASTE OF AMERICAN HAM AND WILL EAT IT WITH ANYTHING, USE ONE OF THE RECOMMENDED TYPES. YOU'LL COMPLETE THIS PREPARATION IN "COUNTRY STYLE", THAT'S IN THE SAUCE PAN.

INGREDIENTS:

1	10 OUNCE PACKAGE FROZEN CHOPPED BROCCOLI
1/2	POUND COPPACOLLA, SLICED AND CHOPPED
4	TABLESPOONS BUTTER
1/2	CUP FRESHLY GRATED PARMESAN CHEESE

METHOD: STEAM THE BROCCOLI, WHILE SIMULTANEOUSLY SAUTEING THE COPPACOLLA IN BUTTER. WHEN BROCCOLI IS DONE, DRAIN AND ADD TO THE COPPACOLLA, STIR TO COAT. ADD DRAINED PASTA TO THE COPPACOLLA/BROCCOLI. TOSS WELL. ADD GRATED CHEESE. TOSS AGAIN, SERVE.

RECOMMENDED PASTA: FANCY TYPES.

SAUSAGE AND CHEESE SAUCE

THIS IS A VERY SIMPLE SAUCE AND QUITE QUICK. YOU MAY USE EITHER A HOT OR SWEET VARIETY OF ITALIAN SAUSAGE IN THIS SAUCE, SO CHOOSE YOUR FAVORITE. AS AN OPTION, YOU MAY WISH TO ADD SOME FRESH, MINCED, LONG GREEN MILDLY HOT PEPPER.

INGREDIENTS:
1	POUND ITALIAN SAUSAGE, SKINNED AND CRUMBLED
2	TABLESPOONS OLIVE OIL OR BUTTER
1/3	CUP FRESHLY GRATED CHEESE, ROMANO OR ASIAGO

METHOD: COOK THE SAUSAGE IN ITS OWN FAT UNTIL IT BEGINS TO BROWN, STIRRING FREQUENTLY TO KEEP IT CRUMBLED. DRAIN OFF SAUSAGE OIL AS IT ACCUMULATES. WHEN SAUSAGE HAS BROWNED, ADD THE OLIVE OIL, BLEND WELL AND REMOVE FROM HEAT. POUR SAUCE OVER PASTA. TOSS, ADD GRATED CHEESE. TOSS AGAIN, SERVE.

RECOMMENDED PASTA: CURLY TYPES.

SHREDDED MEAT SAUCE

(ANOTHER QUICKIE)

THAT'S SHREDDED MEAT, NOT WHEAT, THIS IS NO CEREAL. IT SHOULDN'T BE HARD TO TELL BY THE NAME THAT THIS IS AN ALL AMERICAN SAUCE, THE RESULT OF EXPERIMENTATION BY AN AVERAGE AMERICAN HOUSE WIFE. I WAS GIVEN THE RECIPE BY MY FRIEND "DEL" WHO SWIPED IT FROM HIS SISTER. SHE'S THE BETTER COOK. SO MUCH FOR PLEASANTRIES, ON TO THE SAUCE.

YOU WILL BE USING A PREPARED CANNED MEAT AND IT MUST BE AT ROOM TEMPERATURE.

INGREDIENTS:
1	12 OUNCE CAN CORNED BEEF
1/3	CUP OLIVE OIL
1/4	CUP CHOPPED PARSLEY
1/2	CLOVE GARLIC, MINCED

METHOD: WITH A FORK, CRUMBLE THE CORNED BEEF UNTIL IT IS IN SHREDS, DO NOT MASH IT TO A PASTE. PLACE THE BEEF INTO A BOWL. ADD THE REMAINING INGREDIENTS. STIR AND TOSS TO BLEND WELL. ADD PASTA. TOSS AND SERVE.

RECOMMENDED PASTA: STRINGS OR MEDIUM TUBES.

CHAPTER 20

SAUCES MADE FROM FOWL

(DOES THAT MEAN UNDERHANDED?)

IN ITALIAN COOKERY, AS IN AMERICAN, THERE ARE HUNDREDS OF RECIPES FOR SERVING CHICKEN. MANY ITALIAN RECIPES CALL FOR THE CHICKEN TO BE BROWNED, THEN SIMMERED IN A TOMATO BASE OR CREAM BASE. A THIRD STEP, IF REQUIRED, WOULD INCLUDE A PERIOD OF BAKING. THE CHICKEN WOULD THEN BE SERVED EITHER AS AN ENTREE WITH SOME OF THE SAUCE BEING USED ON A PASTA, OR AS FREQUENTLY DONE IN THE UNITED STATES, THE CHICKEN AND PASTA WOULD BE SERVED TOGETHER. MOST OF THOSE RECIPES ARE BEYOND THE SCOPE OF THIS BOOK. THE FEW SAUCES I'VE ELECTED TO KEEP AND OFFER YOU ARE MORE IN KEEPING WITH THE PREMISE OF THIS BOOK, PASTA SAUCES ONLY.

IF I MAY OFFER A SUGGESTION. IN KEEPING WITH THE CURRENT THINKING BY HEALTH AUTHORITIES, REMOVE AND DISCARD ALL THE CHICKEN SKIN PRIOR TO PREPARING ANY OF THE FOLLOWING RECIPES.

CHICKEN AND TOMATO SAUCE

HERE IS A SAUCE THAT CAN MAKE GOOD USE OF LEFT OVER CHICKEN. IF YOU DON'T HAVE LEFT OVER CHICKEN, COOK SEVERAL MEATY PIECES IN A SMALL AMOUNT OF WATER UNTIL TENDER. YOU'LL USE THE MEAT AND THE BROTH.

INGREDIENTS:

2	CUPS CHICKEN MEAT, DICED
2	CUPS CHICKEN BROTH, FRESH MADE, CANNED OR FROM CUBES
3	TABLESPOONS OLIVE OIL
2	ONIONS, CHOPPED
3	CLOVES GARLIC, MINCED
4	RIBS CELERY, CHOPPED
1	TABLESPOON PARSLEY, CHOPPED
1	16 OUNCE CAN TOMATOES, BLENDERIZED
1	6 OUNCE CAN TOMATO PASTE
1/2	TEASPOON SALT

METHOD: BONE AND DICE THE CHICKEN, SET ASIDE. SAUTE ONION, GARLIC AND CELERY UNTIL ONION IS TRANSPARENT. ADD TOMATOES, TOMATO PASTE, BROTH, CHICKEN AND SALT. BRING SAUCE TO A BOIL, REDUCE HEAT TO SIMMER, LOOSELY COVER AND COOK FOR 1 HOUR. POUR SAUCE OVER PASTA, TOSS AND SERVE.

RECOMMENDED PASTA: STRING TYPES.

FARMER'S STYLE SAUCE

I HAVE NO IDEA WHY THIS IS CALLED FARMER'S STYLE ANYMORE THAN WHY A SIMILAR METHOD IS CALLED CACCIATORE (HUNTER'S STYLE). WITH THIS SAUCE YOU'LL COOK AND THEN BONE THE CHICKEN (YOU COULD ALSO BONE THE CHICKEN BEFORE COOKING) RETURN THE MEAT TO THE TOMATO BASE AND THEN OVER THE PASTA. IF THAT'S MORE WORK THAN YOU WANT TO TAKE ON, LEAVE THE CHICKEN PIECES WHOLE.

INGREDIENTS: 6 TO 8   PIECES OF CHICKEN, (YOUR CHOICE) SKINNED

               SALT

2	TABLESPOONS BUTTER
2	OUNCES PROSCUITTO
1	CLOVE GARLIC, MINCED
	FRESHLY GROUND BLACK PEPPER TO TASTE
2	16 OUNCE CANS PEAR TOMATOES (LEAVE 'EM WHOLE)
1/4	TEASPOON CRUSHED ROSEMARY

IF YOU WISH, BONE AND DICE OR SLICE THE CHICKEN BEFORE SAUTEING. IT'S VERY EASY TO DO, NEATER TOO.

METHOD: SALT THE CHICKEN. SAUTE IN THE BUTTER, CHICKEN, PROSCIUTTO, GARLIC AND PEPPER. WHEN CHICKEN IS NICELY BROWNED, ADD TOMATOES AND ROSEMARY. COVER AND SIMMER FOR 1-1/2 HOURS. REMOVE CHICKEN, BONE AND DICE OR PULL INTO SHREDS, RETURN CHICKEN TO THE SAUCE. POUR OVER PASTA. TOSS AND SERVE.

RECOMMENDED PASTA: STRING TYPES.

WE TRIED THIS SAUCE . . . AND

CHICKEN AND BLACK PEPPER SAUCE

IF BLACK PEPPER HAS A TASTE THAT WHETS YOUR APPETITE, YOU'LL LIKE THIS SAUCE. BUT, BEWARE, CHICKEN IS MILD, BLACK PEPPER IS NOT AND THE OVER ALL TASTE WILL BE THAT OF BLACK PEPPER.

INGREDIENTS:
2   CUPS OF DICED CHICKEN MEAT, FRESH OR COOKED
1/4   POUND BUTTER
1/2   TEASPOON SALT
1   TEASPOON FRESHLY GROUND BLACK PEPPER

METHOD: SALT THE CHICKEN, THEN SAUTE THE CHICKEN IN BUTTER UNTIL COOKED TO YOUR LIKING, OR, ABOUT 20 MINUTES. ADD THE BLACK PEPPER AND BLEND WELL. REMOVE FROM HEAT. POUR CHICKEN SAUCE OVER YOUR PASTA, TOSS AND SERVE.

RECOMMENDED PASTA: RIBBON TYPES.

COUNTRY STYLE CHICKEN AND CREAM SAUCE

IF YOU'VE READ THE AUTHOR'S NOTES, DEFINED AS "INFORMATION YOU CAN'T LIVE WITHOUT", YOU'LL KNOW THAT COUNTRY STYLE MEANS YOU WILL FINISH COOKING THE SAUCE AND PASTA TOGETHER IN ONE PAN.

THIS SAUCE HAS ALL THE EARMARKS OF SOMEONE WITH NO TEETH WANTING TO EAT CHICKEN AND PASTA. INTERESTINGLY, WHILE I'VE NEVER TRIED IT, IT WOULDN'T SURPRISE ME TO FIND THAT YOU COULD USE A COUPLE JARS OF STRAINED CHICKEN BABY FOOD FOR THIS SAUCE. IF YOU HAVE SOME AT HOME, TRY IT, YOU MIGHT LIKE IT. OR, BUY GROUND CHICKEN (NOW THAT IT'S AS READILY AVAILABLE AS GROUND BEEF), MEASURE AS PER THE RECIPE AND USE.
THIS IS THE FIRST OF TWO RECIPES IN THIS CHAPTER CALLING FOR THE CHICKEN TO BE FINELY GROUND INTO A PASTE AND THEN BLENDED WITH SEVERAL ADDITIONAL INGREDIENTS TO CREATE THE SAUCE. IF YOU LIKE THE IDEA, YOU'LL ALSO FIND THIS SAME METHOD OF MAKING A PASTE OF THE MEAT IN CHAPTER 19 OF THIS BOOK.

P.S. THERE IS NO REASON THAT YOU COULD NOT USE TURKEY IN PLACE OF THE CHICKEN, AND GROUND TURKEY IS BEGGING FOR GOOD RECIPES.

INGREDIENTS:

3/4	CUP COOKED OR FRESH CHICKEN MEAT, DICED
4	OUNCES BUTTER
2	EGG YOLKS, BEATEN
1	CUP WHIPPING CREAM
1/2	CUP HALF AND HALF
1/2	TEASPOON SALT
1/2	TEASPOON FRESHLY GROUND BLACK PEPPER
1	CUP FRESHLY GRATED PARMESAN CHEESE

Continued on next page

METHOD: GRIND OR PROCESS THE CHICKEN IN A FOOD PROCESSOR UNTIL IT IS A PASTE.   BLEND THE PASTE WITH THE BUTTER, EGG YOLKS, WHIPPING CREAM, HALF AND HALF, SALT AND PEPPER, STIR IN 1/2 THE GRATED CHEESE.   BRING THE MIXTURE TO A LOW BOIL AND COOK FOR ABOUT 15 MINUTES.   ADD YOUR COOKED AND DRAINED PASTA TO THE SAUCE PAN AND CONTINUE COOKING FOR ABOUT 3 MINUTES.   REMOVE FROM HEAT AND SERVE, WITH REMAINING CHEESE ON THE SIDE.

RECOMMENDED PASTA: MEDIUM TUBE TYPES.

MARSALA CREAMED CHICKEN SAUCE

THIS SAUCE TOO IS A MEAT PASTE SAUCE, I SUSPECT IT TO BE NORTHERN, ALTHOUGH THERE ARE HINTS OF SOUTHERN ORIGINS.

THERE IS NO REASON THAT YOU COULD NOT USE GROUND TURKEY INSTEAD OF CHICKEN, EITHER AS A TASTE CHANGE, OR BECAUSE YOU PREFER IT.

INGREDIENTS:

2	SLICES FRESH OR STALE BREAD
1/2	CUP MILK
2	TABLESPOONS BUTTER
3/4	CUP GROUND CHICKEN
	OR, 6 OUNCES CHICKEN MEAT, MINCED
1/2	CUP CHICKEN BROTH
PINCH	NUTMEG
1/2	TEASPOON SALT
1/4	CUP MARSALA WINE (SCANT MEASURE)
1	EGG YOLK, BEATEN
1	TABLESPOON LEMON JUICE

METHOD: SOAK BREAD IN THE MILK, REMOVE AND SQUEEZE WELL. DISCARD REMAINING MILK. SAUTE GROUND CHICKEN, 1 TABLESPOON CHICKEN BROTH, NUTMEG AND SALT IN BUTTER FOR 5 MINUTES. ADD MOIST BREAD, REMAINING CHICKEN BROTH AND MARSALA. BRING SAUCE TO A BOIL, REDUCE HEAT AND SIMMER FOR 15 MINUTES. REMOVE SAUCE FROM HEAT. SLOWLY ADD EGG YOLK AND BLEND IN WELL. ADD LEMON JUICE AND BLEND IN WELL. POUR SAUCE OVER PASTA. TOSS AND SERVE.

RECOMMENDED PASTA: SHORT TUBE TYPES. (USE ONLY 8 OUNCES).

CHICKEN AND PEAS SAUCE

THIS IS PROBABLY A NORTHERN RECIPE, IT IS A NICE BLENDING OF WHITE CHICKEN MEAT AND GREEN PEAS TOSSED WITH YOUR PASTA. IF YOU PREFER NOT TO COOK FRESH CHICKEN PIECES, YOU MAY USE ANY LEFTOVER CHICKEN, IT WILL EXPEDITE (I THINK THAT MEANS HURRIES?) YOUR PREPARATION.

INGREDIENTS:

1/2	TEASPOON SALT
1	CUP DICED CHICKEN MEAT
2	TABLESPOONS OLIVE OIL
2	TABLESPOONS WHITE OR PINK WINE
1	CUP FROZEN PEAS
2	TABLESPOONS GRATED PARMESAN OR ASIAGO CHEESE
1	EGG, LIGHTLY BEATEN

METHOD: SALT CHICKEN, THEN SAUTE CHICKEN IN THE OLIVE OIL UNTIL THE CHICKEN BEGINS TO COLOR. ADD WINE. COVER AND SIMMER FOR 5 MINUTES. ADD PEAS, CONTINUE SIMMERING FOR AN ADDITIONAL 5 MINUTES. REMOVE FROM HEAT. POUR SAUCE OVER HOT DRAINED PASTA. ADD CHEESE, AND TOSS. ADD BEATEN EGG AND TOSS AGAIN. SERVE.

RECOMMENDED PASTA: THIN STRING TYPES.

DUCK SAUCE

WE'VE ALL HEARD OF DUCK SOUP AND SINCE THE MARX BROTHERS ARE NOT HERE TO SERVE IT UP, WE'LL MOVE OVER TO DUCK SAUCE. THIS IS A SAUCE THAT I SUSPECT ORIGINATED IN LIGURIA, WHERE FRENCH INFLUENCES ON ITALIAN COOKERY ARE MORE COMMON THAN ELSEWHERE IN ITALY. THE FRENCH SEEM TO USE DUCK MORE OFTEN IN COOKING THAN ITALIANS, BUT THEN AGAIN, THE AUSTRIANS AND YUGOSLAVIANS ALSO EAT MORE DUCK THAN ITALIANS. WHATEVER THE CASE, HERE IS A PASTA SAUCE, WITH DUCK AS THE DOMINANT INGREDIENT.

NOT MUCH DUCK MEAT IS NEEDED FOR THIS SAUCE, ONLY 1 CUP, BUT THEN AGAIN, THERE IS NOT MUCH MORE THAN ONE CUP OF MEAT IN A WHOLE DUCK, THE REST IS A VERY FAT LADEN SKIN AND BONE. YOU MIGHT CONSIDER USING THIS RECIPE WHEN YOU'VE HAD ROAST DUCK, AND NOW HAVE LEFT-OVERS.

INGREDIENTS:	1	CUP CHOPPED DUCK MEAT (MORE IF YOU HAVE IT)
	1	DUCK LIVER (IF YOU STILL HAVE IT)
	2	TABLESPOONS BACON FAT, OR DUCK FAT
	1	STALK CELERY, FINELY CHOPPED
	1	ONION, CHOPPED
	1	28 OUNCE CAN PEAR TOMATOES, BLENDERIZED
	1/2	CUP PINK WINE
	1/4	CHOPPED PARSLEY
	1	TEASPOON CHOPPED FRESH THYME, OR
	1/4	TEASPOON DRY THYME, CRUSHED
	1/4	TEASPOON GROUND NUTMEG

METHOD: BRIEFLY SAUTE THE DUCK, (DUCK LIVER) ONION AND CELERY IN THE BACON FAT UNTIL THE VEGETABLES JUST BEGIN TO WILT. ADD TOMATOES, WINE, THYME AND NUTMEG. BRING SAUCE TO A BOIL, REDUCE HEAT AND COOK UNCOVERED FOR 20 MINUTE., POUR SAUCE OVER PASTA. TOSS AND SERVE.

RECOMMENDED PASTA: RIBBON TYPES.

CHAPTER 21

SAUCES MADE FROM FRUIT AND FRUIT JUICES

FRUIT IS SUCH AN ENORMOUS PART OF THE ITALIAN LIFE-STYLE AND IT'S CUISINE, THAT IT WAS INEVITABLE AT SOME POINT SOMEONE WOULD DISCOVER FRUIT FLAVORS THAT COULD BE PAIRED WITH PASTA. WELL, THIS IS THE CHAPTER THAT EXPLAINS IT, AND BRINGS IT TO YOU. CONSIDER THAT ITALY IS A MAJOR PRODUCER OF CITRUS, ASSORTED FRUITS, GRAPES AND NUTS. ALL ARE WELL INTEGRATED INTO ITALIAN COOKERY. THERE IS AN EXTENSIVE USE IN ICES AND ICE CREAMS (INVENTED IN ITALY), PASTRIES, BREADS, COOKIES AND CAKES, THEY ARE USED TO COMPLIMENT MEATS, FISH AND FOWL. THEY ARE ALSO BLENDED INTO HOT AND COLD BEVERAGES, ARE FEATURED IN SALADS, BLENDED INTO MANY MEAT AND DESSERT SAUCES, ARE ALMOST ALWAYS OFFERED AS AN OUT OF HAND FINISH TO A MEAL. IN WINES AND LIQUEURS THEY ARE THE PRIME INGREDIENT. ALL WINES ARE MADE FROM GRAPES OR FRUITS, MOST LIQUEURS ARE MADE FROM FRUITS OR NUTS, (WHISKIES AND BEERS ARE MADE FROM GRAINS OR VEGETABLES).

THERE ARE SEVERAL PASTA SAUCES USING LEMON AND MAY BE FOUND WITH THE CREAM SAUCES, IN CHAPTER 3.

WHILE THERE ARE AT PRESENT ONLY A FEW ACTUAL FRUIT SAUCES FOR PASTA, AND DITTO FOR FRUIT FLAVORED PASTAS, I'M SURE MORE ARE COMING. LIKE ANY IDEA OR TASTE WHOSE TIME HAS ARRIVED, NOTHING WILL STAND IN THE WAY OF CREATIVE COOKS DOING THEIR THING, CREATING. I'M SURE THAT MANY FRUITS WILL LEND THEM SELVES TO SOME MARVELOUS CREATION THAT BECOMES A SAUCE FOR PASTA. TWO, STRIKE ME IN PARTICULAR AS I WRITE THIS, PLUMS (THE DRIER VARIETIES) AND FIGS. PLUMS AND FIGS BOTH STRIKE ME AS HAVING THE CORRECT FLAVOR TO BE OFFERED UP AND SERVED AS EITHER A HOT OR COLD ENTREE.

IF YOU MAKE YOUR OWN PASTA, YOU MAY WISH TO TRY REPLACING THE LIQUID WITH FRUIT JUICE AND/OR PART PUREED FRUIT. THOSE TRIED AND FOUND ACCEPTABLE ARE: ORANGE AND STRAWBERRY. EITHER MAY BE SAUCED WITH A SIMPLE SWEET BUTTER AND GRATED CHEESE, WITH OR WITHOUT WHIPPING CREAM. BE CREATIVE, TRY CITRUS, OR CANTALOUPE, OR OTHER MELONS THAT YOU ENJOY.

WE TRIED THIS SAUCE . . . AND

LOVED IT (   )
HATED IT (   )
MAYBE WE'LL TRY IT AGAIN (   )
WE'LL USE IT FOR UNWELCOME GUESTS (   )

Fresh Apricot Sauce

(Another Quickie)

FRESH APRICOTS OFFER AN INTERESTING SUMMER SAUCE. SERVED AT ROOM TEMPERATURE IT WILL ADD A TOUCH OF ELEGANCE TO A COLD SUPPER OR LUNCHEON. IF YOU DON'T MIND AN ADDED STEP, TRY BLANCHING AND SKINNING THE APRICOTS BEFORE USING.

INGREDIENTS:

1	POUND FRESH RIPE APRICOTS, SEEDED AND COARSELY CHOPPED
1/4	CUP OLIVE OIL
1/4	TEASPOON BALSAMIC VINEGAR
1	TABLESPOON CHOPPED FRESH BASIL
PINCH	FRESH GROUND BLACK PEPPER
1	ZUCCHINI, JULIENNED
1	YELLOW BELL PEPPER, SEEDED AND JULIENNED

METHOD: PUREE 1/2 THE APRICOTS (JUST OVER ONE CUP) IN A FOOD PROCESSOR. ADD THE OLIVE OIL, BALSAMIC VINEGAR, BASIL AND BLACK PEPPER. MIX SAUCE WITH REMAINING APRICOTS AND THE VEGETABLES. POUR SAUCE OVER PASTA. TOSS AND SERVE.

RECOMMENDED PASTA: 1/2 POUND SPIRALS, CURLY STRINGS OR SOLID TWISTS.

FRESH APRICOT SAUCE TOO!

A SECOND OFFERING USING APRICOTS, BUT THIS TIME YOU'LL OFFER IT IN A CREAM BASE BRINGING A TOUCH OF GRACE TO YOUR TABLE.

INGREDIENTS:
1   CHICKEN BREAST, SKINNED, COOKED AND DICED
1   POUND FRESH RIPE APRICOTS, BLANCHED, PEELED*, SEEDED AND CUT IN TO EIGHTHS.
1   CUP WHIPPING CREAM
     SALT TO TASTE

*   IF YOU HAVE NO PROBLEM WITH APRICOT SKINS, LEAVE THEM ON.

METHOD: COOK THE CHICKEN IN A LITTLE LIGHTLY SALTED WATER UNTIL TENDER, COOL, DICE AND SET ASIDE. PUREE 1 CUP OF THE APRICOTS IN A FOOD PROCESSOR. POUR INTO A BOWL, ADD WHIPPING CREAM BLEND WELL. ADD REMAINING APRICOTS AND CHICKEN, MIX WELL, SALT IF DESIRED. POUR SAUCE OVER PASTA. TOSS AND SERVE.

RECOMMENDED PASTA: CURLY STRINGS, SOLID TWISTED OR SPIRALS.

PEACHES AND CREAM SAUCE

(ANOTHER QUICKIE)

EVERYBODY LOVES PEACHES AND CREAM, WHETHER YOU'LL WANT THEM ON YOUR PASTA WHEN YOU'VE PROBABLY HAD THEM SO OFTEN PAIRED TOGETHER IN A BOWL, OR AS PART OF A SHORTCAKE DESSERT, IS A WHOLE DIFFERENT BALLGAME. IF YOU'RE WILLING TO GIVE IT A TRY, THIS IS YOUR RECIPE. YOU MAY WANT TO USE A LIGHTLY SALTED WATER FOR YOUR PASTA WITH THIS SAUCE.

INGREDIENTS:

4	MEDIUM TO LARGE FREESTONE RIPE PEACHES
1/4	TEASPOON BALSAMIC VINEGAR
1	CUP WHIPPING CREAM
*	FRESHLY GROUND BLACK PEPPER TO TASTE

METHOD: BLANCH, PEEL AND SEED THE PEACHES. COARSELY CHOP 2 OF THEM, SET ASIDE. PUREE THE OTHER 2 IN YOUR FOOD PROCESSOR. ADD THE VINEGAR, PULSE ONCE OR TWICE TO MIX. ADD THE WHIPPING CREAM, PROCESS TO BLEND. POUR SAUCE OVER YOUR PASTA. ADD THE CHOPPED PEACHES. TOSS AND SERVE HOT*, OR LET COOL TO SERVE AT ROOM TEMPERATURE.

*IF SERVED HOT, YOU MAY WISH TO SPRINKLE A LITTLE FRESHLY GROUND BLACK PEPPER OVER THE PASTA BEFORE TOSSING.

RECOMMENDED PASTA: SPIRALS, SOLID TWISTS OR CURLY STRINGS.

ORANGE SAUCE

(ANOTHER QUICKIE)

THIS SAUCE FEATURES THE ORANGE, BUT YOU KNEW THAT JUST FROM READING THE NAME. AND WHILE IT IS VERY GOOD AND WILL STAND ON ITS OWN, IT WOULD FURTHER BE COMPLEMENTED BY A FRESH HOME MADE PASTA USING ORANGE JUICE FOR THE LIQUID. IT'S ONLY A SUGGESTION, SO DON'T LET THAT STOP YOU. TRY THIS SAUCE ANYTIME ORANGES ARE EXCITING YOUR TASTE BUDS. I MIGHT SUGGEST THAT FOR THE FIRST EFFORT, YOU TRY IT ON UNSALTED PASTA, OR WITH NO MORE THAN A VERY LIGHT SALTING, AND COOK THE ORANGE PEEL ALONG WITH YOUR PASTA.

INGREDIENTS:
1	ORANGE, JUICED
1	TABLESPOON CORNSTARCH
2	TABLESPOONS TRIPLE SEC OR BRANDY
PINCH	GROUND NUTMEG
3	TABLESPOONS BUTTER
1/4	CUP WHIPPING CREAM

METHOD: THIS IS A TWO PAN SAUCE. MIX THE ORANGE JUICE, CORNSTARCH, TRIPLE SEC AND NUTMEG. BRING TO A BOIL, REMOVE FROM HEAT, SET ASIDE. MELT THE BUTTER, WHEN MELTED ADD THE CREAM. ADD ORANGE JUICE MIXTURE AND SIMMER UNTIL SAUCE THICKENS. POUR SAUCE OVER PASTA. TOSS AND SERVE.

RECOMMENDED PASTA: STRING TYPES, ROUND, SQUARE, OVAL OR HOLLOW.

WE TRIED THIS SAUCE . . . AND

LOVED IT ( )
HATED IT ( )
MAYBE WE'LL TRY IT AGAIN ( )
WE'LL USE IT FOR UNWELCOME GUESTS ( )

VENETIAN MELON CREAM SAUCE

THIS MAY BECOME ONE OF YOUR SUMMER DELIGHTS. YOU MAY KNOW THAT THE ROMANS DEVELOPED THE CANTALOUPE MELON, AND IT HAS BEEN IN GENERAL USE IN ITALY FOR A LONG, LONG TIME. AND AS YOU MIGHT EXPECT, SOONER OR LATER SOMEONE WOULD TRY TO MIX IT WITH PASTA. THIS SAUCE CERTAINLY VERIFIES THAT ASSUMPTION.

INGREDIENTS:

4	TABLESPOONS BUTTER
3	CUPS OF SMALL DICED OR COARSELY CHOPPED CANTALOUPE
1	CUP WHIPPING CREAM
1	TABLESPOON LEMON JUICE
1/2	TEASPOON TOMATO PASTE
	SALT AND FRESHLY GROUND BLACK PEPPER TO TASTE

METHOD: SAUTE CANTALOUPE IN BUTTER UNTIL MELON IS SOFT, ABOUT 3 TO 4 MINUTES. ADD CREAM, LEMON JUICE, TOMATO PASTE, SALT AND PEPPER. BRING SAUCE TO A BOIL, COOK FOR 6 TO 8 ADDITIONAL MINUTES, STIRRING CONSTANTLY. REMOVE FROM HEAT. POUR SAUCE OVER PASTA. TOSS AND SERVE.

RECOMMENDED PASTA: STRING OR WIDE RIBBON TYPES (IF YOU GO WITH THE RIBBONS, BREAK THE PASTA INTO MANAGEABLE SIZE, ABOUT 3 TO 4 INCH LENGTHS).

CHERRY CREAM SAUCE

(ANOTHER QUICKIE)

FRESH CHERRIES ARE A DELIGHT TO EAT ANYTIME, ANYWAY. MY PERSONAL FAVORITES ARE THE BING CHERRIES, FOLLOWED BY THE QUEEN ANNE. THERE ARE A NUMBER OF VARIETIES, SOME SWEET AND SOME TART, I'LL NOT MAKE A DECISION FOR YOU, CHOOSE WHAT IS AVAILABLE, OR YOUR PERSONAL FAVORITE. THIS RECIPE WILL GIVE YOU A DENSE AND VERY FLAVORFUL SAUCE. AND YOU'LL COOK OVER HIGH HEAT, SO DON'T LEAVE IT ALONE!

INGREDIENTS:

1	CUP FRESH PITTED AND QUARTERED (OR COARSELY CHOPPED) CHERRIES*
2	TABLESPOONS MINCED LEEK (WHITE PART ONLY)
	OR
2	TABLESPOONS MINCED SHALLOTS
1	TABLESPOON WINE VINEGAR (FRUIT TYPES ARE OK)
1/4	CUP WHITE WINE
1/2	CUP WHIPPING CREAM (HALF AND HALF IS OK)
6	TABLESPOONS BUTTER (DIVIDED IN HALF)
	PINCH OF SALT, OR TO TASTE

METHOD: PLACE CHERRIES, LEEK, VINEGAR AND WINE INTO A SAUCE PAN. BRING TO A BOIL, COOK RAPIDLY UNTIL LIQUID IS NEARLY GONE. ADD WHIPPING CREAM. BRING TO A BOIL, COOK RAPIDLY FOR 1 MINUTE TO REDUCE. ADD 1/2 THE BUTTER. CONTINUE RAPID COOKING FOR 1 ADDITIONAL MINUTE, REMOVE FROM HEAT. TOSS DRAINED PASTA WITH REMAINING 1/2 BUTTER. POUR SAUCE OVER PASTA. TOSS AND SERVE.

RECOMMENDED PASTA: USE ONLY 8 OUNCES OF THE: FILLED OR TIED PILLOW TYPES.

* TRY THIS SAME RECIPE WITH FINELY CHOPPED SEMI-DRIED FRUITS.

CHERRY SAUCE TOO!

AGAIN YOU MAY USE ANY VARIETY OF CHERRY YOU HAVE OR LIKE. FRESH, CANNED OR EVEN FROM PRESERVES. THE INGREDIENT THAT MAKES THIS SAUCE DIFFERENT FROM THE PRECEDING IS THE ADDITION OF EGGS. AND BECAUSE IT IS COOKED, SOME PUREST MAY CONSIDER THIS TO BE A CUSTARD, ALBEIT A SOUPY ONE.

INGREDIENTS:
2	CUPS WHIPPING CREAM
4	EGGS
1/2	CUP SUGAR
1	TEASPOON VANILLA
1	CUP FRESH OR CANNED CHERRIES, FINELY CHOPPED
	OR
2/3	CUP CHERRY PRESERVES

OPTION: 2 TABLESPOONS MARASCHINO LIQUEUR OR KIRSCH

METHOD: PLACE EGGS, SUGAR AND VANILLA INTO A SMALL BOWL, WHISK TO BLEND. ADD CHERRIES, WHISK AGAIN, SET ASIDE. BRING WHIPPING CREAM TO A LOW BOIL, WHILE STIRRING CONSTANTLY TO AVOID SCORCHING, REMOVE FROM HEAT. SLOWLY POUR WHIPPING CREAM INTO THE EGG/CHERRY MIXTURE WHILE WHISKING. PLACE SAUCE IN THE PAN AND HEAT TO SCALDING (3 TO 4 MINUTES), OR UNTIL IT WILL COAT YOUR SPOON. WHISK IN MARASCHINO LIQUEUR IF DESIRED, POUR SAUCE OVER PASTA, TOSS AND SERVE.

RECOMMENDED PASTA: SMALL FILLED PILLOW TYPES OR A HOME MADE RAVIOLI FILLED WITH DRIED FRUIT (YOUR CHOICE).

MAY I SUGGEST THAT YOU COOK YOUR PASTA IN VERY LIGHTLY SALTED WATER.

CHAPTER 22

SAUCES MADE FROM DRIED TOMATOES

(SUN DRIED OR OTHERWISE)

DRIED TOMATOES ARE IN A CATEGORY ALL THEIR OWN AND ARE ONE OF THE NEW DARLINGS IN AMERICAN COOKERY (THEY'VE HAD THEM IN ITALY FOR A VERY LONG TIME). IT DOESN'T MATTER HOW THEY ARE DRIED, THEY ALL COME TO YOU FULLY DRESSED. THAT IS WITH THEIR SKINS ON, SEEDS AND THE STEM END IN PLACE. THERE ARE ONLY A FEW RECIPES IN THIS CHAPTER, BECAUSE THERE ARE FEW RECIPES PERIOD. IF, AS THE PACKERS WOULD LIKE, THESE DRIED TOMATOES FIND A NICHE IN AMERICAN COOKERY, YOU CAN LOOK FORWARD TO AN EXPANDED CHAPTER IN FUTURE EDITIONS OF THIS BOOK. ON THE OTHER HAND, IF THEY DON'T SELL AS PACKERS AND GROCERS WOULD HOPE THEY WILL. WE MAY FIND IT NECESSARY TO OMIT THIS CHAPTER IN FUTURE EDITIONS. IN THE MEANTIME YOU MIGHT GIVE THEM A TRY, DRAW YOUR OWN CONCLUSIONS, AND, IF YOU LIKE THEM AND ARE A CREATIVE COOK, SHARE YOUR RECIPES WITH ME.

DRIED TOMATOES COME IN THREE FORMS. SOFT DRIED, BRITTLE DRIED AND OIL PACKED. EACH WILL BRING A TASTE DIFFERENCE TO YOUR PASTA SAUCE. DRIERS AND PACKERS ALSO SEEM TO BE USING TWO TYPES OF TOMATOES FOR THEIR PRODUCT. THE SOFT DRIED AND OIL PACKED TYPES ARE FROM THE ITALIAN PEAR OR ROMA TOMATO. IT IS EITHER CUT INTO ROUNDS OR HALVED. THE BRITTLE DRIED TOMATO ARE SLICED FROM THE LARGER, ROUNDER, FULL TOMATO, POSSIBLY A BEEFSTEAK TYPE. YOU'LL GET LESS SKIN FROM THE BEEFSTEAK TYPE PER USE, AND LESS BITTERNESS (THE PACKER TERM IS "INTENSE TOMATO FLAVOR".

(FOR AN HONEST AND UNVARNISHED EXPLANATION OF WHAT "INTENSE TOMATO FLAVOR" MEANS TO ME, PLEASE READ THE INTRODUCTION TO THE FIRST SAUCE IN THIS CHAPTER.)

Continued on next page

PACKERS SUGGEST THAT YOU CAN "PLUMP" OR "RECONSTITUTE" THEIR TOMATOES BY DROPPING THEM INTO BOILING WATER FOR ABOUT TWO MINUTES. THAT'S PART WISHFUL THINKING AND PART BLUE SKY SALESMANSHIP. IT WILL SOFTEN THEM SOMEWHAT, BUT THAT'S ABOUT IT. THE SOFTER CONDITION WILL ALLOW YOU TO SLICE, DICE OR CHOP THEM MORE EASILY INTO A SIZE ACCEPTABLE TO YOU. OR, YOU MAY EXTEND THE COOKING TIME BY THREE TO FIVE MINUTES AND THEN PUREE THEM IN YOUR BLENDER OR FOOD PROCESSOR. IF YOU CHOOSE TO PUREE THEM, REALIZE THAT THEY MAY NOT BE USED AS ANY OTHER PUREED TOMATO.

SUN DRIED TOMATO SAUCE

(ANOTHER QUICKIE)

A FEW YEARS (WAY)BACK . . . , WHEN I WAS A YOUNGSTER, LATE SUMMER AND EARLY FALL WERE VERY INTERESTING TIMES AROUND OUR HOUSE. IT WAS THE HARVEST SEASON, AND ALTHOUGH WE LIVED IN A LARGE CITY, FALL MEANT THAT THERE WERE MANY IMPORTANT THINGS TO DO. FOR THE MEN OF THE HOUSE, IT WAS THE TIME TO MAKE WINE, AT OUR HOUSE IT WAS AN EVENT MARSHALLED BY MY GRANDFATHER, THE MASTER WINE MAKER. HE ALONE UNDERSTOOD THE COMPLEXITIES OF TURNING GRAPES INTO WINE. AND BECAUSE WE LIVED IN A PREDOMINANTLY ITALIAN NEIGHBORHOOD, IT WAS A MAJOR ANNUAL EVENT. TRUCKS COULD BE FOUND UNLOADING THEIR CARGO OF GRAPES AT PRACTICALLY EVERY HOUSE FOR BLOCKS AROUND. IT WAS A FUN TIME, AND EXCITING FOR WILLING, HELPFUL YOUNGSTERS. HOWEVER, BEFORE WE GET TOO FAR AFIELD, LETS GET BACK TO SAUCE MAKING. WELL, ALONG WITH THE GRAPES ALSO CAME THE CROP FOR THE WOMEN OF THE HOUSE, TOMATOES. THIS WAS A HIGH POINT OF PREPARATION FOR THE WONDERFUL PASTA SAUCES TO BE PREPARED BY MY GRANDMOTHER DURING THE COMING YEAR. THE BUSHELS OF TOMATOES WERE DUTIFULLY HAULED INTO OUR BASEMENT, WHERE THEY UNDERWENT THE TRANSFORMATION FROM FRESH TO CANNED INTO THOSE QUART SIZED GREEN MASON JARS. NOW WE'RE TO THE POINT OF THIS STORY! IT WAS DURING THE FIRST STEP OF PREPARATION, BLANCHING THE TOMATOES IN BOILING WATER AND REMOVAL OF THE TOMATO SKINS THAT ALL THE CHILDREN OF THE FAMILY WERE TO RECEIVE A TASTE TREAT OF EXTRAORDINARY VALUE. MY GRANDMOTHER HAD CONVINCED US THAT TOMATO SKINS, LIGHTLY SALTED AND SAUTEED IN OLIVE OIL WERE A TREAT WORTHY OF BEING SERVED TO ANGELS. WE ALL LOVED OUR GRAND-MOTHER, SO WE BOUGHT THE ARGUMENT. BUT, I'M NOT SO SURE I'D BUY IT TODAY. AND . . . , ALTHOUGH THE DRIERS OF TOMATOES WOULD LIKE TO YOU BELIEVE THEIR PRODUCT, DRIED TOMATOES OFFER AN "INTENSE" FLAVOR, THEY OFFER *ONLY* THE TASTE OF FRIED TOMATO SKINS. YOU MAY LIKE IT, EVERY ONE I'VE PREPARED THIS RECIPE FOR, SAID THEY LOVED IT (I'VE CONSIDERED THE POSSIBILITY THAT THEY MAY HAVE LIED TO ME). YOU MAY LOVE IT TOO,

Continued on next page

517

BECAUSE IF YOU WERE DENIED THE OPPORTUNITY TO EAT FRESH TOMATO SKINS, LIGHTLY SALTED AND SAUTEED IN OLIVE OIL AS A YOUNGSTER, THIS TASTE WILL BE A NEW EXPERIENCE FOR YOU.

INGREDIENTS:

3	OUNCES DRIED TOMATOES
1/4	CUP OLIVE OIL
2	CLOVES GARLIC, MINCED
1	TABLESPOON FRESH OREGANO, MINCED
	OR
1/4	TEASPOON DRY OREGANO
3/4	CUP PASTA WATER
	FRESHLY GRATED CHEESE

METHOD: SOFTEN DRIED TOMATOES BY SOAKING THEM IN HOT WATER FOR 2 MINUTES, DRAIN, CHOP OR JULIENNE. SAUTE GARLIC IN THE OLIVE OIL UNTIL LIGHTLY GOLDEN. ADD TOMATOES AND FRESH OREGANO. COOK AN ADDITIONAL 2 MINUTES. SLOWLY ADD PASTA WATER, (IF YOU ARE USING DRY OREGANO, ADD IT NOW). BRING TO A RAPID BOIL, REMOVE SAUCE FROM HEAT, COVER AND LET STEEP WHILE YOUR PASTA IS COOKING. POUR SAUCE OVER PASTA. TOSS, SERVE WITH CHEESE ON THE SIDE.

RECOMMENDED PASTA: STRINGS, RIBBONS OR TUBES.

THERE ARE SEVERAL OPTIONS TO THIS SAUCE YOU MIGHT LIKE TO TRY; YOU COULD ADD UP TO 1 CUP OF SLICED OR HALVED RIPE OLIVES AND/OR YOU COULD USE ONE OF SEVERAL SOFT CHEESES INSTEAD OF HARD GRATING VARIETIES, TRY FETA, SHREDDED MOZZARELLA, OR PROVOLONE.

SUN DRIED TOMATOES AND CREAM SAUCE

(ANOTHER QUICKIE)

MELLOWER THAN THE PRECEDING SAUCE. THE WHIPPING CREAM TONES DOWN THE CHARACTERISTIC BITTERNESS OF THE TOMATO SKINS. AND IT CAN BE TASTE ADJUSTED WITH YOUR FAVORITE LIQUEUR.

INGREDIENTS:

3	OUNCES DRIED TOMATOES
2	TABLESPOONS BUTTER
1	WHOLE SHALLOT, MINCED
3/4	CUP WHIPPING CREAM
1/4	CUP HALF AND HALF

OPTIONAL:

1	TABLESPOON DIJON MUSTARD
	OR
1 TO 2	TABLESPOONS OF COGNAC OR A FAVORITE LIQUEUR

METHOD: SOAK DRIED TOMATOES IN BOILING WATER FOR 2 MINUTES, DRAIN, JULIENNE OR FINELY CHOP, SET ASIDE. SAUTE SHALLOTS IN BUTTER FOR 2 MINUTES, ADD TOMATOES, SAUTE 1 ADDITIONAL MINUTE. ADD WHIPPING CREAM, HALF AND HALF, AND DIJON MUSTARD (IF USED). BRING TO A LOW BOIL. REMOVE FROM HEAT. POUR SAUCE OVER DRAINED PASTA. TOSS AND SERVE.

RECOMMENDED PASTA: 8 OUNCES OF STRINGS, RIBBONS OR MEDIUM TUBES. IF YOU SELECT ANGLE HAIR OR SPAGHETTINI, USE ONLY 4 OUNCES.

PUREED SUN DRIED TOMATO SAUCE

THIS SAUCE WILL REQUIRE SEVERAL STEPS AND TWO COOKINGS OF THE TOMATOES. IT WILL ALSO GIVE YOU A SAUCE WITH LESS BITTERNESS. THE TOMATO SKIN TASTE WILL STILL DOMINATE, BUT IT WILL BE MELLOWER.

INGREDIENTS:

3	OUNCES DRIED TOMATOES
1/4	CUP OLIVE OIL
1/2	CUP ONION, CHOPPED
1	CLOVE GARLIC, MINCED
1/2	TEASPOON SALT OR TO TASTE
1	CUP WATER
	FRESHLY GRATED PARMESAN CHEESE

METHOD: DROP TOMATOES INTO A BOILING WATER FOR THREE TO FOUR MINUTES, DRAIN. PLACE TOMATOES INTO A BLENDER OR FOOD PROCESSOR, PROCESS UNTIL FAIRLY SMOOTH. SAUTE ONIONS AND GARLIC IN OLIVE OIL UNTIL THEY BEGIN TO COLOR. ADD TOMATOES, SALT AND ONE CUP WATER (ADD WATER AS NEEDED IF YOU WANT A THINNER SAUCE). COOK FOR ABOUT 5 MINUTES. POUR ABOUT 1/2 THE SAUCE OVER YOUR PASTA. TOSS AND SERVE WITH CHEESE ON THE SIDE.

RECOMMENDED PASTA: STRINGS, TUBES OR RIBBONS.

SUN DRIED TOMATO AND GARLIC SAUCE

(ANOTHER QUICKIE)

THIS SAUCE IS THE ONLY ONE IN THIS BOOK REQUIRING THE USE OF SUN DRIED OIL PACKED TOMATOES. MY EXPERIENCE HAS SHOWN THAT YOU CANNOT SUCCESSFULLY REPACK DRIED TOMATOES WITH OIL. USE THEM WITH A RECIPE FROM THIS BOOK THAT MATCHES THE CONDITION OF THE TOMATOES AS YOU BOUGHT THEM.

INGREDIENTS:
4	OUNCES (DRAINED) SUN DRIED OIL PACKED TOMATOES
3	CLOVES GARLIC
1	TEASPOON FRESH LEMON JUICE OR WINE VINEGAR
3/4	CUP OLIVE OIL
	SALT AND WHITE PEPPER TO TASTE

METHOD: PLACE TOMATOES AND GARLIC INTO A FOOD PROCESSOR AND WHIRL UNTIL COARSELY CHOPPED. ADD LEMON JUICE AND OLIVE OIL, CONTINUE TO PROCESS UNTIL TOMATO AND GARLIC ARE FINELY CHOPPED. ADJUST SEASONING. POUR SAUCE OVER HOT STEAMING PASTA. TOSS AND SERVE.

RECOMMENDED PASTA: STRING OR RIBBON TYPES.

General Alphabetized Index

Asterisk Denotes (Another Quickie)

See "Contents" For An Index By Category.

( ) Identifies A Second Name For A Sauce.

523

TO THE USER OF THIS BOOK; I WOULD LIKE YOUR COMMENTS: BOTH POSITIVE AND NEGATIVE (IF ANY)! I WILL ALSO GLADLY ACCEPT RECIPES THAT YOU LOVE AND WOULD WILLINGLY SHARE WITH OTHERS. INCLUDE ANY HISTORY OR POINT OR ORIGIN OF YOUR SAUCE IF KNOWN.

SINCERELY,

CHARLES A. BELLISSINO, AUTHOR

ADDRESS YOUR COMMENTS AND RECIPES TO THE PUBLISHER:
MARCUS KIMBERLY PUBLISHERS
2701 WATT AVENUE
SACRAMENTO, CA 95821